THE CONFEDERATE GOVERNORS

THE

CONFEDERATE

GOVERNORS

Edited by W. Buck Yearns

THE UNIVERSITY OF GEORGIA PRESS   ATHENS

Designed by Betty P. McDaniel
Set in 10 on 12 point Century Schoolbook
The paper in this book meets the guidelines for
permanence and durability of the Committee on
Production Guidelines for Book Longevity of the
Council on Library Resources.

Printed in the United States of America

90 89 88 87 86 85   5 4 3 2 1

Library of Congress Cataloging in Publication Data
Main entry under title:

The Confederate governors.

Includes bibliographical references.
1. Governors—Southern States—History—19th century.
2. Confederate States of America—Politics and government.
I. Yearns, W. Buck (Wilfred Buck), 1918–
E487.C727   1985   975′.02   84-154
ISBN 0-8203-0719-X

The title-page illustration is from *The Soldier in Our
Civil War* (1890) edited by Paul F. Mottelay and
T. Campbell-Copeland.

CONTENTS

THE CONFEDERATE GOVERNORS

INTRODUCTION

ne of the recurring problems of interpretation that have bedeviled historians of the American Civil War has been the evaluation of the Confederacy's war effort. The controversy over whether the South should have won its war for independence seems for the moment at least to be settled, but how well it struggled to survive is still debatable. Should it have waged a better war, or did it struggle longer and better than could have been expected? Put another way, the thoroughness of the Confederacy's defeat has caused the focus of investigation to move from the question of why it lost to why that loss was so decisive. In its simplest terms, the pervading question is: How well did the South wage war? And there is no simple answer.

In their search for answers, historians have examined many facets of the Confederacy's history and have usually attempted to assess how they affected the conduct of the war. Probably the most familiar study is Frank L. Owsley's *State Rights in the Confederacy,* in which he argued that the South's extreme states' rights convictions prevented the states and their governments from giving the central government their full cooperation in the prosecution of the war. As Owsley bluntly put it, the epitaph of the Confederacy should be "Died of State Rights."[1] Robert C. Black examined the South's use of its 9,283 miles of railroad and decided that southerners "by no means made the best of what they had."[2] The Confederacy's chief of ordnance commented in April 1861 that "no arsenal, except that at Fayetteville, N.C., had a single machine above a foot-lathe,"[3] and Frank E. Vandiver has traced Josiah Gorgas's desperate efforts to remedy that deficiency.[4] Tom H. Wells showed how administrative inexperience accounted for much of the inability of the Confederacy's Department of the Navy to function properly.[5] Richard Todd's *Confederate Finance* examined all phases of that area, and demonstrated how the South's failure to impose heavy taxes on its citizenry helped bring upon the Confederacy a ruinous and demoralizing inflation.[6] Charles Wesley saw the Confederates' morale collapsing under their multitudinous social and economic problems,[7] while Ella Lonn's *Salt as a Factor in the Confederacy* depicted the real suffering caused by the scarcity of this preservative.[8] Frank L. Owsley's classic *King Cotton Diplomacy* gives a detailed account of the South's diplomacy in which he described how the Confederacy, instead of shipping great quantities of cotton to Europe when it was possible, erroneously calculated that a cotton embargo would force recognition from the European nations.[9] Conversely, Stanley Lebergott contends that cotton diplomacy might have worked, but that the cotton planters, in order to preserve their near monopoly of world cotton production, sabotaged the plan by continuing to plant and export cotton.[10] Paul D. Escott describes Jefferson Davis as a president unable to rally the common people of the Confederacy to a supreme war effort,[11] and Larry E. Nelson describes Davis's failure to profit from the distresses of the North's Republican party in the elections of November 1864.[12] And there are others.

This is not to say that the Confederates made more mistakes than the Federals or that they knew they were struggling against almost insuperable odds. They had the advantage of fighting a defensive war, they had the moral advantage of fighting for their independence, they were more infused with a martial spirit and at first had the more experienced commanders, and they had vast and productive fields and over three million slaves to work them. There is little doubt that most Confederates at first expected complete victory. The purpose of this volume is to attempt to analyze one more element of the Confederacy's war effort: the role of the state governors.

During colonial times the bitter rivalries between the governors and the assemblies had created deep distrust of executive power, and foremost in the minds of those who wrote the first state constitutions was the conviction that all power in government must emanate from the assemblies and that the governors must be restricted.[13] All southern governors were elected by the assemblies. None could immediately succeed himself, and only the governor of South Carolina had a term as long as two years. Each constitution instructed the assembly to elect an executive council whose advice and consent the governor must have before taking significant action and whose journal must always be available for the assembly's scrutiny. Only the governor of South Carolina had the veto power (taken away in two years), and none could recommend legislation to the assembly. The governors had little power of appointment, most of this being the right to fill vacancies in office until the assembly met, and then only with the advice and consent of the executive council. Even the emergency powers that normally accrue to the commander in chief of the militia could only be exercised with the council's approval. These early governors, then, were subordinate to, rather than coordinate with, the popularly elected assemblies. Charles S. Sydnor observed that "it would not be far wrong to regard the governor and council as the executive of the Assembly rather than of the state."[14]

Despite the fact that the first state constitutions violated the principle of the separation of powers of government and that they had proven cumbersome and awkward in prosecuting the Revolution against Great Britain, change was slow in coming. Thomas Jefferson had warned, "An *elective despotism* was not the government we fought for,"[15] but great confidence in popularly elected assemblies was difficult to reverse. Even the model provided by the Federal Constitution of 1787 had few repercussions in the South Atlantic states, though in 1789 Georgia extended its governor's term to two years and gave him the same veto power as that provided for the president, and in 1790 South Carolina abolished its executive council.

Inevitably, however, the course of events brought about some, if not nearly enough, change in this early system of government. Observant minds began to realize that legislative dominance was not automatically the solution for good government. Legislative sessions became longer and more frequent, and the costs of government rose accordingly. In the East it became apparent that an executive council could excessively restrict a good governor in the performance of his duties and might serve as a cloak under which a poor one could escape his responsibilities. Also a constitutionally stronger governor would be able to provide a concentration of authority, a simplicity of organization, and a flexibility in procedure that would be beyond the competence of a legislative body. One with a longer term of office would have more time in which to attempt to fulfill his party's campaign promises. The new western states in particular profited by the model of the Federal Constitution, and their first executives in form were more akin to the national than to the early eastern state constitutions.

By the time Texas entered the Union in 1845, seven states had two-year governorships, five had four-year terms, and the Virginia governor was elected for three years. Five states had a veto procedure like that of the Federal Constitution, four states had a veto which could be overridden by a simple majority of all the elected members in each house of the assembly, and four had no veto. By this date all states but two had governors elected by those citizens eligible to vote for members of the lower house of the state assembly. Virginia adopted this principle in 1851 and South Carolina continued election by the assembly. None of the states that entered the Union after 1789 used the executive council; South Carolina abolished its council in 1790 and Virginia in 1851. Georgia and North Carolina retained their councils, but restricted their authority.

These reforms meant that the governors were becoming more independent of the legislatures, but not that the governors were becoming as strong. One of the convictions of Jacksonian Democracy was that the concentration of great power anywhere, even in the legislature, was detrimental to good government. Nowhere was this more evident than in states where the more populous counties were able to secure legislation for their own advantage and often to the detriment of the less populous districts. The reforms described in the preceding paragraph were designed more to curb the legislative branch than to establish a strong executive branch of government. Other parts of this strategy were to place constitutional restrictions on the assemblies, such as limiting their powers of appointment, and to impose constitutional mandates upon them, such as ordering them to provide public schools. Of course, Jacksonianism was not uniformly triumphant, as the differences in the southern constitutions around 1850 will testify.

To make their governors weak, the first state constitutions not only made them subservient to the assembly but further crippled them by diffusing their authority over the executive branch. Every constitution written in the eighteenth century gave the assembly the right to appoint all the chief executive officers: secretary of state, attorney general, auditor, treasurer, controller, and surveyor general. This meant that the governor had serving under him a group of semi-independent officers, each heading his own department. Only the strongest of governors would be able to coordinate the policies and activities of such departments. Florida, Alabama, Mississippi, and Arkansas adopted the same practice when they entered the Union. Louisiana and Missouri wisely let their governors nominate all their executive officers for the Senate's consideration, and in 1834 Kentucky shifted to this practice. Under these plans, therefore, only three states allowed their governors much direct control over their executive officers.

Eventually four states modified, but did not necessarily improve, the selection of their executive officers. Mississippi in 1832, Texas in its first constitution of 1845, Kentucky in 1850, and Missouri in 1850–51 provided for the popular election of all their executive officers. This may have appeared democratic, but it probably made the proper administration of executive matters even worse. In commenting on the principle of the diffusion of executive authority, Tocqueville wrote, "There are almost as many independent functionaries as there are functions, and the executive power is disseminated in a multitude of hands."[16] Viewing the United States as a whole, Charles E. Merriam wrote that "by the middle of the century public administration, outside the Federal government, had reached the low-water mark of decentralization in the United States."[17] Ralph Wooster has written that "by 1860 the typical governor in the Upper South could do little more than delay legislation passed by the assembly, and possessed little appointive power in the judicial area."[18]

The first constitutions in every state that joined the Confederacy named the governor as the state's commander in chief. Eight constitutions made no statement of what the governor could do in this capacity; five of them stated the obvious: that he could call up the militia to help execute the laws, suppress insurrection, and repel invasion. Probably the writers of these constitutions, as did some of the writers of the Federal Constitution, worked under the assumption that all executives have inherent military powers which are impossible to anticipate.

Once in the Confederacy, none of the states chose to tamper with this part of their constitution, and the war began with the powers of the commander in chief almost untested. In May 1846 the president of the United States had asked for volunteer regiments from the several states to conduct the war against Mexico, and later that year he asked for one more regiment from each of eight states. The governor of each issued calls for volunteer companies, armed them and organized them into a regiment, and then offered it to the president. Federal law specified that each volunteer must furnish his own clothing, but that he would be paid for clothing himself at the rate of $3.50 a month. After the regiment had been organized, the state would be paid for the subsistence of each soldier the sum of fifty cents for each twenty miles that the regiment traveled to its point of embarkation.[19] Thereafter, the state governors and their legislatures considered their contribution to the war effort ended.

Thus, it was with state governors subordinate to their legislatures, inadequately controlling the executive department, and inexperienced in the use of the functions of a commander in chief that the Confederacy began.

For the Confederacy the four years from 1861 to 1865 proved to be years of crisis, and the process of decision making that had operated well enough previously for the state governments quickly proved inadequate. Sacrifices had to be wrenched from a reluctant citizenry; the needs of civilians had to be weighed against those of the soldiers; public figures and private producers had to be badgered or cajoled into giving the war their first priority; soldiers had to be kept in the army and civilians had to be convinced that defeat would be so dreadful as to be unthinkable; the rights of the states and their citizens had to be safeguarded against overzealous Confederate authorities. And each state's image in relation to Confederate survival had to be clearly and symbolically represented. Certainly the Davis administration did provide the basic war measures and the guidelines for implementing them, but even at war southerners would not consent to excessive centralization. Even had they so consented, geography and the economy probably would have prevented much more centralism than actually occurred. In order to wage a successful war, the Confederate government had to have the full cooperation of each of the states. The extent of each states' cooperation can to a large extent be measured by the actions of its governors.

The study of the role of state governors under the Confederacy has been spotty. More than ample attention has been paid to Joseph E. Brown of Georgia and Zebulon B. Vance of North Carolina, who thereby have become almost stereotypes of the Confederate chief executives. A very few others are subjects of biographies, but most have had their records presented only in state studies in which the activities of the governors is a small part of the total picture.

All told, twenty-eight men served as governors of the thirteen states of the Confederacy. Most of them were relatively young men in their forties. All were southern-born except Harris Flanagin of Arkansas and Charles Clark of Mississippi. Without exception, all who served as their state's first Confederate governor were Democrats, and all but three of these had advocated secession upon Lincoln's election as president. But as the tide turned against the Confederacy and discontent and even disaffection emerged, voters in the southern states turned mainly to ex-Whigs and former Unionists. Most of the governors had pursued legal careers, with almost half of them being college or university graduates. Most had done well in their profession, and generally had interests both in land and in slaves. Most had had political experience either in their legislatures or in Congress before the war. Six had had military experience. As a whole the Confederate governors seem to have been quite representative of mid-nineteenth-century American political leadership.

A people fighting against great odds to establish their independence must use all their resources and abilities if they expect success. But continued sacrifice is physically and morally exhausting. It becomes intolerable if it seems to be unavailing. In such circumstances the aura of leadership may be pivotal. It must appear as a symbol of the nation to be, an image of hope. The question of how effectively Jefferson Davis personified the South's struggle for independence has always intrigued historians,[20] and the extent to which the Confederate governors collectively represented their states' war effort was hardly less critical. All of the first governors except John Letcher of Virginia had been secession leaders, which suggests that they must have had both the attention and the respect of their people. As the war progressed and intensified, the responsibilities of the state executive branch increased dramatically, and the visibility of the governors increased proportionately. How well each of them appeared to dedicate himself and his administration to victory would inevitably offer guidelines to the people of his state. Though the pattern was not perfect, for in some instances the people of a state ignored such guidelines, generally they responded to the war as their governor seemed to be doing. With certain exceptions the governor, more than any single individual, represented the collective sentiments of his states' population.

As depicted by the authors of the following chapters, Alabama, Florida, Louisiana, Kentucky, Mississippi, Tennessee, Texas, and Virginia began their Confederate experience with governors visibly dedicated to victory and both willing and able to marshal their resources toward that objective. Each man attempted to project—and for the most part succeeded in projecting—the image of a practical, hardworking executive, conscious of the martial spirit prevailing in 1861 and determined to exploit it. They made good preparations for war, and when it commenced they met it decisively and innovatively. They sought to preserve the proper balance between the rights of the states and individuals on one hand and the need for sacrifice on the other, and with certain exceptions their people recognized and accepted this position. Possibly Pettus of Mississippi was so overzealous as to be counterproductive, but in late 1861 he was overwhelmingly reelected and was always the center of the Mississippi war effort. And apparently Andrew B. Moore of Alabama from the very first had malcontents in his state whom he could neither beguile nor intimidate. Nevertheless, both Pettus and Moore deserve high ratings for dedication. While these eight governors, all of whom had been secession leaders, were probably no better nor worse managers than the other five original Confederate governors, they seem to have had a symbolic quality that the others lacked. One might say that by their very nature they established state rapport with the Confederate war program.

The other secession governors failed in varying degrees to become charismatic Confederate leaders. Brown of Georgia deliberately rejected the role and swiftly earned the image of a near-foe of the Confederacy. Events is Missouri went too fast for Claiborne Jackson to handle well, for he lacked both skill and tact. John Ellis of North Carolina, though he did yeoman work in taking his state from the

Union and did fairly well in preparing it for war, was both pedestrian and sickly. Francis W. Pickens of South Carolina rested upon his laurels as secessionist leader and was later rejected by the electorate. Henry M. Rector of Arkansas tried hard for greatness, but he was self-centered, too radical for the moderates, made several unwise compromises with opponents, and tended generally to be out of rhythm with public opinion. Except for Brown, then, none of these six governors was able to establish any great identification for himself as a state leader in the Confederacy.

Only eight of the postsecession governors succeeded to office early enough or served long enough for their image to be of much consequence. John G. Shorter of Alabama and John Milton of Florida entered office when the Confederacy was less than a year old and quickly established themselves as strong protagonists of both state and nation. Allen of Louisiana, Lubbock of Texas, Smith of Virginia, and Bonham of South Carolina took office midway through the war with matters grim but not hopeless. All four were hardworking, fair-minded, and determined, and it would be difficult to imagine men operating under such trying circumstances to have been more successful. None of them—except possibly Allen—had the compelling personality that makes a great leader, but they notably projected the quality of grim determination that was becoming the last hope of the Confederacy. Their states' steadfastness during these times is a partial tribute to the governors. Vance of North Carolina quickly acquired an almost hallowed image as a guardian of state and personal rights, regardless of how they might affect the Confederacy, and both he and his state appeared actually anti-Confederate despite their enormous contributions to the war effort.

The quality of Confederate leadership exhibited by the remaining nine governors varied greatly but mattered little. The tenures of Clark of North Carolina and Allison of Florida were too brief for them to make their mark. Watts of Alabama, who served seventeen months, was the only one with even an outside chance of becoming a rallying symbol for the Confederacy. He might have done so had his term come earlier, but by 1864 disaffection was so firmly entrenched in Alabama that Watts's moderation seemed pro-Confederate to Alabamians and pro-Alabama to the Richmond authorities. Hawes of Kentucky, Charles Clark of Mississippi, and to a lesser extent Reynolds of Missouri attempted to contribute to the war effort, but Clark's efforts were largely wasted because most of Mississippi by this time was in Federal hands, while Hawes and Reynolds were refugee governors. Flanagin of Arkansas, Magrath of South Carolina, and Murrah of Texas took office very near the end of the war, and their inactivity and/or obstructionism was important only to their memory.

But while the quality of a governor's image might help set the morale of his state, what he did was of course far more important. Even a pedestrian public servant could contribute workmanlike and valuable services to the Confederate war effort. One of the more lasting controversies of Confederate historiography has been the extent to which the states cooperated with the central government. While few historians still accept Owsley's idea that the Confederacy "Died of State Rights," there is still the gnawing possibility that had the states cooperated better with Richmond the war somehow might have ended differently.[21] But insofar as a state's cooperation can be measured by the actions of its governors, this part of the Owsley thesis has little validity.

The Confederate governors, like their northern counterparts, found themselves enmeshed in a world of changing political power. They had been bred on states' rights doctrines and reared in a prewar political atmosphere which, for all the arguments to the contrary, still left a great deal of power at the state level. But the exigencies of wartime changed all this, and with certain notable exceptions the southern governors accepted the changed base of power. The pattern that developed is roughly as follows. Upon the enactment of such extreme war measures as conscription, impressment, suspension of the habeas corpus, regulation of state blockade-runners, and taxation in kind, most governors automatically protested. Some—Brown and Vance in particular—did so so stridently that they have been condemned more for their words than for their deeds. But after making their points loudly and clearly, and at times forcing a slight compromise, the governors were generally cooperative and, even more, seem to have been satisfied. As Paul Escott has pointed out in his excellent monograph on the Davis administration, the initial "groundswell of support for the Confederacy [was] truly impressive."[22] Obviously this about-face could not have been completed in so short a time, and it is evident that the cooperation of some governors like Pettus of Mississippi waned as conditions worsened. But the belief that the differences between Brown and Vance on one hand and the remaining governors on the other was one of degree rather than kind is erroneous.

The following chapters seem to indicate that of the twenty-eight Confederate governors, fifteen cooperated with the war policies of the central government to a commendable degree. In fact, several of them were so much more nationalistic than their legislatures or their citizenry that they suffered politically for it. These men were Letcher and Smith of Virginia, Pickens and Bonham of South Carolina, Perry and Milton of Florida, Moore and Shorter of Alabama, Pettus of Mississippi, Moore of Louisiana, Clark and Lubbock of Texas, Jackson of Missouri, Johnson of Kentucky, and Harris of Tennessee. Of course, all these men occasionally bickered with Richmond about something, but as a rule they consistently placed national over state interests when conflicts of interest existed.

This certainly should not imply that Confederate laws were necessarily well executed by the presence of a cooperative governor. The novelty and stringency of the wartime programs, southern individualism, poor communications, and the poverty of the people were inherent obstacles. No governor, nor even an entire state government, could overcome them. But within recognized limits these fifteen governors earned good marks for nationalism.

Ellis and Clark of North Carolina almost qualify for the above category, but their cooperation with the Confederate government was probably too passive to deserve high marks. Allen and Rector wanted to work closely with Richmond, but the Confederate government's neglect of the Trans-Mississippi Department forced them to work almost entirely alone. As refugee governors, Hawes and Reynolds had little opportunity to participate in Confederate affairs. With the exception of North Carolina's constant complaints of being left undefended, none of these six men engaged in any serious controversy with the central government.

The remaining seven governors are the ones on whom is founded the charge that the Confederacy was too divided internally to wage war effectively. But how damaging was their position? Five of these men took office when it is known now that the Confederate cause was obviously lost. Flanagin recognized this and gave up, while Watts, Magrath, Murrah, and Charles Clark still hoped to salvage something either by separate state action or by even continuing the war in the Southwest. But whatever they or their governments did or did not do made no difference to the outcome of the war.

Brown and Vance remain as the only governors who significantly damaged the Confederate war effort. Both were jealous guardians of local rights, and when Confederate policies infringed on them the two men protested unremittingly. Whether their constant carping was more a cause or a reflection of public discontent is debatable, but it is clear that both Brown and Vance willingly shouldered their citizens' resentments. Both men quarreled with Richmond over much the same matters, but of the two Brown was the more destructive. Vance won the right to control the exemption of state officials and the cargoes of the *Advance;* on all other disputes he gave grudging but full cooperation. As Professor Escott so well documents, Brown differed with the Confederacy more often, quarreled with it more violently, and won more victories than did any of the other southern governors.

Even more significant than the charisma and cooperation discussed above was how a governor handled the numerous and complex problems which the war had provoked at home. The time had not yet arrived when a national government could perform well at the local level, and this was especially true of the South. The Confederate government simply did not have the experience, the money, or even the inclination to inject itself very far into social or economic affairs. Such areas had traditionally been left to the states and for the most part remained so during the Civil War. About all the Richmond authorities asked was that the states cooperate fully on some matters and shift for themselves elsewhere. So it was vital that the states have both able and active executive leadership in local matters as well. As Professor Wooster comments, the Texas war governors were "required to expand the powers of their office far beyond those exercised by the state's antebellum governors,"[23] and they moved into areas in which prewar Texas chief executives had little experience.

This does not mean that the governors became local wartime dictators. Prewar governors had found themselves contending far more often with their own legislatures than with the government in Washington. When war broke out, the independence which legislatures could exhibit, even in time of crisis, is well demonstrated by the difficulties that Governor Letcher, Governor Pettus, and others had in wresting wartime sacrifices from reluctant legislators. It can also be seen by the appointment by several legislatures and conventions of military boards to coordinate their war effort and in the creation of a plural executive in Florida and South Carolina to monitor an unpopular executive. But none of these artificial restraints was effective. The modern pattern of acting in an emergency was beginning to emerge. There would be an obvious and probably sudden need for a new program or a new appropriation; the governor would inform the legislature precisely what was needed; and, unless there were some overwhelming reason to the contrary, the legislature would give him what he wanted. Thus the national pattern also became the state pattern.

The Davis administration originally planned for a volunteer army of only one hundred thousand men, but after First Manassas it adopted the more realistic figure of four hundred thousand. This number would have been almost impossible to attain in a reasonable time if the state legislatures and conventions had not already authorized their governors to set in motion machinery for raising, organizing, and training the militia. Some governors even acted without legislative instruction, and Mississippi had sixty-five militia companies organized even before the Confederacy was created. The governors protested bitterly when the War Department at first accepted only three-year volunteers or

twelve-month volunteers who were already armed, leaving over two
hundred thousand militiamen idling in camp at state expense. But the
fact remains that these less desirable companies were available at a
moment's notice to the War Department's call.

Generally the legislatures and conventions also gave their governors
instructions to establish "local defense" forces of companies not received by the Confederacy or, later, of able-bodied men outside the
draft age. There was considerable experimentation here, but in every
instance except that of South Carolina the governors were in almost
total command of such forces. The ineffectiveness of these state troops
is a familiar, but only half-told, episode in Confederate history. Probably the concept of an effective state army was as difficult to imagine
then as it is now.

Arming, outfitting, and supplying its troops was another critical
problem for the War Department, and it would be difficult to imagine a
Confederate government with the means or ability to do this unaided.
One of the greatest contributions that state governments made, even
under the leadership of Brown and Vance in the East and of all the
governors in the neglected West, was in these areas. Such work was
largely a matter of ad hoc administration and improvisation. The Confederate governors suddenly found themselves saddled with a variety
of duties for which there was little precedence: organizing the collection of guns and other weapons; negotiating contracts for the manufacture of clothing and army accoutrements; sending out purchasing
agents and often blockade-runners to buy everything from meat to
muslin; begging contributions of clothes from individuals, churches,
and ladies' organizations; and the like. One problem with these operations was that state agents operated in competition with Confederate
purchasing agents and prices rose accordingly. Also, states that acquired good supplies by these means used them for their own troops,
leaving to the hard-pressed War Department the responsibility of outfitting the less fortunate soldiers. This of course is selfish localism, but
if the amount of collectibles ferreted out by swarms of state agents
were to be weighed against the antagonism that they provoked with
Richmond, the judgment seems unclear.

All governors found that the war had promoted them to quasi commanders in chief, far beyond the limits envisioned by their own state
constitutions. Mention has already been made of the ineffective state
"army" that each governor established from men unqualified for regular military service and that he had at his disposal. Those who had
Federal forts or arsenals in their jurisdiction seized these installations
generally independent of the Confederacy's War Department. Those in
states outside the main battle zones unwillingly had to take charge of

most of their own defense plans and constructions. Generally they had newly formed military boards to advise them here, and all of the governors impressed slaves and free Negroes to work on defense construction. Collectively, the Trans-Mississippi governors met from time to time to formulate and coordinate their strategies; individually they established local systems of frontier protection against Indians. Most governors obtained from their legislatures, or simply preempted, the right to restrict cotton planting, to buy cotton for export, to arrest peace activists, and even to declare martial law, to ban distilling, to restrict hoarding and speculation. The governors of Texas, Georgia, and South Carolina even ventured into foreign diplomacy.

All these war programs inevitably caused state expenses and indebtedness to soar unprecedentedly, and conservative antebellum financial guidelines had to be abandoned. No sooner would a legislature vote a tax increase or a new appropriation than its governor would report that more was needed. The legislature would then either raise taxes or authorize a new issue of fiat money, often both. The Georgia state budget for 1863 exceeded the state's appropriations for the entire period of the 1850s. Refugee governors virtually carried their state treasury in their saddlebags and spent it at their own discretion. One can observe in reading the following chapters that, with rare exceptions, the necessary financial legislation was far more the governor's decision than the legislature's. This abdication of joint responsibility for taxes and expenditures was but another illustration of executive domination in times of trial.

Obviously much of these expenditures were of a military nature, but the manpower drain, the deprivation, and the inflation caused by the war created such distress among civilians that for the first time in American history individual welfare was considered a major responsibility of state government. The pattern which generally developed was for the legislature to authorize in the most general terms a new relief policy, finance it as well as possible, and then leave its implementation to the best devices of the governor. This was yet another way in which the governors, to repeat Professor Wooster, were "required to expand the powers of their office far beyond those exercised" by the antebellum governors.

Some of these policies were startlingly modern. Probably the most revolutionary was the allocation of money and/or food to soldiers' families as well as to other needy civilians. Some states, like Arkansas, failed in their direct relief efforts; others, like Georgia, succeeded; but all tried. Possibly success or failure depended on whether the money was available, for in Georgia the welfare costs dominated the state's budget for the last two years of the war. Salt was a vital preservative, and it appears that every governor had almost carte blanche authority to acquire this precious commodity. So many different techniques were used that the one unifying principle seems to have been to get salt to the people at cost. Cotton and wool cards were both necessary and scarce. Some governors imported them; others succeeded in having them manufactured; still others failed in both efforts. As slight as these relief efforts seem today, it is difficult to see how the Confederate home front could have survived nearly as long as it did without them.

Some of the above observations on the Confederate governors and their governorships may be at variance with the intended interpretations of the authors of the following chapters or of other readers. Each author is a recognized authority on Civil War history in his state and has been given no guideline except that of brevity. A fuller account of the Civil War in each state is easily attainable elsewhere, and other works by these historians is suggested. I have simply sifted through the thirteen chapters and attempted to extract what seems to me to have been the significant developments in government and administration which resulted from the war. I must confess to having lifted several ideas from the authors and wish to give them full credit for them. Some of my other observations have clearly been reached subjectively, and on this I make no comment.

W. BUCK YEARNS

ALABAMA

Malcolm C. McMillan

ndrew Barry Moore, the first of Alabama's three Civil War governors, had only about eleven months left in office when Alabama joined the Confederacy early in 1861. Born in Spartanburg District, South Carolina, on March 7, 1807, the son of Captain Charles Moore (a Revolutionary War and War of 1812 soldier), he was reared on a South Carolina cotton plantation. When their land wore out the family moved west, settling at Marion, Alabama, about 1823. Perhaps because of his schooling, Andrew did not join them until 1826. After teaching school for two years, he read law and began to practice in 1833. His law practice prospered and he soon began cotton planting as well. In 1837 he married Mary Goree, daughter of a local planter.[1]

Moore was elected as a Democrat to the state House of Representatives in 1839 and every year from 1842 to 1845. He served as speaker for the last three years, demonstrating marked ability to deal with rival factions of his party. A contemporary described him as "about six feet in stature, stout and well built, with good features and florid complexion." He found Moore "frank, cordial, moral and full of public spirit," always a popular favorite and demanding "the highest respect."[2] A fellow legislator wrote that Moore was "a clever fellow but scary, has a good opinion of himself and is on the fence between the Hunkers and the Chivalry [conservatives and states' righters]."[3] In 1851 Governor Henry W. Collier appointed him to the circuit bench, and he was reelected until nominated for governor in 1857. At that time Moore was a moderate on the sectional issue and triumphed over his extremist rivals only after twenty-six ballots.

In the election which followed, he had no opposition, the Whigs and Americans being too weak to organize. Dissension among the Democrats increased, however, and in 1859 the Southern Rights wing of the party ran William F. Samford against the more conservative incumbent. Moore's overwhelming victory indicated that Alabamians still trusted the national Democratic party to defend southern rights, though after John Brown's raid at Harpers Ferry in October 1859 this trust began to waver. In December of that year Moore himself devoted most of his second inaugural address to the rights of the South, an issue which he had not even mentioned in his last message to the legislature. He said that he had been deluded by the Kansas–Nebraska Act and the Dred Scott decision into thinking that peace was at hand, but now knew that he was wrong.[4] Upon his recommendation, the next session of the legislature provided for the organization of a volunteer corps in each county, appropriated $200,000 for defense, and established scholarships for two young men from each county to attend military schools and learn to train troops.[5]

Although now thoroughly aroused, Moore still sought to avoid the issue of secession. In mid-1860 he received joint resolutions of the South Carolina legislature proposing a southern convention to consider secession; at the same time the "fire-eaters" in the Alabama legislature were demanding resolutions providing for a state convention in case a Republican was elected president. Moore saw the Alabama resolutions as the lesser of two evils, for, as he put it, "if a Republican victory does not occur, there will be no necessity for a convention."[6] When the contingency resolutions passed almost unanimously, Governor Moore wrote Governor William H. Gist of South Carolina that Alabama favored a separate state convention upon the contingency cited and a southern convention later.[7]

However, subsequent events, including the Democratic party split at Charleston, soon convinced Moore of the likelihood of a Republican victory. Moore wrote E. C. Bullock of Eufaula that Lincoln's election now seemed assured and that he was asking his lawyer friends to review his conviction that since the electoral college officially elected the president he should not call a convention until after it met in December. Moore stated he wished to be on sound legal grounds so as not to give the submissionists an issue in the election for the convention or the convention itself. He added that "the convention should be convened at the earliest day the law will permit."[8]

After Lincoln's election, pressure began to build for the governor to announce his intentions. On November 14, 1860, he told a committee which waited on him that although he would not issue a convention call until December 5 he could say unofficially that the election for convention delegates would be on Christmas Eve and that those elected would gather in Montgomery the following January 7. He thus added three weeks to a campaign which would otherwise have been far too short.[9] Although Moore did not take sides in the campaign, the public knew full well that he considered Lincoln's election to be sufficient cause for immediate secession. Meanwhile, he sent sixteen commissioners to confer with the officials of other slaveholding states, ostensibly to consult but in fact to coordinate and urge secession. Moore thus had much influence on this movement by his early initiative and emphasis on the need for coordination. The commissioners also kept him abreast of events in the other southern states.[10]

After several weeks of planning and after ascertaining that all Federal forts in Alabama were dilapidated and almost undefended, Moore, working through Major General Thomas J. Butler of the state militia, ordered the militia to seize the arsenal at Mount Vernon and Forts Morgan and Gaines in Mobile Bay.[11] The attack began on January 3, 1861, and was made with overwhelming force to prevent bloodshed. By January 5 all were in Alabama hands. Moore later told the convention that he had assumed "great responsibility" in seizing the forts. "For my justification," he said, "I rely upon the propriety and necessity of the course I have taken, and upon the wisdom and patriotism of the convention and the people of Alabama."[12] Even as he gave the orders for seizure, Moore was preparing a letter to President James Buchanan. He explained the seizure as a measure "to avoid and not to provoke hostilities," a precaution taken upon evidence that the Federal government was moving to reinforce the forts. Moore later dispatched Thomas J. Judge to Washington in order to negotiate with Buchanan a division of the public property and debt, but the president refused to see him.[13]

After Lincoln's election, uncertainty about the future brought on a financial crisis. On December 4 Governor Moore by circular letter pressured all banks in the state to suspend specie payments and guarantee at least one million dollars in their vaults to the state. This was an emergency measure to be legalized later by the legislature, which Moore argued could not be called together at the time because it would cause a run on the banks and defeat the purpose. Most banks suspended specie payments, and all promised to guarantee the state their share. In February 1861 the legislature authorized the earlier suspension provided the banks buy a fixed quota of state bonds at par value against which they could issue their notes. Thus the government secured nearly all the specie in the state to finance the war in return for state bonds which were later to become worthless.[14]

In the meantime Governor Moore was seeking arms in fierce competition with other southern states. Under the Military Bill passed by the last session of the legislature, volunteer companies were springing up in most counties and Moore was hard-pressed to furnish them with arms. He had several purchasing agents in the field, the most diligent of them J. R. Powell, mail contractor and stagecoach owner-promoter and later a builder of Birmingham. Powell traveled east to Washington, New York, and Boston in November and December of 1860, buying $46,452 worth of arms, mostly small arms, but also cannon, gun carriages, and caissons. On December 14 Moore called him home by telegraph, saying "Your purchase of muskets has created great dissatisfaction." Actually Powell's trip had received more publicity in the press, both North and South, than the governor or his agent wanted. This was to be only the beginning of Moore's quest for arms as he was besieged by volunteers, by the Confederate government, and later by some of the border states.[15]

Governor Moore's relations with the secession convention which met in Montgomery on January 7, 1861, were amicable, perhaps because the immediate secessionists controlled the convention. He had promptly reported to and asked the blessings of the convention on his appointment of commissioners to the slaveholding states, his seizure of the forts and his letter to Buchanan, his circular letter to the banks, and his purchase of arms. When Governor M. S. Perry of Florida called on Moore to send five hundred armed troops and, later, five hundred stands of arms to Pensacola, a majority of the convention supported the move. When a stalemate developed at Pensacola and the cooperationists tried to recall the troops, the same majority supported the governor. The cooperationists struck back at Moore by introducing an ordinance based on the South Carolina plan which would create a council of state to advise him on military matters, but it was defeated by a vote of 52 to 40.[16]

On January 14, 1861, Governor Moore called the legislature into special session in order to implement actions taken by himself and the convention. He exhorted it to place Alabama "as early . . . as possible upon the most efficient war footing." In response it legalized the suspension of specie payments and the forced purchase of state bonds, but only by a close vote. But there was no reorganization of the armed forces, and the system of depending on volunteer companies to replace the militia system was continued. The legislature authorized the chief executive to issue treasury notes, an action which fortunately Moore, unlike his two successors, largely ignored. The governor asked the House of Representatives to give up its chambers to the Confederate convention, which arrived on February 4 to find a newly carpeted and generally refurbished hall.[17]

Moore had a ringside seat at the birth of the new nation in Montgomery. The Confederate congressmen seem to have been impressed by his hospitality. One member wrote: "Governor Moore has treated us mu-

nificently . . . [and] with every manifestation of respect."[18] According to
another account, Moore played a key role in the selection of Jefferson
Davis to head the Confederacy. He had the Alabama commissioners to
Virginia promise Alabama's support for the more conservative Davis
for the presidency over the fire-eater William L. Yancey, whom Virginians feared, in return for movement toward a convention in Virginia.[19]

The last nine months in office found Moore's time packed with work
and decision making. He even had to hire an extra secretary to answer
his mail. The legislature created a military board of three members to
serve at his pleasure and give advice when asked. The governor appointed the able Duff Green as state quartermaster general. Green
held the position throughout the war and became an important cog in
Alabama's war effort. Upon authorization by the legislature, Moore
dispatched J. W. Echols to the Northwest on a successful mission to
buy commissary stores. As Alabama troops became Confederate regu-
lars, many of these supplies went with them, as did arms purchased by
the state.[20]

The United States fleet blocked the inner channel between Mobile
and New Orleans, and Moore, along with the governors of Mississippi
and Louisiana, launched a temporarily successful effort to open it.
When the owners of the *Florida,* a merchant vessel in Mobile Bay,
would not agree to her conversion to a gunboat under lease, Moore had
the vessel seized, leaving payment to a board of appraisers.[21]

Nearly all the home-front problems, which later became more acute,
emerged under Moore. Scarcities of certain necessities developed early
in the war and speculators and extortioners appeared. Moore quickly
proclaimed their activities "unpatriotic and wicked." When salt rose
from one dollar to ten dollars a bushel the governor without legislative
warranty used part of the military fund to purchase and distribute salt
to the poor families of soldiers. He also encouraged its production by
leasing the state-owned salt springs to private companies and individuals. He attempted to help indigent families of soldiers by authorizing courts of county commissioners to levy a local tax and to appoint
agents to buy and distribute food to such families.[22]

Under ordinances passed by the convention, Moore transferred the
Federal forts and arsenal to Confederate ownership along with most of
the arms captured at Mount Vernon, approximately twenty thousand
stands. But defense of the coast continued to be a major concern. As
large numbers of Alabama troops were moved to the Virginia and
Kentucky fronts, South Alabama clamored that Mobile was being neglected although then threatened by a powerful United States fleet.
The governor resisted all pressure "to make application for the recall of
Alabama regiments in Virginia and Kentucky." But after two regi-

ments were organized and accepted from the Mobile area, Moore declared that he would receive no more companies from Mobile. Mobile was in an exposed position and fairness demanded that it "should have the means of protection constantly in reach." Privately he admitted that he disliked the large number of troops leaving the state and threatened to treat as deserters all who resigned from state units to join the Confederate army.[23]

When the governor of Florida called for aid, Moore rushed the Second Alabama Volunteers under the command of Tennent Lomax to Pensacola. On January 13 Lomax was instructed to assume command, if offered, and to take Fort Pickens even "at a sacrifice." But Governor Perry of Florida placed William H. Chase, an old army officer who had constructed Fort Pickens, in command. Moore did not give up easily. When he dispatched the First Regiment of Alabama artillery to Pensacola on February 7 he instructed its commander to try to get command, but the opportunity never came. Moore believed that "no other place on the Gulf is safe while the federal troops hold possession of the commanding fortifications at Pensacola." It exasperated him not to have command there, so close to the Alabama line and where most of the troops were Alabamians.[24]

Scholars have argued that after secession all factions in Alabama came together to support the Confederacy, but the Moore correspondence does not support that position. On July 16, 1861, a correspondent in Blount County wrote that "a very considerable number of the inhabitants of the counties of Winston, Marion and Morgan are disaffected toward the Confederate government and are actually raising and equipping themselves to sustain the old government of the United States." Other letters add Lamar, Walker, Shelby, Randolph, and Tuscaloosa counties to the list of those with disaffected people. Moore, wondering whether he should use force to put down the opposition, dispatched former Congressman George S. Houston to the area. Houston did not think force necessary and advised the governor that because of old factions there the worst thing he could do was to send in troops recruited from North Alabama counties. During the crisis Moore wrote one of his informers in Walker County that "as long as I am governor of the state the laws against treason and sedition shall be faithfully executed if it takes the whole military power."[25]

Moore allowed his strong states' rights convictions to emerge on two matters. In the early months of the war, arms were so scarce that he had the sheriff of each county searching homes for old militia weapons. But soon the Confederate War Department began to pressure him, as it was doing other state governors, to turn over all arms to the Confederacy. Moore did give up those taken from the Federal arsenal, but he kept and allocated to himself those purchased by the state. While this policy kept arms at home badly needed elsewhere, it may be said in Moore's defense that public clamor to retain arms was tremendous and that eventually many of the locally obtained arms units went into the Confederate army. Another states' rights position emerged when Moore refused to allow state agents to collect Confederate taxes.[26]

On October 28, 1861, Moore proudly told his last legislature that "your state has given to the defense of the Confederacy full 27,000 men." Twenty-three regiments were already in the field and five others were near completion. "Of these troops Alabama has armed more than 14,000 and equipped nearly half that number." He concluded by saying, "It is a source of much gratification to be able to say that there is no state in the Confederacy which has done more in proportion to its means . . . than Alabama."[27]

Constitutionally barred from seeking a third term, Moore left the governorship but not the war effort. He worked tirelessly as special aide to his successor, recruiting troops, rushing supplies to beleaguered Confederate forces, urging planters to lease their slaves for railroad construction, and buying corn for indigent families. His health began to fail, however, and he spent the last months of the war quietly at home in Marion.[28]

On May 16, 1865, Secretary of War Edwin M. Stanton directed General E. R. S. Canby to "arrest and imprison Moore . . . and have him confined in a secure military prison," the correspondence revealing a bitterness toward "the secession governor" not displayed toward his two successors.[29] He was arrested in or near Marion and taken to New Orleans, where he was sent by steamer to Fort Pulaski in Savannah. Finally released in August 1865, in part at least because of failing health,[30] he returned to Marion where he practiced law until his death on April 5, 1873. He was buried in Fairview Cemetery in Perry County.[31]

John Gill Shorter, the man who succeeded Andrew Moore as governor of Alabama, was born in Monticello, Georgia, on April 3, 1818. In 1833 his physician-planter father, Reuben Clarke, took the family to Irvinton (now Eufaula), Alabama. John Gill finished at Franklin College (the University of Georgia) in 1837 and followed his father to Eufaula, where he was admitted to the bar in 1838. In 1843 he married Mary Jane Battle, daughter of a wealthy Barbour County planter. Shorter soon became one of the best-known lawyers in Southeast Alabama, and his remunerative practice enabled him to invest heavily in cotton land and slaves in Barbour County and in Quitman County, Georgia.

In 1844 he was appointed solicitor for the Eufaula District, and the next year he was elected to the state Senate as a Democrat from normally Whig Barbour County. He refused to stand for reelection, but in 1851 was persuaded to become a candidate for the lower house. He won the seat, but soon gave it up when appointed circuit judge of the Eufaula District. Shorter was elected judge in his own right in 1852 and again in 1858.[32] A disciple of William L. Yancey and an admirer of John C. Calhoun, he represented Alabama at the Nashville convention of 1850 as an ardent secessionist. Throughout the fifties he was a member of the "Eufaula regency," about a dozen lawyer-planters of Barbour County whom one historian has called "the most consistent secessionists in the state during the fifties," men who refused "to make any concessions to preserve the Union." As soon as the Alabama secession had taken the state out of the Union, Governor Moore sent Shorter as commissioner to Georgia to urge its secession. On January 16 he sent a message to the Georgia Secession Convention "inviting the people of Georgia and other slaveholding states to meet the people of Alabama, by their delegates in convention on the 4th day of February, 1861, at the city of Montgomery."[33]

While in Georgia, Shorter was elected to the Confederate Provisional Congress and served until he resigned to become governor. While in Congress he established a reputation as being a "Davis man," consistently supporting the president's policies. In the gubernatorial election of 1861 the press replaced the traditional nominating conventions, the consensus being that traditional politics should be suspended for the war. Some six names were brought forward, but eventually Shorter became the favorite of the Democratic press and Thomas H. Watts of the Old Whig and American papers. On August 10 Shorter won over Watts by a vote of 37,894 to 27,121. Ironically he ran best in North Alabama, where secessionism had been weakest. The vote indicated that party geographical links were still holding despite secession and war, and, more significantly, that secessionists were not yet being blamed for having disrupted the Union. The glorious days of First Bull Run were still fresh in people's minds.[34]

Shorter was inaugurated on December 2, 1861. In his inaugural address he called for building up state fortifications and war industry. He warned that the war would bring "unaccustomed burdens," but promised that it would also bring "a deliverance . . . from all commercial dependence upon, as well as from all social and political complications with a people who appreciate neither the value of liberty nor the sanctity of compacts."[35]

Shorter's first priority on taking office was to strengthen the forces of Albert Sidney Johnston, then facing a desperate situation to the north.

Shorter sent former Governor Moore, whom he made a military aide with the rank of colonel, into North Alabama to raise and arm troops, and soon Shorter was able to send Johnston two regiments and a battalion as well as five hundred slaves to work on fortifications. But the Kentucky and Tennessee fronts crumbled rapidly, and in April 1862 that part of Alabama north of the Tennessee River fell into Federal hands. With the exception of a brief respite in the fall and winter of 1862–63, North Alabama remained a battlefield. The area had been predominantly Democratic and pro-Shorter in 1861, but by 1863 the horrors of war had turned the political situation around.[36]

The invasion of North Alabama so stunned Shorter that it was two weeks—a delay for which he was later criticized—before he called for the formation of four cavalry companies to harass the enemy. But with the defeat at Shiloh, the state almost destitute of arms, and most Alabama troops fighting in Virginia, there was little that the Confederacy or the governor could do. When the Federals withdrew from North Alabama, after five months of occupation, they left behind a bitter people. And when reports of the ruthless "rape of Athens" reached Montgomery, the governor was powerless to help. In January 1863 Shorter made his only trip to the Tennessee Valley to assure the people of his interest and to try to get them to form volunteer units for local defense. But when he returned to Montgomery due to pressure of business instead of surveying the devastation throughout the valley, the people were offended.[37]

Like his predecessor, Shorter considered the defense of Pensacola as important to Alabama as to Florida. However, when he heard in March 1862 that the Confederate government planned to evacuate the town, he rushed there to see what could be salvaged. He ascertained that "it would be physically impossible to remove the guns, ammunition and other public stores . . . within the time limited for its abandonment," and by a joint telegram with the officer in command induced the War Department to postpone the evacuation.[38] Shorter then sent seventeen companies from Confederate regiments to help with the evacuation, and he called on the planters to furnish slave labor to repair the Alabama and Florida Railroad, over which war materiel could be brought to Alabama. Though still opposing evacuation, when Pensacola was abandoned on May 10, 1862, Shorter sought and secured his share of its cannon to fortify Mobile and its river defenses. His overall activities were invaluable to the war effort, and also allowed many private citizens to escape with their personal belongings.[39]

The transfer of Confederate troops from Pensacola to Tennessee meant that not only would Pensacola be lost but that Mobile would only be protected by its forts and would be vulnerable to a land attack.

When Federal troops landed on Ship Island equidistant between Mobile and New Orleans, great excitement and confusion reigned in Mobile at the city being "left to the mercies of the federal fleet." Shorter persuaded the secretary of war to send to Mobile troops then forming in the state, where they were joined by the state militia of that area. The strong defenses later built about Mobile did not exist at this time and it was saved only because the enemy chose to attack New Orleans.[40] With tension eased, Shorter allowed some militia units to return home for spring planting provided they would turn over their arms to the state. The state paid for these guns and Shorter used them to arm the Confederate regiments forming in Mobile, though he was charged with unnecessarily calling up the militia as "a mere pretext or scheme to obtain their arms."[41]

Although Mobile was temporarily safe, its Committee of Public Safety continued to pressure the governor for better protection. He in turn applied the same pressure to the War Department, arguing "our Gulf coast is abandoned now, having sent out of state all the public arms the state had, and contributed them, with our brave troops to the common cause."[42]

In Shorter's opinion Alabama's critical problem was "not in procuring men but arms and ammunition." His predecessor had let twenty thousand stands of arms leave the state, and on March 28, 1862, Shorter telegraphed the secretary of war: "I have not a single regiment which has arms and equipment, hardly clothing."[43] When the governor received no satisfaction from Richmond he asked his legislature to empower him to impress arms from civilians, but it refused on the grounds that possession of arms was a sacred right of the people. Shorter was obliged, therfore, to send agents through the state to gather militia muskets, which the governor insisted were still the property of the state, and to buy "country arms" of all kind, even flintlock rifles, which could be bored out or altered from flint to percussion.[44] Out of desperation Shorter turned to home manufacture. Shops and small foundries through the state were given contracts, the largest being made with the newly formed Alabama Arms Manufacturing Company in Montgomery, to whom the state loaned $250,000 to be paid back in manufactured arms. Despite these efforts, however, the arming of Alabama troops remained a major unsolved problem. Some eighteen months after the contracts were let, the governor had to report to the legislature that no arms had been delivered to the state by any of the contractors.[45]

Shorter did manage, however, to send arms to the University of Alabama. The school had instituted military training in 1859, and after the fall of Fort Donelson there was an exodus of cadets from the campus. But Shorter refused to let them volunteer in new regiments, sending them instead to camps of instruction where they helped train raw recruits. He also sent President L. C. Garland to Richmond with a letter to Jefferson Davis, asserting that these cadets had drilled twelve thousand of the eighteen thousand troops raised in the state since he took office. He boldly declared that they were a military unit under his control and were not subject to the Conscription Act. The secretary of war tacitly accepted this position, the cadets continued as drill masters, and the University of Alabama remained open.[46]

Though volunteers were slow to reenlist in 1862 and the Federal army continued to press on all fronts, Shorter at first opposed conscription. "If we are to depend upon . . . [conscription] to maintain the liberty of the South, I should almost despair of our ultimate triumph," he said. After the conscription law was adopted, he counseled the secretary of war "that the enrollment should be postponed as long as possible until the grain and provision crops" could be gathered. He warned that this was especially important in North Alabama, the granary of the state, where opposition to the law would be most pronounced.[47]

Shorter correctly predicted the opposition to the draft in the mountain counties of North Alabama and the wiregrass of Southeast Alabama. When armed resistance to conscription broke out in Randolph County in September 1862, the War Department suggested to Shorter that he send in a force commanded by state officers. While the governor agreed that the law "should be enforced at every hazard," he maintained that it should be done solely by Confederate officers. Upon his suggestion, Confederate cavalry moved into Randolph and the trouble subsided, but three months later he was forced to telegraph the secretary of war that "Randolph County defies enforcement of the conscript act" and urged speedy action or else "deserters from every quarter will increase."[48]

But the problem was uncontrollable, and as the war lengthened Toryism and desertion in North and Southeast Alabama increased. By August 1863 one estimate placed eight thousand in the hill country alone. As an original secessionist Shorter had little influence with these people, so he tried to reach them through loyal Confederates who had opposed immediate secession, among them being Robert Jemison of Tuscaloosa and Robert Patton of Florence. He also made his brother, ex-Congressman Eli Shorter, an aide. The governor himself persuaded President Davis to let him enlist conscripts and deserters in Southeast Alabama into a special army to defend the Gulf coast, which meant the suspension of conscription in that area. The ploy was successful because it meant staying close to home. But it made good Confederate soldiers out of very few; some of them later mutinied.[49] Meanwhile,

Shorter asked all Alabamians to "give no shelter to deserters" and to give "aid to the proper officers in arresting and coercing those who yield to no gentler means."[50]

The threats of Federal attacks against Mobile during the spring and summer of 1862 had revealed serious weaknesses in Alabama's local defense forces. In March, Shorter had called out the militia from the southwest counties, but the better companies were fighting far afield and most of those at home failed to respond. The conscription act of April depleted the militia even more, and Shorter realized that the only hope of forming an adequate state force was to extend the militia age limits. In October he recommended to a special session of the legislature that the militia be so organized as to "embrace all ablebodied citizens of the state above the age of sixteen and under the age of sixty years" not subject to the draft.[51] But the legislature, dominated by localism at this time, failed to act. It did pass a law making militia officers subject to conscription, but this only further weakened the militia. After the legislature adjourned, the governor appealed to the people to form volunteer companies, but the response was disappointing. The truth was that there was no longer much manpower for the militia. In desperation Shorter even tried to force substitutes and certain other men into the militia, but they sought "pretexts in every manner to avoid duty, even to a resort to a habeas corpus before ignorant justices of the peace, who have no jurisdiction of their cases."[52]

In August 1863 Shorter convened the legislature in special session for the sole purpose of providing militia for state defense. He urged that all white males without exception between the ages of sixteen and sixty and not in the Confederate army be drafted into a military force to protect the state and enforce the law against stragglers and deserters. Opponents of the governor's proposal centered on the argument "that young men under 18 and old men over 45 would be inefficient as soldiers and that their services were required at home." Its proponents finally agreed to a cumbersome compromise in which boys sixteen and seventeen and men between forty-five and sixty would be organized as "County Reserves," liable to service only in their respective counties and therefore almost useless. Men from eighteen to forty-five and not in Confederate service were to be organized as "State Reserves," which included a few thousand exemptees, details, and substitutes. Shorter disliked the bill, but signed it because "it was the best I could get."[53] Nevertheless, the system remained intact for the duration of the war.

Perhaps no problem on the home front worried the governor as much as the growing number of indigent families of soldiers, many of them near starvation. Bessie Martin in her *Desertion of Alabama Troops* found this to be the major cause of desertion by Alabamians.[54] In October 1862, Shorter called a special session of the legislature to consider remedies. In response to his dramatic appeal, the legislature appropriated $2 million to be disbursed to the probate judges of each county, who would distribute the relief under the supervision of the court of county commissioners. Each judge would also make a survey of the needs of soldiers' families and report his findings to the state as the basis for future relief. The legislature also empowered county commissioners to levy a local tax to supplement the state's relief work.[55]

When the legislature met in November 1863 the number of indigent families had trebled, and the legislators once again responded generously to Shorter's plea for relief appropriations. But inflation was now eroding the value of money so rapidly that Shorter placed more emphasis on the purchase of supplies by the state for distribution. Soon the governor had numerous purchasing agents in the field competing with speculators for scarce provisions. There was actually plenty of grain in the Black Belt throughout the war, and on one occasion former Governor Moore bought a supply of corn for the state at $1.25 a bushel when the market price was $3.00. But the state's deteriorating railroad system often made transportation of such purchases impossible, and Shorter even considered impressing teams to haul grain to the North Alabama counties. By 1863 "corn women" from North Alabama, walking with sacks on their backs, were a familiar sight in the Black Belt.[56]

But food at reasonable prices was a concern of almost everyone. On March 1, 1862, Shorter asked the people to "plant not one seed of cotton beyond your home wants, but put down your land in grain and every other kind of farm product and raise every kind of livestock." In December of that year the legislature upon his recommendation imposed a tax of ten cents a pound on all cotton grown above 2,500 pounds of seed cotton per hand.[57] On his own authority Shorter banned the distillation of alcohol except that which he would license for medicinal and war purposes. In the same month he obtained legislative authority "to have distilled only such amount of grain as he thinks consistent with the common defense and the general welfare of the state." Under the law the governor licensed distillers only in counties with a surplus of grain, the license fee to be used for the support of the poor. Since the right to make liquor was a proverbial one in the frontier South, the law was inevitably poorly enforced and almost unworkable.[58]

Shorter continued his predecessor's efforts to alleviate the salt shortage. In fact he devoted so much attention to this single problem that some of his contemporaries held that so much energy could have been better spent in securing arms. He leased the state-owned salt springs in Clarke and Washington counties to Figh and Company, and even leased springs in Saltville, Virginia. He began the State Salt Works in Alabama with A. G. McGehee as salt commissioner. And he threatened to seize private salt works if they overcharged for their product. Overall his efforts should be considered successful, though they were often hampered by poor railroad facilities and even by the cutting of railway lines by Federal troops.[59]

The extent to which Shorter was willing to risk his political career for the sake of the Confederate war effort is best demonstrated by his vigorous impressment of slave labor for war work. At the beginning of the war, planters offered free slave labor for such work, and in December 1861 the governor raised without difficulty five hundred slaves to work on the fortifications at Fort Henry in northern Tennessee. But stories of neglect and abuse soon began to circulate, and in October 1862 the otherwise loyal planters of west-central Alabama began to withdraw their slaves from work on the Alabama and Mississippi Railroad (Selma to Meridian). Shorter, however, contended that these slaves were treated better than soldiers and received twice their pay. He sent former Governor Moore, probably his most indispensable aide, to reason with these planters and eventually they furnished enough slave labor to complete the railroad.[60]

In October 1862, therefore, the legislature gave the governor the power to impress slaves for work on fortifications and defenses, and a system developed whereby the military commanders would inform the governor how many laborers they needed, the governor would requisition them, and the Confederate government would pay the owners for their hire. The gradual loss of forts on the Mississippi and its tributaries made the heartland of Alabama vulnerable to attack by Federal gunboats, and in February 1863 Shorter requisitioned 2,100 slaves to help place obstructions at strategic points in the rivers to slow enemy gunboats so that they could be destroyed by cannon on nearby bluffs, particularly on Owen and Choctaw Bluffs. But the most feared invasion was through Mobile, and between February and October 1863 Shorter provided nine thousand slaves for work on its defenses.[61]

Apparently the military was more interested in getting the job done than anything else. Shorter wrote General D. H. Maury, commander at Mobile, that among the slaves working there "there have been fully five hundred deaths, in many instances caused by sheer neglect." He claimed that in many cases no records were kept, that slaves were underfed and not returned to their owners on time, and that sickness was ignored. He also charged that impressed wagons and tools were either torn up or never returned.[62] But despite the governor's constant exhortations, little improvement occurred. After the passage of the

Confederate Impressment Act of March 26, 1863, Shorter seriously considered saving himself politically by leaving all impressment activities to the Confederate government, but apparently his honor and patriotism forced him to continue his cooperation. After his defeat for reelection, he wrote that it was the impressment of slaves "which carried the state so largely against me."[63]

Neither Alabama's governors nor its legislatures ever faced up to the need for higher taxes, and for a year Shorter was able to avoid asking the legislature for an issue of paper currency. But in November 1862 he faced the almost impossible task of obtaining the $2 million needed for indigent families; and he also informed the legislature that the privately issued change bills—"shinplasters"—had become such a public nuisance that the state needed "some kind of paper currency." The legislature obediently authorized him to issue $2 million (later in the same session raised to $3.5 million) and the state was on its way almost overnight to financing the war by printing fiat money.[64]

To keep Alabama's credit good in England, Governor Shorter sent through the blockade $155,000 in specie as interest on state bonds held by British investors. This was done with the permission of the Federal squadron off Mobile, which allowed a British ship to pick up the money. However, the United States decided to make an issue of the matter with Great Britain, which because of the pressure dismissed its consul in Mobile through whom Shorter had made the arrangement. This incident became a part of the larger controversy over accreditation of British consuls in the Confederacy that ended in the expulsion of all in late 1863.[65]

As the election of August 1863 approached, Confederate Attorney General Thomas Hill Watts wrote a friend that although he would not campaign he would accept the governorship of Alabama "if called by the people." Although Shorter had become the scapegoat for almost every problem brought by a bloody civil war, he said that he did not "feel at liberty to decline serving the state for a second term, according to past usage." If he stepped aside under pressure his enemies could say that all charges were true. In an address to the people he stated his intention to run again and reviewed his administration. He said that he was aware of complaints against him, "but believed them to be undeserved." Time, he said, would "disclose my record and vindicate my course." However, the people voted Shorter out of office by the overwhelming majority of 28,215 for Watts, 8,415 for Shorter, and 1,471 for James Dowdell. Shorter carried only four North Alabama counties and lost his own county of Barbour by four hundred votes. In 1861 he had been elected by heavy majorities in northern and eastern Alabama; he lost both areas in 1863. On July 24 he wrote Braxton

Bragg that he was "afraid our reverses in the west will affect our election," but a long, hard, self-sacrificing war had had the most telling effect.[66]

The Confederacy possessed too few men of the quality of Shorter. In 1872, the year of Shorter's death, historian William Garrett wrote: "In justice to Governor Shorter, it may be said that it was virtually impossible for any man to fulfill the public expectations and to satisfy all complaints during the war. . . . The sentence against him was harsh indeed." After the election Shorter wrote a friend: "I have been stricken down for holding up the state to its high resolves and crowding the people to the performance of their duty."[67] In most of his letters after defeat, however, the governor showed no bitterness.

Shorter retired to Eufaula for the remaining years of his life. Despite the assertion by several historians, there is no evidence that he was arrested and imprisoned at the end of the war. He continued his law practice and appeared briefly at Conservative Reconstruction meetings in Montgomery. His health had always been delicate and in January 1872 he caught a severe cold which finally developed into tuberculosis. He died on May 29 and was buried in the family burial ground in Eufaula.[68]

Thomas Hill Watts, who became governor of Alabama on December 2, 1863, was born January 3, 1819, the oldest of twelve children. His father, John Hughes Watts, had moved from Georgia to what is now Butler County, Alabama, a year earlier. After attending an old field school near his home, young Watts entered Airy Mount Academy in Dallas County. In 1836 he asked for a college education instead of part of his father's estate and spent the next four years at the University of Virginia. He read law at home for the next year, passed the bar examination, and began practicing at Greenville. Successful from the start, in 1848 he moved to Montgomery and joined Thomas J. Judge and others in a firm which became one of the best known in the state. By 1860 Watts was a wealthy lawyer-planter, owning 179 slaves and a plantation valued at $200,000. The variety of cash crops, foodstuffs, and livestock produced on his estate indicated a self-sufficiency rare among plantation owners. He was a large and affable man, "social and quite popular with all classes." His habits were prudent and he maintained good health by daily physical exercise.[69]

Watts had been elected to the lower house of the state legislature as a Whig in 1842, 1843, 1845, and 1849. In 1853 he went to the state Senate, where he sponsored initiatory steps toward a geological survey of the state. As the Whig party disintegrated in the middle fifties he found temporary refuge in the American party, which in 1855 nominated him as its candidate for Congress from the Montgomery District. Though he lost by a small margin, it was evident that he was becoming one of the acknowledged leaders of the Democratic opposition. In 1860 Watts campaigned for the Bell-Everett Constitutional Union ticket in an effort to save the Union, but he let it be known that he would advocate secession if Lincoln were elected. And he rejected the cooperationist position that safety demanded that all the seceding states leave the Union at the same time, arguing that a sovereign state should leave the Union as it entered—alone. As a delegate to the Alabama convention, which met on January 7, 1861, Watts worked for immediate and separate state secession. And even before the passage of that ordinance he favored the immediate seizure of all Federal property in Alabama and cooperation with neighboring states in their seizure of Federal forts and arsenals.[70]

In June 1861 the Montgomery *Daily Post* nominated Watts as a candidate for governor in the August elections. Soon there were four others running, but by July all but Shorter had withdrawn to prevent any appearance of former "partyism" continuing in the Confederacy. The *Daily Post* soon renominated Watts, however, and he eventually agreed to serve if elected. Shorter won by a 3 to 2 majority, though Watts ran well in the traditionally Whig central and southern counties. Watts then organized the Seventeenth Alabama Regiment and was elected colonel. He served with the regiment at Pensacola and at Corinth, but just before the battle of Shiloh word reached him that Jefferson Davis had appointed him attorney general of the Confederacy.[71]

Watts took his oath of office in Richmond on April 9, 1862, and found his job to be a taxing one. He wrote his son-in-law that besides the legitimate business, which in itself "was sufficient to keep a pretty good worker busy," he had to "entertain all Alabamians who ever knew or heard of me" and to attend to their business with the government.[72] Nevertheless, he ran his office well and once informed his staff that "incivility even to a beggar" was the quickest way to get demoted. In his eighteen months as attorney general Watts wrote over one hundred carefully documented decisions, most of them favorable to the central government. For instance, he declared that all officers of state troops called into Confederate service should be appointed by the president, that conscription was constitutional, and that foreigners giving evidence of remaining in the Confederacy were subject to conscription. Though Watts's rulings sometimes angered the War Department, the best judgment of his ability ranks him as one of the most important of all the members of Davis's cabinet.[73]

As the election of August 1863 approached in Alabama, Watts's friends prepared to nominate him again for governor. Though strongly tempted to remain in Richmond, Watts considered state duty more important and agreed to run. Once again he played the reluctant candidate and refused to campaign, but promised to serve if elected. Shorter himself did little campaigning but issued a circular to the press defending his administration. Watts's friends then issued a handbill attacking Shorter for not driving the enemy out of North Alabama and for neglecting the families of soldiers, two unfair charges. This time it was Watts who won overwhelmingly, and since Shorter had been an able and energetic war governor the sharp reversal can only be interpreted as a protest against secession, the conduct of the war, and the Democratic party. There was a strong feeling that a new administration was needed because things could not get worse and might become better.[74]

More foreboding for the Confederacy, however, were the other elections. Alabama sent six enemies of the Davis administration to the Confederate House of Representatives, and the new legislature would soon replace Clement C. Clay and Yancey in the Senate with men of a different stripe. The legislature itself was composed of a large number of "obscure peace men" who would refuse to cooperate in the future prosecution of the war. Merely because he had opposed Shorter, Watts was, through no fault of his own except his absence from the state and his failure to delineate the issues clearly, assumed to lean toward reconstruction. This was grossly inaccurate, but the disgruntled electorate had read into the situation what they wished.[75] After the election Watts made a speaking tour through northern and middle Alabama to combat the belief that he favored reconstructon. Apparently he convinced his listeners that he was a "war man all over," for after the new governor's speech in the reconstructionist stronghold of Talladega, the local editor wrote disgustedly that he had heard only the "old state rights, state sovereignty and secession arguments."[76]

William Garrett, writing in 1872, said that never was there a more trying and critical juncture in the experience of a public man than that suffered by Watts during his governorship.[77] It began with the enemy holding North Alabama and much of Mississippi in the west. Mobile was obviously the next attack point in the Gulf, and soon Sherman's mighty army would be threatening from the east. Little help could be expected from Confederate forces desperately engaged far afield.

The governor was helpless to organize a strong militia to meet any attack because of the Militia Act of August 1863. Boys and older men could not be ordered out of their county, and the Confederate draft laws left too few ablebodied men for effective State Reserve units. When Federal troops began to threaten Mobile in February 1864, Watts issued appeals asking county reserves and all other available men to join the state reserves. He issued similar appeals in July and August during the period of Rousseau's raid from North Alabama against the Montgomery and West Point Railroad, which Rousseau reached with ease and which permitted him to destroy the road from Tuskegee to Opelika. But the response to these appeals was negligible, and Watts was forced to call the legislature into extraordinary session during October.

Watts devoted his entire message to the need for reorganizing the militia, and the response was devastating. The Troy *Southern Advertiser* summarized the arguments against Watts's request, and some of these were as follows: "an organized militia will be absorbed by the Confederate army"; "without a home producing force everything will be lost"; "it is very easy for a man like Governor Watts who is far removed from the rural districts . . . to come to the conclusion that everybody is doing as well as himself"; and so on. After reviewing these arguments the *Southern Advertiser*'s editor added, "We trust the legislature will not sanction the policy of the Governor,"[78] and this was the result.

The situation must have been embarrassing for the governor. Georgia was calling for help against Sherman, and Confederate forces desperately needed help to defend Mobile. President Davis himself felt that Watts "already possesses full power on the subject of the militia,"[79] but he was mistaken. In the fall of 1864 Watts begged the regular session of the legislature for militia reorganization, but again was rebuffed. Historian Walter L. Fleming admitted that the "stupid conduct of the legislature" did not affect the outcome of the war, but he believed that reorganization "would have allowed the Governor to control outrages by lawless factions."[80]

The Confederate Conscription Act of February 1864 made matters even worse for Watts, for it extended the draft age to include most of the troops composing Alabama's volunteer companies and state reserves. Not only was local defense further weakened but experienced state troops would suffer both loss of position and morale when they were summarily drafted and lumped together with raw recruits. Now the governor's frustration turned to anger. He had been a nationalist as attorney general, but as governor the reality of local problems revived his old state's rights position. And this time the legislature backed him. It imposed both a fine and imprisonment upon conscript officers who forced members of state volunteer organizations into Confederate service.[81] When Jones M. Withers, commander of the Confederate State Reserves, tried to force all eligible men into his command, a showdown occurred. Watts wrote the president that he considered such action by the War Department "a great calamity." In harsher tones he wrote Secretary Seddon a few days later, "Unless you order the commandant of conscripts to stop interfering with such companies there will be a conflict between the Confederate and state authorities." Confronted so bluntly, Seddon virtually conceded Watts's position. He agreed that in such cases "it would seem proper to receive the companies as organized either in the reserve or active force." Watts had won his point. His companies would not be broken up, and until called up either by the governor or by Confederate authorities they could remain at home in productive labor.[82]

But individual cases continued to arise under the provision of the new conscription law drafting men between forty-five and fifty. Watts contended that the Confederacy had no right to conscript anyone already in state service within that age range until the state had discharged them, and he instructed state commanders not to give them up.[83] He wrote General Withers that, in addition, some of the latter's men were enrolling state officers certified as exempt both by the governor and by the Confederate commandant of conscription. Watts's broad definition of "state officers" included even city policemen, and he warned the secretary of war that he would "protect my state officers with all the forces of the state at my command." Watts's thinking, basically, was that the Confederacy had done little to drive the enemy from North Alabama and that he could use troops more effectively than the Confederacy to protect the remainder of the state. Secretary of War Seddon finally commented that the question scarcely entitled the governor to "take up arms" against the War Department and called on Watts to let the courts decide it. Watts agreed and when the state supreme court decided against him the dispute was over.[84]

Meanwhile, desertion was steadily increasing, especially in the wiregrass and in North Alabama, and public opinion made all legislation against harboring deserters irrelevant. In the winter of 1864–65 a dinner was given in a wiregrass town for fifty-seven deserters; subpoenas were issued for their arrest, but the arresting officer refused to serve them. Outlaw-deserters burned the courthouse in Coffee County and murdered four of its best citizens.[85] North Alabama was infested with deserters, but it was almost impossible to catch them. An officer sent to arrest them wrote Watts that in the thick woods there "you would as soon catch a flea" as a deserter.[86] Though the legislature promised to secure pardons for any deserter who would return to the army and Watts pled with them to do so, few complied.[87]

Watts was less than enthusiastic about several of the Confederate economic policies. Certainly his attitudes were based on genuine differences of opinion on policy, but there was also the concern that as governor he was the most visible official in Alabama and people would blame him for unpopular Confederate policies as they had blamed Shorter before him. For instance, he disliked the entire impressment system. When General Maury asked for even more slaves to work on Mobile's fortifications, Watts agreed to encourage planters to offer such labor. But he refused to commit state officials to the execution of the Confederate labor impressment law, and declared that he himself was not "the high sheriff to execute the laws of Congress." He also refused to let General Withers impress blacks hired by the state to work at salt making. Watts even opposed the Confederacy's impressment of foodstuffs for its armies, believing that the practice caused so much ill will among the civilians that it would be better to pay double the market prices than incur such hostility.[88]

In April 1864 Watts and other Confederate governors protested the regulation which allocated to the Confederate government half of all the cargo space on ships running the blockade, even though chartered or owned in part by a state. Watts himself felt that he must have the right to implement an act of his legislature instructing him to sell cotton abroad with which to buy blankets and clothing for Alabamians in the army or in northern prisons. Congress quickly passed a law exempting state-owned or state-chartered vessels from the regulation, but the president vetoed it, and an angry group of governors met at Augusta, Georgia, in October to protest. They formally asked Davis to have the restrictions removed, but most of their other resolutions were supportive of the war effort. Watts was in essential agreement with all the proceedings except one, that advising the use of Negro soldiers. He was called home by illness in his family before the latter resolution came to a vote, but later told the legislature that he would have opposed it.[89]

Despite Watts's increasing states' rights stance, as governor he maintained the cordial relations with President Davis that he had established as attorney general. But this cordiality did not carry over to General Braxton Bragg, whom Davis sent to Alabama in July 1864 to confer with Watts about the military situation there. Apparently angry with the Confederacy in general and Bragg in particular for neglecting Alabama's defenses, Watts agreed to see Bragg, but added, "If I were to consult my private feelings alone, I should have no conference with you." Bragg stormed back to Richmond without seeing Watts, and informed Davis that the governor was trying "to make him [Bragg] a scapegoat in order to escape the withering criticism of his fellow citizens for the situation" in Alabama.[90] Even then, when Davis spoke before the legislature in Montgomery in September he paid a "glowing tribute to the capacity, gallantry and patriotism" of Governor Watts.[91]

As best he could, Watts continued Shorter's efforts to supply needy civilians with scarce necessities. He had to concentrate his salt-making activities along the Florida coast, but Federal vessels and bands of outlaw-deserters harassed the operations constantly. Watts could not protect them very well because of the strict regulations against sending the militia out of state. Cotton and wool cards continued to be scarce, but Watts occasionally succeeded in getting some of them through the blockade. In December 1863 and in October and December 1864 the legislature appropriated a total of $8 million for the relief of indigent families of soldiers, and probate judges were instructed to buy corn and distribute it instead of money, if possible. But transportation of corn was a major problem, and Watts was authorized to buy corn along the railroads and swap it to the Confederacy for tithe corn where it was close to needy families. He continued the restriction on the distillation of grain into whiskey.[92]

The growing number of scarcities, the breakdown of authority, the drain of manpower, and the dwindling hope of victory gradually brought the same desperate war weariness to Alabamians that was settling over much of the Confederacy. Inevitably "peace party men" emerged, and in August 1863 so many were elected to county positions that Watts was never sure of local support for any war measure. By the fall of 1864 reconstruction was being openly discussed in some newspapers and Lewis Parsons had become the leader of a Peace party in the legislature.[93] In addition to its policy of continued obstruction, this Peace party in October 1864 seemed on the verge of pushing through the legislature resolutions in favor of peace and reconstruction. They were deterred, however, by a powerful speech from Watts in which he asked if they wished to join a government with "those who have murdered our sons, outraged our women, and destroyed our property." The legislators finally passed a halfhearted resolution "to sacrifice, if necessary, all our resources to the common cause."[94] Watts himself had filled his message to the regular session in November with opposition to reconstruction in general and especially to the plan proposed by the northern Democrat's Chicago platform of 1864. The governor was well aware of his unpopularity and vulnerability by this time, and he wrote Governor Magrath of South Carolina that "I fear a new election shall place in power other men."[95]

Watts never condoned the peace movement or reconstruction, though late in the war he and Governor Magrath discussed establishing a possible common front. While the details of this discussion are lost, one of Watts's letters indicates that their concern was the "usurpation by the Confederacy which the war engendered" and the best manner of "admonishing the Confederacy for these usurpations." Watts agreed that more watchfulness by the states might prevent future errors and that possibly the other governors should be asked to join in a statement of remonstrances.[96] But apparently they did not discuss reconstruction.

Military events moved swiftly in the last few months of the war. Commodore David G. Farragut captured Mobile Bay and its forts and thus deprived Alabama of any further significant use of the Gulf. General James H. Wilson's Federal cavalry command destroyed the heartland in early 1865 when he raided Selma to destroy its valuable war works and its industrial and mining sites. One of Watts's correspondents in Sparta wrote: "I regret that the people at home are not disposed . . . to cooperate with you," but were "using every effort to sustain the Legislature [against you] because they have determined not to fight."[97]

Nevertheless, the governor remained optimistic until the end. In an emergency meeting at the Montgomery Theatre on February 25, 1865, he maintained that the Confederacy was stronger in munitions and in many other ways than it had ever been. When a "croaker" in the audience loudly disputed him, Watts retorted, "Give me liberty or give me death."[98] But Wilson's raiders were now moving toward Montgomery, and brave words could not stop them. And when General Richard Taylor, commander of that military district, decided not to defend the city, Watts gathered up some of the state archives and moved the seat of government to Eufaula. Montgomery surrendered on April 12, and soon Wilson started for Columbus, Georgia. A few days later Watts went to Union Springs, where remnants of the Confederate military forces were concentrating, and there he was arrested on May 1 by Union General T. J. Lucas. Apparently he was sent to Macon, Georgia, for a short time, but the Montgomery *Mail* of June 19 reported that he "has been released and has returned to Montgomery."[99]

Watts was now bankrupt. His cotton and his houses had been burned and he was $100,000 in debt, most of it incurred as surety for other people. Nevertheless, he remained an ardent Confederate veteran and never tired of extolling the virtues of the men who fought in gray. He resumed his law work in Montgomery with great success and had a greater practice before the Alabama Supreme Court than any other man. He was eventually able to pay off all his debts and before his death had again become a man of some wealth. He became a Conservative Democrat, but was elected to office only once, this time to the legislature in 1880. Partly because of the key role he had played in the overthrow of Radical Reconstruction, Watts aspired to the United States Senate. His name was considered by the legislature in 1882, but when it became evident that he could not get a majority of votes he withdrew his name. On September 15, 1892, he collapsed at work of a heart attack and died the next day. He was buried in Oakwood Cemetery in Montgomery.[100]

All of Alabama's Civil War governors belonged to the slaveholding class which, because of its political clout in the secession convention, was able to take Alabama out of the Union in 1861. But as governor each of them found that a majority of their constituents were small white farmers or poor whites. Each made appeals to all the people of the state and in doing so faced a leadership test which none was able to pass. They simply could not command and keep the trust of the non-slaveholding whites who composed a majority of the population.

Since the governors belonged to the large planter class they were suspect in regard to the charge that the Civil War was "a rich man's war and a poor man's fight." The Confederate Congress in 1862 exempted one white man on every plantation working twenty or more slaves, and until January 1864 one who had the money could escape conscription by hiring a substitute. Although none of the wartime governors or their families personally benefited from these exemptions, they belonged to the class which sometimes used them to escape service.

In addition to the class lines that separated the governors from a majority of their people, they all faced the age-old sectionalism between North Alabama and South Alabama, based on geography and the resulting interests of each section. Unfortunately, this divisiveness was accentuated in the war period by differences as to the right and mode of secession and the prosecution of the war. Sectionalism grew by enormous proportions after Alabama north of the Tennessee River was occupied by the Federals following the Battle of Shiloh. From April 1862 on, North Alabama demanded that the enemy be driven from its bounds, but neither Governors Shorter nor Watts had the men or the arms to do so. Shorter supported the Confederate policy of consolidating the army on the Virginia and western fronts, declaring that North Alabama would be free from occupation if the South won the war. Although not as vocal in his support, Watts acquiesced in the same policy because of his lack of manpower and arms. Shorter was the most earnest Confederate among the governors, giving Davis unqualified support while in the Provisional Congress and the governorship of Alabama.

Shorter lost the governorship by a landslide vote in August 1863. The election occurred after the tide had turned against the South and the vote was a protest against Shorter the secessionist and the Democratic party which the electorate felt bore most responsibility for the long, hard, and apparently unsuccessful war. Since Shorter was an ardent supporter of Davis, the outcome was also determined in part by the unpopularity of the president in some sections of the state.

Shorter did not win in 1863, but neither was it a real victory for Thomas H. Watts or the policies for which he stood. Watts was a one-time Whig who had decided to support immediate secession at the eleventh hour when it became apparent that Lincoln would win. Naturally, in the election of 1863, he attracted peace advocates who were now on the move against the former secessionist Democrats. The election of August 1863 in Alabama turned on the wishful vote for peace by thousands of Alabamians. This was shown by the large number of men inclined toward peace elected to the Congress, the legislature, and county governments. A big factor in the election was that the electorate knew too much about Shorter; they did not know enough about Watts. The governor-elect did not disclose the fact that he was "a war man all over" until after the election when he came to Alabama on a speaking tour to combat the widespread rumor that he was for peace and reconstruction. This tour shattered the hopes of thousands that he might somehow turn the situation around in favor of ending the war. From the time of Watts's inauguration, the state had a "war governor" but a legislature and many county officers wanting to "wind down the war." Watts's war policies were stymied by a rebellious and uncooperative legislature. The best example of this struggle was the refusal of the legislature to reorganize the militia so that it could be used effectively to keep order at home and stop Federal armies invading the state.

Desertion from the army should be placed at the top of all the problems which finally caused the home front to collapse. Although there were many causes for desertion, desertion to take care of one's family proved to be the most serious because it turned good soldiers into outlaws and bushwhackers. Before the end of 1864, deserters and resulting disorders had turned at least half the counties in Alabama into lawless areas unfit for human habitation.

Desertion was caused in many instances by the inability of the state and local governments to care for soldiers' families. The state and county governments made heroic efforts to feed and clothe the destitute. The state government alone appropriated some $11 million for that purpose between 1862 and 1865. As the relief was granted by the state merely printing more paper money, however, the relief added to the inflation spiral that was taking place all over the Confederacy— thus destroying the economy. Nothing in the Confederacy escaped the baneful effect of the depreciating currency. As the currency became worthless the Confederacy had to resort to the impressment of private property and the onerous tax-in-kind. These measures provided goods to continue the war for a time, but eventually turned many people against the undemocratic despotism of their own government.

The "peace society" grew rapidly after 1863 and since they could not control Watts they determined to oust him in the election of 1865. Watts could not have been reelected as he was as unpopular by the fall of 1864 as Shorter had been in August 1863. Despite the fact that Watts was attorney general in Davis's cabinet where he upheld Confederate policies against opposition from the states, he became an ardent states' righter while governor of Alabama. Although he did not play as large a part as Joseph E. Brown of Georgia or Zebulon Vance of North Carolina in bringing the Confederate government to its knees, his opposition to Confederate policies contributed to their failure.

ARKANSAS

Michael B. Dougan

ike all frontier states, Arkansas had an early reputation for violence. But while other states outgrew their pioneer days, Arkansas did not. Economic development languished after the failure of the state's banking ventures in 1843, while in popular culture "The Arkansas Traveler," in story, song and print, came to symbolize backwoods society to nineteenth-century Americans. As late as 1857, one newspaper lamented that outsiders still thought of Arkansas as the home of "the bloody bowie knife, assassins, cut throats, and highway robbers."[1]

Politically, socially, and economically the state failed to transcend the image prior to the Civil War. The election of its two Confederate governors reflected a division within the state between the traditionalists and the modernizers. The first of the wartime governors, Henry Massie Rector, was a traditionalist marked by an idiosyncratic personality; his successor, Harris Flanagin, although a modernizer, possessed a legalistic personality entirely unsuited to a revolutionary cause. Since the state was remote from the Confederacy's chief concerns, both governors had open to them a wide range of options. None of the Trans-Mississippi generals prior to the arrival of Edmund Kirby Smith in 1863 had as much power, for good or for ill, as did the two war governors of Arkansas.

Henry M. Rector, the first wartime governor of the state, was born in Louisville, Kentucky, on May 1, 1816. He was the son of Elias Rector, one of eight brothers who moved westward with the frontier into Illinois, Kentucky, Missouri, and Arkansas. When Elias died in 1822, his wife Fannie married Stephen Trigg, who operated a saltworks in Saline County, Missouri. Young Henry received the rudiments of an education from his mother, but spent most of his youth hauling wood for the fire at the saltworks. His formal education was limited to the years 1833–35 when he attended Francis Goddard's school in Louisville.[2]

At age nineteen Henry went to Arkansas to further a land claim, inherited from his father, to the Hot Springs. In 1838 he married Jane Elizabeth Field, daughter of Little Rock postmaster William Field and niece of Governor John Pope. In 1839 his relatives found Henry a place as teller in the State Bank, a job that he lost the following year when the bank failed. Hurt by the panic of 1839 and the subsequent depression, he moved to Saline County, where he farmed and studied law. Two years later he was appointed by President John Tyler as Federal marshal. His appointment caused one Whig editor to complain that all the offices in Arkansas were being monopolized by a "reigning Dynasty" which included two of Rector's cousins, United States Senator Ambrose H. Sevier and Governor James Sevier Conway. After losing his marshalship to his cousin Elias Rector in 1845, he attempted to practice law in the state capital. Finding the climate uncongenial in the aftermath of Arkansas's flush times, Rector returned to "Midland," his Saline County farm near Alexander.[3]

He emerged in 1848 to serve a term as state senator from Perry and Saline counties. In 1852 he was a Democratic elector for Franklin Pierce and actively supported his cousin Elias N. Conway's successful gubernatorial bid. His reward was the appointment as surveyor general of Arkansas. Once in office he took an independent course, and reportedly broke with Conway over the governor's reluctance to grant state aid to railroads. In 1854 Rector moved to Pulaski County and served a term in the lower house of the legislature representing that county. By the late 1850s he had become a well-to-do planter with agricultural interests in several counties. In Pulaski County in 1860 he owned over a thousand acres, eight town lots, and twenty-one slaves. His kinship connection remained considerable and included, besides the Rectors, Seviers, and Conways, Ben T. DuVal, a brother-in-law and Fort Smith politician; Edmund Burgevin, another brother-in-law who was chief clerk of the surveyor general's office; and a number of cousins in minor positions. In 1858 the dominant faction of the Democratic party, still called the Dynasty or "family," engineered Rector's elevation to the state supreme court.[4]

As a judge Rector was sadly miscast. He was frequently absent and wrote few opinions, mostly on inconsequential cases. In those, Rector's convoluted language and muddled thinking defy easy analysis. His resignation from the court, an anonymous but obviously informed correspondent claimed, "was considered by all as a case of necessity on his part as the only way to save himself in a manner from public disgrace."[5]

If Rector had not made a success out of the judgeship, it was perhaps because he had wider ambitions for which judgeships were not the usual stepping-stones. When state gubernatorial politics were being discussed in early 1860, the Van Buren *Press* observed that Rector was an available candidate. But a handpicked state Democratic convention in April 1860 nominated Richard H. Johnson, editor of the party organ, the *True Democrat*, and brother of United States Senator Robert Ward Johnson. Rector, in the "family's" judgement, was not gubernatorial material. With Arkansas Democrats divided over national issues, weakened by factionalism, and with no Whig or opposition party offering a challenge in a state which had never elected anyone but Democrats, Johnson found the convention's nomination "not worth a fingersnap."[6]

There was discontent with Johnson for at least two reasons. First, he stood as a symbol of the "family," whose control over Arkansas politics was increasingly resented. Second, the Johnson faction argued that the state's lawful debts incurred by the failures of the Real Estate and State Bank should be paid. A substantial number of influential men with still unpaid debts would thereby be embarrassed.[7]

Opposition to the "family" was perennial but had not heretofore been successful. The current "disorganizer" was First District Congressman Thomas Carmichael Hindman. Elected to Congress in 1858 with "family" support, Hindman had demanded a share of the patronage. He made himself popular with the masses by staging a theatrical revolt highly publicized by his own paper, defying Senator Johnson, surviving assassins' bullets, and hurling forth a level of bombastic demagoguery never before reached in Arkansas, although not that uncommon in Mississippi, the state from which Hindman came.[8]

Hindman's state strategy and Rector's ambitions came together in May 1860. Since Richard H. Johnson's nomination, "family" members had been watching for a move from Thomas Fletcher, considered a potential "disorganizer." Thus Rector's announcement for governor caught many people off guard. "Who is Henry M. Rector?" *Old Line Democrat* editor Thomas C. Peek, soon to be Rector's nephew-in-law, asked:

A poor honest farmer of Saline county, who toils at the plow handles to provide bread, meat, and raiment for his wife and children. Do you not know him? There are many among the people who do—who have seen him laboring in the field, earning his bread with the sweat of his brow. But possessing the impress of manhood from nature, and from nature's God, at his country's greatest need, he arose like Cincinnatus of old and did his duty.

An old acquaintance, Fayetteville wag and cartoonist William (Bill Cush) Quesenbury, could hardly resist adding a flourish: "Always at the close of any public duty he rushes to the handles of his plough and holds on to them until the people drag him away."[9]

Rector issued a circular explaining his stands on state affairs. Besides attacking "family" dictation and corruption, he raised only two substantive issues. First, he favored education. But when his plan of distributing state monies for schools to the counties on a white per capita basis was criticized as injurious to slaveholders, he reversed himself and called for a tax cut instead. His second argument was that the state should aid in the construction of railroads. State internal improvements was a Whig issue, and retiring Governor Elias N. Conway was commonly called "Dirt Road" Conway for his stand. Rector's idea was to give state aid to the railroads in return for which the railroads would assume the state debt. Even Rector's friends could not find anything understandable or practicable in the plan, and his definition of it seems to have shifted in each speech.[10]

Rector and Johnson took to the stump in a series of appearances. Johnson was a poor public speaker, "slow, dry, and prosy"; as for Rector: "His fault is that he is too wordy—his sentences are crowded with big six syllablers [sic] and that he dilutes his ideas until they are sometimes rather thin. He is an orator of the ka-larruping style, as shown in the following sentence: 'I stand on my pedestal, shorn of the abominations and malpractices whereon they relied to cast the nomination upon the present nominee of the Democratic party.'" It was a hard-fought battle in Arkansas's summer heat. In what proved to be an accurate summation of Rector's style, William Quesenbury noted: "Henry is a violent man and fights people."[11]

Laurels crowned Rector's brow in the August state election as he defeated Johnson 31,948 to 28,847. A close analysis of the election results indicates that his support came from various sources. One main group included ex-Whigs and ex-Know-Nothings, especially those who had recently arrived in the state. A second group included all the minor Democratic politicos who saw their path to advancement blocked by the "family" and opened by Rector. A third group consisted of those who, seeing the prospects of a civil war, wanted to support a Union man. At Bentonville, in mountainous Northwest Arkansas, Rector was reported to have said, "though Seward *himself* were elected to the Presidency of the United States, it were no justifiable grounds for secession, and nothing short of an overt act on the part of the North would justify such a step."[12]

On November 15, 1860, Rector took over as governor and immediately plunged the state into controversy. News of Lincoln's election preceded Rector's inauguration, and the governor used the opportunity to seize the leadership of the secession movement in Arkansas. The

North, by electing a sectional candidate, had, he reasoned, "revolutionized the government," thus dissolving the Union. Arkansas, he proclaimed, was now independent and would act accordingly.[13]

In contrast to Rector's idiosyncratic secessionism, the state legislature completely ignored the governor and began considering candidates to fill the vacancy in the United States Senate. Robert Ward Johnson had declined to seek reelection. Rector, unable to frustrate this activity or even to effectively promote one of his own followers for the office, repeated his views on the national question in an address on December 12, this time calling for the summoning of a convention to effect the separation. He also urged the legislature to pass a law prohibiting slave owners from the border states from bringing their slaves into Arkansas. This, the governor thought, would encourage secession in those states.[14]

Over the next month the legislature dallied, electing a U.S. senator, Charles B. Mitchel, an alleged "family" man. Meanwhile, Robert Ward Johnson, Albert Pike, Thomas C. Hindman, and lesser lights all publicly urged secession. After South Carolina broke the traces and the other cotton states followed, the legislature reluctantly consented, with the convention bill finally passing the state Senate on January 16, 1861, at the very end of the session. Rector felt that his vital role in the movement was in jeopardy. Thus in late January he again assumed an aggressive posture, this time against the Federal arsenal located in Little Rock and manned by Captain James Totten and sixty-five men of the Second U.S. Artillery.[15]

The arsenal crisis began when Rector informed Totten that neither the arrival of reinforcements nor the removal of the arms would be permitted by state authorities. When unfounded rumors of Federal reinforcements reached Rector, cannon were placed on the Little Rock wharf as a defensive measure. Shortly thereafter armed companies began to converge on the capital from all of South Arkansas, allegedly in response to the governor's orders and for the avowed purpose of seizing the arsenal. Little Rock militia units were called out "and marched around a little." Perhaps Rector planned to start the Civil War in Little Rock.[16]

In fomenting the arsenal crisis Rector was opposing the dominant sentiment in the state capital and ignoring the state's secessionist leaders. Senator Johnson and Senator William King Sebastian telegraphed repeatedly from Washington that no reason existed for taking the arsenal, and the Little Rock city council demanded of the governor a public explanation. On the other hand, the armed bands swore to take the arsenal before they would leave Little Rock. Fortunately for Rector, Captain Totten failed to receive any instructions from Washington and so decided to agree to an abandonment of the arsenal, the governor guaranteeing safe conduct and acting as receiver for the arsenal supplies. On February 8 a jubilant Rector led a march to the arsenal to obtain possession, and made a speech. A diarist left this description of the event: "[Rector] acknowledged that he ordered the cannon to be brought to the wharf. A company from one of the counties swore that if they did not enter the arsenal grounds first they would make a charge on the Little Rock Company. They went first. Very exciting times."[17]

The arsenal seizure gratified the extremists in the slaveholding counties, but no one else; instead it touched off a wave of rejuvenated Unionism which in the convention election on February 18 gave the Unionists a majority of the delegates. One observer offered this explanation for the secessionists' defeat: "They say the secession movement would be more popular if Rector was not at the head."[18] In Little Rock itself Rector was in particular disfavor. By contrast, Totten was given a hero's farewell and a sword engraved to him from the ladies of Little Rock. Meanwhile, Rector, with control over the state treasury and state arms, paid the "volunteers" for their services and supplied secession companies with weapons.[19]

On March 5, the day after Lincoln's inauguration, the secession convention assembled. Rector addressed the body on March 8, reiterating his well-known stance. The convention demanded of him a complete accounting for all the expenses entailed in the arsenal seizure and then fought with him over the convention's prerogatives. The election in Fulton County had resulted in a tie vote, which the convention resolved to decide by holding another election. Rector told the body that they lacked the power, and they responded that as sovereign representatives of the people they possessed infinite power. Rector gave in and ordered the election, the first in a series of retreats which marked the subsequent course of his gubernatorial career. The convention adjourned with Arkansas still in the Union as the debate continued.

While Senator Johnson, Albert Pike, and Congressman Hindman stumped the state, Rector remained in Little Rock strangely quiet. His alliance with Hindman had ended in December when Hindman made his peace with the "family." Although Hindman's now unemployed editor married Rector's niece, the funds to establish a Rector paper were not forthcoming. The Arkansas State Gazette, a Unionist organ edited by C. C. Danley, and the True Democrat, run by Richard H. Johnson, criticized the governor at every turn.[20]

On April 12, 1861, the firing on Fort Sumter produced a crisis in Little Rock. To President Lincoln's call for 780 Arkansas soldiers, Rector indignantly and with unconscious irony replied: "The people of this commonwealth are freemen, not slaves, and will defend to the last extremity their honor, lives and property against Northern mendacity and usurpation." Most Arkansas Unionists were of the conditional variety, and in the emergency felt that they must support the South. Rector heard a report that the Fort Smith arsenal was to be reinforced, and recruited a force to ascend the Arkansas River and seize the installation. Unlike the previous arsenal episode, little opposition greeted the governor's move, though the Federal garrison had already left.[21]

Meanwhile, the secession convention was preparing to reassemble. In its ranks were many "conditional" Unionists who, while prepared to vote for secession, nevertheless blamed men like Rector for the crisis they could not prevent. In a private letter to one delegate, *Arkansas Gazette* editor C. C. Danley suggested a course of action: "I think the conservative men of the convention should take charge of the affairs of the state and prevent the wild secessionists from sending us to the Devil." Thus after the ordinance of secession was passed on May 6, the "family" secessionists and the conservatives formed a unified front against Rector; Rector's supporters could be counted on one hand. There was even some talk of deposition. A note in Rector's handwriting reads: "Col. Webb says that when the convention meets they will try to declare my office vacant. Oh Hell." Rector was spared, apparently through the good offices of Hindman and Richard H. Johnson, but was shorn of his powers. Hindman drafted a military board bill which removed the war power from the governor's prerogative to a three-man board. The convention also appointed the officers to command the state army. Rector fought both measures ineffectively. His major ploy was a decision to reconvene the legislature. The convention ordered him to stay the order, and he again gave in. Finally, the convention drafted a new constitution and by careful wording scheduled the next election for certain offices of state, including the governor, for October 1862. On June 1 the convention ended its labors. Critic J. William Demby thought that despite the scars of battle Rector was still convinced "he had the ability to govern the world, to lead armies, and manage an empire." The succeeding months offered him his chance.[22]

Rector's vision of the war centered around his belief in states' rights, which, however sincerely held, nevertheless emphasized his role as governor. Each state should defend itself by maintaining its own army. The convention had created an Arkansas army, but with the intention of turning the men over to the Confederate authorities if any would bother to come to Arkansas. When no one came, military board member C. C. Danley went to Richmond and negotiated a transfer, only to have the other two members (Rector and B. C. Totten) reject it. The troops remained under Rector's control during the critical summer months of 1861.[23]

While Rector controlled the state establishment, the "family" held sway with Richmond, using their influence to get Hindman made first a colonel and then a brigadier general. Criticism of Rector was constant. The first appointed western commander, General Ben McCulloch, reported to Richmond that affairs in Arkansas were in a deplorable state, thanks to the governor. This view was echoed by David Hubbard, the Indian commissioner. Rector insisted that Arkansas troops be used to defend Arkansas, that they not be transferred to the Confederate service without their permission, and that their arms be retained by the state. Secretary of War L. P. Walker would offer only the "watchful care of the Government." When General Nathaniel Lyon began his struggle for control of Missouri and thus threatened the West, McCulloch called for Arkansas volunteers to come to his assistance in the Indian Territory. Rector, insisting that only a governor could raise troops, retaliated by offering a shorter term of service for volunteers joining the state army.[24]

The arrival in Arkansas of General William J. Hardee on July 25 signaled a change in Richmond's thinking. Hardee assumed command in the northeast at Pitman's Ferry and agreed to let the Arkansas soldiers vote on whether to accept transfer to the Confederate army. Rector's friends, Edmund Burgevin and James Yell, generals in the militia, addressed the men so successfully on the governor's point of view that large numbers went home. Before the transfer of the other half of the army in the Northwest could take place, the Arkansas army fought in its only battle, Wilson's Creek (Oak Hills), and acquitted itself splendidly. The soldiers marched back to Arkansas and threatened to lynch Rector's brother-in-law, Paymaster Ben T. DuVal, until he finally paid them in state bonds. Disgusted by state mismanagement and certain that the war was over, all but eighteen men voted to disband. By the fall of 1861 Arkansas's state recruiting efforts of over four months had been almost totally erased. While criticism swirled around Rector's head, the Federals recovered from Lyon's defeat at Wilson's Creek and secured Missouri for the Union.[25]

In the fall of 1861 politics again flourished. The electors for the Confederacy's one presidential election were chosen without consulting the governor: two conservatives and two "family" men. Rector finally found the funds to establish a newspaper with his nephew Thomas C. Peek as editor. Intended to influence the fall session of the legislature, the paper had a short life. The governor addressed the legislature at the opening session, making few positive suggestions and criticizing his opponents. In language hardly conciliatory he declaimed: "More treason lurks in Arkansas, under the garb of patriotism, than most men conceive of. Libelous traduction of its authorities, gloatingly sought for, and swallowed by snarling cormorants of newspaper filth, well attest this fact."[26]

The attack brought forth even greater unity between the conservatives and "family" men. Tensions ran high. The *Gazette*'s language toward General Burgevin grew so severe that Burgevin challenged the crippled editor C. C. Danley to a duel. Rector, in violation of state law, carried the challenge. Danley chortled in refusing: "It has seldom, if ever, been the lot of an editor to receive a challenge from as low a vagabond, or to have it borne by so high a public functionary." The legislature, which nephew-editor Peek finally called "completely Johnsonized," abolished Peek's patronage job as penitentiary inspector, while Richmond eliminated him as military storekeeper at the arsenal. Since the governor made no suggestions concerning the pressing problems of relief for soldiers' families, a sagging currency, and a breakdown in local law and order, the legislature passed mostly trivial laws.[27]

In selecting two Confederate senators the legislature heard the claims of a number of men before sending Robert Ward Johnson and Charles B. Mitchel to Richmond. Rector's friends James Yell and Napoleon Bonaparte Burrow received only thirteen and six votes respectively.[28]

After the legislature adjourned, Rector faced another problem, the "peace society" movement. This early example of dissension in the Confederacy occurred in the Ozarks in the form of secret societies of mountain men who resolved to be neutral in the struggle. Rector considered this attitude treasonous and caused hundreds to be arrested. The evidence to prove treason in a court of law was lacking, so he browbeat the prisoners into enlisting in the Confederate service. The hysterical reaction to the peace societies by the governor and some secessionists formed the prologue for the bloody guerrilla warfare which enveloped the mountains the following year.[29]

During the winter of 1861–62 serious wartime inflation hit Arkansas. When ex-United States Senator and now Confederate Colonel Solon Borland attempted limited price controls in response to a food shortage, Rector was furious and succeeded in getting the War Department to disallow Borland's order. The governor even went so far as to issue his own proclamation against the unfortunate colonel, commenting: "Repeated acts of insult, injustice, and wrong have by the subordinate officers of the Confederate States been contumaciously and without provocation insultingly offered to the State of Arkansas." Confederate neglect of Arkansas prompted Rector to revive his pet plan for a state army, this time utilizing the militia. In January 1862, in the midst of spring plowing, he ordered militia musterings. Total insubordination greeted the governor's order, and criticism mounted. The Helena *South-ern Shield* observed that Rector had "shown himself a miserable apology for a high public functionary."[30]

In the spring Richmond sent General Earl Van Dorn to Arkansas to straighten out the tangle. Unfortunately Van Dorn, an overgrown adolescent whom even his biographer could not admire, was hardly the type of man to cooperate with the suspicious governor. Van Dorn called on Rector for troops, threatening Confederate conscription if the state did not meet its quota. It was too late. The Federal army of General Samuel Curtis entered the state and met Van Dorn at the Battle of Pea Ridge (Elkhorn Tavern) on March 6, 1862. This "Gettysburg of the West" began the process of the Confederate abandonment of Arkansas.[31]

If it was too late to recruit an army, it was also too late for the legislature to do effective work. Nevertheless, that body persevered, and in a March special session tried to put Arkansas on a war footing. Prohibition laws were passed to protect foodstuffs; sales of public lands were halted; counties were authorized to aid the poor; and restrictions were placed on cotton production. Rector, so vigilant about states' rights, apparently thought little of farmers' rights. Advising South Carolina Governor Francis Pickens, he observed: "Cereals should be grown exclusively, cotton *abolished*." Planters ignored the act, planted cotton as usual, and helped to starve a state that was a food importer even before the war. The legislature also abolished the militia system and set up a new one. Rector vetoed the bill but accepted a separate appropriations bill, channeling it for his own purposes. The perpetual chorus of criticism again mounted but to no avail.[32]

After the Battle of Pea Ridge, Van Dorn took Arkansas and Missouri soldiers east of the Mississippi, leaving Arkansas defenseless against Curtis's slowly advancing Federals. With the extension of Federal control down the Mississippi as far as Memphis, the mountains and the waterways were both equally open to attack. All parties in Arkansas were alarmed by the situation, but it was Rector who took steps. Calling all citizens to rally to his state army, he promised, in a probably unconscious pun, to "build a new ark and launch it on new waters." Once again Rector was in advance of public opinion and was roundly condemned in the state press, as Van Dorn reported that Rector "stood almost alone."[33]

With General Curtis making his way down White River, capturing Batesville, and scouting within thirty miles of Little Rock, General P. G. T. Beauregard responded to Senator Johnson's pleas by detaching General Thomas C. Hindman to return to Arkansas. Hindman seized supplies on his way to Little Rock, conscripted Rector's army, established manufactories, and set up a system of martial law, all without the slightest official approval, or, as it turned out, even a legitimate jurisdiction in Arkansas. Rector was completely overawed, and for once did nothing.[34]

When the Federals threatened Little Rock, Rector ordered the removal of the state archives to Hot Springs. This presumed abandonment of the capital gave editor Richard H. Johnson his chance to accuse the governor of cowardice. Rector retorted by charging Johnson with treason, and Johnson replied that he would answer to any legal tribunal. After more heated exchanges Rector challenged Johnson to a duel, but the seconds never came to terms.[35]

The arrival of Hindman shifted the war emphasis away from the governor. It was Hindman who quarreled with General Albert Pike in Indian Territory, who was cursed by the planters for his cotton policy and denounced by many for his violations of civil liberties. After a month and a half Hindman was superseded by General Theophilus Hunter "Old Granny" Holmes, a friend of President Davis. Rector had his own troubles. When it became apparent that he would not call the election for the offices of state specified by the 1861 constitution, Danley and Johnson obtained a writ of mandamus from the supreme court against Rector. Thus the fall of 1862 witnessed another gubernatorial election.[36]

Rector announced as a candidate in a circular defending his administration in all particulars and denouncing his many enemies. Just before the election a newspaper called the *Patriot* was instituted in his behalf in Little Rock with Edmund Burgevin as the unlisted editor. Another candidate was James S. H. Rainey of Camden. More dangerous to Rector was the candidacy of Harris Flanagin, who was presently a colonel in the Second Arkansas Mounted Rifles in Tennessee and whose nomination was a public letter signed by virtually every leading conservative and "family" Democrat in Arkansas.[37]

With Flanagin in Tennessee, the campaign attracted little attention. The *Ouachita Herald* tried to stimulate some Rector support by portraying Flanagin as an Irishman and a Yankee. Although four counties were occupied by Federal troops, the election elsewhere was conducted regularly. Rector received 7,419 votes to Flanagin's 18,187 and Rainey's 708. When the results were announced, Rector addressed the legislature in singularly caustic terms, culminating his speech with his resignation. The remaining two weeks of his term were filled by Thomas Fletcher.[38]

Rector had become governor with great expectations, but left office in bitterness. A man embodying the individualism and violence of the frontier, he took out his frustrations on those around him. A teacher who made the mistake of disciplining one of his children received a visit from the governor: "He struck me on the side of the head with his fist & nearly knocked me down & before I got straight he hit me again & said, 'Just as you I strike you, you God damned son of a bitch, you damned stinking Yankee, you Yankee dog. You strike my son like I would a negro, you god damned miserable Yankee dog.' He had his hand on his pistol & if I had endeavored to make any resistance he would have shot me."

In public affairs Rector's temper kept him from building up a following either by reuniting with the "family" or by conciliating the conservatives. His views on the war were characterized by an extreme devotion to states' rights which was hardly representative of the state as a whole. Perhaps because of Rector's fanaticism, both the conservatives and the "family" men were generally solid supporters of Jefferson Davis despite the president's policy of malignant neglect towards the Trans-Mississippi.[39]

Rector's war strategy can be best illustrated from his letter of April 11, 1862, to South Carolina Governor Pickens. Rector blamed the problems of the Confederacy on the central government's ignoring state authorities and proposed a convention of state executives to decide Confederate policy. He criticized Davis for underestimating the southern people, for relying on European aid, for his "insane adoration of West Pointism," for bad appointments to the War and Navy departments, and for "undertaking an impossibility—a defensive warfare." At the same time Rector asserted that state troops should stay at home to defend their states. On one occasion he told the Arkansas legislature: "Arkansas owes protection to her people and their property at every point." Rector's thinking was neither coherent nor consistent, but it was typical of many persons in high office, in the army, and at home.

After his resignation Rector disappeared from politics, although he continued to support the Confederacy. In March 1864 he attended a public meeting in Washington, Arkansas, called to endorse a vigorous prosecution of the war. He also served as a private in a Confederate reserve corps.[40]

Harris Flanagin, who succeeded Rector as governor of Arkansas, was born at Roadstown in Cumberland County, New Jersey, on November 3, 1817, the son of James and Mary Harris Flanagin. His early education was in Quaker schools in New Jersey and seems to have been thorough. At age eighteen he was made professor of mathematics and English at Clermont Seminary, Frankfort, Pennsylvania, where he taught for a year before opening his own school at Paoli, Illinois. While in Illinois he commenced the study of law, and after two years was admitted to the bar. In 1839 the young lawyer arrived in Clark County, Arkansas, to seek his fortune. The county's 1845 tax books reveal that Flanagin owned 120 acres and no slaves; eight years later his acreage had increased to 2,720 and he also owned thirteen town lots. His ownership of that property plus six slaves, $1,500 worth of furniture, four cows, and a carriage made him one of the largest taxpayers in the county. This success did not stem from the practice of law but rather from an association with Benjamin Duncan, a friend from Pennsylvania, in real estate speculation.

A Whig, Flanagin had a modest political career in Democratic Arkansas, serving a term in the lower house of the state legislature in 1842–43 and winning a hotly contested race for the state Senate in 1848 against the county's leading Democrat, Hawes H. Coleman. He also served in the state militia during the Mexican War. After the Compromise of 1850 and the collapse of the Whig party, Flanagin retired from politics. He married Martha Elizabeth Nash on July 3, 1851. During the 1850s he served as city alderman of Arkadelphia and was a trustee for the state's first institute for the blind, which opened in Arkadelphia.[41]

On February 18, 1861, Flanagin was elected as a delegate to the secession convention from Clark County. Officially he was classified as a secessionist, but in debate his reluctant attitude was obvious and his friendships were largely with the conditional Unionists who dominated the convention prior to the firing on Fort Sumter. After the war started, Flanagin was chosen captain of Company E of the Second Arkansas Mounted Rifles and saw action at Wilson's Creek and Pea Ridge. Following the death of Colonel James McIntosh in the latter battle, Flanagin was elected colonel. He was serving in Tennessee during the fall of 1862 when his friends entered him against Governor Rector. Older histories claim that Flanagin was unaware of his nomination and election until a telegram reached him after the election. But other Arkansas soldiers in the Army of Tennessee were apprised. One wrote: "I would not have Colonel Flanagin beaten for governor for anything in reason."[42]

In his inaugural address Flanagin called for aid for indigent soldiers' families and a renewed dedication to the war effort. Under his direction the legislature completed work on virtually all the possible wartime legislation. It strengthened the liquor laws, allocated $1.2 million for poor relief, and made adjustments in the court system. The scarcity of salt and cotton cards prompted an appropriation of $300,000 to assist manufactories. Unfortunately the state was bankrupt. Only the printing press supplied Arkansas with money, and even paper was in short supply. The suspension of tax collection meant that no new revenue would be forthcoming. Like the rest of the Confederacy, Arkansas financed the revolution by mortgaging the future.[43]

As Arkansas's chief executive, Flanagin inherited several problems. He refused to join the civil rights chorus of complaints mounting against Holmes and Hindman. After Hindman's defeat at Prairie Grove on December 7, 1862, he was transferred east of the Mississippi River, and the great effort to modernize and regiment Arkansas to win the war lapsed into Holmesian senility. Flanagin, a strict constitutionalist if not a strong states' rights man, did involve himself in the administration of the conscription laws. Nothing in Arkansas was more unpopular than conscription, arraying the rich against the poor, the slaveholder against the nonslaveholder, and the influential against the powerless. When conscription officers attempted to induct the clerk of the state supreme court, the court protested and Flanagin agreed: "[It is] the duty of the Executive to ask and insist upon those rights of the State which she undoubtedly possesses."[44]

Flanagin did not take such a strong line on other matters. That nothing was actively done on the executive level to enforce the liquor laws led a Baptist minister friend to write Flanagin in 1864: "I have had it said to me, 'your governor loves whiskey too well to get him to stop still houses'" Similarly, rampant inflation, profiteering, and wide-spread crime went unchecked by the state authorities.[45]

The winter of 1862–63 was not a happy one in Arkansas. Hindman's defeat at Prairie Grove in December was followed by the fall of Arkansas Post in January, prompting the governor to issue a call for volunteers for sixty days to defend the state. The potential of a revived state army did not exist; the volunteers were to bring their own weapons. The fall of the post was merely a byplay in the great Mississippi campaign centered on Vicksburg. The failure of the Confederates to coordinate their defense, a failure largely due to the policies of Jefferson Davis, prompted a futile diversionary attack on the Federal post at Helena the same day Vicksburg surrendered.[46]

The fall of Vicksburg convinced many that Confederate defeat was inevitable. The rush to save property by moving to Texas now became general. Confederate military authorities added to the pessimism by removing supplies and machinery from Little Rock. Flanagin protested: "If the state be abandoned again, she may well ask to be protected from her friends." The realists, among them Senator Johnson and C. C. Danley, urged turning to guerrilla warfare and giving the new Trans-Mississippi commander, Edmund Kirby Smith, extraordinary powers without waiting for Richmond. Jefferson Davis, who lived with the bugbear of a seceding Trans-Mississippi and who believed in making all decisions himself, quarreled with Senator Johnson over the issue. Privately Flanagin may have believed that the war was over, and even received what amounted to treasonous correspondence from one of his friends.[47]

None of this stopped the Federal advances from Indian Territory in the west and up the Arkansas River in the east. In September of 1863 both Little Rock and Fort Smith fell to the bluejackets, and the greater part of the state passed under nominal Federal control. Flanagin again attempted to rally a state defensive force of old men and led them himself, but the war enthusiasm was gone. After about a month, during which the governor was in Arkadelphia, the state government reassembled in Washington, Arkansas, in the Hempstead County courthouse.[48]

For the next six months Flanagin did nothing except pardon convicted soldiers. The state government did not lapse without some protest. Even many of the most conservative men were convinced that Flanagin was not up to the crisis. In a quarrel with Senator Johnson, Flanagin claimed that "the clamor that has been raised against me arises from disappointed applicants for position." He castigated the aggressive war governor of Louisiana, Henry Watkins Allen, as "a governor who acts without or contrary to law." Flanagin played a minor role in the somewhat sordid politics of Kirby Smith's little fiefdom. Generally he supported the military authorities. In contrast to Senator Johnson, he agreed with them that it was useless to attempt to recapture the Arkansas River Valley. There was not enough food to feed an army even if it won, and the transportation did not exist to get the supplies from Texas.[49]

Since the governor would not act outside the law, the logical step was to change them. A session of the legislature was made possible by the supreme court declaring that a quorum consisted of two-thirds of those present. Thus in September of 1864 the rump legislature heard the governor declare that the war effort had failed. State relief to soldiers' families had stopped after December 1863; the cotton card manufactory had never materialized; the laws were unenforced and unenforceable. The legislature's response was to appropriate more nonexistent monies ($35,000 in gold and silver and $1 million in paper for cotton cards and medicine, $200,000 for salt) and to substitute the lash and the pillory for the use of the now Federally occupied penitentiary.[50]

After the legislature adjourned, new elections were held for the next regularly scheduled session to meet in the fall of 1865. That body never assembled and Flanagin was left alone to preside over the demise of state government. "The outcry against your policy has been so general," a friend wrote, "that a careful and scholarlike exposition is necessary to show that your action is in accordance with the law and the constitution of the state." Another advised Flanagin to do something to show the people "that our Governor is not as slow a man as they took him to be."[51]

The total collapse of the Confederacy in the spring of 1865 occurred in the East. Confederate leaders in the West were still discussing their options at a conference at Marshall, Texas, when the privates dissolved the army by going home. Flanagin professed a desire "to restore quiet to the country at the earliest possible day." A delegation from Washington conferred with the Federals in Little Rock on Flanagin's proposal to summon the legislature, repeal all acts of secession, and then resign. Flanagin urged the Federals to recognize existing county governments in the Southwest. However, the only thing the Federals would permit was for Flanagin to return the state archives to Little Rock and to retire unmolested to his home at Arkadelphia.[52]

Neither of Arkansas's wartime governors had been effective. Henry Rector failed to unify and lead the state. His overwhelming desire for political aggrandizement was the altar upon which the resources of the state of Arkansas were sacrificed. There was a healthy balance in the treasury when Rector took office, and he proceeded to spend it to develop his pet state army. Its dissolution was a vital factor in the early collapse of the Confederate Trans-Mississippi. Rector's devotion to the Confederacy clashed with his ideas of the rights and powers of the governor of a sovereign state. Finally, he totally failed to anticipate the obvious wartime problems of food supply, salt, and civil disorder.

Harris Flanagin inherited a lost cause and made it more hopeless by his inactivity. Not as overbearing as Rector, and much more sympathetic to the sufferings of the poor, he nevertheless felt compelled to follow the letter of the law, even if it destroyed him, his government, and his people.[53]

Both men came to power in unusual circumstances, and neither played much of a role in state politics after the war. Flanagin was consulted during the period of Reconstruction, and was a delegate to the constitutional convention of 1874 which ended Republican rule. "You have never sold out to the enemies of your country and people," one well-wisher wrote him. On October 23, 1874, just after returning from the convention, Flanagin was stricken and died. His eulogy was pronounced by ex-Governor Rector, also a delegate: "He has fallen a martyr in public service."[54]

Rector suffered a different kind of martyrdom. His richly stocked plantation near Little Rock was left in ruins by the war, with only two massive charred gateposts, a pile of debris, and the remnants of an orchard left to indicate previous habitation. Most of his extensive land holdings fell to the tax auctioneer's hammer during Reconstruction, as Rector devoted himself to the great passion of his life, the vindication of his father's claim against two other contenders and the Federal government to the ownership of the Hot Springs. In 1875 the United States Supreme Court ruled against all the private claimants. A commission set up to settle the claims awarded Rector's buildings to the occupants, sending Rector back into court again, this time successfully. Stories of this episode were indelibly fixed in the public mind. For many years when a shot was heard in town someone would say, "Look out, old Governor Rector is collecting his rent." Rector served in the 1874 constitutional convention, and reportedly was offered the gubernatorial nomination of the Greenback party in 1878 but rejected it. In Rector's old age the Confederate experience began to be suffused in the haloed light of the Lost Cause. Arkansas annalists ignored Rector's shortcomings but praised his courageous defiance of President Lincoln's call for troops in April 1861. A proper assessment of his role has been long delayed.[55]

FLORIDA

W. Buck Yearns

hen Lincoln's election as president of the United States brought the sectional crisis to the breaking point, radical democracy was in full control of Florida. In the early 1850s the Whigs had been viable rivals, but their compromising position on slavery in the territories soon spelled their demise. In the mid-1850s the American party, with its antiforeignism and its cheap-land platform, became a potent political force. It did well in the election of 1856, losing to the Democrats by only small margins, but the threat of the Republican party with its antisouthern position soon drove most Americans into the protective folds of the Democratic party. Thus, as the nation reeled under the shock of John Brown's raid on Harpers Ferry and the election of a purely sectional president, Florida was firmly in the hands of a leadership dedicated to state and southern rights. This leadership had its geographic and political origins in South Carolina and Georgia, had come to Florida to enter railroading and planting, and during the secession crisis had at least the temporary loyalty of the yeomanry.[1]

Representative of this leadership and head of the so-called South Carolina Ring was Governor Madison Starke Perry.[2] Born in Lancaster District, South Carolina, in 1814, Perry moved to Florida as a young man and began operating a plantation near Micanopy in Alachua County. He soon developed an interest in politics and was known as one of the best orators of his area. In 1849 he was elected to the Florida House of Representatives as a Democrat and in 1850 to the Senate. In 1856 he was Democratic candidate for governor on a strong states' rights and pro-southern platform, and defeated the American party candidate by a vote of 6,208 to 5,894. He did not take office until October 5, 1857.

During Perry's governorship several new counties were created, many of the Seminole Indians still living in Florida were moved to Indian territory, and the Florida Railroad was completed. Always an agrarian, Perry feared the coming of corporations to Florida and warned citizens there not to "bow the willing neck to the yoke of unscrupulous monopolies." He also predicted in 1858 that the reopening of the foreign slave trade was only a matter of time.

As early as 1858 Governor Perry had tried to begin preparing his state for the possibility of secession. Following the Lincoln-Douglas debates, in which Lincoln emerged as a dangerous man and the Democratic party a doubtful guardian of southern rights, Perry asked the legislature to reorganize the state militia and see that it was better armed and equipped. Nothing resulted, and following John Brown's raid in 1859 Perry reiterated his demands. He added that he himself was in favor of "eternal separation from those whose wickedness and fanaticism" posed such a threat to the South.[3] This time the legislature responded a little, reorganizing the militia somewhat, increasing the patrol systems, and even authorizing the governor to act in concert with other slave states in the event of Lincoln's election. Meanwhile, volunteer military organizations began to increase their activities: drilling, holding reviews, and collecting arms.[4]

After Lincoln's election several Florida newspapers demanded immediate secession and cooperation with other states in forming a southern confederacy. Governor Perry was in complete sympathy with them, and in his message of November 27, 1860, to the regular session of the General Assembly he warned against waiting for any overt act by the incoming president. "For myself," he stated, "I do most decidedly declare that the only hope the Southern States have for *domestic peace and safety* . . . is—Secession." He advised an immediate convention call and the further strengthening of Florida's defenses.[5] By now the radical spirit was affecting even the opposition in the legislature. With but one dissenting vote that body called for a convention to meet on January 3, 1861, and appropriated $100,000 for the purchase of arms. As soon as he was able Perry hurried to South Carolina to make the necessary purchases and also to confer with secessionist leaders who had gathered there. He brought several of them back to Florida with him, and they spoke before the convention, advising immediate secession. Caught up in the hysteria of the moment, the convention on January 10 voted 62 to 7 for secession.[6]

Even as the convention was considering Florida's relationship with the Union, its secession leaders were preparing for possible war. On January 4 they met secretly and authorized the governor to seize Fort Marion at St. Augustine, the arsenal near Chattahoochee, and the Navy Yard at Pensacola. Thoroughly in accord with the plotting, Perry sent the Quincy Guards, with orders "to act with great secrecy and discretion," to take the arsenal. That installation, defended by three men, fell on January 6; the next day another company took Fort Marion, defended by one elderly sergeant.[7]

The Navy Yard and Fort Pickens in Pensacola Bay were somewhat better defended. Nevertheless, Perry correctly judged the rising martial spirit in his state and asked nearby governors to send troops to supplement his own militia. Soon fifteen hundred volunteers from Florida and four other states were in the area ready for action. Commodore James Armstrong surrendered the Navy Yard without resistance, but Lieutenant Adam Slemmer and his eighty officers and men gave every indication of making a fight. For Florida to have precipitated war at this time would have been most imprudent, and upon the advice of Florida's senatorial delegation to Washington, Governor Perry decided to do nothing and let the future Confederate government handle the matter.[8] Meanwhile, troops continued to arrive and a period of watchful waiting began.

Until this time Florida's militia system had been in poor shape because of the state's small and scattered population. Perry's repeated appeals for improvement had aroused little interest in the legislature, but the prospect of war now dispelled this indifference. On February 4 the governor asked the legislature to raise, arm, and equip "such a number . . . as may be equal to our defense." He added, "Is it not our duty to prepare to sustain, by arms, what we have determined upon in our councils?"[9] On February 14 the legislature passed an act authorizing captains and lieutenants then holding commissions to recruit every ablebodied male over the age of fourteen and willing to volunteer. The men were to furnish their own clothing and to be armed by the state or the Confederate government. Companies and regiments were to choose their own officers, and the governor was to appoint a brigadier general over the entire force. The convention meanwhile was appropriating enough money to provide for the defense of Florida's coastal positions until their defense could be assumed by the Confederate government, a faulty ordinance because when that government failed to defend Florida properly the state was left almost defenseless.[10]

By mid-March mobilization of the militia was well under way. Volunteering was heavy, and Perry moved the men into camps of instruction as rapidly as such camps could be established. The problem was that preparing thousands of men for combat was beyond the resources of the state. But with what little money the legislature was able to provide him, the governor struggled to arm and outfit the men. He even sent a personal representative to buy arms from the state of North Carolina, but without success. Blockade-runners brought in a considerable amount, soldier-aid societies were helpful, and the governor requisitioned much from private citizens, but there was never enough. Considering these deficiencies of materiel, Perry found it inadvisable to wait until a regiment was fully organized and ready for service before offering it to the Confederate government. Instead he permitted unattached companies and even individuals to volunteer into Confederate service when they were properly armed and equipped. This obviously worked to the advantage of the Confederacy, for during 1861 Florida sent five thousand troops into Confederate service. On the other hand it stripped the state almost bare of local defense forces, for in January 1862 the state militia numbered only 762 troops.[11]

Perry's term as governor ended on October 7, 1861, and assessments of his administration vary. He might be praised as the extreme Confederate nationalist, for he uncomplainingly offered Florida's manpower and resources to the Richmond authorities for the prosecution of the war elsewhere. His correspondence with the War Department was so small that one might envision a governor struggling in the backwash of the Confederacy to meet Richmond's requisitions, even though they left his state stripped bare and defenseless in the process. Perry's only show of exasperation emerged for a moment in a telegram to the secretary of war asking that two regiments of Florida volunteers be assigned to its coastal defenses, the telegram ending with the acerbic comment: "If Florida is to take care of herself, say so."[12]

Florida's leading historian of the Civil War, John E. Johns, views Perry differently. In an indictment documented entirely from the letters of John Milton, who disliked Perry intensely, Johns claims that Perry was a poor administrator, gave army commissions on the basis of friendship rather than competency, spent money unwisely in buying arms but still sent troops into service poorly armed, ruined Florida's local defense system by compliance with Confederate manpower requisitions, and left the state almost bankrupt.[13] Unfortunately the Florida Civil War records are too sparse to make this or the previous interpretation definitive.

After his governorship Perry served as a colonel of the Seventh Florida regiment until he was forced to resign because of illness. He retired to his plantation and died there in March 1865.

Perry's successor as governor of Florida, John Milton, was born in Louisville, Georgia, on April 20, 1807. His father was a planter of moderate circumstances and sent his son to the academy in Louisville. After his studies there and after being graduated from the University of Georgia, Milton read law in the office of Roger L. Gamble and following his admission to the bar began the practice of law at home. Two years later he moved to Columbus, Georgia, and a little later to Mobile, Alabama. He practiced law in Mobile and in New Orleans for the next several years except for the period of his service as captain of volunteers in the Seminole War. In 1845 Milton moved to Florida, bought a plantation in Jackson County, and lived there the remainder of his life. By 1860 he owned fifty-two slaves and over seven thousand acres of land. In 1826 he married Susan Amanda Cobb of Cobbham, Georgia; after her death he married Caroline Howze of Marion, Alabama, in 1840.

In 1833 Milton ran for Congress in Georgia as a nullifier, but was defeated. In 1850 he was elected to the lower house of the Florida General Assembly, and it was there that he revealed his moderate tendencies. Instead of exploiting the tempestuous sectional issues of the day, he devoted his energies to Indian affairs, the judiciary, and school and college matters. He did not stand for reelection, but had made his mark as a conscientious public servant. In 1860 he was chairman of the Florida delegation to the Democratic national convention in Charleston and worked to keep the party united. But when it split over the question of slavery in the territories he took a strong prosouthern position and was now popular with both radicals and conservatives in Florida.[14] The South Carolina Ring, led by Governor Perry, opposed Milton's nomination as governor, but he won the nomination with ease and then defeated his Constitutional Union opponent by a seven to five majority.

Milton spent much of his time as governor-elect in familiarizing himself with conditions in Florida and found much to displease him. Most prominent was his conviction that Perry's military appointees lacked both ability and leadership.[15] The defense of the Apalachicola River basin was his chief concern. After considerable machinations he was finally able to replace Perry's chief appointees there with his own men and to persuade the Confederate government to refuse to accept an artillery battalion headed by yet another Perry appointee. And when the Confederate government ordered General James Trapier to Florida as Confederate commander, the acting commander, Colonel William Scott Dilworth, was also placed in check.[16]

These were costly victories for Milton, however, for they united the Radical Democrats against him. These men, angered at so many of their ilk being replaced by moderate Democrats and even ex-Whigs, decided to use Florida's financial problems as an excuse to limit the governor's authority. In a surprise move they had the convention reassembled on January 14, 1862, and from that vantage point launched their attack.[17] In November 1861 the General Assembly had enacted a law proposed by Milton banning any speculation or monopoly. The convention invalidated that law despite Milton's warning that this would unleash untold "villany."[18] The convention then charged him with concealing $21,000 of the state treasury. Milton easily proved that he had concealed the money only to prevent the revelation that this was the total amount in the treasury, but a shadow had been cast over his honesty.[19] The convention then created an executive council composed of the lieutenant governor and three members of the convention. The ordinance specified that the council was to share fully the "power conferred" upon the governor, which in effect made it the governor's equal in both decision making and administration. Finally the convention attempted to sabotage Milton's consuming interest in state defense by ordering the state militia to be disbanded by March 10, 1862.

This strategy of trying to limit the governor's authority, however, backfired on the radicals. The council met only five times and spent most of its time unanimously approving resolutions letting Milton prosecute the war as he wished. Some of these authorized him to seize private weapons, use the coast guard for local defense, remove telegraph lines and railroad facilities from danger of enemy capture, declare martial law, and regulate blockade-running. The council even ordered state troops, whom the convention had ordered disbanded, to remain on duty at Apalachicola until relieved by Confederate troops. The members gradually stopped attending meetings, and in November Milton informed the legislature that he had not seen a council member since May. The legislature recognized the obvious and quietly repealed the convention ordinance establishing a plural executive. The result of this unwarranted experiment was that Radical Democrats lost their dominance of government and Milton now controlled the political situation in Florida.[20]

As already mentioned, Milton began his governorhsip with an almost empty treasury. When Florida seceded, there was little ready capital in the state, and both the assessment and collection of taxes was poor. On February 14, 1861, the legislature authorized the governor to issue $500,000 in state bonds and a similar amount in treasury notes.[21] But neither Perry nor Milton was ever able to sell many bonds, and Perry's hasty efforts to place Florida on a wartime basis had almost exhausted the issue of treasury notes. Soon Florida, as other states and even the Confederate government were doing, began to rely on repeated issues of treasury notes. Milton blamed the inevitable inflation that resulted on blockade-running and unnecessary government spending. He asked the Florida delegation to the Confederate Congress to see that the number of government employees be de-

creased and that the "villainous traffic which is carried on by speculators under the plea of furnishing the people . . . with the prime necessities of life should be suppressed."[22] In 1864 he belatedly asked the
legislature to double Florida's tax rate, but all his advice fell on deaf
ears. By the end of the war $1,857,270 in Florida treasury notes was in
circulation.[23]

Florida's exposed and almost helpless position put Milton's strong
Confederate nationalism to its severest test. An early aggravation to
him was the latitude with which his predecessor had allowed volunteers to enter Confederate service and the readiness with which the
War Department had accepted them. He wrote President Davis to "sol-
emnly protest, the tendency of the assumption . . . of such power by the
Confederate Government," as it sapped "the very foundation of the
rights of the States." His pique must have been largely personal, however, for he was easily soothed when General Trapier asked his permission to retain "troops already mustered" into Confederate service.[24]

Milton's chief concern during the winter of 1861–62 was the defense
of the Florida coast. On November 27, 1861, he asked the legislature to
revitalize the remnants of the militia left from Perry's administration
by enrolling every man from sixteen to sixty in state defense units.[25]
Meanwhile he was begging arms and munitions from the War Department for his prospective state army. But his hopes were soundly
dashed. Not only did the legislature reject his proposal of massive
enrollment, but the convention for reasons of economy required the
transfer by March 10, 1862, of all remaining militia companies to
Confederate service or their disbandment. Worst of all, because of recent military disasters in Tennessee, the Confederacy transferred to
the Tennessee front all its troops then defending the Florida seaboard
except those defending the mouth of the Apalachicola.[26] R. E. Lee himself wrote Milton that "unless troops can be organized in Florida for its
defense, I know not whose they can obtain."[27] Even then Milton wrote
the secretary of war that "if the sacrifice of Florida is necessary, there
is not a man, woman or child in Florida, but what will say Amen."[28]

Despite these reverses Milton still remained possibly the most cooperative Confederate governor in regard to conscription and exemption
programs. When Congress enacted its first conscription law on April
16, 1862, he urged all Floridians to volunteer before being drafted. It is
true that he did ask the Florida congressmen to see that subsequent
laws permitted some ablebodied men to remain at home for local defense, and that skilled workers like millers and tanners be exempt, but
he never tried to force either point.[29] Generally he disliked favoritism
to any interest group. When Congress allowed conscripts to hire substitutes, he wrote his delegation: "Shall the sulking coward be favored by

a legal exemption?"[30] And when Congress finally succumbed to states' rights pressures and let every governor exempt every state employee considered necessary for good government, Milton was responsible for only 109 of the 18,843 eventually exempt.[31] The only strong position taken by Congress which Milton deplored was one drafting certain overseers. Florida's chief contribution to the war effort was food, and in Milton's opinion drafting any overseer would threaten both the state's production of food and its control of its large slave population.[32] Considering such cooperation, Secretary of War Seddon had every justification for thanking Milton for "the cordial support you have habitually given to all measures for the common defense."[33]

The Confederate policy that caused the greatest dissatisfaction among Florida civilians was that of impressing army supplies from individuals or stores and paying less than market prices. Governor Milton at first interpreted state laws quite loosely in order to avoid any conflict between state property and Confederate impressment laws. But by mid-1863 impressment agents had begun to use the most arbitrary tactics conceivable, and the problem was compounded when unscrupulous men began seizing property under the guise of Confederate agents.[34] In November 1863 Milton now excoriated Congress for passing such a law and the army for abusing it. He asked for "the interposition of State authority to protect the rights, lives, and liberty of citizens against the military orders of Confederate officers." He next wrote the chief commissary officer of Florida predicting adverse effects upon Floridians in service if their families "shall be made to suffer by impressments unnecessarily or illegally made." In turn, the legislature adopted a resolution describing impressment practices then being used as a "serious evil, unauthorized by law," and ordered that any person unlawfully impressing property be jailed for from one to five years.[35] As he did in the cases of other governors making the same complaint, Secretary Seddon conducted an immediate inquiry into such charges, which gave satisfaction to no one.[36]

But even here Milton did not let his concern for the rights of citizens hamper the prosecution of the war. At the beginning of the war Florida had no rail connection with the rest of the Confederacy. The need for Florida foodstuffs, particularly beef, increased as the war dragged on, and the Confederacy began developing plans for a line from Lawton, Georgia, to Live Oak, Florida. By the end of 1862 the roadbed was almost complete, but there was little rail or rolling stock available. Meanwhile, much of the 155 miles of the Florida Railroad had been torn up to prevent enemy use of it, and late in 1862 Milton conceived the idea of cannibalizing what was left of it for the Lawton–Live Oak Connection. The Florida Railroad was able to stave off the impressment of its line for several months, but in the spring of 1864 the War Department began seizing some of its rails. The aggrieved company filed suit in the Alachua County court for the recovery of its rails and the court granted an injunction in their favor. But when the War Department ignored the ruling and the governor gave no sign of any support coming from him, the court dropped the case.[37] Milton himself wrote the judge of the Alachua court: "Nothing can justify a conflict between the State and the Confederate Government but an absolute necessity for the protection of civil liberty."[38]

Milton was even more hostile to private and state blockade-running than was the Confederate government. Both believed that it weakened the Confederacy's effort to wrest recognition from European nations by withholding cotton from them and that it also led to the importation of too many nonmilitary items. But Milton also argued that it led to speculation and extortion, and he was able to get the legislature on December 4, 1863, to ask its congressional delegation to outlaw all private blockade-running.[39] On one occasion he tried to prohibit several vessels from leaving Apalachicola, but Secretary of Navy Stephen R. Mallory informed him that cotton exportation could only be stopped to prevent it from falling into enemy hands.[40] Under a law of Congress passed February 6, 1864, President Davis ordered all vessels to assign half their cargo space to Confederate account. Governor Joseph E. Brown of Georgia invited the other Confederate governors to join with him in protesting this law, but Milton refused. He wrote Brown: "My judgment . . . does not approve of any direct attempt by persuasion or otherwise to be made by the Governor of a State . . . to influence the legislation of Congress. . . . It is best . . . to avoid all conflicts and competition between State and Confederate authorities."[41]

Since food was Florida's chief contribution to the Confederacy, what the state planted was of paramount importance. At first its planters voluntarily complied with the Confederate government's urging that they plant food rather than cash crops. By the spring of 1862, however, there was a general feeling over the South that the war was about won, and Florida planters once again turned to cash crops. The subsequent disasters in Tennessee again changed southern thinking, and on February 24, 1863, Governor Milton appealed to the planters to emphasize food production. Patriotic elements even urged him to call a special session of the legislature to regulate planting by law, but Milton refused. He explained that the legislature of 1862 had discussed and then rejected such a statute, and even if the call were made, spring planting would have been completed. He also questioned the legality of such an act. Fortunately everything worked out well, for the strong appeals that he and the press had made took effect. Little cotton was planted in

1863. When the legislature met later that year and restricted cotton to one acre and tobacco to one-quarter acre for each hand, its purpose had already been achieved.[42]

When Florida left the Union its only important industry was sawmilling, and with all the state's deficiencies there was little that anyone could do to increaase or diversify industry in the state. The Bailey Cotton Mill in Monticello was a struggling company, and the state's largest leather factory was in Madison. Together they employed ninety-one workers. For a while Governor Milton considered having the state take them over, but after an investigation he decided that they could operate best under completely private management.[43] In 1862 the legislature appropriated $20,000 for the purchase abroad of cotton and wool cards, to be sold to needy families at cost. Milton did not follow through with the project since he considered the imported items far too expensive. Instead he contracted with four local investors for the manufacture of cards and arranged to buy them at six dollars each. Problems of labor, machinery, and material kept both the quality and quantity of the Florida Card Manufacturing Company's products quite poor, but it operated until the end of the war.[44]

It was not long before the lack of the preservative salt became a problem even to ocean-bound Florida. The best location for making salt from sea water was on the Gulf coast between Tampa Bay and Choctawhatchee Bay, where the coast was broken by inlets and bays partially hidden from prowling enemy vessels.[45] When speculators began buying large tracts of land there for resale to would-be salt makers, Governor Milton withdrew from sale all public land in the area and gave individual producers free use of the water and wood there. He also tried to help workers for the larger companies defend themselves by organizing them into militia units and promising them guns. This worked badly, however. He was able to provide only forty-three guns for five hundred men, and since most of the younger workers were army deserters they were uninterested in defending themselves.[46]

Florida began its Confederate experience with few Unionists in the state, most of them concentrated in Key West and on the East Florida coast. But starting with the first conscription law and progressing through the increasing distresses of war caused by taxation, impressment, and scarcities of almost everything, disaffection among civilians and desertion by soldiers gradually increased. Together they were more than Governor Milton and his small support of Confederate troops could handle.

Halfway through the war Milton tried to appease the disaffected by providing state support to county relief programs. In December 1861 county commissioners had been given the authority to levy a separate tax to be used for the relief of needy families of soldiers. When the amount of money raised in this way proved insufficient, the legislature on December 6, 1862, appropriated $200,000 for the needy and gave the governor essentially a free hand in spending it.[47] Milton ordered the probate judges and justices of the peace in each county to make lists of needy families of soldiers. He then instructed the county commissioners to buy basic foods with the state money and distribute them at state expense.[48] But the money was insufficient to feed the thirteen thousand needy families existing in Florida by 1864, and even more money probably would not have helped. Enough food was not to be had at any price, and in April Milton was informed that many families were still "perilously near starvation."[49]

The most damaging element of the disaffected was the bands of deserters which increased in number and size as the war dragged on. For the most part they avoided open combat with troops sent to apprehend them, but used the numerous swamps and sparsely settled areas as bases from which they stole slaves and cattle, robbed mail and wagon routes, disrupted local government, and even plotted to kidnap Governor Milton. By 1864 they had become so disruptive that the Confederate government determined to stamp them out if possible.[50] In March Lieutenant Colonel Henry D. Capers with infantry and cavalry units raided a deserter camp near the mouth of the Econfina River. Finding only sixteen women and children there, the frustrated officer hauled them to a camp near Tallahassee and placed them under guard in rude cabins.[51] Milton had long been urging the War Department to wage war on the deserters, but at this development insisted, "I cannot approve of a warfare upon women and children."[52] He had them delivered to a Union blockading vessel and the ridiculous episode was over. Milton's few state militiamen occasionally captured a few straggling deserters, but for the remainder of the war deserters were virtually unthreatened.

In the summer of 1864 Confederate strategists decided to abandon the defense of the coast, but to resist any enemy attempt to penetrate the interior of the state. To assist the small Confederate force remaining in Florida, Milton on July 30 and with legislative authority called on all males capable of bearing arms to organize themselves into militia units. Three thousand men volunteered and the War Department was able to provide them with fifteen hundred guns. By this time, however, the United States was concentrating its attack elsewhere, and for the rest of the life of the Confederacy warfare in Florida consisted of small raids by the two opposing forces against each other. On April 1, 1865, Milton, realizing that the war was lost, took his own life.[53] His successor, President of the Senate Abraham K. Allison, had only to turn the state over to the Union forces.

GEORGIA

Paul D. Escott

merican politicians, as a type, are rather predictable figures. Instead of initiating change or breaking old customs, they generally conform to the expectations of their era and reflect the existing forces of their day. In a democratic system, after all, the politician survives by adapting to the realities of power, not by defying them. Yet politicians, in their role as conduits for underlying social forces, can hold great interest for historians. As they play out their limited role, political figures sometimes reveal the structure and nature of their society. Leaders who are especially adept at sensing and responding to centers of power may help us penetrate to the heart of a social system and understand the forces at work there. Such a man was Georgia's Joseph Emerson Brown. Blessed with great sensitivity and political skill, Brown held office in a period of immense and fundamental change that challenged the operating assumptions of his society. In responding to this challenge he brought sweeping changes to the government of Georgia and simultaneously laid bare the internal contradictions of the Confederacy.

There were few indications at the outset of the Civil War that Brown would play so important a role. In 1861 he was the young and undistinguished governor of a state whose politics focused on matters of limited and parochial interest. Not yet forty, Joseph E. Brown had come to high office only because Georgia Democrats had deadlocked in 1857 over the choice of more prominent men and had turned to a relative unknown who met the requirement of hailing from the upcountry or Cherokee region. Compared to Robert Toombs, Howell Cobb, and Alexander Stephens, Georgia politicians of national stature, Brown was a pigmy among titans. That he could be elected, however, was understandable; for in contrast to the great questions of union or disunion, slavery or free labor, state politics before the war was also limited in scope. Mundane issues such as taxation and management of the state-owned Western and Atlantic Railroad dominated the scene. Whigs, who generally represented planters and urban commercial interests, usually fought for higher taxes and modest expansion of governmental expenditure to spur business and provide services; Democrats, who drew their strength principally from subsistence farmers, typically opposed new taxes and programs.[1]

By 1865 both governor and state government had changed tremendously. Joe Brown rapidly developed into a formidable politician, one who repeatedly challenged Jefferson Davis and conferred as an equal with Alexander Stephens on ways to change basic Confederate policies. While dominating state politics and twice winning easy reelection, he transformed the prewar state government into an effective relief agency that served both soldiers and thousands of suffering citizens. Brown charted his successful course by keeping in touch with vital elements of the electorate and responding to their needs. This perceptive politician expressed the grievances of both planters and yeomen and found ways to serve their interests, even when these were opposed to the needs of the southern government. In the process he won growing popularity within Georgia while the national cause declined, and his stands illuminated major issues within the Confederacy.

The crucial questions confronting the southern nation grew out of its class system and concerned the character of the planter class and its relationship to the yeomen. Would the planters' ideology of states' rights permit an effective southern government? Could nonslaveholders be convinced to fight for the planters' interests? Which classes in society would make sacrifices for the war effort and to what extent? In dealing with these questions, Brown proved keenly sensitive to both planters and yeomen. Under the stress of wartime conditions each group became seriously discontented and posed major difficulties for the Confederacy. Although members of the South's slaveholding elite had led their region into secession, they often opposed the Richmond administration and resisted any infringement of their privileges or freedom of action. Far too many of them wanted only to protect their slave property and accustomed style of life, and lacked a positive conception of national goals or purpose. Consequently, when the Confederate government demanded significant sacrifices—such as conscription or the impressment of slaves and private property—as the price of winning the war, many planters turned their backs on the government they had created. Meanwhile, thousands of nonslaveholders encountered economic privation and suffering that raised the stakes of their sacrifice. These yeomen began to ask how far they must go for the Confederate government, especially when the rich and influential re-

ceived preferential treatment while poorer men had to bear the greatest burdens. As both groups grew restive, their support of the Confederacy dwindled.[2]

With uncommon sensitivity and frank opportunism Brown managed
to serve these two masters at once—the planter elite and the masses of
nonslaveholding yeomen farmers. To win the planters' support, he became chief critic of the Confederacy and a determined foe of the policies
of Jefferson Davis. To appeal to the yeomen, he became the champion
of their economic interests and the servant of their needs. Brown opposed policies that damaged the privileges or position of the planters at
the same time that he stood up for the little man who was making
extreme sacrifices in the war. Thus he served established centers of
power while he also drew attention to the necessity of meeting the
needs of the masses. These techniques were inconsistent with Confederate survival and with each other, for they reduced support for the
war and both promised and denied social justice between the classes.
But they proved effective in the short run and spotlighted the flaws in
the southern social system. Thus Brown demonstrated that it was possible for an astute politician to stay very much afloat while his
society—which cherished both independence and states' rights, sacrifice and privilege, democracy and aristocracy—sank into defeat.[3]

Brown's wartime activities proceeded naturally from his personal
experience and character. Not born into the elite, he exhibited
throughout his life an acute perception of the routes to success in his
society. But, while climbing upwards, he retained from his origin an
understanding of the feelings of the common man that would prove
invaluable to his political career. Brown was born at Long Creek,
South Carolina, on April 15, 1821, into a middle-class farming
family that settled in North Georgia and aided his efforts to obtain
an education. After attendance at a southern academy, he was
graduated from Yale Law School and began law practice in Georgia
in 1847. That same year he married Elizabeth Grisham, a woman
from a prosperous background. A successful lawyer, he soon began
to invest in real estate and built up his fortune through steady
appreciation of land values and occasional windfalls.[4]

From the beginning, however, Brown felt an attraction to politics,
and in 1849 he won election to the state Senate. Undaunted by lack of
experience, he spoke out boldly and quickly became "the acknowledged Democratic leader" in his chamber. Then, after achieving
such early renown, he chose a less active role in politics and threw
himself into making money. Perhaps, having tested his abilities and
found them ample, he perceived that real political prominence required a more substantial financial foundation. In any case, he de-

voted himself during the early fifties to building his law practice and using the proceeds to speculate in farm land and extensive mineral properties. Securely on the road to wealth, Brown eased back into a public role by becoming a circuit judge in 1855. He was in that position when the stalemate at the 1857 Democratic convention catapulted him into the governorship.[5]

From the first, Brown displayed two significant qualities that marked his four terms as governor: bold, colorful leadership and advocacy of certain key issues that appealed to both the elite and the masses. He promptly silenced the question "Who is Joe Brown?" by assailing the state's banks, most of which had suspended specie payment in the aftermath of the Panic of 1857. Brown proposed to enforce an existing statute that would strip offending financial institutions of their charters, and he vigorously fought the legislature when it passed a bill virtually forgiving the banks. Though he eventually lost, Brown, to all appearances, had struggled like Andrew Jackson against financial monopoly and for the common man. Planters, too, soon had reason to feel that they had a staunch friend in the capital as Brown staked out uncompromising positions in the sectional crisis. From the beginning of his career he had defended slavery, and in the 1850s, he also became a slaveholder. As Congress debated the admission of Kansas under a proslavery constitution, he seized the opportunity to assure Georgia's congressional leaders that he was "safe" on slavery. At one point he threatened to call a secession convention if Congress rejected Kansas, and after Abraham Lincoln's election, he strongly backed secession and argued to nonslaveholders that leaving the Union was essential to their interests. In this manner, and through profitable management of the state-owned railroad, Brown entered 1861 as a popular executive enjoying his second term.[6]

Brown believed in the fundamental importance of state sovereignty, and even before Georgia joined the Confederacy he demonstrated his determination to make this principle a reality. In the short interval between secession and admission to the new southern government, he dispatched T. Butler King as a diplomatic representative to seek recognition for the sovereign state of Georgia from Queen Victoria, Napoleon III, and the king of Belgium. Such a heady conception of states' rights accorded with the inclinations of men like Stephens or Toombs, who often stated their states' rights convictions strongly, or in the latter case, belligerently. It was also likely to produce collisions with the Confederate government.[7]

These were not long in coming. From the first, Brown jealously sought to keep all the state's guns under his exclusive control, even though the Confederacy was struggling to create a southern army from virtually nothing. Brown threatened to disarm Georgia soldiers as soon as they left the state, and he also schemed to keep the appointment of as many officers as possible in his hands. Despite the fact that the Confederacy needed battle-ready units, the governor repeatedly offered only skeleton regiments that had a full complement of officers, with all those through colonel appointed by Brown, and few simple foot soldiers. This device allowed the crafty governor to confer impressive military titles on a greater number of Georgians. He also tried to please the mass of his constituents by insisting, whenever possible, that the state's soldiers be allowed to elect their company-grade officers, rather than accept commanders appointed by the Confederacy.[8]

Further, Brown took several steps early in the war that showed his concern for the economic welfare of the comman man. For those in the army he bought blankets, clothing, shoes, and other supplies, and he insisted that the state continue to clothe its troops even after the central government was ready to assume the task. Citizens at home needed cloth, and thread could not be spun until cotton cards untangled the fibers, so Brown set the penitentiary to work manufacturing cards. These efforts won popular approval, but the most dramatic act was his response to a shortage of salt that occurred in the state before the end of 1861. On November 20 of that year he ordered the seizure of all salt that was selling for more than five dollars per sack, and asked the legislature for the future authority to impress essential items. Armed with this power, and through hastily arranged manufacturing in Virginia, he began to supply salt to the poor. This commodity was indispensable in the days before refrigeration, and the governor's actions gained him the gratitude of widows and soldiers' families when they received salt either free or far below market price. In his distribution of salt Brown established a system of priorities that he followed throughout the war: soldiers' wives and widows and the parents of dead soldiers came first, then the poor and heads of families generally.[9]

As the war went on, Brown expanded his service to the interests of both rich and poor. The Confederate administration, acting on Jefferson Davis's belief that the central government should exercise its constitutional war powers, moved to take control of the war effort. The adoption of conscription in April 1862 gave startling proof of the government's intention. To many states' rightists this law was an act of tyranny, and Brown wasted no time in condemning it and leading an assault on Davis's policy. He declared that conscription was unnecessary, demanded the exemption of a long list of state officials and citizens, ordered Georgia enrollment officers to refuse to cooperate with Confederate officials, and protested that the law constituted power "to destroy the civil government to each State." Warming to his subject, the governor next declared that conscription was "subversive of [Georgia's] sovereignty, and at war with all the principles for the support of which Georgia entered into this revolution." Through complicated examination of precedent he maintained that the Confederate government had no right to draft most southerners since a state's militia consisted, according to his definition, of everyone who was not in regular service.[10]

When Davis responded that conscription obviously had been necessary and was part of the constitutional power to raise armies, Brown readied his counterarguments. After Davis stated the general principle that Congress should judge whether its laws served a specific constitutional purpose under the "necessary and proper" clause, Brown pounced on the unwary chief executive, pointing out that Davis had raised the same issue debated earlier by Hamilton and Jefferson in the controversy over establishing a bank. Jefferson's views had become southern dogma, and here the president of the Confederacy had taken the wrong side. Davis's view, Brown wrote, had been "first proclaimed . . . almost as strongly by Mr. Hamilton." Stressing that he stood in the superior company of Jefferson, Madison, and Calhoun, Brown condemned the president's exegesis of the Constitution and charged that conscription represented "a bold and dangerous usurpation by Congress of the reserved rights of the States, and a rapid stride towards military despotism." Apparently conscription was not despotic when undertaken by Brown himself, for the governor had drafted Georgia men without legal authority. These facts, however, only seemed to help him detect tyranny and usurpation in others.[11]

The second conscription act, passed in September 1862, provoked even greater ire in Brown. The governor charged that this act, which extended the maximum age of eligibility from thirty-five to forty-five, "strikes down [Georgia's] sovereignty at a single blow" and was worse than anything passed by the U.S. Congress before secession. Eventually Brown submitted to the operation of the law, but he never ceased to protest. The battle over conscription set him clearly against the Confederate government and inaugurated an extended campaign that he waged against the policies of the Richmond administration, ostensibly on grounds of principle.[12]

Brown's hostility toward the Davis government reached its peak in his opposition to the suspension of the writ of habeas corpus. By 1864 the pugnacious governor had decided that the fight against this measure should be made the vehicle for controlling the expansion of Richmond's legal powers, augmenting the power of the states, and bringing the war to a peaceful conclusion. After careful planning with Alexander and Linton Stephens, Brown and the two half-brothers addressed a special session of the state legislature. Linton Stephens denounced the suspension of the writ as "a dangerous assault upon . . . the liberty of the people," while Brown denied that Congress had legally suspended the writ and accused Davis of making *illegal and unconstitutional arrests.*" This coordinated attack on Confederate policies included legislative resolutions that endorsed negotiations as the means to peace and invited the people to act "through their state organizations and popular assemblies" to end the war. Technically the Confederate and United States governments would still have the opportunity to enter the peace process, but this plan, if it meant anything, represented an attempt to supersede constituted authority.[13]

These contentious episodes frustrated Jefferson Davis and crippled some of his policy aims, destroying in particular the image of a determined and united South that he was trying to project in 1864. They also promoted confusion and disunity within the struggling South. Beyond this their main effect was to strengthen Brown and establish him as a leader in the ranks of Georgia's slaveholding politicians. The unknown from Cherokee County had now arrived as an equal among the plantation aristocrats. His letters from the earlier period of his governorship, for example, show him as respectful, solicitous, and ingratiating toward a major figure like Stephens; but by the middle of the war these two dealt with each other on an even plane. In the realm of policy and practice Brown's protests ultimately were unsuccessful, for the Davis government sustained both conscription and the suspension of habeas corpus. In a key area of political support, however, the governor's actions had great value.[14]

While cultivating the elite in this manner, Brown did not fail to identify new and effective means of serving the common people. In November 1862 he urged the state legislature to award one hundred dollars to the family of each soldier who owned taxable property worth less than one thousand dollars. This measure gave tangible relief to those suffering most in the midst of a difficult war, and the governor went further by asking the lawmakers to rescind the poll tax for soldiers and allow a one-thousand-dollar exemption on the property tax. At approximately the same time he supported the campaign to shift agriculture from cotton to grains, so that the southern masses would not suffer for bread. A new statute limited cotton planting to three acres per hand, and Brown repeatedly pressed for a lower limit of only one quarter-acre per hand. Thus, while some haughty planters, including a callous Robert Toombs, scorned the common man's problems, Brown showed that he was concerned and determined to help. A law to prohibit distilling, which he vigorously enforced, showed a similar concern[15]

Brown waged a relentless war on distilleries and won many supporters through his energetic actions. The Rome *Weekly Courier,* for
example, had always been unfriendly to the governor, but by the fall of
1863 his aid to suffering citizens began to compel a change in editorial
attitude. On November 12, 1863, the newspaper ran a headline asking
"WHAT SHALL WE DO FOR SOMETHING TO EAT?" Food was criti-
cally short, yet some people in North Georgia were distilling whiskey
from grain under a contract with the Confederacy. In a short while Joe
Brown had intervened, spoken out against distilleries, and warned the
Confederate government to cease its violation of a state law. The *Courier* expressed warm gratitude to Brown on this issue and continued to
criticize him in other areas; it is probable that many of the *Courier's*
readers felt gratitude of a less restricted sort.[16]

To serve Georgia's fighting men, Brown displayed tireless energy.
He dispatched purchasing agents throughout the South and Europe,
and in 1864 began an export-import operation that supplied these
agents with ample funds. Chartering steamers and loading them with
state-owned cotton, Brown sent these ships through the blockade to
Caribbean ports where their cargoes were sold. On the return voyage
these Georgia blockade-runners carried blankets, clothing, and medicine earmarked for men on the battlefields. Five million dollars worth
of cotton was exchanged in this way, and only Zebulon Vance of North
Carolina rivaled Brown in supplying state troops.[17]

These activities amounted to a substantial record of achievement,
and Governor Brown was not one to stand humbly by and eschew
publicity. With well-aimed rhetoric he reminded the common people on
every possible occasion of what he had done for them, educated them
on the subject of who was their friend, and exploited their class resentments. He often credited the ordinary citizens in a democracy with
making the greatest contributions and praised the common people,
"the hardy, wayworn veterans of Georgia who are kept in the front,
and have no comfortable office, and no command in the rear, who left
their wives and little ones to defend [the aristocrat's] large inheritance, as well as their own log cabins." To recognize such sacrifice
Brown took a firm stand on financing the war: since the poor "have
generally paid their part of the cost of this war in military service,
exposure, fatigue and blood, the rich, who have been in a much greater
degree exempt from these, should meet the money demands of the
Government." His numerous other services to the ordinary Georgian
confirmed this interest in equity and surely Brown had reason for
pride when he pointed out in 1864 that "the Governor and Legislature
of your State . . . have appropriated for this year nearly $10,000,000 to
feed and clothe the suffering wives, and widows, and orphans, and

soldiers, and to put shoes upon the feet and clothes upon the backs of soldiers themselves, who are often destitute."[18]

Brown's efforts to aid the poor were in fact so extensive that they transformed the state government. To accommodate military needs and the governor's welfare activities, the state budget expanded tremendously. "Georgia's wartime expenditures," writes the closest student of this subject, "dwarfed all its ante-bellum state budgets." In a single year, 1863, the state's appropriations exceeded the total for the decade of the 1850s, and in the latter years of the war it was common for many important budget items to equal an entire budget from a prewar year. Inflation, to be sure, accounted for some of this increase, but the role and scope of the government truly expanded. At the beginning of the war the majority of expenditures went for military needs, but as the war continued, "the larger items of state spending became expenditures to support civilians—the state's (white) poor generally, but particularly the families of soldiers." Welfare costs dominated the budget in the last two years of the war, and by the time of surrender total welfare spending almost equaled the aggregate of military expenditures.[19]

Examination of the annual state budgets reveals how the aid promoted by Brown both increased and became more specific. In 1863, for example, the legislature approved such items as $1 million for the military fund, $1 million for debt, $1.5 million for soldiers' clothing, and $2.5 million to aid indigent soldiers' families. Aid to soldiers' families increased to $6 million in 1864 and to $8 million in 1865. Brown took the lead in obtaining this money, even though it meant an annual property tax of 10 percent. In addition to relief for soldiers' families, the governor distributed salt and cotton cards, and targeted food for certain depressed localities. Three special acts in 1863 gave aid to North Georgia, where fighting had diminished provisions; $800,000 was spent to furnish corn for the poor there in 1864; 10,000 bushels and 97,500 bushels were appropriated on two other occasions.[20]

In financing these unusually large expenditures, Brown kept the plight of the common man in mind. Normal functions of government were curtailed in order to save money, and the governor recommended that revenues from the state-owned railway be committed to aid for soldiers' families. In 1863 Georgia adopted a progressive income tax on net profits from manufacturing or sales of nonagricultural products. While many yeomen gained an exemption from poll and property taxes, Brown urged a confiscatory tax on the surplus production of cotton, which some profit-minded planters were growing instead of grain. Before he was done, Brown had supported property taxes that were fifteen times the prewar tax rate and the highest in the Confederacy, yet he had shielded the state's poorest citizens from these burdens.[21]

Even many of his states' rights protests brought dividends to the common man. As Brown elaborated his program and sensed a growing disillusionment with the war, he found many ways to serve rich and poor simultaneously. Conscription, for example, presented numerous chances to assist yeomen, for the laws that planters fought on principle were also those which forced ordinary men to leave their families and fight in the army. In the case of one-man farms, this often produced economic hardship for wives and children, and the induction of skilled craftsmen could have a detrimental effect on an entire community. Petitioners from Tatnall and Montgomery counties backed up their blacksmith when he explained that "if I am takein of [off] the farmers will be lefte intirly desitute of a smith." Crops had been poor, and the farmers stood "in grate grate need of a smith to repair their plows to prepair their lande for a small grain crop." Similarly, millers provided an essential service in rural localities, and many Georgians asked their governor to protect these men from the draft. Beyond such pleas for craftsmen and physicians, many counties simply needed manpower to raise and harvest the crops. A typical petitioner, from Cave Springs, Georgia, begged that the local company of volunteers be allowed to remain home until after "the growing crops are made. . . . There is no supply of provisions in this country for the future, and the growing crop is our only dependence for future supplies.[22]

Brown was sympathetic to such entreaties and frequently tried to exempt soldiers himself or pleaded their case before the Confederacy. On several occasions he wrote President Davis and explained the local conditions that made some special treatment wise and necessary. Abuses by Confederate officials, such as irregualr impressments or unauthorized foraging by the army, brought a quick retort from the watchful executive.[23]

As a result Brown became known as the man to whom Georgians could turn for help. Planters received the same kind and courteous attention as yeomen, and in time even obvious malingerers felt justified in writing to the governor. Impressment of slaves to work on fortifications or do fatigue duty in the army stimulated many protests to Brown, and one writer indicated clearly that the governor's popularity grew directly from his opposition to such unpopular Confederate policies. Slave owners assumed they could find a sympathetic ear in the governor's mansion, as evidenced by a letter early in 1862 from Senator Benjamin H. Hill. Hill explained that militia duty for overseers was inconvenient because it took them briefly away from their duties and, although it caused little real danger, made women and children on the plantations *"feel* a little insecure." Men who had lost their substitutes to the draft and faced actual military service often wrote to the governor, and many hoped for safety through a commission in the state forces. One man sent in his name and address with the terse explanation that a newspaper had reported "that you have ordered all Commissioned officers of the State of Georgia to report to you and you will protect them against the Conscription law." Through stubbornness and bureaucratic resistance Brown did manage to protect over eight thousand Georgians from the Confederate army—more than any state except North Carolina. Among these thousands of men, states' rights principles, reluctance to endure sacrifice, and simple war weariness surely mingled as motivations.[24]

By 1864 the way in which Brown's opposition to the Confederacy expressed a variety of motives was especially evident. His attacks on Confederate shipping regulations and the suspension of habeas corpus appealed to states' rightists, the common man, and the growing number of southerners who had lost their enthusiasm for the cause and sought only some relief from the burdens of war. Late in 1863 the Confederacy began to requisition one-third to one-half of the cargo space on outgoing ships, and soon made this practice compulsory in order to obtain vital war materials. On its face this policy was offensive to states' rightists due to the centralization that it entailed, but there were other causes for objection. Governor Brown and Governor Zebulon Vance of North Carolina stood to lose the ships that they used to conduct their extensive import-export programs. Brown protested on grounds of states' rights, but his concern rested equally with hard-pressed citizens at home who received aid through these shipping operations. Here, as at other junctures, Richmond's determination to wage an effective war collided with the need of ordinary citizens for some degree of security and economic welfare. Brown won warm support through serving their need, so he naturally opposed a Confederate policy that might destroy his ability to aid the people.[25]

Brown's attack on suspension of habeas corpus also had several dimensions beyond states' rights. By 1864 morale had plummeted throughout the Confederacy and people cried out for peace. In congressional elections the year before, established figures and ardent secessionists had been thrown out of office in favor of new faces who had opposed secession and who often supported peace. North Carolina had a peace candidate for governor and rumors flew that the Old North State might pull out of the Confederacy. Conditions were not much better in Georgia. The people were despairing, and many had lost faith in their government. Class resentments focused on some of Jefferson Davis's policies, and war weariness grew irresistibly. In this setting

Brown's assault on the supension of habeas corpus became an outlet for people's anger at their government and its leaders as well as a gesture toward the desideratum of peace. Brown did more than criticize a single policy; he became a symbol of and spokesman for the numerous resentments and frustrations of the people.[26]

What made it increasingly possible for Brown to function effectively at these different levels and before these different audiences was identification of the Davis government as the chief source of all problems. The needs of yeomen and planters were not truly compatible, because in the long run redress of the yeomen's grievances would require some limitation of the privileges that planters fought to retain. Nonslaveholders would not want to fight on and sacrifice unless the slaveholding elite bore an equitable burden and surrendered some of its privileges, such as substitution or exemptions for overseers.[27] But for the short term, anger at the Davis government obscured these social fissures. A "wool hat boy" from the Cherokee district could hate Davis for pampering the rich while a Black Belt planter could rage at the president for restricting his privileges, and both could join the mass in its displeasure with the poor results of a long, bloody, and terribly burdensome war. After a point, tired and harassed southerners realized that the Confederacy was always demanding another sacrifice or calling on them to bear another burden whereas their state government tried to help them and offered relief. Thus, as long as the central government appeared to be the enemy, Brown could obscure divisions, ignore contradictions, and satisfy each class by supporting its quarrels with the Confederacy

By the end of the war Brown had accomplished a remarkable feat of political prestidigitation. While the southern ship of state sank in stormy seas, his popularity and influence rose continually higher. All around him were signs of chaos and disaster. A selfish and short-sighted ruling class had led its region into secession and then proven unwilling to make sacrifices or to surrender its privileges for independence. Lack of a national vision and an obsession with preserving the world of the past made the slaveholders incapable of rule in the revolutionary world they had created. Yeomen, who had generally responded to their region's crisis, soon staggered under the loads they were forced to carry, grew resentful of the preferential treatment given others, and withdrew their support from the war. A central government which recognized the steps required for independence discovered that its leadership class had largely gone into opposition and failed to give sufficient attention to the needs of the poor.[28] Yet Joseph E. Brown became ever more appreciated, more respected, and more popular. A skillful opportunist, Brown offered no overall solution to the Confederacy's malaise, but he knew how to respond to its symptoms. The visibility and effectiveness of his responses brought him political success while the political system in which he moved rushed toward failure.

As the war drew to a close Brown, with his catlike ability to land upright and on his feet, may have been casting about for a new role to play. Any honest southerner could see that the reality of a postwar world was rapidly overtaking the wartime context in which Brown had functioned so adroitly. Professor Joseph Parks suggests that Brown determined to maintain the distance that he had established from Jefferson Davis, whose image might not fare well in a world of defeated and impoverished southerners. Yet Brown could not place himself in a position of disloyalty, and so he declined to meet and negotiate with General William T. Sherman. To the end he maintained his ties with the slaveholding class by condemning the Confederate proposal of emancipation, and to mitigate the sufferings of the yeomen he gave serious consideration to the calling of a convention and separate state action, ideas which were gaining support and even public endorsement by groups of citizens. Yet there are some situations that even the wiliest and most creative of politicians cannot master and Brown had to watch, inert, while the final scenes of Confederate defeat unfolded.[29]

Federal authorities imprisoned Brown for almost a month at the end of the war, but after the period of Reconstruction had begun he started once again to give his resourcefulness and inventive energies full play. His greatest skill was adaptability, and he early discerned the future direction of economic life and arranged his affairs to conform to it. By 1866 this longtime Jacksonian foe of banks had become a well-paid lobbyist for important banking interests. With his talent for making the most of a situation, Brown built upon these connections and turned himself into an exemplar of the New South's political economy. His law practice flourished in Atlanta, and by 1868 he was a spokesman for the pro-industry, pro-tariff, pro-internal improvement point of view. In 1870 he became head of the Western and Atlantic Railroad, and subsequently he assumed such titles as president of the Dade Coal Company and president of the Southern Railway and Steamship Association.[30]

The postwar political puzzle was more difficult to solve, but Brown attacked it with the same boldness and cold-headed intelligence that had benefited his earlier career. After a visit to Washington in 1867, he accurately concluded that the South's rejection of the Fourteenth Amendment had made black suffrage inevitable, and he urged Georgians to accept that fact rather than resist further and bring about even sterner measures. These views made him unpopular with many Georgians but not with the Republicans, whom he joined in 1868. Though he was no friend of the freedman, Brown worked industriously to win Republican support from white yeomen farmers and later urged appeals to the moderate wing of the Democrats as well. Though defeated for the United States Senate, he gained appointment as chief justice of the state supreme court. In 1870 he resigned that position and two years later became a Georgia Democrat once more. He contributed his legal talents to the national Democratic party during the dispute over the 1876 election results and finally, in 1880, achieved both vindication and the height of his ambitions. Through a complicated deal involving greed, Atlanta boosterism, and the linkage of railway systems, Brown engineered his appointment to the U.S. Senate, where he remained for ten years. While in that office he combined his pro-industry views with advocacy of Federal aid to education and retained his popularity with the common people.[31]

Brown died in Atlanta on November 30, 1894, not covered with honors perhaps, but surely remembered for a colorful and astonishing record in public life. Throughout his long career he had spoken of principles and acted without them. He was a premier example of the amoral but eminently sucessful man in both politics and economics. His years of public service produced no social innovation or new institutions, yet his significance is great because he was an indicator of forces greater than himself. As Civil War governor his actions underlined and illuminated the two basic tendencies within the Confederacy's body politic: the planter elite's willingness to allow the preservation of privilege to frustrate effective government and independence, and the tendency of nonslaveholding yeomen to withdraw their support from the war as a result of poverty and class resentments. Brown had helped the slaveholders effect their folly while he ministered to the common man's problems and championed his social position. Such political leadership met real human needs and pleased the voters, although it could not overcome the inherent contradictions in the southern social system. Joseph E. Brown was not a great man who rearranged social forces, but he was one of America's most perceptive politicians, and one who responded to the existing social structure with remarkable artistry.

KENTUCKY

Lowell H. Harrison

entuckians were sharply divided when the secession crisis forced them to assess their relationship to the Union. In view of their differences, the neutrality adopted in the spring of 1861 made sense, although no one should have expected it to continue indefinitely. Neutrality may in fact have insured Kentucky's continuance in the Union. The secessionists' best chance of taking the state out of the Union came during the excitement that followed the attack on Fort Sumter, but the adoption of neutrality blunted that hope and during the summer of 1861 the Unionists clearly gained the ascendancy. Many states' righters were appalled when impetuous General Leonidas Polk occupied Columbus and rejected their pleas that he withdraw. Union forces also moved into the state, but the legislature demanded the withdrawal only of the Confederates.

Pro-Confederate Kentuckians longed to be in the Confederacy, but the Frankfort government was Unionist, and the cherished doctrine of states' rights held that secession could be attained only by action of a sovereignty convention called by the legislature. Some Confederate soldiers and civilians held an assembly in Russellville on October 29–30 at which they denounced the Frankfort government and appealed to the right of the people "to alter, reform, or abolish their government, in such manner as they think proper." A committee was appointed to prepare for a sovereignty convention to meet in Russellville the following month. The 115 delegates who assembled there on November 18 represented sixty-eight counties, but most of them were soldiers or civilians who had fled to the Confederate lines. The convention denounced the Frankfort government and declared Kentucky "a free and independent state, clothed with all power to fix her own destiny, and to secure her own rights and liberties."[1]

The delegates quickly drafted a provisional government with a governor and ten councilmen, one from each congressional district, elected by the convention. The governor was to appoint other officials with the advice and consent of the council. The state constitution and laws that did not conflict with the work of the convention and council were declared valid. Bowling Green was designated as the capital for the new government, but the governor and council were authorized "to meet at any other place that they may deem appropriate." A convention of one hundred members was to be convened, "so soon as an election can be held, free from the influence of the armies of the United States," to provide for a permanent government. Meanwhile, admittance into the Confederate States of America was to be sought.[2]

Both President Jefferson Davis and some members of the Confederate Congress were concerned by the irregularity of the Kentucky proceedings. But, as Davis wrote Howell Cobb, president of the Congress, "the conclusion to which I have arrived, is, that there is enough of merit in the application to warrant a disregard of its irregularity."[3] On December 10, 1861, Kentucky was admitted into the Confederacy.

George W. Johnson, the first governor of Confederate Kentucky, had played an active role in the independence movement. He was born in Scott County on May 22, 1811, the son of William Johnson, and after attending local common schools enrolled in Transylvania University. He received an A.B. degree in 1829, the L.B. in 1832, and an M.A. in 1833.

In 1833 Johson married Ann Eliza Viley, daughter of Captain Willa Viley, one of the state's noted breeders of thoroughbreds. Johnson began a law practice in Scott County, but he soon abandoned it in favor of his agricultural interests. His Kentucky farm of over three hundred acres, located three miles from Georgetown, was worked by twenty-five slaves. He also acquired a cotton plantation of over a thousand acres near Helena, Arkansas, where he usually spent several months during the winter. George Johnson's gracious hospitality kept his large mansion crowded with visitors. He was especially fond of children, and two large ponds on his Kentucky farm were well stocked with fish for the amusement of his young friends and his own children.[4]

A popular figure in central Kentucky, Johnson was frequently urged to seek public office. He was elected to the state House of Representatives in 1838, 1839, and 1840, and in 1852 and 1860 he was a Democratic candidate for presidential elector. But he had a strong aversion to holding office, and rejected other requests. However, Johnson was keenly interested in politics and his political sagacity made him an important figure in the state Democratic party.

Although he believed in both slavery and states' rights, Johnson loved the Union, and he sought ways to avoid secession and war. He believed that if Kentucky joined the Confederacy the balance of power would be so even as to preclude war. On May 10, 1861, the State Rights Democrats in the legislature selected him as one of their two nominees to serve on a proposed five-man commission that would direct the state's military forces. The Unionists initially rejected the proposal, and when the commission was established two weeks later Johnson was not a member. In August, Governor Beriah Magoffin sent Johnson to Virginia to secure President Davis's pledge that Kentucky's neutrality would not be violated.[5]

When the state's neutrality ended in September 1861, Johnson fled the state to avoid arrest. Then fifty and with a crippled arm, he seemed precluded from any active military service. While he may have held rank in the state militia, Johnson had had no military experience that would compensate for his other handicaps. After a brief stay in Virginia he joined the Confederate army under General Simon Bolivar Buckner that had occupied Bowling Green on September 18. Johnson served as a volunteer aide to his friend Buckner and shared a house with him.

The situation in the state was still confused, and Johnson was consulted frequently on political-military affairs. Embarrassed by Kentucky's failure to secede, he was instrumental in staging the Russellville meeting of October 29–30 and the sovereignty convention of November 18–20. As a delegate from Scott County he was an active participant in the convention, and he was elected provisional governor. One of his first official acts was to request that Kentucky be admitted into the Confederate States of America, "to offer you [the Confederacy] our assistance in a common cause, while peril surrounds us both, and to share with you a common destiny."[6]

Even before word arrived that the request had been granted, Governor Johnson and his associates were busily engaged in attempting to establish a viable government. Fortunately, he worked well with Albert Sidney Johnston, Buckner, and John C. Breckinridge (his wife's cousin), for the provisional government had no jurisdiction outside the limited areas occupied by Confederate troops.

Finance was an urgent problem for the Johnson administration. The council directed the governor to take possession of the banks within the Confederate lines. Private accounts were protected, but the Confederates seized some funds that belonged to the state. By an act of December 11, 1861, sheriffs and other revenue collectors were ordered to deposit their collections with the treasurer of the provisional government. When Sheriff Pleasant J. Potter of Warren County protested the law, he was removed from office. Merchants were required to take out licenses, and other small sums were obtained. The provisional government probably raised less than $250,000, and that sum was woefully inadequate. The financial stability of the government depended primarily upon a $2 million "loan" from the Confederate government.[7]

The Johnson administration had already started recruiting troops before Secretary of War Judah P. Benjamin wrote on February 3, 1862, that a recent act had called for the enlistment in each state of enough soldiers to equal 6 percent of the entire white population. Kentucky's quota was forty-six thousand men, who were to serve for three years or the duration of the war. Always a realist, Benjamin added that "under the peculiar circumstances in which Kentucky is placed and the difficulties which embarrass her authorities I cannot hope that you will be able at present to meet this call, which it is, however, my duty to make."[8] The assigned quota could not be met, for most Kentucky men were Unionists and many avid Confederates had already volunteered. And, while Confederate leaders wanted men to assure victories, many southern sympathizers waited for victories before committing themselves to the Confederate cause.

Arms were lacking for some of the volunteers, and the Johnson administration required all white males between eighteen and forty-five who did not volunteer for military service to deliver their weapons to a county inspector of arms. Anyone with taxable property worth five hundred dollars who did not have a gun to turn in was required to pay twenty dollars. Noncompliance made the offender subject to a fine of fifty dollars and imprisonment until the money was paid.[9] This act produced a little money, an interesting assortment of ancient guns, and much evasion.

Near the end of December the council made preparations for the election of Confederate congressmen on January 22, 1862. The state was divided into districts, but voting was by general ticket since elections could not be held in much of the state. Johnson was empowered to appoint officials to conduct elections in the Kentucky regiments, and sometimes the soldier votes were the only ones cast.[10]

Some local officials abandoned their positions as the Confederates arrived, and others were replaced by men loyal to the southern cause. Included among the departed were a number of justices of the peace. During the next few months some of their successors performed marriages, the legality of which became suspect when the Confederates withdrew from the state. The Union legislature finally ended some apprehensions and perhaps destroyed some hopes by ruling that such ceremonies had been legally binding.[11] Less permanent was the changing of the name of Wolfe County to Zollicoffer to honor the general who had been killed at Mills Springs.

While Johnson disclaimed any knowledge of military affairs, he was in frequent consultation with the Confederate generals. He interceded with General Johnston upon one occasion to support John Hunt Morgan's request that two light-artillery pieces be attached to his company. Johnson had no confidence in General Lloyd Tilghman, whom he described as "vain and incompetent," and the governor tried unsuccessfully for months to get him removed from command.[12]

While Johnson and the council worked diligently to create a government, their political structure collapsed when the Confederate army withdrew from the state in February 1862. The exiled governor wrote his wife, "I go now with the army and intend to remain constantly in the field. . . . We will soon be ready to return." A newspaper reported in late March that "Gov. Johnson and the Provisional Government of Kentucky, are with Gen. Crittenden's brigade; the capital of Kentucky now being located in a Sibly tent, near the headquarters of that General."[13]

The long retreat ended at Corinth, Mississippi, and on April 6, 1862, Johnston attacked the Union army at Shiloh. During the day's savage fighting George Johnson served as a volunteer aide to his friend Breckinridge and to Colonel Robert B. Trabue, commander of the Kentucky Brigade. When his horse was shot from under him, the governor refused another mount. Instead, he joined Captain Ben Monroe's E Company of the Fourth Kentucky Infantry Regiment, and that evening he insisted on being sworn in as a regular member of that unit. "I am determined to share the dangers of the battle with these boys," he explained to those who protested his decision. "They are my friends and relatives, and I feel better with them."[14]

During the early afternoon of April 7 the elderly private was shot through the body and in the right thigh. He lay unattended until the following morning when he was recognized by General A. McDowell McCook of the Union army; McCook had Johnson carried to a hospital ship, where he received the best possible care, but the governor died on Wednesday morning, April 9. In a death message dictated to a friendly chaplain, Johnson repeated the creed that had governed his conduct during the nation's crisis: "I wanted personal honor and political liberty and constitutional state government, and for these I drew the sword."[15]

Federal officials expedited sending the body to Kentucky. A few determined Unionists questioned the propriety of holding the services in the Georgetown Baptist Church and burying Johnson with Masonic honors, but the love and respect that he had enjoyed swept aside such objections, and he was buried at Georgetown on April 18, 1862.

The constitution adopted at Russellville provided that the council should fill the office of governor if it became vacant. No qualifications were prescribed, and the only restriction was that the council could not select from among its own members. Soon after Johnson's death the council elected Richard Hawes of Bourbon County as his successor.

Hawes was born in Caroline County, Virginia, on February 6, 1797, the son of Richard and Clara Walker Hawes. The elder Hawes had served several terms in the Virginia legislature before moving to Kentucky in 1810. Young Richard attended Transylvania University, then read law with Charles Humphreys and Robert Wickliffe. When he was admitted to the bar in 1818, he began practice with Wickliffe. In 1824 he moved to Winchester, where he combined hemp manufacturing with his legal profession. In 1843 he moved to Paris, Kentucky, his home for the rest of his life. A successful lawyer, Hawes was one of the state's political leaders. His advancement was probably assisted by his 1818 marriage to Hetty Morrison Nicholas, the youngest of seventeen children of George Nicholas, one of Kentucky's most prominent citizens prior to his death in 1799.

Hawes was a leading member of Kentucky's Whig party and a devout supporter of Henry Clay. He was elected to the Kentucky House of Representatives in 1828, 1829, and 1836, and he represented the famed "Ashland District" in the national House of Representatives in 1837–41. After the dissolution of the Whig party in the 1850s Hawes became a Democrat and supported James Buchanan in 1856 and John C. Breckinridge in 1860.

Hawes played an active role during the secession crisis. In May 1861 he was one of three representatives selected by the States' Right party in the legislature to work with their Unionist counterparts to devise an acceptable policy for the state. The group recommended the policy of neutrality and the creation of a bi-partisan five-member board to direct Kentucky's military force.

When the state's neutrality ended, Richard Hawes joined the exodus of Confederate sympathizers who left Kentucky to avoid arrest. His military experience consisted of limited service during the Black Hawk War, when he was sixty-four years old (Hawes was commissioned a major). For several months he served as a brigade commissary in General Humphrey Marshall's command in eastern Kentucky. Thus Hawes did not participate in the formation of the provisional government. Selected state auditor, he declined the post in order to continue his military duties.[16]

Despite his limited military experience, Major Hawes corresponded directly with such leaders as Adjutant-General Samuel Cooper and Secretary of War Benjamin. Marshall may have been irked by his subordinate's disregard for the chain of command, for in late January

1862 he recommended acceptance of Hawes's letter of resignation with no note of regret. A few days later Hawes was seriously ill, but he soon recovered and in May accepted his election as Johnson's successor.[17]

In the spring of 1862 there could be no pretense that the Confederates actually controlled any part of Kentucky, but during the summer rumors of a Confederate offensive in the west led the exiles to hope for a return home. On August 27 the council resolved that Hawes should be requested "to visit Richmond and lay before the President the views of the council" favoring an invasion of Kentucky. Hawes conferred with Braxton Bragg and Buckner near Chattanooga on August 27 and concluded that his government should follow Bragg's army. Before doing so, however, he went to Richmond to confer with President Davis and other Confederate officials, including the Kentucky members of Congress. Hawes told Davis that he and the council hoped they could soon assume the civil administration of at least a large portion of the state. Meanwhile, he inquired about the availability of the money that he understood had been appropriated for the use of the provisional government. The sum allocated for military purposes, he suggested, could be put to good use in forming large bodies of Kentucky troops.[18]

As a result of the Richmond trip Hawes and the council did not leave Chattanooga until September 18. When they caught up with General Bragg in Kentucky he seemed more interested in installing the provisional government than in securing coordination of the forces under his command. On October 3 Bragg, then at Frankfort from which the regular government had fled, wrote, "Tomorrow we inaugurate the civil Governor here, and transfer to him all that department."[19]

But Bragg had already lost control of events. Don Carlos Buell had moved out from Louisville with unexpected speed, and even as Bragg completed plans for Hawes's installation Confederate commanders were retreating hastily to avoid being overrun. Since Hawes had taken the oath of office when elected governor the ceremony was not actually an inauguration, but Bragg attached much importance to it. In his speech to the crowd that overflowed the hall of the House of Representatives at noon on October 4, Bragg assured Kentuckians that he would hold the state and the provisional government would thrive under his protection. Governor Hawes assumed that Bragg was correct, and his address gave an optimistic picture of what his administration hoped to accomplish. But Union artillery began to shell the town in early afternoon, and the governor and his civil associates left Frankfort "in dignified haste."[20] The dinner and ball planned for the evening were never held.

A few days after the battle of Perryville the Confederate government of Kentucky left the state for the second and last time. When Bragg blamed "cowardly Kentuckians" for his retreat, Governor Hawes replied in the Richmond *Examiner* that the campaign failed because of Bragg's military incompetence.[21]

During the rest of the war Hawes and the council attempted to function as a government, sometimes in Richmond but more often with the Kentucky troops in the Army of Tennessee. Hawes sent suggestions and recommendations to Confederate civil and military authorities, but the pretense of governing became increasingly pathetic as the war moved toward Confederate defeat. Hawes had to admit in 1863 that he was "almost powerless" in raising troops or securing supplies from Kentucky.[22]

The Hawes administration lacked the de facto status of the Confederate governments in the eleven formally seceded states, and it simply disappeared when the Confederacy collapsed. Richard Hawes made his way home and resumed the practice of law in Paris. His popularity was attested to by his 1866 elections as Bourbon County judge and then master commissioner of the circuit and common pleas courts, the position he held until his death. In early 1867 he delighted most of his constituents by declaring void the apprenticeship contracts of the Freedmen's Bureau in Kentucky. The bureau, ruled the ex-Confederate governor, did not have jurisdiction in Kentucky because the state had not been in rebellion. Richard Hawes died on May 25, 1877, and was buried in the Paris Cemetery.[23]

LOUISIANA

Vincent H. Cassidy

hen the results of the presidential election of 1860 were known, Governor Thomas Overton Moore of Louisiana called a special session of the state legislature which convened in Baton Rouge on December 10. Two days later Henry Watkins Allen, a representative from West Baton Rouge Parish who had earlier sponsored resolutions calling for secession in the event of a Republican victory, introduced secessionist Wirt Adams of Mississippi to a joint session of the House and Senate. The end result was provision for a state convention which met on January 23, 1861, and which three days later voted to dissolve the bonds holding Louisiana to the Union.[1]

It is tempting to comment on how these few men, in an effort to resist change, voted to change the lives of thousands, but the responsibility was hardly theirs alone. The course was already determined and history's inevitability had set in. The bulk of the elected delegates were secessionists who had received a substantial, although not overwhelming, share of the vote. Their moves were predictable; the decision already made. The vote was announced, the doors of the convention swung open, and Henry W. Allen entered, carrying the flag of the state. Behind him came Governor Moore; behind the governor, Braxton Bragg; and behind Bragg, a host of other secessionist supporters. It was as if a monumental tragicomedy had begun and the key players were being introduced.

Moore, who had taken office as governor of a Federal Louisiana a year earlier, was about to become head of an independent state. In a short time he would become Louisiana's first Confederate governor. His duties would range from commanding its armed forces to showing proper concern for the design of an appropriate flag. Allen had already enlisted in a local militia company, the Delta Rifles, which on the orders of Governor Moore had helped occupy the United States arsenal in Baton Rouge. He would eventually see action and sustain wounds, be commissioned as a brigadier general in the Confederate army, and become the second and last of Louisiana's Confederate governors. Bragg, the commissioner of public works, would become a full general and a favorite of the Confederate president, Jefferson Davis. An 1837 graduate of West Point who had seen service in the Indian war in Florida and in the Mexican War, Bragg had in 1856 resigned his commission in the army and retired to a plantation in LaFourche Parish. Moore, Allen, and Bragg were all sugar planters. In the struggle to follow, Bragg would be a continuing factor in the lives and administrations of Moore and Allen.

Thomas O. Moore was born in Sampson County, North Carolina, on April 10, 1804. On his father's side there was a tradition of rebellious reaction to tyranny, the family having moved in succeeding generations from participating in the Irish Rebellion to figuring prominently in the American Revolution. His great-grandfather, John Moore, served as governor of the Carolina colony. On his mother's side, the Overtons of Tennessee had served in the Revolution and in the War of 1812. His uncle, Walter H. Overton, had been on Jackson's staff at the Battle of New Orleans, and when the war was over had settled in Rapides Parish, Louisiana.

Thomas Moore spent his early years in North Carolina. That he had some educational advantages is apparent but not documentable. In 1829 he moved to Louisiana to become plantation manager for his Uncle Walter. Then, as thereafter, it was comfortable to be a member of the "Overton Dynasty," although that would not always be a political advantage. In 1830 Moore became a plantation owner in his own right and steadily increased his holdings. Until 1852 his main crop was cotton; that year he moved into sugar cane production and by 1860 he was the largest sugar planter in Rapides Parish.

Moore's interests would also expand in other directions. He entered politics actively in 1842 as a police juror. He became a state representative in 1848, a state senator in 1851. Throughout he remained a staunch Democrat. He consistently supported education. He was a sponsor of the State Seminary of Learning, although the proposed location, in Rapides Parish, may suggest mixed motivation. He also was, and here the motivation is not clear, opposed to further importation of slaves. The struggle in the Louisiana legislature takes on a personal note in a comment scribbled on the back of an unrelated plantation document, dated March 14, 1858: "Last night defeated the African Bill. Thank God nearly through."[2]

In May of 1859 Moore finally would emerge from a badly split Democratic party convention as their nominee for governor by a unanimous vote. However, delegates who had been refused recognition refused in turn to accept the convention's decision. They advanced Thomas J. Wells, a friend and neighbor of Moore in Rapides Parish, as their nominee. The campaign was carried in the columns of newspapers; neither candidate campaigned in his own behalf. Moore even took time for a month's vacation in North Carolina. He still won easily in November and assumed office January 23, 1860. The victory was not unexpected. Moore had spent much of the previous year getting his sugar plantations and other interests in order. For example, on August 11, 1859, he wrote to E. W. Halsey, who was in charge of the editorial department of the *Louisiana Democrat,* in which Moore seems to have had the major interest, proposing to lend Halsey the "press, type & other fixtures" in exchange for which he was "to continue editing a good Democratic paper during the time you have the same in your possession." Halsey was also to have whatever profits accrued.[3] His editorial duties continued even when nine months later he was pressed into service as the governor's private secretary.

In his inaugural address Governor Moore pointed out that he had not sought the office, that he had no political debts, and that he intended to be governor of all the people. He promised economy in government made possible by an efficient administration, and then turned to the problems posed by the growth in the North of the anti-slavery Republican party and of the threat it posed to the slaveholding states and thereby to the Federal Union. Although his own position was clear, his language was restrained. (Some of his closest friends had counseled a policy of conciliation.[4]) He concluded by recommending a reorganized state militia, just in case.

During the sixty-day legislative session which followed, activities were diffuse rather than concerted. A bill to move the state capital to New Orleans failed to pass, and provision was made to build an executive mansion in Baton Rouge. Baton Rouge also was to be headquarters for a revived Louisiana Historical Society which the legislature incorporated. Allen, who had spearheaded the move, would become president of the society in February 1861. Another of Allen's projects, a bill concerning a geological survey of the state, died in the Senate. Other measures toward a levee system and flood control were also swept over by the turmoil of the times. Making the State Seminary of Learning into a military academy and establishing an arsenal there seemed more to the point.

The fever was rising. In the presidential election of November 1860 Breckinridge won the state, but Lincoln, who was not on the Louisiana ballot, won the country. Then pandemonium. Within two weeks, Governor Moore called for the special session of the legislature which convened on December 10. In his message Moore announced that the Federal union was dissolved. "I do not think it comports with the honor and respect of Louisiana to live under the government of a Black Republican President." He called again for a reorganized militia, for the provision of military arms and equipment, and recommended a state convention. It was on December 12 that Henry Allen introduced Wirt Adams, commissioner from Mississippi, to the legislature in joint session. Adams eloquently urged Louisiana to cooperate with its sister southern states. A convention was voted, delegates were elected, and on January 23 the convention assembled in Baton Rouge. The regular session of the legislature in the interim proffered little but oratory. The governor, however, was busy. Without the mandate documentable which he rightly assumed existed, Moore ordered state troops to occupy the forts commanding the Mississippi below New Orleans, the barracks and arsenals at Baton Rouge, and Fort Pike on the Rigolets. On January 13 the Delta Rifles, the company in which Allen was a private while still in civilian dress, occupied the Federal arsenal in Baton Rouge, lowered the star-spangled banner and raised the ensign of the state.

The governor's actions were approved after the fact. His problems were just beginning and he applied himself to each. Approval would not follow all of his proffered solutions, but history would hardly notice. Moore deserved more credit than he ever would receive and he would never fail to preserve his dignity in an impossible situation. He did not make it happen, but he happened to be there. He guided Louisiana into the Confederacy, an on-duty helmsman faced with unknown rapids.

The state convention, after adopting the Ordinance of Secession, would spend nearly two months on business which secession required. Six delegates were elected to represent Louisiana at the convention of southern states called for February 4 in Montgomery. Provision was made for Federal officers and employees who were properly sympathetic to retain their positions. Similarly existing offices and laws would remain in effect under Confederate aegis. Federal property, citizenship, the creation of a larger military force, and public lands were all of concern. With the ratification of the Confederate Constitution on March 21, 1861, the Louisiana convention's duties were over. All that had been Federal and acquired by the state was ceded to the Confederacy, including a half million dollars in gold and silver.

It was up to Moore to implement the decisions of the convention and at the same time to protect Louisiana's interests within the Confederacy. He protested inadequate fortifications and when there was no response stopped the flow of munitions and arms from the state. He feared invasion, especially an attack on New Orleans. The Confederate secretary of war, however, was convinced that Pensacola was the imminent target, and nothing was done to protect New Orleans. On April 12 Fort Sumter was fired upon. The war had begun.

Louisiana's quota, when President Davis called for volunteers, was promptly filled. Within six months an estimated thirty thousand men would leave the state.[5] Many would see service in the Army of Northern Virginia. Henry Allen and four companies of the Fourth Louisiana Regiment would occupy Ship Island, strategically located off the Mississippi coast. Those in the field away from the state would remain a concern to Thomas O. Moore, who was not only governor but a reluctant commander-in-chief.

Moore's overview of the state and all its problems was comprehensive; his task, however, was extremely difficult since he had to serve both as political and military leader. There was much to be done. Guns and munitions were in short supply. Louisiana had turned these, along with all other seized United States property, over to the Confederacy and now found itself poorly armed. Moore ruled that no further arms should be sent. The material needs of the troops in the field had to be considered. Here much depended on the women of the state. Moore called for blankets and clothing, but for fairness in distribution asked that they all be funneled through one agency. The state militia had always been one of his concerns; now the problem was crucial. So also, the governor felt, was the problem of traitors and "Tories" in their midst. Each solution he proffered to the latter two problems, which were intertwined, was more stringent. He asked that businesses close on drill days at 2 P.M. so that all between the ages of eighteen and forty-five could participate. All not taking part were to be blacklisted. To provide the militia with weapons, an inventory of all firearms in each parish (county) was to be made and all weapons turned over to the military authorities. Those who refused to release their weapons were to be treated as traitors. Trading or corresponding with the enemy was treason. The homes of known traitors would be burned. To supplement the military, a women's "auxiliary" was organized, and the women seldom failed him. Supply depots were established. Most of these, sooner or later, would be raided by "friendly" forces or overrun by Federal troops.

Many problems were major; some were minor; all took time. Braxton Bragg was particularly bothersome. In March Bragg had been made commanding general at Pensacola and among his troops were two Louisiana regiments. In spite of his admission to Moore in a letter that "your troops are better supplied than most others, and are the best organized and by far the best officered in my army," weapons and ammunition were mismatched and he needed .58-caliber ammunition left behind in Baton Rouge. Supplies were not only short but the horses, mules, wagons, etc., purchased and sent from New Orleans were, Bragg said, the "greatest swindle ever perpetrated." Furthermore, his two aides, Garvet and Ellis, both from Louisiana, were payless. "Discarded by their State and not recognized by the Confederacy, they occupy a most unpleasant position."[6]

Five days later, on May 7, Bragg wrote again. The ammunition problem was pressing. "You sent me all the rifled muskets of caliber .58 of an inch, the ammunition for them can be of no use to you, and the arms are of no use to me without it." On July 25 he wrote again, this letter to be delivered by Aide-de-camp Ellis in person, to plead for all the artillery and caissons that could be spared, explaining that Pensacola was Louisiana's first line of defense. In return he could send some guns which could be used to arm towboats. "They are strong and would make as good gun boats as the enemy could get." On August 2 the problem had to do with promotion and other decisions concerning rank in the Louisiana forces. On August 13 it was the need for more troops for a possible offense. "I need at least 5000 men well armed and equipped as infantry. How many can you spare me—say for two months?" September's problem was personnel. In October Bragg expressed dissatisfaction with the appointment of General Mansfield Lovell to command in New Orleans. "The command at New Orleans was rightly mine. I feel myself degraded by the action of the government and shall take care they know my sentiments." In the same letter he complained to Moore of the treatment accorded Ellis, his aide-de-camp, by the military in New Orleans,[7] a subject which would be returned to in November when he forwarded a long letter of complaint by Ellis to the governor.[8] It can be assumed that the .58-caliber ammunition was sent since it ceases to be mentioned as a problem. There is no indication that artillery was forthcoming or that towboats were armed. A later letter from Bragg, however, indicates that Moore and others had taken pains to placate him about Lovell's appointment.[9]

Moore's message to the legislature in November 1861 was predictable—finances topped his list. Two-thirds of the taxes due the state, a million dollars, had not been paid. Steps should be taken to assure a valid currency. Money was needed to pay back the emergency loans he had contracted and to run the government the coming year. As for the military, he estimated that 24,093 Louisiana men were in service outside the state, and the problem of supplying them with blankets and clothing was increasing with the advent of winter. Some of the money he had borrowed had been for this purpose. He recommended that all males at home between the ages of eighteen and fifty be subject to compulsory mustering with no exemptions. Further, he recommended the creation of a Special Military Department. Finally, he advised against the passage of a "Stay Law" which would prohibit civil suits pertaining to mortgaged property, recommending instead that such suits go to trial as usual, and that the compulsory sale of property of soldiers in active service be delayed.

The legislature responded favorably to most of the governor's requests. Among other things a "Stay Law" bill was introduced but was passed in the modified form recommended by Moore. The governor was given the power to borrow up to $7 million at his discretion. An association was established for the relief of sick and wounded soldiers. The only discordant note was a "Cotton Bill," passed by both houses, which was to provide relief to cotton planters with a $10 million loan with future cotton crops as security. This legislation was vetoed by the governor as being both unwise and unconstitutional.

On the first anniversary of secession, January 26, 1862, Moore reviewed his troops, the state militia, on parade in New Orleans. At the governor's request, banks and business houses closed for the occasion. There was a feeling of impending disaster. A few days before, General Lovell had written Jefferson Davis deploring the inadequate provision for New Orleans's defense. In the days that followed, the New Orleans Committee for Public Safety and the governor would also write to Davis describing the immediacy of danger. Among other things, the size of the naval force stationed in New Orleans had been greatly reduced. Finally, despairing of help from Richmond, Moore used his now confirmed right to incur indebtedness and to spend state funds at his discretion to purchase twenty thousand rifles and thirty thousand rounds of extra ammunition. This shipment, however, was landed on the Florida coast, whereupon the governor of Florida had it seized. Half remained in Florida; the other half was sent to the War Department in Richmond.

Moore's outrage was understandable. On April 1, 1861, he protested to Davis: "This unpardonable and unparalleled outrage is nothing short of robbery and just as bad. . . . I have given all the arms I had, expecting that these would be in the hands of my own troops. Now that thirty-seven enemy sails are in the river, in God's name, in the name of my State, I ask you to order them sent to me immediately."[10]

Two weeks later the Federal fleet began to move in. Resistance was ineffective. Lovell ordered all cotton and tobacco burned to keep it from Federal hands. All coin was removed from New Orleans banks. Lovell tried, but the odds were impossible. On April 24 Farragut's fleet succeeded in passing the two forts on the river guarding New Orleans, and on April 26 the city fell.

Preparations began immediately to move the capital from Baton Rouge, which the Federals would occupy the following month. The state archives were moved to Opelousas. Uncertain as to how far or how fast the enemy would penetrate beyond New Orleans, Moore issued an order that cotton, tobacco and other supplies should be burned if they could not be moved in time. Federal success should be as barren as possible. Moore followed the archives to Opelousas. He joined others in hoping that a general would be sent to relieve his governorship of military duties, but meanwhile he continued as commander in chief with the problems intensified. Once again he ordered guns and munitions. These were seized by the Federal forces while en route to Opelousas. Some 350,000 pounds of powder and 4,500 muskets were lost. Next, without waiting for permission from Richmond, he organized thirty-seven companies of "Partisan Rangers," setting up training camps at Monroe and Opelousas. He wrote to the secretary of war for permission after the fact and it seems to have been tacitly granted. To equip his new army, the governor ordered ammunition and 2,720 rifles. These were confiscated by Confederate General Earl Van Dorn as they crossed Mississippi. Moore's complaint to Richmond this time brought the response that the materials seized would be forwarded to Louisiana and that it would not happen again.[11] On June 11, Moore asked Davis that a commissary officer be assigned to Louisiana, adding "not an honest one, that would be an impossibility—but one that will not take more than half of what I may get together."[12]

In July the governors of Louisiana, Arkansas and Texas conferred and jointly requested of the president a commanding general for the newly designated Trans-Mississippi Department, a treasury west of the river, and a supply of arms. Davis replied that no general was available, that he did not have authority to establish a separate treasury, and that some arms were on the way.

For a few months, one part of Louisiana was attached by the War Department to a general based in Texas, another part to a general with headquarters in Jackson, Mississippi, a third to a general whose activities centered in Little Rock, Arkansas. The third general was Thomas C. Hindman. On July 8, Moore wrote the secretary of war another letter asking consideration for Louisiana. He also protested:

I have not been informed that General Hindman has any command over any portion of my State. The only notice I have had of his pretending to exercise any authority here is the visit of a Captain Taylor with a party of armed men, about the 24th of last month, who came to Alexandria, south of Red River, and seized private property, entered houses of private citizens, brutally practiced extortion and outrage and with bullying and threatening language and manner spread terror among the people and disgraced the service upon whose errand he came.[13]

Two weeks later he wrote the president: "We have had but one Confederate Officer South of Red River. He came to commit an outrage, and supported by ten men the only Confederate force in this section of the State, succeeded."[14] Moore had already in the previous letter advised the secretary of war that:

With Butler below and Hindman above, each of his officers committing the same outrages, I am forced to self protection. I have ordered a force of militia at Alexandria to prevent any similar raid. I have directed that any similar expedition shall not only be stopped, but the whole party arrested, and if their boat will not stop I have cannon planted to fire into her and sink her. I have selected men to command this force who are fully impressed with the indignities we have suffered and who will carry out my orders.[15]

Soon after, if not concurrent with, Moore's protest (for which he apologized) General T. H. Holmes was placed in charge of the Trans-Mississippi Department with headquarters at Little Rock.

In August 1862 Moore finally got one wish granted. Major General Richard Taylor, son of Zachary, was made commander of the Department of West Louisiana. He and the governor worked well together. Although all the problems of weapons, ammunition, and enforced service remained, these were now primarily Taylor's responsibility. An additional camp was established at New Iberia with no justification other than convenience. Arms and munitions again were purchased by the governor, this time in Mexico, but the shipment failed to arrive because transportation was unavailable. A semblance of order prevailed, but unfortunately it was all on paper.

In June 1862 Moore addressed the people of Louisiana. Trade with the enemy was forbidden, communication could no longer be allowed with citizens in occupied Louisiana, New Orleans was out of bounds, and there would be no tolerance for spies, informers, or "Tories," who, "though very few in number, . . . exist, and with a hate of our government not exceeded by the hate of their predecessors to the Government of George Washington." Moore went on to discuss the necessity of trusting Confederate currency, of destroying riverboats that were in danger of falling into Federal hands, of every citizen being prepared for immediate armed service. He called for a "swarm" of "armed patriots to teach the hated invader that the rifle will be his only welcome on his errands of plunder and destruction."[16]

This message, which was about as violent an exhortation as Moore would make, solved few of his problems. His constituency would continue to be a disordered one. Infantrymen would petition the governor to have the War Department release them when they were forced to serve beyond their term of enlistment.[17] A precinct in Rapides Parish would petition him to leave enough ablebodied men at home to transport necessary supplies. "Unless your Honor grants this our prayer . . . there will be great suffering in our vinage."[18]

At the governor's call the legislature met in special session at Opelousas on December 15, 1862. The major problem was defense of the Red River. The legislature provided for the drafting of ablebodied slaves between the ages of eighteen and forty-five with or without the consent of their owners for work on defense projects. Materials, tools, carts, wagons, and horses might also be subject to requisition, noncooperative owners to being arrested. New troops were sought with inducements such as a fifty-dollar bounty, a grant of eighty acres of state land, and release from military duty outside the state, but no blood came from the turnip. Nonavailable money was also appropriated. The General Assembly's most successful action, considering the endangered location of Opelousas, was to establish the capital in Shreveport. In the interim the governor and the archives paused just south of Alexandria and Moore's plantation was the capital. From there, the governor issued orders that all men between seventeen and fifty were to be called to serve. Resistance continued, however, and Moore reluctantly allowed exceptions.

There had not been time to implement the plans to defend the Red River, and shortly after Moore and the archives moved to Shreveport, General Nathaniel P. Banks and his Yankees moved north. For a short while Federal raiders even occupied Moore's plantations. Many of his Negroes fled toward freedom, slaughtering beeves and hogs before they left. The departing raiders took five teams and twenty-eight mules, along with sugar, molasses, and hundreds of cattle. John H. Ransdell, a Rapides neighbor, did what he could to restore order and kept Moore informed, at the same time pleading, "Come home at once if you expect to make a crop, as you alone can set matters to rights." Moore's overseer also wrote to say that crops were being made although he was shorthanded. With one or two exceptions, "all of the good Negroes were gone."[19] Although the governor's duties kept him away, the process of salvage continued, and in June Mrs. Moore returned to look after their interests.[20]

By this time nineteen of Louisiana's parishes were occupied by Federal troops and the legislature had difficulty achieving a quorum, but it finally met in Shreveport in May 1863. The legislators made another attempt to provide additional manpower, but Moore himself must have known that it was futile. He admitted to those assembled that more Louisiana men were already in service outside of Louisiana than had ever voted in a state election. The new laws were more stringent and penalties for noncompliance were more severe, but enforcement was impossible. The governor showed his weariness by asking that a quartermaster general and other disbursing officers be assigned to handle problems of military expenditures. The legislature complied but, at the same time, instructed him to take bids on two ironclad gunboats which might later be sold to the Confederacy at cost. There is no indication that this was done. Moore advised the legislators that half of the $20 million of treasury notes he had been empowered to issue were not yet in circulation and recommended that the remaining $10 million not be printed to avoid further inflation. He also suggested that the bulk of the money voted in Opelousas for needy families of soldiers be spent to buy cotton cards. These cards would then be sold to indigent families at cost, so that they might provide for themselves and not feel like the recipients of charity, and so that their activity might reduce the shortage of cloth. Spiritous liquor should be taxed out of existence to preserve foodstuffs as foodstuff, the governor said. He concluded by reminding the legislature that if the price were paid, failure was impossible. All of Moore's recommendations were followed. Before adjourning, the General Assembly ordered that it convene the next January and every January thereafter.

Ransdell continued to write Moore about plantation problems with an occasional reference to the larger world. On June 6 he referred to what was on everyone's mind: "We are in considerable anxiety about the result in the neighborhood of Vicksburg. If we succeed in destroying Grant's army there, I think we will soon see the beginning of the end."[21] Much depended on Vicksburg, but on July 4, 1863, it fell, followed by the surrender of Port Hudson a few days later, and the Confederacy was divided. The Trans-Mississippi governors met with General Edmund Kirby Smith, military commander of the department, to determine what could and should be done to continue resistance with only limited help from across the river. They planned for increased self-sufficiency, efforts to arouse their citizens to a vigorous patriotism, and the granting of extraordinary powers to the commanding general. Back in Shreveport, finally relieved of many military responsibilities, Moore would spend his last months in office trying to implement procedures and policies already decided upon.

Governor Moore's successor, Henry W. Allen, had been born in Farmville, Virginia, on April 29, 1820, and remained there until his thirteenth year, when his father moved the family to Farmville, Missouri. Relatives preceding them accounted for the community's name. It was a pioneer existence. Allen spent some time as a store clerk and then for two years attended nearby Marion College, which he left in 1837 to follow the Mississippi River south. He disembarked at Grand Gulf, Mississippi, where he secured employment as a tutor. He later opened his own school and studied law at night. He began practicing in 1841 but took time out the next year to serve the Texas Republic from April until October as captain of his self-organized "Mississippi Guards." Back in Grand Gulf he resumed his law practice, dabbled in real estate, and in 1844 eloped with Salome Ann Crane, the daughter of a Claiborne County planter. The bride's frail health—and possibly the unfortunate wound which Allen sustained in a duel—ruled out the possibility of children. When his wife died in 1851, Allen crossed the Mississippi River to try to establish a plantation in Tensas Parish, Louisiana. Later that year he recrossed the river to take the waters at Cooper's Well, where he met and profoundly impressed an aged sugar planter from West Baton Rouge who, the next year, on most liberal terms and with no down payment, made him half-owner of one of the largest sugar plantations in Louisiana. As "Allendale" prospered he made extensive tours of the South, the Northeast (with a hectic session at Harvard), and Europe. Between tours he found time for plantation affairs and for local politics, developing his considerable skill as an orator.

Allen began as a Whig. He was elected to the Louisiana legislature in 1857 as a Know-Nothing and once again in 1859 as a Democrat. Though for a while he was under indictment for the illegal importation of slaves, he seemed destined for a bright political future. One of his legislative side interests was the landscaping of the state capitol grounds. When he returned from a quick trip to Cuba to collect shrubs and seeds for the project, Louisiana had seceded and joined the Confederacy.

Ever impulsive, Allen enlisted as a private in the Delta Rifles, but he was soon elected lieutenant colonel of the Fourth Louisiana Regiment, and then colonel. At Shiloh he was wounded by a rifle ball through the mouth, and in the Confederate attack on Union-held Baton Rouge in August 1862, he had both legs badly torn and his horse shot out from under him while charging Federal cannon. He was forced to resign his commission, but after several months' recuperation asked for and received his old command. In August 1863, still in pain and on crutches, he was promoted to brigadier general and ordered to report to the Trans-Mississippi Department. Early in the fall he learned that he had been nominated as governor of Louisiana in absentia, and in November he was forced to resign his commission when overwhelmingly elected. To ascertain the extent of the problems with which he would have to deal, Governor-elect Allen spent the next two weeks touring unoccupied Louisiana in an ambulance wagon, crutches by his side. When he had an audience he stopped to speak, devoting much of his address to trying to raise the morale of his listeners and everywhere earning applause from the audience.

On January 18, 1864, Governor Moore addressed the legislature for the last time. Though he expressed concern about conditions at home and the inequities of certain Confederate war measures, he stressed the necessity of sacrifice and struggle and urged the organization of "Minute Men" for local defense. He concluded by praying that by "passing through the sharp ordeal of war and suffering, may we learn to value the blessings of Independence, which at no distant day will be secured to Louisiana and the States with which she has confederated."[22]

In his inaugural address a week later, a pale and emaciated Governor Allen thanked his audience for their confidence and promised to serve them well. Peace with the Federals, perpetrators of atrocities, was impossible. Victory was within sight, he said. His recent tour of the state had convinced him that priority should be given to cotton cards and medicine. After complimenting the women of Louisiana for their efforts in clothing Louisiana's soldiers, he proposed that every woman in the state be given a pair of cotton cards. He then asked to be empowered to do whatever was necessary to see that medicine was available to all. But while need was the state's first consideration, the question of loyalty was second. Soldiers must do their duty, and so too the legislature and those at home. Charity was an obligation of all who were not destitute. The status of the Negro and slavery would not change, although the Negro might, after he realized the Yankees would treat him as a "driveling outcast" or "mendicant wanderer," serve the Confederate army. Future historians might report that "master and slave were found in the ranks, side by side, fighting bravely, shoulder to shoulder, for the independence which they have so gloriously achieved." Every needy dependent of a soldier in service should be provided sustenance, Allen said. Every wounded soldier should receive a pension of eleven dollars a month. "Let every man who owes service to his country go to the army. Let every man who stays home do his duty. Be true to yourselves, and leave the rest to God."[23]

The legislature granted almost everything that Governor Allen asked of it. Some facets of the program had been on his mind for a long time. He asked for a geologic survey of the state to exploit whatever lead, iron or sulfates existed. He wanted a mining and manufacturing bureau, to which would be attached a laboratory for producing indigenous medicine. The legislators appropriated a large amount of uncommitted funds for the governor's use. Food, medicine, and cotton cards were imported and paid for by the sale of cotton, purchased within the state through the back door of the Confederacy, Browns-ville, Texas. Legality was stretched, but the ploy worked. Any other possible outlet was also acceptable. Cotton cards were soon being manufactured within the state. As for medicine, Allen turned to his former physician, Dr. Ami Martin, and appointed him surgeon gen-eral of Louisiana. He was to be in control of the medicinal laboratory and the store which would dispense medicine. Agents in Mexico pur-chased supplies which could not be produced in the state, such as mercury, licorice, and phosphorus.

The actual manager of the medical laboratory was Dr. Bartholomew Egan, drafted from the State Seminary of Learning at Alexandria. On February 24, 1864, Allen advised him: "You will purchase and put up such machinery as you may think proper to meet the needs of suffering people." By November Egan was producing medicinal whiskey. By January of 1865 the state had in operation two turpentine distilleries, one castor oil factory, one factory making carbonate of soda, two dis-tilleries, and two laboratories for producing indigenous medicines. All available sources for salt were exploited. An iron foundry was set up in Shreveport. State charity was to be dispensed "without distinction." The relief agencies were "not [to] inquire into the past and present status" of those in need, and the "families of those in the Confederate, Federal and Jayhawker service were all supplied alike." Any area which suffered enemy depredation was supplied immediate relief with-out petition. According to a Natchitoches newspaper, the governor pro-vided "as much as near fifteen thousand pounds of flour, five thousand pounds of sugar, seven thousand pounds of bacon, and five thousand barrels of corn," all of which were free to those unable to pay. Between June 30, 1864, and the end of the war, $11,000 of the governor's contin-gent fund went to destitute families and wounded soldiers. Attempts were also made to get relief to captured Louisiana soldiers.

Allen established a state store with household articles, clothes, shoes, utensils, and groceries, which not only filled a need but made money: $400,000 in 1864, $1.5 million in 1865. When it became obvi-ous that the war was lost, the governor directed the state store to put all of its stock on sale for state money. Confederate currency was not acceptable.

The state guard which the legislature authorized Moore to raise in 1863 never materialized. Allen attempted to implement the law, but found that it conflicted too much with the extended Confederate draft law. Nevertheless, the state had enough officers and men to participate in the battles of Mansfield and Pleasant Hill in April 1864 when Banks was on the move again.

Allen's interests were far-ranging. He directed that a *Louisiana Almanac* be published and suggested that space be provided for testimony "concerning the conduct of the enemy during their brief and inglorious occupancy of a part of West Louisiana." He even instructed Edmund Halsey to compile a Louisiana English grammar and a Louisiana spelling book. Schoolbooks were to be distributed free to any pupils whose parents could not afford them. Allen imported newsprint from Mexico and planned to establish paper mills. His year had been busy. He planned another one.

The pattern is easily discernible. Louisiana's Confederate governors were both able men. Moore was a firm and staid father, a strict disciplinarian; Allen was an understanding and generous uncle. Moore was reticent; Allen dominated conversations. A visitor to the governor's mansion gave an account of two elderly pipe-smoking women, soldiers' mothers, who called on the governor. Allen got out his pipe, sat, and smoked with them. They said they had received corn, but had no hoes or plows with which to plant it. Turning to his secretary, Allen said, "Mr. Halsey give these ladies an order for a plow and two hoes, free of charge." The conversation continued. They also needed meal, meat, sugar, and molasses. Halsey was instructed to write out another order. As the women were leaving, one turned at the door and said, "Well, Gov., we hate to bother you so much. You are the best man alive. We are all going to name our next grandchildren after you." Then one of them remembered; they also needed a well-rope and a pig. "Ladies," said Allen smiling bemusedly, "you shall have the well-rope but at present, *we are out of pigs.*"[24]

Allen, just as Moore, was in almost constant correspondence with Jefferson Davis, most frequently about impressments and violations of civil rights. The governor also had his problems with General Kirby Smith, sometimes because of military intrusion in civil affairs, more frequently because of Allen's "cotton trade." This latter resolved itself, however, as the general began to get necessary funds the same way.

When Allen addressed the legislature in January, his thoughts on the use of blacks as soldiers had crystallized. Blacks should be freed and armed. He had, in fact, already written Secretary of War Seddon urging this. He told the legislators that the public mind had some adjusting to do. "Shall we," he asked, "continue to fight on, in a long protracted war with slavery, or shall we give it up and have peace and independence? Louisiana will rise en masse and say without hesitation, 'we will abolish the institution—we will part with slavery without regret—if necessary to gain our independence.' "[25]

Not all of his listeners agreed with him but, nevertheless, the entire body joined in a vote of thanks to the governor for all he had managed to accomplish the previous year. The newspapers joined in the chorus of praise, as did people from Texas, Missouri, and Arkansas who had also shared his bounty. His friend Sarah Dorsey reported that he had nearly arbitrary power but did not abuse it. "The people idolized him! If the blessings of the poor could give soft slumbers, his head ought to have rested very quietly on the pillow of his hard couch . . . which did not even boast a coverlet."[26]

The times were desperate. Allen, before the legislature met, had joined with General C. J. Polignac, with Kirby Smith's blessing, in seeking intervention by Napoleon III of France, whose black troops, incidentally, had impressed Allen in Paris years before. Allen's message was presented in person by Colonel Ernest Miltenberger. The emperor's reply was that he had considered such action but now it was too late.[27]

When news of Lee's surrender reached the West, the initial reaction was to carry on. Smith exhorted his troops. Governor Murrah of Texas pleaded with Texans "to redeem the cause of the Confederacy." In a proclamation on April 29 Allen declared the cause was not lost, that the Trans-Mississippi Department was in better shape than it had ever been, and foreign aid might yet arrive. That same day he elaborated on these themes before a mass meeting in Shreveport.[28]

On May 8 Kirby Smith refused proferred terms of surrender, but gradually second thoughts began to emerge. Allen's reconsideration apparently began when he talked to the Federal officers who had brought the surrender terms to Smith. He asked these officers to stay in Shreveport until the Trans-Mississippi governors could meet in Marshall, Texas. On May 13 this group authorized Allen, as soon as safe conduct was guaranteed, to go to Washington to negotiate the terms of surrender.

When the Federal peace commissioner could not guarantee safe passage, Kirby Smith refused to surrender. Allen continued to await notice that it was safe to enter the Union lines, but privately counseled, "there will be a cessation of all hostilities. . . . *The War is over.*" Kirby Smith left for Houston to rally his forces, but his weary troops had already begun to go home and his officers advised him that within a few days there would be no Confederate army. There was nothing to bargain with; Allen's role as a negotiator was bypassed, for on June 2, 1865, Smith signed the peace agreement in Galveston and ended the Civil War.

At the end of his term of office, ex-Governor Moore had returned to his plantation, but in March Federal troops under Banks again ravaged his plantation, damaging it so much this time that he decided to take what was left and move to Texas. He remained near Crockett for more than a year, and on June 7, 1865, Governor Allen joined him. Uncertain of their fate in Federal hands, the two men fled southward in Allen's ambulance and reached Mexico City in August. Allen remained there and edited an English language newspaper subsidized by the imperial government, the *Mexican Times*. He planned some further travel, but his wounds, which had never completely healed, continued to plague him. He died in Mexico City on April 22, 1866, and was buried in the American Cemetery there, then taken to New Orleans the following year. In 1885 his remains were interred on the grounds of the capitol at Baton Rouge which he had helped to landscape.

At the end of the war, Moore left almost immediately for Cuba, where in September he took the oath of allegiance to the United States at the U.S. Consulate. He received a full pardon on January 15, 1867. He returned to his plantations south of Alexandria, which he found in ruins. He salvaged all he could and gradually conditions improved. In September 1868 he became president of the "White Man's" Democratic party in Rapides Parish. In 1874 he was a delegate to the state Democratic convention. But his health began to fail, and he died on June 25, 1876.

MISSISSIPPI

Robert W. Dubay

n early October 1859, Democrat John Jones Pettus, characterized as "a disunion man of the most unmitigated order," was
elected governor of Mississippi by the wide margin of 24,251
votes over an Oppositionist (Whig) opponent.[1] Pettus's resound-
ing triumph, along with victories by candidates for other high
offices who held similar views, offered dramatic proof that the destiny
of the state was in the hands of the fire-eater, secessionist wing of the
Democratic party. But such developments did not transpire overnight.

During the decade preceding the Civil War, Mississippi underwent a
profound political metamorphosis which culminated in the virtual ex-
tinction of a viable two-party system. Primarily because of its appeal
for moderation in sectional affairs, the state's Whig party was able to
maintain parity with the Democrats for a brief period following the
Compromise of 1850. After 1853, however, and for the next three state
elections, Whig fortunes registered a steady decline as its members
found themselves increasingly hampered by factionalism, the lack of a
national party, ineffective leadership, and a political philosophy that
proved less and less attractive to voters.[2]

Conversely, the same years saw Mississippi Democrats sharpen the
themes of southern nationalism and states' rights and champion a
progressively more inflexible position relative to the protection and
expansion of slavery. Each new issue or crisis with sectional overtones
enhanced the Democrats at the expense of the Whigs. By the close of
the decade, secessionist ideology had become such an accepted principle that a sizable body of Mississippians was ready to turn the reigns of
government over to a proponent of such dogma.[3] And John Jones Pettus personified this trend.

A second son and one of seven children, John Pettus was born in
Tennessee on October 9, 1813, while his father was serving in the

Creek Indian War. Shortly afterward the family moved to Alabama. Following the death of his father in 1822, Pettus settled briefly in Sumner County, Mississippi, before establishing a permanent residence in Kemper County, where he engaged in the practice of law. He also grew cotton, devoting sixteen hundred acres and twenty-four slaves to that enterprise.[4]

An inelegant, tobacco-chewing, woodsman type of man with limited formal education, Pettus could have easily been a character out of a Horatio Alger story. His rise to prominence began in 1843 when he was elected to the state House of Representatives. After serving two terms he moved on to the Senate, remaining there for a decade. Further distinction came his way when he was twice chosen president of the Senate (1854 and 1856) and when by virtue of office he became governor ad interim (January 5–11, 1854) following the resignation of Governor Henry Stuart Foote.[5]

When the time came to select candidates for state office in 1859, John Pettus had little difficulty securing his party's gubernatorial nomination. His legislative years had enabled him to cultivate the friendship of numerous influential Mississippians, including politicians, businessmen, and newspaper editors. The fact that he was a distant cousin of Jefferson Davis, who had been secretary of war and who was now in the United States Senate, did not hurt, either.[6] His standing among common men was strong, for in previous government service he had earned a reputation for progressivism by supporting the University of Mississippi, public schools, railroad expansion, bridge and road construction, banking legislation, and the creation of a state historical society.[7] Perhaps the paramount appeal that Pettus possessed was the he was no Johnny-come-lately to states' rights, having taken such a stance as far back as the late 1840s. After the Kansas–Nebraska controversy, Pettus assumed the secessionist mantle.[8]

Nominated for the governorship in early July 1859, he conducted a thorough and rigorous campaign. Although he was not an eloquent speaker, large and enthusiastic crowds heard him attack abolitionism and defend black servitude. In keeping with the state party platform, he pledged to work for the reopening of the slave trade and the acquisition of Cuba as a slave state. Concerning secession, he left little room for misunderstanding. Advocating "armed neutrality in the face of Northern opposition to slavery," he implored the legislature to "fill the arsenal with arms" so that Mississippi might be ready to maintain its rights and property in the event a Republican became president.[9]

For their part, the Whigs, or Oppositionists as the Democrats labeled them, failed to agree on either a platform or a slate of candidates until early September of that year. Thus allowing themselves only a month for campaigning, Whig-Oppositionist forces spent what was left of their precious time before election day engaging in internal partisan quarrels, and in the end they circulated a ticket in only twenty-five of the state's sixty counties. A crushing defeat by better than a three-to-one margin at the polls came as no surprise to anyone and caused one pro-Opposition writer to summarize the fire-eater victory as "an evident mass of approaching disaster."[10]

Pettus was not formally installed as governor until November. In his inaugural address he spoke of continued sponsorship of education and internal improvement projects and promised to limit his exercise of the veto. But since John Brown's infamous raid into Virginia had occurred little more than a month earilier, it was inevitable that the governor would devote much of his text to the sectional struggle. Declaring the "scene at Harper's Ferry . . . [to be] only the beginning of the end of this conflict," Pettus reviewed the growth of the antislavery movement and blamed the Federal government for being either "unwilling or unable to guard the rights or redress the wrongs of slaveholders." He warned of the consequences that the election of a "Black Republican" president would have for the perpetuation of the Union. Stopping short of charting a course for immediate secession, Pettus nevertheless urged that vigorous defensive measures of a military nature be taken. The cotton states must be garrisoned by men who were unafraid of meeting an "irrepressible" situation. As if to show northerners that the South meant business, he called for a meeting of representatives from slaveholding states to determine common policies during these perilous times.[11]

Pettus spent his first weeks in office attempting to promote a southern conference plan which, he envisioned, needed the backing of Virginia to ensure success. The governor, however, lacked the authority to appoint a commissioner to go to Virginia to lobby in favor of a slave state gathering in Atlanta. The Mississippi legislature did not get around to granting permission to send an envoy to Richmond until mid-February 1860.

Pettus's efforts to woo Virginians were supplemented by similar actions on the part of South Carolina. Both endeavors, however, met a cool response due to pending national political developments. And, in point of fact, only Governor William H. Gist of South Carolina expressed willingness to have his state represented at a proposed Atlanta meeting.[12] So convinced of the necessity for southern solidarity was Pettus that he offered to circulate a temporary cancellation notice or to transfer the site to Richmond in order to avoid the stigma of failure. In the end, it was Governor Andrew B. Moore of Alabama who best summed up the majority view among state chief executives when he stated that it was "unnecessary to take any steps . . . until after the Charleston convention [had] met and acted."[13]

The first month of the new administration also witnessed a change in Pettus's thinking on the outcome of sectional difficulties. Initially, he seemed to trust in a political solution to such differences, so much so that an offer to sell the state three thousand firearms was declined.[14] But when a distressing Senate committee report on the resources of the state arsenal reached him, he reversed himself. With requests for armaments from local militia units becoming commonplace—and knowledge that the state held a mere 344 rifles, 14 pistols, 118 swords, and 2 cannons—a change of attitude was not unexpected, and he promptly asked lawmakers to appropriate $150,000 for the purchase of military supplies while he personally placed an order for four thousand guns.[15]

Throughout the better part of 1860, presidential politics captivated the attention of Mississippians. Spokesmen took to the stump on behalf of all the candidates except Lincoln, with Governor Pettus campaigning for John Breckinridge. Labeling Republicans as untrustworthy as Comanche Indians, Pettus denounced Lincoln and predicted that members of the legislature might as well "set out for the Capitol . . . the next minute" if a Republican won the presidency. Disunion would surely follow.[16]

Despite the fact that Mississippians gave John Breckinridge a 15,000-vote majority over John Bell, news of a national Republican triumph brought an expected reaction from the governor's office. Following the election Pettus maintained a steady stream of correspondence with other southern governors relative to the course of action each intended to pursue. "We have opened the wall," Gist of South Carolina wrote of his state's secessionist momentum. "Will not Mississippi stand by her side?"[17]

Pettus needed no prompting and issued a directive for a November 26 extraordinary legislative session to deliberate the "propriety and necessity of providing surer and better safeguards for the lives and liberties" of Mississippians. He also felt obliged to augment political developments with an order for nine thousand rifles and two hundred thousand cartridges from the Federal arsenal in Baton Rouge, Louisiana.[18]

If the governor waxed bold in public, he displayed more thoughtfulness in private. Since he had not specifically directed the legislature to consider the secession question, he sought to establish guidelines for his own conduct when that body convened. The counsel of Mississippi's congressional delegation was requested and a two-day caucus produced unanimity on whether to ask the lawmakers to call a secession convention. Nevertheless, a vigorous debate ensued over the timing of secession, be it to transpire unilaterally or in concert with other states. With Pettus in the majority, a vote of 4 to 3 cast the die for a "no pause or tarrying" position, as Representative Reuben Davis noted.[19]

On November 26, 1860, state solons assembled in Jackson and heard the governor proclaim that the South could find no safety in a Union soon to be run by men of "violence and bad faith." Black Republicanism, "a cesspool of vice, crime and infamy," made it mandatory that Mississippi "go down in Egypt while Herod rules in Judea." In short order the legislators sanctioned a December 20 special election for the purpose of sending delegates to Jackson in January to vindicate the "sovereignty of the state." Furthermore, the legislature passed a Pettus-backed resolution calling for the appointment of emissaries to every slave state in order to seek as much disunion cooperation as possible.[20]

The Opposition press did not take such matters lightly and depicted Pettus as some kind of madman intent on plunging the state headlong into war. But the governor was not going off half-cocked and took precautions to see to it that if Mississippi left the Union and Alabama and Louisiana did not, the state would still have access to a seaport. Toward this end, Pettus dispatched agent Wirt Adams to Baton Rouge and instructed him to stress the absolute necessity of maintaining close commercial relations among the contiguous states. The desired assurances were forthcoming, along with similar promises from the state of Alabama, which were personally delivered by Edmund Winston Pettus, John's brother,[21]

Preparing for any eventuality, Governor Pettus overlooked few opportunities to acquire military hardware. In mid-December he wrote Jefferson Davis in Washington and predicted secession would be a reality in a matter of weeks. Therefore, Davis was directed to arrange the purchase of fifteen thousand pounds of gunpowder and forty thousand pounds of lead. The supplies had to be paid for with state treasury warrants, as tax dollars were not yet in hand.

When no word was received concerning the weapons order, Pettus became nervous and harbored second thoughts on disunion. His apprehension was compounded when he learned that President James Buchanan had ordered the completion of a Federal fort on Ship Island. Since the stronghold was located in the Gulf of Mexico a short distance from shore, its menace to sea traffic and Mississippi soil was obvious. Faced with the problem of not being able to "convert auditors warrants into rifles," which were much in demand by volunteer companies forming in every county, Pettus wondered whether secession should be postponed "until other states can get ready."[22]

On January 7, 1861, amid a serious yet almost festive atmosphere, delegates to the Mississippi convention met in Jackson. The majority of the members were men of above-average financial means, either attorneys or farmer-planters, small slave owners, and below the age of fifty. Twenty-three of the one hundred seats were occupied by individuals who listed a Whig affiliation. But the disunion impulse transcended party lines, and, by a vote of 84 to 15, and ordinance of secession was adopted on January 9.[23]

Although the election and convention proceedings held center stage for several weeks, the governor was also active. Pettus was on hand to greet Jefferson Davis at the Jackson train depot and present him with a commission as major general, head of the armed forces of Mississippi. With the consequences of separation from the Union still very much on his mind, Pettus also insisted that seventy-five thousand firearms should be acquired, and he even took the crafty step of writing to Secretary of War John B. Floyd to request that Mississippi be sent its quota of Federal arms for a year in advance.[24]

Government affairs sometimes went lacking for unity and direction during the early months of 1861—with the governor, the legislature, and the secession convention often functioning at cross-purposes. Greatly adding to the vagueness of the Mississippi political climate at this stage was the fact that, technically, the legislature and the secession convention were in session at the same time. The former body accomplished little and left most government realignment work to the convention. Especially in seeing to military matters, the new Republic of Mississippi suffered from unfortunate, but not unexpected, disorganization. A majority of legislators and convention delegates apparently held the opinion that splitting the Union would not provoke a military response from the Buchanan administration. Moreover, several individuals believed that the ordinance of secession was merely "a demonstration inviting concession" on the part of the North and that the "disrupted Union [would be] fully restored within the next twelve months." In fact, numerous constituents were more concerned about the status of mail delivery than the likelihood of hostilities.

Much evidence exists relative to the low priority that military preparations had in early 1861. The convention, it seems, declined an offer to "sell the state the finest machinery for manufacturing small arms in America," and the legislature debated a plan which would have curtailed the governor's military powers and prerogatives.[25]

Governor Pettus, known to be "a man of strong and decided convictions," lived up to his reputation, particularly when it came to defense. On his own, he acted to set up an armory, sent troops to help capture Federal installations in Florida, and forwarded seven militia companies to Mobile—telling Alabama Governor Moore to "call on us" for futher resources.[26] Additionally, Pettus's soldiers stationed at Vicksburg fired a warning shot across the bow of a ship on January 11, and the governor advocated the seizure of the U.S. gunboat *Silver Wave* on the same day. His reason for desiring to accomplish the latter was to employ the vessel's guns in defense of Ship Island, which he planned to occupy.[27]

In the middle of January, Adjutant General Sykes rendered a glowing report of Mississippi's military conditions. Sixty-five militia companies had been organized, contracts for weapons were being concluded, and many of the "old arms and accouterments (a pile of rubbish) in the arsenal were overhauled and examined, cleaned, and stored away for an emergency."[28] This positive assessment brought small comfort to the governor, however. For without his permission an overzealous group commandeered Ship Island, and he did not have the means to defend it. Further contributing to his woes was the fact that some of the Mississippians sent to Florida and Alabama returned home because of lack of funding and confusion over who should command them, or for displeasing the host states by demanding use of excessive force against Federal strongholds.[29]

For reasons of jealousy over legislative prerogatives and fear that the governor's enthusiasm might get entirely out of hand, thus invoking needless bloodshed, the secession convention took steps to curb Pettus's unbounded martial spirit. On January 23 it appointed a three-man council to advise the chief executive concerning military matters until such time as the state should enter the Confederacy. Only one division of troops was ordered raised, and although one million dollars in interest-bearing loan certificates was approved, the meager amount of one thousand dollars was all the convention saw fit to appropriate for immediate military expenses. In a further effort to restrain Pettus, a five-member Military Board was created, whose consent was necessary on any armed services matter.[30]

As for Pettus, he chose not to stand idly by while either the legislature or the convention inhibited his interpretation of executive duty. With secession a reality, any device of war that could be obtained seemed worthy of the effort. Besides, it was a reelection year for him and he would accommodate the wishes of the people, who for months were clamoring to get into uniform and have at the Yankees.[31]

Trouble soon surfaced between the executive and legislative branches of government in other quarters as well. The governor was continually notified that an increasing number of persons were hungry and destitute, being too preoccupied with politics to grow crops.[32] Lawmakers hardly addressed this problem at all, providing relief for only one county—a grand total of $1,500.[33]

With the advent of secession, Governor Pettus had been directed to muster four regiments of twelve-month volunteers. The subsequent response was underestimated and enlistments proved "very rapid." Before long the governor exceeded his authority and accepted the services of eighty companies. As the number of units continued to expand, it became apparent that there was little for them to do. Although Confederate Attorney General Judah P. Benjamin was authorized to call forth seven Mississippi regiments, a restlessness among the remaining companies was evident.[34]

On top of this dilemma John Pettus had other troubles, such as trivial arguments within the Military Board over uniform specifications. More important, Jefferson Davis's resignation as major general in order to assume the Confederate presidency likewise became a bone of contention when the governor appointed Bolivar County planter Charles Clark, a future governor, to replace Davis.[35] Soon afterward Clark, in a speech at Natchez, defended Pettus's war preparations and "pitched into" two local militia units for daring to criticize the governor's leadership. The outspoken general did not become a local favorite when he alluded to the "Home Guards" and the "Silver Greys" as "occupying positions that women with broom handles could succeed in."[36]

The Clark incident soon passed, but the problem of having allowed too many volunteers into the ranks did not. Although Pettus managed to dispatch seven hundred troops to Forts Morgan and Pickens (Alabama and Florida), provide two regiments to the Confederate army, and prevail upon the Military Board to forward twenty-three companies to Pensacola for training, the riddle of what to do with the other idle soldiers was far from being solved. Faced with an ever increasing number of enlistments, Pettus sought to curtail the flow by friendly persuasion. But this policy only generated more protest.[37]

Perhaps the real heart of the issues with which the governor had to contend was simply the cumbersome and often illogical framework that he was forced to operate under. Not only were his hands partially tied by the necessity of obtaining approval from the Military Board for many of his actions, but the members of that board did not always attend called meetings. The acquisition of weapons was usually difficult enough, but the convention, incredibly, ordered a shipment of arms from Baton Rouge sent to the Confederate government. And even as war loomed on the horizon, the power for organizing and disciplining the state militia was still reserved for the legislature. The governor, although allowed to "call forth the militia," could not hold troops for more than one year, nor draw unsanctioned money for their support. No changes in the executive's military authority were authorized during the first half of 1861, and only reluctantly did lawmakers go so far as to agree to allow the governor the jurisdiction to convene the legislature in some place other than Jackon, should the need arise.[38]

To make matters worse, the state convention, upon reconvening in March, refused to shoulder any responsibility for maintaining customs-houses, hospitals, fortifications, and lighthouses within the borders of the state. These burdens were consigned to the central government. The governor was left virtually penniless, and since the previously endorsed bond sales could not be offered until mid-March, conditions were not likely to improve much.[39]

Amid uncertainty, and in the absence of clear-cut authority, Governor Pettus was often forced to operate unilaterally. To get Confederate courts functioning and open customshouses, he relied upon the new national government for support. But if state politicians often refused to confront pressing matters, dealings with Confederate officials proved equally frustrating. Messages between Jackson and Montgomery were occasionally lost or delayed, or involved decisions for which guidelines were not yet formulated.[40]

Along military lines, John Pettus continued uninhibited, but evidence of naivete surfaced. Contacting his chief of ordnance, he revealed a grand strategy for defeating the Federals. Ostensibly the plan was to equip soldiers with shotguns. Although skeptical, ordnance director Samuel G. French placed orders for this type of firearm. When the guns arrived it was noted that "the god of war never beheld such a collection of antique weapons. . . . There were guns without a vent, to be fired with a live coal, guns without ramrods, barrels without stocks, stocks without barrels, guns without cocks, cocks without pans." Worse still, Pettus gave every indication of actually daring the "pestiferous Yankees" to invade so that he could ambush them.[41]

Spring found the popular subscription of volunteer companies maintaining a fever pace, especially following Lincoln's inauguration. The difficulty with such readiness was inactivity and it was not long before criticism found its way to the executive mansion. Pettus, with no power to veto a Military Board decision to accept all volunteers, was reminded by friend and state Brigadier General Reuben Davis that the growing discontent could well have political implications.[42]

With a keen eye toward the fall elections, as well as in an attempt to stabilize the situation, Pettus turned to the War Department for relief. "Companies fuller than expected," he wrote in one dispatch, and on another occasion he sent two hundred more men than asked for, noting: "I hope the Pres. will receive them." Again, on April 13, he informed Secretary Walker that thirty companies were impatient for service. When he received no answer, Pettus wired that he had learned southern property was being confiscated at Cincinnati. "It is difficult to restrain river people. I wait instructions for retaliation," he said.[43] None came.

In an attempt to dissipate some of the mounting dissatisfaction, the chief executive visited several units, inspected them on parade, and handed out a few rifles. This did little good and by May, with ninety-three companies in state service, loud complaints relating to the enrollment of certain groups ahead of others and to the acquisition of weapons, pay allotments, buttons, clothing, and supplies were recorded daily. Even three companies of artillery called up for Confederate service had to go along without horses or harnesses.[44]

Before long, newspapers were openly chiding the administration's handling of military affairs, with one calling for an end to the "imbecility" at Jackson and another putting forth names of likely candidates to run against the incumbent the coming fall.[45] Faced with such pressure, Pettus redoubled efforts to end the dilemma. By threat and persuasion he prevailed upon the Military Board to grant a temporary halt to enlistments. He then sent direct appeals to Jefferson Davis and General Gideon J. Pillow for swift action. For all his labor, the result was paltry—just two regiments, "armed with heavy Double-Barreled Shotguns," were mustered.[46]

As if Pettus's dilemma was not overwhelming enough, another politically dangerous situation arose in early June when Charles Clark tendered his resignation as major general. The next individual in seniority for the post was James Lusk Alcorn, a Whig who had opposed unilateral session. Instead, Pettus appointed Reuben Davis to the position, believing he would bring additional aggressiveness to the military program.[47]

During June the clamor for repeal of the volunteering moratorium heightened. Disgusted, Pettus explained that "arms manufactured especially for war cannot be secured in sufficient numbers to arm all who are willing and anxious to take part in the present conflict." At least twenty-five thousand troops would be needed soon and it was highly probable that Mississippi "will be called upon to put forth her full military strength." To aid him in resolving current stresses, he would call a special July legislative session.[48]

Pettus's decision came not a moment too soon, for the Military Board, bowing to public pressure, suddenly threw open the volunteer floodgate again and by the time lawmakers reached Jackson 125 companies were on the muster rolls.[49]

The governor addressed the legislators and vented his wrath by charging them with ineptness. Noting that some of his actions had been arbitrary, he felt justified in doing as he had because of the emergency of the times. By way of specifics, the executive urged enactment of a stay law to protect soldiers from debt collectors, new tax legislation, and a law to permit troops to vote in the field. He scolded the Military Board and announced an agreement with the governors of Alabama and Louisiana for the procurement of gunboats to patrol the Gulf coast.[50]

Apparently many state solons did not share the governor's sense of urgency and contended that the war would soon end. Unbelievably, a bill was introduced to dismantle the Military Board and drastically reduce the state's armed forces. Governor Pettus and Reuben Davis were unalterably opposed to such irresponsibility. The latter, acting under directive, attempted to browbeat the legislators into defeating military cutbacks by warning that the state was about to be invaded. This scheme having failed, Davis waxed belligerent and threatened to force the lawmakers from the capitol, and "perhaps hang them."[51]

The legislature, in retaliation for such heavy-handedness and out of lack of concern for contemporary affairs, failed to enact a single piece of worthwhile legislation which would in any way eliminate the already rampant difficulties.

Regardless of whose fault it was, the unsatisfactory military situation and corresponding discontent with things in general began to have a serious impact on the political atmosphere. Since taking office, the Mississippi governor had made numerous efforts to create a sense of unity among opposing political factions by appointing several former Whigs and moderates to responsible positions. When he selected I. M. Partridge, former editor of the antisecessionist Vicksburg *Whig,* to head a division of the state militia, members of his own party denounced him. A short while later the governor received another setback when a foreign journalist's unfavorable report circulated throughout the state. William Howard Russell, an employee of *The Times* of London, visited Mississippi and found a "grim, tall, angular" executive living in a mansion with broken windows, "ragged" carpets, spartan furnishings, and "walls and ceilings discolored by mildew." Russell characterized Pettus as a "silent man, tobacco-ruminant, abrupt-speeched." When the governor talked, he would sometimes pause and spit tobacco juice toward a receptacle, just missing the target, but acting "with the air of a man who wished to show he could have hit the centre if he liked." During their conversation the reporter noted that there was constant commotion as all types of people wandered "in and out of his room, looking around them and [acting] in all respects as if they were in a public-house."[52]

Amid "a good deal of dissatisfaction," Pettus was renominated by party caucus in July because it was generally conceded that he was the best choice avaiable.[53] Several of the governor's friends called to his attention a list of names pledged to support the candidacy of

Madison McAfee, state quartermaster general and longtime foe of the governor on the Military Board.[54] Clearly, reelection was not a foregone conclusion.

By August, Pettus's political fortune mirrored the festering military issue. He even discussed the propriety of withdrawing from the contest, but Reuben Davis advised against such action. In an effort to take the heat off his commander, Davis offered to announce for Congress and canvass on a platform calling for the governor's vindication.[55]

Pettus took heart and was soon in the thick of things once again. Madison McAfee, his foremost rival, was temporarily disposed of by being sent to Richmond under the pretext "of procuring an adjustment of accounts due from the Confederate Government." McAfee, sensing the discomfort of his position, withdrew from the contest a month later and even defended the administration by stating that he too was "equally responsible" for whatever failures had occurred.[56]

Still on the offensive, Pettus circulated a public appeal asking voters to investigate the charges leveled at him. The accusations, he maintained, were little more than personal attacks by individuals who still opposed secession. He had "labored diligently, faithfully, and zealously for the safety, prosperity and happiness of the State."[57]

While the quandary of what to do with surplus troops remained the administration's primary stumbling block, Gulf coast citizens offered another, more serious, challenge. Since early in the year the importance and exposed position of the region were known. Among the points of contention was concern for Ship Island, which had never been completely fortified by the state. Cause for alarm increased in mid-September when personnel from the U.S.S. *Massachusetts* dislodged Confederate troops stationed there and then succeeded in cutting a telegraph cable between Shieldsboro and Pass Christian.[58] Confederate General T. E. Twiggs encountered a "positive refusal" from local citizens to enroll in the army, due to prevailing opinion that an invasion was imminent.[59]

Notwithstanding Gulf coast reversals, John Pettus's campaign began a dramatic turnabout in early September with the arrival of War Department telegrams hinting that Mississippi troops would soon be mobilized on a large scale. Rather than release this good news immediately, the governor sought to enhance his chances for victory by shrewdly withholding until September 28 a general call for ten thousand men to assemble at Grenada and Vicksburg and for another twenty companies to rendezvous at New Orleans.[60]

The outcome of the October 7 election was never in doubt after the release of the muster orders. Incumbent Pettus carried every county but four, three of which were located on the Gulf coast. His nearest rival, Jacob Thompson, a moderate Democrat and former member of the Buchanan cabinet, received only 3,556 votes to Pettus's 31,169.[61] The governor's total might have been even higher had arrangements been made for absentee voting, as there probably was more than one trooper who could not comprehend why it was that Mississippi lawmakers could be "so unpatriotic as to disfranchise its soldiers."[62]

On the surface, it would appear that the election of 1861 exonerated John Pettus's handling of political and military affairs. Certainly, had a more dynamic opponent been in the picture and the muster orders not arrived when they did, the balloting might have been different. Be this as it may, two things were apparent by late 1861: many Mississippians, including legislators, held a rather naive view of the realities of the day, and Pettus, often without guidance or support, seemed to acquit himself in an acceptable manner.

Although preoccupied with his own political aspirations, Governor Pettus did not neglect the duties of office. In matters involving the Confederate government, his was a policy of notable cooperation, except when it came to weapon acquisitions.[63] The governor also helped state railroads arrange financing and worked out contracts for the shipment of salt from Alabama.[64]

Despite a son's death at the recent Battle of Ball's Bluff, Pettus managed the strength to address the legislature on November 4, 1861. Much of his discourse dealt with the summation of the issues that had dogged him since secession, and he complained of not being given the authority to better prepare the state troops. Bonds brought in scant revenue and were no longer considered a good risk. Mississippi, he insisted, must develop "some well-digested financial scheme." For remedy, he proposed that the national government be the only source of paper currency, that the Military Board be abolished, and that a "less expensive and less complicated" defense system be devised. Surely, the "magnitude and duration of the war" had not been fully appreciated by the lawmakers, he said.[65]

Pettus's straightforward message bore fruit. The Military Board was terminated, all twelve-month volunteers were ordered to remain in service for an indefinite period, $250,000 was appropriated for gunboats, and volunteer and militia units were combined into a single command structure. One question not dealt with was a Pettus recommendation for limits on cotton cultivation, a move designed to encourage food production for wartime needs.[66]

By 1862 the state's precarious financial condition was apparent. The sale of bonds to Virginia lenders proved sluggish, and with munitions dealers demanding cash-on-the-line, Pettus was forced into economy moves, such as having military units serve for less time and directing police boards to seize all available firearms.[67] Hard times also found businessmen refusing to accept paper money, inflation gathering momentum, and increasing reports of military desertions for lack of pay.[68]

Wartime disillusionment often meant that self-interest, profiteering, and speculation took precedent over state needs. When hearing of such things, the governor called upon the citizenry to "silence those who love money more than their liberties." Efforts to curtail cotton production were futile, thus forcing Pettus to issue an unpopular executive order limiting the planting of cotton to "not more than one acre to the hand." Grain was to be raised on the remaining land.[69]

Except for minor engagements, fighting spared Mississippi until the spring of 1862. During the interim the governor saw to the fortification of Vicksburg and offered the War Department "any amount of labor" toward this objective. His toil elsewhere was discouraging, however. A joint project to procure gunboats floundered due to contract and specification conflicts. To compound things further, a gun factory at Aberdeen burned to the ground.[70]

The realities of war began to materialize after the Battle of Shiloh when Union forces occupied Corinth. Not unexpectedly the governor and Confederate officials were criticized for "much talk, but no definite action." One pungent indictment condemned all politicians who sat "in a comfortable chair and put up forts" but won only paper victories.[71]

From May through the mid-summer of 1862, Federals periodically menaced Vicksburg. At the first sign of trouble Pettus called out two thousand troops and dashed to the scene. Later he wrote General Earl Van Dorn that he could hear "the heavy guns from your beleaguered city," and promised resistance to the last man. However, a local newspaper noted that that community was not interested in consigning itself to flames, as the governor would surely advocate.[72]

Although this Federal threat proved temporary, Vicksburg became a source of contention between Confederate and state authorities. A special adjutant, sent by President Davis to demonstrate Richmond's concern for the city, found defense preparations so adequate that he recommended the reassignment of Confederate troops. The governor strongly objected to this and insisted that his state be fully protected.[73]

It was at this stage that John Pettus began to reevaluate previously cordial executive relations with the central government. Although initially supporting Confederate conscription, for instance, he had second thoughts when officers accomplished their task with special zeal and seized numerous planters and overseers. The inherent dangers were obvious, there not being "white persons sufficient to keep the slaves in subordination." When desertions grew more common, the governor elected not to enforce the penalties for such things.[74]

Struggles to procure Confederate military aid were likewise exasperating and President Davis freely admitted being unable to "provide for the military wants" of Mississippi. Pettus, always short of patience, resorted to hijacking weapons bound for government troops.[75]

The scarcity of salt was yet another point of controversy. Need for the item caused the governor to authorize the trading of cotton to the enemy. When rebuked by Confederate Secretary of War George W. Randolph for doing so, he bluntly replied: "Our people must have salt." Insisting that he had the power to make such transactions, the governor made it clear that he was "disposed to exercise this right to the amount of fifty thousand sacks."[76] In reality, Pettus did little more than officially sanction practices that were already widespread.

The closing months of 1862 furnished little cause for optimism. While on a tour of Louisiana's New Iberia saltworks, a procurement agent found that supply subject to constant Federal harassment. Troops defending the saltworks were of low caliber and could not be made to stand and fight. When salt was available, transportation difficulties ensued, either because railroad officials were dubious about hauling cotton to exchange for it or because state and Confederate personnel vied for the use of the rolling stock, thus preventing salt shipments altogether.[77]

Although the Federals were operating in several sections of the state, defense preparations suffered due to a lack of coordination. When the governor, for example, issued a call to impress slaves to build fortifications, agents found planters unwilling to part with their chattel. One commissioner was unable to "raise any negro men," as Richmond's staff had already "made the rounds" and collected large numbers. Owners also grumbled about unfair reimbursement and complained that too many slaves ran away while under Confederate supervision.[78]

Another growing problem at this juncture was desertion. Certain conscripts not only disliked forced service but found camp life little short of starvation; others, including family men, persisted in fleeing homeward to assist destitute kin. So alarming was the manpower drain that the Confederate commander in Mississippi, John C. Pemberton, appealed to Pettus for permission to allow convicts to enlist in the army.[79]

Incapable of singlehandedly contending with such an array of adversity, the governor again summoned the legislature and personally implored Jefferson Davis to visit the state because everything that had previously given "attractive coloring to the soldier's life" had now faded into a "cold, gray shadow with nine tenths of the army." "A weak spirit" was afoot, he wrote Davis, and "something must be done to inspire confidence." Troubled by the prognosis, the president soon spent four days reviewing troops, inspecting Vicksburg, and calling for an end to "rumors of alarm and trepidation and despondency."[80]

It was not until December 1862 that the legislators could muster a quorum and hear Governor Pettus present a lengthy list of proposals for improving the conduct of the war and alleviating civilian suffering. Legislation seeking to conscript men up to age sixty, arrest deserters, prevent grain hoarding and the distillation of cereals into spirits, increase military expenditures, and mandate slaves from planters who "refused to contribute anything" was introduced.[81]

The legislators, displaying neither the tardiness nor disinterest so characteristic of them on earlier occasions, backed the governor. Impressment was authorized, the manufacture of alcohol was forbidden, local sheriffs were to be paid five dollars for each deserter apprehended, and $500,000 was allocated for the purchase of salt.

But when it came to giving the governor more flexibility in military matters, it was quite another story. Instead, lawmakers required that troops could be placed in service outside the state for only limited periods and that units could be put under Confederate command for only short, specified times. Pettus was likewise ordered to supersede Richmond's conscription policies as he saw fit.[82] For all their good intentions, the solons ultimately succeeded in further rupturing state and Confederate relations. Newly appointed Secretary of War James A. Seddon voiced disapproval of such states' rights posturing and said flatly that the times were "too critical for any interference."[83]

Bickering with the central government was not the only irritation for John Pettus during the first months of 1863. Manifestations of disloyalty and noncooperation with the war effort surfaced throughout the state. Groups of deserters, draft-dodgers, and bandits sometimes rode so freely and menacingly in the countryside that by mid-March the governor had to send troops into four counties to quell these unruly elements.[84]

In spite of the existence of legislation, some planters continued to refuse the state the use of their Negroes. Aside from needing the labor for spring planting, owners whose slaves had already performed service declined to deliver them a second time. Impressment officers were coerced and it was not unknown for one to resign for fear of his life.[85]

As Union activity gave promise of intensifying, the number of Mississippians seeking to avoid draft induction did the same. Frequent pleas for disbanding state militia units and petitions for wholesale furloughs were common. Sheriffs, who had the local task of arresting AWOL soldiers, were either inefficient at the job, or, due to intimidation, found it more convenient to collect taxes. One conscientious law officer had double difficulty because deserters were hard to catch, and once apprehended, were freed by friends who came "and broke them out of jail."[86]

Spring 1863 brought an understandable revitalization of cooperation between Jackson and Richmond as the military scene shifted increasingly to Vicksburg, where native Mississippian Earl Van Dorn had been replaced in command by Major General John Pemberton on October 1 of the previous year.[87] Almost from the very first, Pemberton, from Philadelphia, Pennsylvania, was distrusted and many residents were "inclined to question his loyalty" to the southern cause. Further, he was considered "a feeble and ineffectual general whose outstanding characteristic was doing things by half measures."[88]

Pettus and Pemberton were on good terms and the general was persuaded to transfer his headquarters from the capital to Vicksburg. Simultaneously, the governor and his Alabama brother conducted a tour of the area. As fate would have it, John Pettus was present when some of the Union Admiral David Porter's gunboats attempted to pass the Vicksburg batteries and a foolish commander of one of the vessels brazenly requested the city's surrender. Surprised, Pettus "unhesitatingly returned . . . [the] answer that he would defend Vicksburg until it was laid in ruins and then keep up the fight amid the ruins." In any event, the governor and the people were satisfied that the defenses were sound and he was praised for having made the place the "Gibraltar of the Western Hemisphere."[89]

Some individuals, including the governor's brother who was stationed there, did not share the same sense of security. Edmund Pettus was "not favorably impressed with the spirit of the people." Aside from the army being hampered by poor communications, there was much evidence of "trading with the Yankees" and a preference on the part of many persons "to exercise their patriotism at home." Another observer inferred that certain military officers were more party-minded than fighting-oriented.[90]

The war soon quickened. On May 2 Pemberton warned that Union forces were on the move and advised the transfer of state archives from Jackson, a likely target. John Pettus was determined to stand his ground and ordered every Jacksonian to turn out with his slaves to help fortify the capital by digging rifle pits and erecting earthworks. Many did as asked, but a few had first to be assured that they would be paid for the services of their blacks.[91]

Endeavoring to warn citizens of the deepening crisis, Pettus dispatched propagandists to urge upon them the necessity of a full commitment to the cause. Sent on such a mission, his secretary discovered that people were aroused to the danger but "divided as to what ought to be done."[92] Many were fleeing to Alabama.

The governor, while projecting optimism, nonetheless felt despair. A newspaper reporter sensed it and when Pettus telegraphed Jefferson Davis: "Hour of trial is on us. We look to you for assistance. Let it be speedy," the suspicion was confirmed.[93] A May 5 proclamation conveyed the impression that a decisive turning point was in the offing and sacrifice needed, so that the state flag would not be "dragged in the dust by barbarian hordes." If the people failed to rally, the governor would personally seek out the cowards and see to it they "hereafter wear the disgraceful badge of the dastardly traitor."[94]

In late April the Federal plan to reduce Mississippi began to unfold. The design was to begin operations south of Vicksburg and then proceed toward Jackson. With the capital thus threatened, Pemberton would be ordered from Vicksburg to defend Jackson—thereby avoiding a siege of the former city. News of the bluecoat advance reached the capital and touched off intense excitement. A correspondent recently released from Jackson's Marble-Yard Prison viewed the scene with interest and humor, noting "a panic of the most decided kind." The mayor called for calm, hammered up a proclamation to that effect, but became a fugitive himself "before the paste on his defiant pronunciamento" was dry. "If citizens were flying to arms," wrote the reporter, "they must have concealed them somewhere in the country, and have been making haste in that direction to recover them."[95]

Offering only token resistance, Joseph E. Johnston, the Confederate commander in this theater, withdrew his force of fifteen thousand men and allowed the Federals to enter the city on May 4. This decision was based in part on the fact that for all the positive talk regarding the state's security, Governor Pettus had blundered immensely by neglecting to prepare this important political, rail and munitions center for defense. A British observer who arrived in the capital a few days later told of finding "great numbers of pikes" to be used as weapons and "a mild trench, which was dignified by the name of fortifications of Jackson."[96] During the advance on Jackson the governor left town under the pretext of moving the capital to Enterprise.

On May 17 the Federals withdrew and marched off toward Vicksburg. Before departing they tore up railroad tracks and, while not harming government buildings, put factories, foundries and a hotel to the torch. The propaganda effect of an enemy army occupying the "capital of the great secession state of Mississippi, and home of the President of the Southern Confederacy" was obvious. Indeed, it was a heavy blow to morale and threw "a damper over the spirits of the people."[97]

From Jackson the center of war shifted westward where the struggle for Vicksburg became protracted. Pettus returned to the capital and underscored the seriousness of the times by allowing state convicts to join the army. He appealed to Richmond for financial aid to rebuild the capital and, more important, told Jefferson Davis that unless reinforcements were "strong enough to fight their way in" Vicksburg might soon be lost.[98] Also accentuating the crisis, Johnston and Pettus issued a joint manifesto calling for Mississippians to support the army which was "to fight the battle on which your liberties, your homes and property depend" and assuring the soldiers "that they fight for a people worthy of their protection."[99]

Meanwhile, using Jackson as a staging area, Johnston tried to assemble fifty thousand troops to effect an eleventh-hour linkup with Pemberton's encircled army. Realizing this, the Federals sent a force to harass the capital. The governor concluded that *he* was the main target of the expedition and, in something less than a valiant display, fled the city nightly. The pressures of the moment apparently got the better of him and he soon abandoned Jackson altogether—much to the displeasure of reinforcements which arrived to find the "Governor's family gone, his mansion deserted, the entire machinery of his government removed, and . . . [themselves] left without the assistance, support, countenance or even the presence of its head."[100]

John Pettus was naturally depressed by the surrender of Vicksburg on July 4. However, he was not ready to concede defeat and five days later called upon the city's defenders, who had been paroled by the Federals, to rearm and fight again. In this way "Mississippi *may yet be saved*," he told Jefferson Davis. The president declined.[101]

After the middle of July, Jackson was in enemy hands once more. Outnumbered, and with inadequate fortifications, many of which contained only sham or wooden guns, Johnston had no alternative than withdrawal. With the evacuation, Mississippi Unionists appeared in Jackson and began to plan for peace and new government.[102]

Following the loss of Jackson and Vicksburg, Mississippi's direct significance to the Confederacy was virtually nil. Yet the state was not entirely conquered, and tribulation and fighting continued for another year and a half. The governor devoted his remaining time in office to regrouping the state's military forces, but dwindling manpower, the complete disarray of records, and the well-worn conflict with Richmond over conscription prevented him from accomplishing much.[103]

In his last address to the legislature, which convened in Columbus, Pettus offered a gloomy forecast for the times ahead. Noting a growing trend toward disloyalty and the fact that modest numbers of citizens were taking the oath of allegiance to the United States, he insisted that the conflict continue and that the state spend its resources "in manly fashion [rather] than permit [them] to become the prey of plundering invaders." Independence or death were the only alternatives, as there was "no half-way house of rest in this revolution."[104]

Pettus's political career came to a close with his departure from office. Although there was talk the previous spring of his seeking a Confederate Senate seat, this did not materialize. Instead, Pettus went into hiding for a brief period and watched helplessly as Union troops freed his slaves. Undaunted, however, he enrolled as a private in an infantry company and took to the battlefield. By August 1864 he was commissioned a colonel and placed in command of two troop-staging centers.[105]

The October state elections of 1863 were necessarily influenced by the course and conditions of war. No less than a dozen men offered for the post of governor and the results of the voting revealed new trends. Reuben Davis, long an associate of Pettus and known to be equally hawkish, ran a distant third. Absalom West, of Whiggish bent, received 4,863 ballots and finished second. Planter, soldier Whig-turned-Democrat, Charles Clark won the governorship with 16,428 votes (70 percent). What was interesting, aside from the fact that so many people were able to vote, was that conservatives, moderates, and former Whigs were elected to office and even elevated to such important positions as Confederate senator and speaker of the state House.[106]

Clark differed markedly from his predecessor. The third of ten children, he was born into a Lebanon, Ohio, Methodist household on May 25, 1810. Upon completing a degree at Kentucky's Augusta College in 1831, a steamboating uncle took him to Natchez, where he decided to remain. To earn a livelihood he turned to teaching, but an epidemic closed the school and forced him to move to the town of Benton, where he resumed teaching and also took up the practice of law.[107]

In his early Mississippi years Clark's family urged him to return to Lebanon, and apparently he gave some thought to the practice of dentistry. He entered politics for the first time in 1833, offering for the state House as a Whig candidate. Although unsuccessful and warned by his father that failure was "a kind of drawback," he proved victorious in 1838 and several times thereafter.[108]

During the next decade Clark served briefly as an officer in the Mexican War, then divided his time between the legislature and establishing himself "as an able and brilliant trial lawyer." It was in this latter capacity that he acquired large land holdings as payment for his services in the "John Doe vs. Richard Roe" court action which grew out of a land-grant recovery case resulting from the Choctaw Indian cession of 1830. In fact, his Bolivar County plantation, "Doro," owed its name to that proceeding.[109] In 1860 he owned three thousand acres and fifty-three slaves, and had assets valued at $170,000.[110]

With the coming of secession, Clark first served as major general of the Army of Mississippi and then became a brigadier general in Confederate service. He saw action in Kentucky and Virginia and received a right shoulder wound at Shiloh. In the Confederate attempt to take Union-held Baton Rouge in the summer of 1862, a bullet smashed his right thigh bone and led to his capture. A prisoner exchange released him later that year.[111]

Charles Clark's accession to the governorship brought not the "smallest disposition" for surrender. Any doubt that he was as strong-minded as Pettus in this regard was immediately erased by an energetic inaugural speech in which he warned that "reconstruction" would be "the climax of infamy." The people were asked, "like the remnant of the heroic Pascagoulas when their braves were slain, [to] join hands together, march into the sea, and perish beneath its waters."[112]

Like Pettus before him, Clark's primary concern was for the protection of the state. Recognizing the futility of large-scale efforts, however, the new governor was determined to end military "play-time" and prepare his troops to "repel raids, not make them." Toward this end, realignment and efficiency were called for and reliance was placed upon cavalry.[113]

Clark's time for restructuring the military was limited. Instead, within a month the capital had to be moved to Macon and he was soon plunged headlong into controversy with the Confederate government over impressment and the use of the writ of habeas corpus.[114] The legislature became embroiled in the former issue again and passed measures making Richmond authorities responsible to the state on such matters and authorized the governor to disregard Confederate priorities.[115] The impressment issue raged on until the end of the war.[116]

Governor Clark's message to the legislature in March 1864 was one of deep economic foreboding. Telling lawmakers that it was "no time to cavil about nice questions of constitutional construction," he amplified Mississippi's "ill digested" financial picture. Taxes were going uncollected, and he predicted that $2 million more would soon be needed.[117]

Far and away the most serious issue throughout 1864 was the near-complete breakdown of law and order, a good deal of which was traceable to military desertion. Reports of such activity flooded the chief executive. "Our own Soldiers," complained one LaGrange resident, are no more than "robbers and thieves." General Samuel J. Gholson and others were distressed by bands of five to eight hundred AWOL troops who caused "great alarm and much suffering" and were considered "far more dangerous and destructive than . . . the Yankees." So engulfing was the problem that by year's end Governor Clark had to agree to grant amnesty to deserters who would promise to join the militia for the purpose of hunting down other deserters.[118]

Certainly aiding the lawless atmosphere was the almost total disappearance of the normal systems of civil and criminal enforcement of judicial proceedings. Sheriffs, for instance, had their lives threatened or became refugees. Courts ceased to function and judges quit riding circuit. Conversely, civil officials did not attempt arrests because grand juries refused indictments. In reply to all this, the governor threatened sheriffs with "indictment, forfeiture of office, fine and imprisonment."[119]

One of the few bright spots for Governor Clark was his ability to induce older men into the ranks, especially those over fifty. He also established a solid and good relationship with Confederate General Nathan Bedford Forrest.[120] Forrest's cavalry command no doubt prolonged the war in Mississippi and also fit nicely into Clark's strategy.

From late 1864 throught the first months of the following year Charles Clark personified the hapless condition of his state. Railroads were at a virtual standstill. Although he could "impress the cars," he had "no power over the employees." The executive no longer had "means to supply the state troops." "I cannot even procure a blanket," he said, and disgustedly concluded that he "must disband or furlough" the army. No more bonds would be issued or sold, as this "hereafter" might place the state in a "delicate and embarrassing position." The state treasury was empty.[121]

On May 22, 1865, Clark wrote from Macon to Union General E. D. Osband: "I will not attempt to resist the Armed force of the United States in taking possession of the premises."[122] Mississippi had surrendered.

Mississippi's wartime governors were as different after they left office as they were upon entering it. Following surrender, Governor Clark was taken to Fort Pulaski, an installation near Savannah, for internment. There, on September 2, 1865, he signed the oath of allegiance and was soon paroled.[123] He then returned home and remained aloof from politics until shortly before his death on December 18, 1877.

At war's end John Jones Pettus went to Arkansas in the hope of uniting with Jefferson Davis and others for the purpose of migrating to Mexico and continuing hostilities on a guerrilla basis. Because of his ties to Davis and his reputation for radicalism, Pettus was wanted for questioning concerning a possible role in Lincoln's assassination. Consequently he stayed in hiding, but on three separate occasions did apply for amnesty—even signing the oath of allegiance. With citizenship never restored, he died of pneumonia in Lonoke County, Arkansas, early in 1867.[124]

MISSOURI

William E. Parrish

he brilliant hues of autumn still lingered over the Ozarks as an uncounted remnant of the Missouri General Assembly gathered late in October 1861 in the small county-seat town of Neosho. Recently deposed in a legally questionable action by the same state convention that earlier had decided against secession, they came in response to a call from Governor Claiborne Fox Jackson, who had been similarly removed the previous July. Military forces loyal to the governor and his legislature held only small areas of southwestern and southeastern Missouri while Federal troops from Kansas, Iowa, and Illinois occupied the rest of the state. Yet the main army of the Missouri State Guard, as Jackson's forces were officially know, had won impressive victories at Wilson's Creek and Lexington during the past two and a half months. Hopes remained high that with the help of Confederate forces from Arkansas a concerted pincers movement might still regain Missouri and restore Jackson to his capital at Jefferson City.

On October 28 the assembly—later commentators claimed the absence of a quorum—passed an ordinance of secession officially taking Missouri out of the Union. The news was quickly telegraphed to Richmond, where two of Governor Jackson's emissaries were hammering out an alliance with the Confederacy which they signed three days later. Meanwhile, the legislature, having adjourned to nearby Cassville, ratified the provisional Confederate constitution, made provision for Missouri representatives in the Provisional Congress, reorganized the State Guard, and authorized the governor to issue $10 million in defense bonds to underwrite the cost of Missouri's war effort. Exactly where the money to back these bonds might come from seemed of little concern. On November 28 the Confederate Congress formally received Missouri as the twelfth state in the new nation.[1]

The governor who had led Missouri to this point of division came from strong southern antecedents and had pursued a staunchly pro-slavery policy in the General Assembly and in Democratic politics since the late 1840s. Claiborne Fox Jackson had been born on April 4, 1806, in Fleming County, Kentucky, of Virginian ancestry. He had gone to Missouri at the age of twenty and eventually settled at Arrow Rock. There he engaged in various business pursuits, chiefly mercantile and banking, but politics was his first love. Jackson served in the Missouri House from 1836 to 1848 and then in the Senate from 1848 to 1852. He allied himself initially with Senator Thomas Hart Benton, who dominated Missouri Democratic politics, and he became a leader in the so-called Central Clique, which generally controlled affairs at Jefferson City.

Following the Mexican War he helped engineer Benton's downfall through resolutions in the legislature which called for the extension of slavery into new territories and demanded compliance by Missouri's senators. Benton balked at that kind of instruction and split the party. Although they continued to have their differences throughout the 1850s, the Democrats always managed to come together every four years to retain the governorship. By the end of the decade Jackson had become state Democratic chairman as well as Missouri's first state bank commissioner.[2] A contemporary described him as "tall, erect and dignified; a vigorous thinker, and a fluent and forcible speaker, always interesting, and often eloquent . . . with positive opinions on all public questions, and the courage to express and uphold them."[3]

Jackson's turn for the governorship—something for which he had long been grooming himself—arrived in 1860. But no sooner had he secured his party's nomination than he confronted the national Democratic schism. Although sympathizing with the Breckinridge party, he and running mate Thomas Caute Reynolds wisely backed the regular Democrats of Stephen A. Douglas and thereby managed to eke out a narrow victory over the Constitutional Unionists. Most Missourians wished to stay on middle ground in the emerging national crisis and hence found Douglas and John Bell much more to their liking than Breckinridge or Abraham Lincoln.[4]

At his inauguration in early January 1861, however, Governor Jackson quickly made his real sentiments known. He warned the North against any coercion and indicated that such action would cause Missouri to join her sister southern states in secession. He asked the legislature to call a convention to determine Missouri's course for the future and sought "a thorough reorganization of our militia."[5]

Lieutenant Governor Reynolds had just returned from Washington where he had held secret meetings with various southern congressional leaders to determine the best path to secession. Reynolds would prove even more ardent for the southern cause than Jackson, if such were possible. Born in Charleston on October 11, 1821, he had graduated from the University of Virginia and then had studied at Heidelberg where he received his doctor of laws *(summa cum laude)*. Following a brief diplomatic career he joined a leading law firm in St. Louis, served as United States district attorney, and became active in Democratic politics. One contemporary described him as a brilliant man who "bored into the heart of every question with the pitiless auger of common sense."[6]

In the early months of 1861 Reynolds organized a prosouthern paramilitary group in St. Louis to counter a similar pro-Union outfit which Congressman Frank Blair had established. In the assembly he worked assiduously to push through the convention bill. When that body met in early March, however, it was dominated by conditional Unionists who adopted a wait-and-see attitude while appointing a committee to call them into later session if things changed.[7]

A month later Fort Sumter exploded across the national scene. When Governor Jackson received President Lincoln's request for Missouri troops, he rejected it curtly as "illegal, unconstitutional and revolutionary; in its objects inhuman and diabolical." Blair promptly volunteered his group to fill the state's quota and was accepted.[8]

Jackson now called the legislature into special session in an attempt to secure the reorganization of the militia with unlimited gubernatorial powers over it. He also ordered that organization into statewide encampments during the first week in May. This latter move served as a cover-up for a proposed attempt by the St. Louis militia to seize the United States arsenal there. The governor secretly dispatched agents to both the Confederate government at Montgomery and the recently seceded state of Virginia seeking arms. These received a sympathetic ear with Jefferson Davis ordering that four guns be sent upriver from the Baton Rouge arsenal. The Confederate president assured Jackson that "our power to supply you with ordnance is far short of the will to serve you," while simultaneously requesting a regiment for service in Virginia. The governor replied that the latter would come with time.[9]

mand of Federal forces at St. Louis, had thwarted Jackson's arsenal dreams by thoroughly securing all the approaches to that facility. Nevertheless, the militia proceeded to muster for a week's stay in an encampment named for the governor. To this outpost came the Baton Rouge ordnance in boxes carefully marked "marble Tamaroa," which were never unpacked. A concerned Lyon now determined to seize the "traitorous" militia whom he outnumbered better than ten to one.

Ignoring the protests of its commander that they had done nothing illegal, he demanded surrender on the final day of the encampment. The state forces capitulated without a struggle but as they were being taken to Jefferson Barracks a riot broke out among the civilians gathered along the line of march. Before it was put down, twenty-eight persons had been killed. War had come to Missouri.[10]

While St. Louis remained in tumult all weekend, the legislature was galvanized into action. Amid unfounded rumors that Lyon and Blair were pushing on to Jefferson City, it approved the entire military package of Governor Jackson calling for the enrollment of all ablebodied males in the state's defense and giving him virtual carte blanche as commander in chief of what would now be known as the Missouri State Guard. Funds were diverted from the state's schools and charitable institutions, and loans and defense bonds authorized.[11]

At the insistence of Lieutenant Governor Reynolds, Jackson appointed former Governor Sterling Price to head the new State Guard. A popular hero of the Mexican War, Price had recently chaired the convention. He and the governor quickly organized the Guard to prepare for the state's defense. Reynolds meanwhile decided that for all this activity a firmer tie to the Confederacy was needed. Strangely, communication between him and Governor Jackson broke down at this point. Jackson told Reynolds he already had an emissary at Montgomery, without going into details, but the lieutenant governor determined to go south anyway and seek troops from Davis with which to hold the state. Price accompanied him to the depot, en route to an appointment with General William S. Harney, who had reassumed command in St. Louis, and endorsed his errand. To his dismay, Reynolds later learned that Price had signed what amounted to a neutrality agreement with Harney whereby each would seek to keep the peace within his respective area.[12]

This agreement lasted ten days and failed to satisfy extremists on either side. Reports flowed into St. Louis of harassment of Union citizens by pro-southern men in other parts of the state. Thomas W. Knox, the correspondent of the New York *Herald,* visited Jefferson City and noted Confederate flags very much in evidence around the town. Rumors were rife there of behind-the-scenes maneuverings by Jackson to take Missouri into the Confederate camp. Finally Blair and Lyon used their pipeline to President Lincoln to secure an order removing Harney at the end of May. This precipitated a final confrontation in St. Louis between Jackson and Price on one side and Lyon and Blair on the other. Lyon made it clear that he had no intention of honoring the Harney–Price agreement, that he would move Federal troops into the state as he thought necessary, and concluded dramatically: *"This means war."*[13]

Jackson and Price returned quickly to Jefferson City where the governor called for fifty thousand volunteers to defend Missouri against Federal encroachment. The two officials, in consultation with others, now decided that the capital was not readily defensible should Lyon move upriver. Hence they retreated to Boonville on June 13. From this time forth theirs would be a government in exile.[14]

Two days later Lyon occupied Jefferson City where he remained only twenty-four hours before pursuing the Jackson forces. The latter were soundly routed at Boonville and now retreated into the southwestern corner of the state to regroup and organize the new recruits they confidently expected to flock to their banner. They also hoped that contact could be made with Confederate troops in Arkansas. Lyon meanwhile secured the line of the Missouri River while Federal forces poured into Missouri from three sides.[15]

The two sides continued to maneuver militarily during July, with Lyon occupying Springfield and General Ben McCulloch reluctantly agreeing to move his forces up from Arkansas to join Price in a countermove. Simultaneously Confederates also advanced into southeastern Missouri under Generals Gideon J. Pillow and William J. Hardee to cooperate with State Guard units there being organized by M. Jeff Thompson.[16]

Even as these movements went forward, political maneuvering also got under way on both sides. Governor Jackson, accompanied by former Senator David Rice Atchison, visited Richmond in mid-July. Jefferson Davis, distrustful of the governor after the Harney–Price agreement, had been dragging his feet on cooperation; and Jackson wanted to tie down a specific agreement. Through the intercession of Atchison, a longtime friend of Davis and Secretary of State Robert M. T. Hunter, he was successful in allaying Davis's doubts about his integrity. The Confederate president urged Jackson to take the necessary steps leading to secession and the ratification of the Confederate constitution and promised to pay Missouri forces in the field as soon as Congress appropriated the necessary funds.[17]

Jackson and Atchison returned to newly occupied New Madrid to learn that in their absence the old secession convention had reconvened at Jefferson City and deposed the state's top three officials together with the General Assembly. In their place it established a provisional government to rule Missouri in cooperation with Union military authority. Undaunted, Jackson issued a proclamation declaring Missouri a free and independent state under authority given him earlier by the legislature. Returning to Memphis, he learned that the Confederate Congress had appropriated one million dollars for Missouri troops cooperating with its armies. He now urged General Leonidas Polk to launch a pincers movement up from southeast Missouri in coordination with Price and McCulloch in the southwest, but Polk demurred on the ground of insufficient strength.[18]

Jackson and Atchison hastened through Arkansas to rejoin Price, arriving too late for the battle of Wilson's Creek (August 10), in which Lyon was killed and his Union army sent into retreat. They caught up with Price on the eve of the battle of Lexington, and in the wake of that victory Jackson called the legislature to meet at Neosho. Sterling Price had won two significant battles within six weeks. Recruits flocked to his banner; he increased his force to eighteen thousand—half again as many as he had come with. He found himself unable to hold this tenuous line to the Missouri River, however, without McCulloch's help. This the latter refused to give because of his distrust of Price's military ability and his fear of stretching his support line too far from his base.[19]

So Price and Jackson retreated back to southwest Missouri to prepare for the legislative session already described. Once Missouri's admission to the Confederacy had been definitely secured in late November, the governor traveled to New Orleans where he procured arms for the State Guard and managed to float the recently authorized defense bond issue. Union forces finally pushed Price out of the state in February 1862. Over the preceding eight months his troops had marched more than eight hundred miles, had fought in five battles, and engaged in approximately thirty skirmishes. He had yet to lose a fight, but his army was ill-equipped and poorly trained. McCulloch continued to refuse to support him and after an amnesty offer from the provisional government in mid-October his troops tended to melt away. When Price crossed over into Arkansas he took with him only seven thousand men.[20]

In the meantime, he had become a storm center of controversy. His exploits had captured the imagination of many southerners seeking positive battlefield news. Jackson had begun pushing him as commander of the Trans-Mississippi in the hope of getting more positive efforts from the Confederacy for a Missouri campaign. Yet McCulloch and the Arkansas men would have nothing of him. Finally Davis appointed Earl Van Dorn as a compromise candidate.[21]

The new commander barely had time to pull together the remnants of the various forces in northern Arkansas, which included some two thousand Indians from present-day Oklahoma, before being confronted by Union General Samuel Curtis at the battle of Pea Ridge on March 7 and 8, 1862. Poor tactics led to Confederate defeat and ended whatever hope there might have been for a new movement back into Missouri. Shortly thereafter Confederate forces also withdrew from southeast Missouri, and the state became the backdrop for intense guerrilla warfare.[22]

Price and most of his men were now enrolled in the Confederate army with their leader being given a commission as major general. In anticipation of the Shiloh campaign they were transferred east of the Mississippi but arrived too late to be of help to Albert Sidney Johnston.[23]

Governor Jackson, who had rejoined Price just before Pea Ridge, remained west of the river, apparently establishing a temporary capital at Camden. He had brought his wife and family south sometime during the winter, accompanied by twenty handpicked slaves, and had settled them in Red River County, Texas. July found him at Marshall, Texas, conferring with his counterparts from Louisiana, Texas, and Arkansas on the problems of the Trans-Mississippi. They urged a unified command for their area, with greater attention to its particular needs, something in which President Davis acquiesced. Later that fall Jackson established reception camps along the border for those Missourians going south to join the Confederate service as a result of the activities of guerrilla recruiters who had been active in Missouri all summer.[24]

In mid-November the governor contracted a bad cold which quickly developed into pneumonia. He had suffered from tuberculosis for several years, and it is believed that he had stomach cancer. Whatever the case, the pneumonia proved fatal. Death came at Little Rock on December 7, 1862, after a confinement of several weeks.[25] However one may judge the actions of Claiborne Fox Jackson in terms of practical wisdom in 1861, it must be said that he had chosen the course he sincerely believed to be best for his state and for the South and that he was deeply attached to both.

With the death of Governor Jackson, Lieutenant Governor Thomas Caute Reynolds assumed control of Missouri's government in exile. Because of disagreements with Jackson and the lack of any real function, Reynolds had retired to his native South Carolina at the end of 1861 to pursue the private practice of law. Now he hurried to Richmond to confer with Missouri's congressional delegation and to reestablish a long-standing friendship with President Davis. The need for continuity was evident. On February 14, 1863, Reynolds issued a proclamation to Missouri's Confederate sympathizers and soldiers, formally announcing Jackson's death and his own assumption of power.[26]

Reynolds discovered that his predecessor had allowed the reins of power and the channels of communication to erode badly in his last few months. The records of government were scattered all the way from the Jackson home in Texas to the presumed "capital" at Camden, to Jackson, Mississippi, where General Price had centered his official operations. The latter proved to be Reynolds's most pressing problem. For months the general and many of the Missourians under his command had been pressing for transfer back to the Trans-Mississippi. With Reynolds on the scene at Richmond, Price now came east to make a personal appeal; and the new governor, through his friendship with Davis and Secretary of War James Seddon, finally negotiated the change.[27]

Reynolds remained in Richmond for two months establishing strong liaison with Confederate officials, handling the Price affair, and beginning the reorganization of Missouri's government in exile, of which he really knew little, to suit his own style. Then in mid-March he traveled west to consolidate his authority with those Missouri troops still remaining east of the Mississippi—after Price's transfer—and with the remnant of Jackson's bureaucracy at Camden. En route he also stopped at Shreveport, Louisiana, to confer with General E. Kirby Smith, newly appointed commander of the Trans-Mississippi, with whom he would work closely in the final two years of the war. Upon his arrival at Camden he found the situation there deteriorated to the point that it would "irritate the mildest saint." He immediately set to work to systematize his administration and clear up the government's tangled finances.[28]

Sorting out the latter proved to be one of Reynolds's biggest headaches. Such coinage and United States treasury notes as the Jackson government had been able to carry away from Jefferson City had long since been exhausted. So, too, had the few loans rendered by sympathetic banks. What remained were the unexpended portions of the Missouri Defense Bonds, authorized by the Neosho legislature, amounting to some $6 million, and the unused residue of $3 million appropriated at various times by the Confederate Congress for the use of Missouri during its transition from "independence" to Confederate statehood, including the full mustering of the State Guard into Confederate service. This latter amounted to approximately $200,000 in Confederate notes.[29]

Slowly Reynolds brought order out of chaos. Throughout he placed strong emphasis on the need for close cooperation with Confederate civil and military officials. At least two improvements for the Trans-Mississippi which he recommended to President Davis received implementation: a "Western Preferred Mail" system and a treasury branch which could handle claims against the Confederacy without prior referral to Richmond and could engrave and sign government notes and bond.[30]

General Smith looked upon the exiled Missourians as a cooperating military establishment and afforded them all of the courtesies and privileges which such a group might expect. In August 1863, Reynolds attended a meeting with other governors and state officials at Marshall, Texas, from which he emerged as chairman of a Committee of Public Safety whose purpose it was to organize county volunteer organizations for emergency situations. This post gave him ready access to General Smith. Following the fall of Little Rock in September, he wandered briefly through Arkansas and then in early November established a permanent capital at Marshall, only thirty miles from Kirby Smith's headquarters at Shreveport. This remained the seat of Missouri's government in exile for the rest of the war.[31]

From there Governor Reynolds maintained his liason role between Confederate authorities and Missouri troops in the field. He served as the covert agent for Confederate guerrillas recruiting back in Missouri. As vacancies occurred in the ranks of Missouri's delegation to the Confederate Senate, Reynolds named replacements. And when the Confederacy held nationwide congressional elections in May 1864 the governor coordinated balloting for Missouri's House delegation among the various camps and stations where his constituency was located.[32]

As time went on, the legality of Reynolds's status came into question, for Missouri's constitution provided that in cases such as his a new election for governor must be held within eighteen months. This was obviously impossible so Reynolds fell back on the proviso that an executive hold office for his specific term or until a successor should be duly elected and qualified. In this he received the reluctant support of General Price and others.[33]

For this and other reasons Reynolds and Price had been urging upon Kirby Smith a Confederate raid into Missouri. They hoped such an effort would divert Union support from General William T. Sherman in Georgia, rally supposed Confederate sympathizers in the state, and possibly reinstate Reynolds at Jefferson City so that at least some kind of quasi election might be held. Smith finally gave his support in August 1864 and chose Price to lead the movement. Reynolds opted to go along. The raid turned out disastrously, however, with Price being driven back into Arkansas after six weeks of maneuvering which saw him reach the Missouri River and engage in two battles and numerous skirmishes.[34]

Reynolds became convinced that Price was responsible for the debacle by the loose way in which he had managed the campaign and leveled a public blast at the general upon their return. Price demanded a court of inquiry to which Kirby Smith agreed. But nothing had been concluded by the time of the final Confederate surrender.[35] There had been tensions of various sorts between the two throughout Reynolds's administration, but it is unfortunate that this final break could not have been avoided.

After the war Reynolds went with Price and a number of other Missourians to Mexico City, where his excellent knowledge of French and Spanish served him well. He became involved in railroads and served unofficially as an adviser to Maximilian. Following the collapse of Maximilian's empire, Reynolds returned to St. Louis and resumed his law practice. He served a term in the legislature in the 1870s and under Grover Cleveland acted as United States trade commissioner to Central and South America. He took his life on March 30, 1887, leaving a note in which he said that he was afraid he was losing his mind.

Thomas Caute Reynolds, and to a lesser extent, Claiborne Fox Jackson, had performed a difficult task well, exercising tact and skill to keep Missouri a viable entity within the framework of its agreement with the Confederacy. In the end, Missouri furnished some thirty thousand troops to Confederate service—as contrasted with over one hundred thousand in the Union cause—but the agents of the government in exile and the Confederacy itself caused untold turmoil throughout the Union-controlled state in the form of endless acts of guerrilla warfare. While Governors Jackson and Reynolds maintained their shadow government in Arkansas and Texas, Missouri's representatives played an active role in the Confederate Congress at Richmond. Hence, for all the difficulties of administration and the lack of actual territorial control, it can truly be said that Missouri was "the twelfth Confederate state."

NORTH CAROLINA

John G. Barrett

ohn Willis Ellis was governor of North Carolina when the
state seceded from the Union in the spring of 1861. He was
born on a plantation in eastern Rowan County, November
23, 1820.[1] After early schooling at home and in neighboring
Lincoln County, Ellis attended Randolph-Macon College in
Virginia but was graduated from the University of North Carolina in
1841. He then read law under the distinguished North Carolina jurist
Richmond M. Pearson and was admitted to the bar in 1842. He set up
practice in Salisbury.[2] In 1844, 1846, and 1848 he represented his
county in the North Carolina House of Commons. Ellis, however, did
not complete his final term because in December of 1848 he was elected
a state superior court judge by the General Assembly. He returned to
politics in 1858 as the Democratic nominee for governor. With the
support of the slaveholders and gentry in his party, Ellis easily defeated D. K. McRae for the governorship and two years later was reelected to the same office, this time defeating John Pool of Pasquotank
County.

The General Assembly which convened on November 19, 1860, following the election of Lincoln to the presidency of the United States,
heard the governor call for the reorganization of the militia, the recruitment of additional troops, and the convening of a conference of
southern states "to enter into consultation with us, upon the present
condition of the country."[3] He also recommended that "a convention of
the people of the State be called." The intent of his message, the
governor maintained, was a plea for the "prevention . . . of Civil War,
and the preservation of peace amongst us."[4] On the other hand, im-
plicit in his call for a convention was the assumption that this was
the necessary first step toward secession.[5] Ellis was in fact an ardent
secessionist.

Governor Ellis was formally installed in office for his second term on January 1, 1861. The inauguration ceremony, due to the troubled times, was brief, and scarcely had it ended before the governor was confronted by a delegation from Wilmington which had just arrived in Raleigh by special train. The group requested permission to seize Forts Caswell and Johnston on the lower Cape Fear to prevent them from being garrisoned by Federal troops. At the time these installations were occupied only by caretaker ordnance sergeants. Ellis refused to consider the proposal. He did not question the patriotic motives behind the request; his concern was its legality. To seize the forts while North Carolina was still in the Union would be, in his opinion, unlawful. Consequently, when he learned the next week that a detachment of "Cape Fear Minute Men" had taken possession of the forts anyway, he ordered Colonel John L. Cantwell of the Thirtieth North Carolina Militia to Smithville (Southport) with orders to restore the property to the Federal government. At the same time he kept President Buchanan informed of developments. The president assured Governor Ellis that he had no intention of sending larger detachments of Federal troops to the Cape Fear region.

Amid the excitement surrounding the disposition of the forts, the legislators returned to Raleigh. The House wasted little time in passing a $300,000 military appropriation bill which the Senate had accepted before the holiday recess. The General Assembly also established a military commission to help the governor administer the sum, and by January 19 Ellis had dispatched Lieutenant C. C. Lee northward with a long list of military needs and instructions for buying them.[6] Also, by this date four more states of the Deep South—Mississippi, Florida, Alabama, and Georgia—had joined South Carolina in leaving the Union, and pressure was mounting on the legislators to call a convention to consider secession.

It was the Fort Sumter crisis, however, that took the state out of the Union. For most North Carolinians Lincoln's call on April 15 for seventy-five thousand troops to suppress an insurrection in the South was an attempt at coercion. So when Lincoln's secretary of war called on North Carolina to furnish two militia regiments for this purpose, Governor Ellis replied emphatically that he "could get no troops from North Carolina" for "this war upon the liberties of a free people."[7] Furthermore, he ordered Forts Caswell, Johnston, and Macon, the latter on Bogue Banks, to be seized along with the United States Arsenal at Fayetteville and the Branch Mint at Charlotte. In less than a week's time all of this valuable property was in state hands.

Meanwhile, the governor had issued a call for the General Assembly to meet in special session on May 1. He also asked the president of the

Confederacy to visit the state. On the seventeenth he had wired Jefferson Davis: "I am in possession of forts, arsenals, etc., come as soon as you choose. We are ready to join you to a man. Strike the blow quickly and Washington will be ours."[8] By this time Union sentiment in the state had all but disappeared. Unionist and secessionist alike urged resistance. The governor's boldness in meeting the secession crisis seems to have met with the approval of most North Carolinians. At the same time, however, the demands of the office were killing him. Suffering terribly from consumption, Ellis oftentimes had to conduct the affairs of state from his sick bed. Certain, nevertheless, that withdrawal from the Union was only a matter of time and the drafting of certain documents, he set about putting the state on a wartime footing. General W. H. C. Whiting was made inspector general in charge of defenses. Military companies were hastily organized, and an encampment named for the governor was established near Raleigh.

When the General Assembly met in special session on May 1, Ellis reported on the action he had taken to meet the emergency. He also noted the programs that needed to be instituted immediately, such as the manufacture of munitions at the Fayetteville arsenal, and finally, "with the view . . . of the secession of North Carolina from the Northern Government, and her union with the Confederate States at as early a period as practicable," he recommended "that a convention of the people be called with full and final powers."[9]

It took the General Assembly only an hour and a half to pass a convention bill calling for the election of delegates on May 13 to convene in Raleigh on May 20. The legislature then proceeded to authorize a division of ten thousand men consisting of ten regiments of state troops to serve for the duration of the war. The governor was to appoint all commissioned officers, and captains were to raise their own companies. Two days later, May 10, legislation was adopted which allowed the governor to accept as many as fifty thousand twelve-month volunteers. During the process by which these North Carolina volunteers were turned over to the Confederacy, a number of serious problems developed, forcing Governor Ellis to send Thomas Ruffin and William A. Graham to Richmond to discuss the situation with the Confederate secretary of war.[10]

The General Assembly adjourned on May 13 after voting its thanks to the governor for his efforts to prepare the state for war. Although very sick, Ellis felt that it was now mandatory that he talk with Virginia's leaders, and he made a trip to Richmond where he was well received. The governor was back in Raleigh by the evening of the fifteenth and shortly afterwards D. H. Hill's First North Carolina Volunteers (Bethel Regiment) was on its way to the Old Dominion.[11] Prior to this, Dr. Charles E. Johnson had been appointed surgeon general of North Carolina troops.

The convention which assembled on May 20 was a distinguished gathering with many of North Carolina's ablest men present. This body wasted little time in unanimously adopting an ordinance of secession. The Raleigh *State Journal* reported that on the afternoon of the twentieth, "amid the ringing of bells and the booming cannon, mingled with the deafening shouts of thousands of loyal voices," the state left the Union.[12]

Governor Ellis, his health rapidly failing, journeyed to Red Sulphur Springs, Virginia, the latter part of June in an effort to regain his strength. It was too late. He died on July 7 at the age of forty-one.[13] His body was returned to the family cemetery in Davidson County, North Carolina, for burial.

John Willis Ellis was certainly one of North Carolina's favorite sons. Although a wealthy slaveholder and a secessionist, he was, as one historian has noted, "always a moderate in his views and actions and never compromised his state beyond the law and the will of the people."[14]

The death of Governor Ellis greatly complicated the situation over the governorship. In the absence of a lieutenant governor,[15] the speaker of the Senate, Henry Toole Clark,[16] a Democratic secessionist planter from Edgecombe County, became the state's chief executive officer.[17] The convention, having decided that a vacancy in the office of governor would exist at the expiration of Clark's term as senator, passed an ordinance during its fourth session providing for the election of a governor on August 6, 1862. Soldiers in camp could cast their ballots a week earlier. The inauguration was set for the second Monday in September, and Clark was to continue to serve until his successor qualified.[18]

Clark was born on his father's plantation along Walnut Creek near Tarboro, Feburary 7, 1808, and received his early education in private schools in both Tarboro and Louisburg. In 1822 he enrolled in the University of North Carolina and was graduated four years later. Clark was admitted to the bar in 1833 but rarely engaged in the practice of law, devoting most of his time, instead, to the management of his father's plantation and business affairs. Neither did he take much interest in politics until 1850, when he was elected to the state Senate. That same year he married his widowed cousin, Mary Weeks Hargrave. Clark remained in the Senate for eleven years. He was elected speaker of that body in 1858.

Though North Carolina left the Union reluctantly, once the move was made there was no looking back, little indecision in support of the

Confederacy. The state sacrificed mightily for the southern cause. Yet few people have ever been less prepared for war. Northern and English markets provided North Carolina with virtually all manufactured goods.[19] This state of unpreparedness was of great concern to both the General Assembly and the governor. Clark informed the convention early that the $5 million appropriated by the legislature for public defense had already been spent and that an additional $6.5 million was urgently needed. For him it was to be a policy of "the last man and the last dollar," if necessary, to win the war.[20]

During the early months of the war equipment was more sorely needed than men. North Carolina youth volunteered in such large numbers that it was extremely difficult to provide them with arms. The state retained most of the thirty-seven thousand muskets seized at the Fayetteville arsenal, but many of them were antiquated flintlock models that had to be altered. It was the fall of 1861 before the arsenal began the manufacture of rifles. Cannons were even more scarce. Other then several antiquated artillery pieces taken at Fayetteville and the coastal forts, North Carolina entered the conflict with only a few old smooth-bore guns.[21]

The shortage of ammunition was equally critical. In an effort to alleviate the situation Clark, in accordance with legislation passed by the General Assembly, advanced George B. Waterhouse and Michael Bowes $10,000 toward the construction of the Raleigh Powder Mills. The plant was erected but was soon destroyed by an explosion. At the governor's insistence, additional money was advanced to Messrs. Waterhouse and Bowes for a new mill which was to manufacture seven hundred pounds of powder a day at a profit of fifteen cents a pound.[22]

During the first year and a half of the war North Carolina attempted to clothe its own troops under a compensatory agreement with Richmond. By a law of September 20, 1861, the governor was required to furnish the state's soldiers with suitable clothing and make arrangements with the Confederacy for commutation money. The entire output from local textile mills was purchased by the state. Also, agents were sent to other areas to buy materials, and a factory was set up in Raleigh to manufacture uniforms and overcoats.

From the outset this operation was unpopular in Richmond and with many mill operators as well. Confederate Quartermaster General Abraham C. Myers complained to Clark that North Carolina was not living up to its agreement with the Confederacy, and therefore the production of its mills should be shared by all. Francis Fries of F. & H. Fries Co., Salem, claimed that "to the neglect of our customers and our interest we have from the beginning of our troubles made all our business yield to the demands of the army."[23]

Salt, indispensable to preservation of food, was in very short supply early in the war. The state not only established factories on the coast for making salt by evaporating sea water, but it also purchased salt in Virginia. In the summer of 1862 Governor Clark arranged a contract with Stuart, Buchanan and Co. calling for 300,000 bushels per year from the mines at Saltville in western Virginia.[24]

Although North Carolina made tremendous contributions to the Confederacy in materials of war, its greatest contribution was in manpower—"the huge number of soldiers who bore the brunt of scores of battles."[25] In the process, however, numerous conflicts developed with Confederate officials over the raising of troops. For at least a year it was generally held in Raleigh that all troops furnished Richmond should be "tendered to the Confederate government through the governor or some other authorized agent." As a consequence, Clark objected strongly to President Davis's policy of "independent acceptance," maintaining that it "interfered with the State filling its own quota and that it overruled the Governor and compromised the dignity of the State."[26]

There was also the question of who was to commission officers for North Carolina's various regiments. The matter became very touchy after the passage of the conscription acts of 1862. Governor Clark claimed the exclusive right to commission officers, fill vacancies, and make promotions according to the laws of the state, not only in the first ten regiments which had been recruited to serve for the duration of the war, and which were usually referred to as "State Troops,"[27] but also in various other units. Since Confederate authorities would not accept this contention, the governor sent his assistant adjutant general, W. B. Gulick, to Richmond to make arrangements with the War Department "as to what Regiments under the conscript law are to receive the commissions of their officers from the Confederate Government and which are to be commissioned by the Governor of the State." Gulick talked with the secretary of war, who told him that the department "was in the habit of issuing commissions to all the troops under its orders upon application."[28] This by no means settled the issue. It was long a matter of considerable controversy.

Conscription created problems for Clark other than the commissioning of officers. What was to be the status of Quakers under the law and was the militia to be used to enroll conscripts, as Confederate authorities desired?[29] These were but two of many questions confronting the governor. One of his aides wrote in the summer of 1862 that Clark never ordered, nor had any intention of ordering, the militia officers to enroll the conscripts, but that he had no objection to it.[30] Neither did the governor object at this time to the "colonels" arresting or enrolling

Quakers as long as it was done under Confederate authority. Members of this peaceable faith were not automatically exempt under Confederate law. Complicating matters considerably, however, was a convention ordinance adopted earlier freeing Quakers from military service, provided each one exempted paid $100 to the state. If a member were unable to pay, the governor could have him help with the manufacture of salt or work in a state hospital.[31]

As war governor, Clark had the unenviable task of preparing the state for possible invasion. From the outset of the fighting North Carolinians feared an attack upon their coastal region, and shortly after secession became a reality, preparations were made to defend the area. Existing fortifications were strengthened, and new ones built. Since Hatteras, on the Outer Banks, was one of the state's busiest ports and an ideal base for privateers, Forts Hatteras and Clark, which guarded the inlet, were of primary importance.

The possibility of an attack on Hatteras had not been overlooked by North Carolina authorities. A member of the Military Board wrote: "As we are taking prizes . . . the U.S. will certainly make some effort to break up the nest." On August 27, therefore, the governor should not have been surprised when he received the following message from a Confederate officer in Norfolk: "The enemy's fleet . . . left last evening; passed out of the capes and steered south, I think to the coast of North Carolina." Hatteras fell on the twenty-ninth after the forts had "sustained," in the opinion of Clark, "the heaviest and most incessant firing that the country ever witnessed."[32]

When it became known that Federal authorities intended to hold Hatteras Inlet for future operations, the citizens of eastern North Carolina bombarded the governor with petitions asking protection for their part of the state. It was thought that Roanoke Island, commanding the entrance to Albemarle Sound, would be the next target.

Governor Clark, in a most difficult position, could promise the people little. The coastal fortifications were now under Confederate control, and most of the state's troops were on duty in Virginia. Yet he was severely criticized by many North Carolinians. One thought him "still in a stupor." Another, while not questioning his patriotism, remarked that "his total incapacity is so enormous that it is becoming the subject of everyday remark."[33]

The governor did the only thing he could do. He pressed the need for arms and troops upon Richmond. His efforts bore little fruit even though he pointed out to the secretary of war that the "best population" of the undefended region was now serving in North Carolina regiments in Virginia. "We see," he wrote, "just over our lines in Virginia, near Suffolk, two or three North Carolina Regiments, well-armed, and well-drilled, who are not allowed to come to the defense of their homes." Clark also noted for the secretary that North Carolina not only had armed "her own volunteers in Virginia" but also had loaned the state thirteen thousand stands of arms. This "liberality," he complained, "has exhausted our supply and I am trying to buy rifles and shot guns." Still, the governor made it clear that he would make all the preparations in his power to repel an invasion, and this despite the fact that his resources were "restricted almost to militia . . . unarmed, undrilled, and some not yet organized."[34]

Though unable to provide the badly needed arms and men, Richmond authorities did transfer a number of established Confederate officers to North Carolina. Generals R. C. Gatlin, D. H. Hill, and J. R. Anderson arrived in the state to take over command of the defenses. The situation, nevertheless, remained critical, and in January of the new year Clark asked the Confederate government to return the large quantity of arms that had been taken from the state to Virginia. Later he issued a proclamation prohibiting Confederate agents from purchasing arms in the state or impressing any kind of equipment. He threatened the use of force to protect the citizens against such activities.[35]

The long-awaited invasion of eastern North Carolina finally came in February 1862. A large Federal expedition under General Ambrose E. Burnside successfully landed on Roanoke Island on the eighth.[36] From there the Federals moved to the mainland, and by the end of April New Bern, Fort Macon, and much of coastal Carolina were in Federal hands. Burnside planned to move on the important rail town of Goldsboro. However, before the operation could be launched, he was ordered to Virginia. General J. G. Foster was left behind to hold the Federal gains in North Carolina.

During the summer of 1862 Federal activity in eastern North Carolina was minimal, but Governor Clark remained fearful that Foster might at any moment leave his base at New Bern and push toward Goldsboro, which was virtually undefended. Accordingly, he urged General R. E. Lee to send an expedition to the state to drive the Federals out of New Bern, Plymouth, and Washington, "now swarming with Yankees, Negroes and traitors." Clark felt that Lee appreciated the importance of protecting the rail lines at Goldsboro, but he was not certain that the general realized the extent of "individual and state loss" in property and crops to the occupying forces. Lee, after replying that he had no troops to spare, pointed out to the governor that "the safety of the whole State of North Carolina depends . . . in a measure upon the results of the enemy's efforts in [Virginia]." Lee also made it clear that he fully appreciated the injuries suffered by North Carolinians. He had seen the depredations carried out by the Federal army in Virginia.[37]

Clark's troubles with Confederate authorities were not confined to the critical situation in eastern North Carolina. As early as the fall of 1861 he had become disturbed over conditions in the western part of the state. In November of that year he wrote Richmond that he was receiving "numerous communications from the North Carolina counties bordering on East Tennessee" requesting help against traitors.[38]

The mountain people owned few slaves and had generally been opposed to secession, but when the war started they volunteered for service in unusually large numbers. This stripped many areas of young men and made it difficult for those at home to protect themselves against native Unionists (Tories),[39] East Tennessee raiders, and bands of deserters who gathered in the area to rob and steal.

The problems of the mountain people were eased none by the bitter party spirit that developed in the gubernatorial campaign of 1862. By this time many North Carolinians had become convinced that the war was being poorly managed, as evidenced by defeats on the battlefield. People were also upset over the social and economic dislocations produced by the "scarcity [of goods], high prices, conscription, and wartime taxes." Such conditions created an opportunity for the disgruntled, mostly former Whigs and Union Democrats who had opposed secession until the outbreak of war, to join forces as the Conservative party. In response the Democrats quickly transformed themselves into the Confederate party and nominated railroad executive William J. Johnston of Mecklinburg County for the governorship.

The Confederates were composed primarily of "original secessionists," who, believing that military success was essential for independence, zealously supported the Davis administration. Editor W. W. Holden of the Raleigh *Standard,* leader of the Conservatives and outspoken critic of President Davis as well as Governor Clark, selected Zebulon Baird Vance, youthful colonel of the Twenty-sixth North Carolina, to head the Conservative ticket.

The campaign that followed was one of the strangest in the state's history. It was conducted chiefly in the press. Johnston remained with his railroad and Vance with his regiment in Virginia. The Confederate press claimed that the issue was between Union and secession and insisted that Vance's election would be taken in the North "as an indubitable sign that the Union sentiment is in the ascendancy in the heart of the Southern Confederacy." The Conservatives professed to be amused at this argument, pointing out that Vance was in the army while Johnston stayed home. They attempted, however, to capitalize more on the public discontent with war measures such as conscription and the suspension of the writ of habeas corpus.

Vance won a sweeping victory at the polls, carrying all but twelve counties in the state. In his inaugural address, delivered September 8, 1862, he eliminated all doubts as to his devotion to the Confederacy, pledging a vigorous prosecution of the war until the invader was driven from the soil of the Old North State. He urged the people to forget party differences and to work together for victory.[40]

In the contest of 1862 Governor Clark had not sought the nomination on the Confederate ticket and after the election he returned to Edgecomb County. In 1866 he was elected to the state Senate but remained active in North Carolina politics for only a short period. Other than serving as chairman of the county court of common pleas and quarter sessions, he was out of public life until his death on April 14, 1874. During his last years Clark spent much of his time studying North Carolina history and corresponding with many of the state's leading figures.

Henry Toole Clark was a capable individual devoted both to his state and to the southern cause. He performed his duties as war governor faithfully. Yet he was never able to lead forcefully the people of North Carolina in time of civil crisis.[41] That remained for his successor in the governor's chair, "Zeb" Vance.

The new governor faced a herculean task. His predecessors, Ellis and Clark, had served only partial terms, and neither had had sufficient opportunity to come to grips with the monumental problems associated with guiding an independent-minded state through a bitter and devastating civil war. A majority of North Carolina's constructive war measures consequently are attributable to Vance. Either their inception or their effective implementation can be traced directly to him.[42]

Vance was born on May 13, 1830, in Buncombe County, North Carolina, on Reems Creek about twelve miles north of Asheville. He attended Washington College in East Tennessee and the University of North Carolina at Chapel Hill. In 1852 he was licensed to practice law, but the legal profession never brought forth his best endeavors. For Vance law was primarily preparation for politics, which was his passion. He understood people better than he did judicial matters.

Vance entered politics as a Whig but joined the American or Know-Nothing party when the Whigs folded. He served one term in the House of Commons of the North Carolina General Assembly and in 1858 was elected to Congress to fill a vacancy created by the resignation of Thomas L. Clingman. He was reelected the next year to the thirty-sixth Congress, but left his seat to join the army.

Vance never questioned the legality of secession, only its wisdom under certain circumstances. He stoutly defended the Union up to the firing on Fort Sumter and Lincoln's call for troops. In later years he wrote: "For myself, I will say that I was canvassing for the Union with all of my strength. I was addressing a large and excited crowd, large numbers of whom were armed and literally had my arm extended upward in pleading for peace and the Union of our Fathers, when the telegraphic news was announced of the firing on Sumter and the President's call for seventy-five thousand volunteers. When my hand came down from that impassioned gesticulation, it fell slowly and sadly by the side of a Secessionist."[43]

Rather than run for the Confederate Congress, Vance raised a company of "Rough and Ready Guards" and marched off to war with a captain's commission. By June 1861 the "Guards" had become Company F, Fourteenth North Carolina Regiment, and were on duty in Virginia. Elected colonel of the Twenty-sixth North Carolina in August, Vance took command of the regiment the next month at Fort Macon. His first experience under fire came the following March in the Battle of New Bern, where he and the Twenty-sixth performed well. Vance's military career in the field came to an end late on the afternoon of July 1, 1862, at Malvern Hill, the final engagement of the bloody Seven Days before Richmond. Ransom's brigade, to which the Twenty-sixth North Carolina was attached, lost heavily on that day, but Vance came through the battle unscratched.

The harsh realities of war, however, never diverted Vance's attention far from politics and public affairs. Furthermore, by this time he had become something of a hero in his native state, especially in the Conservative newspapers which had the Clark administration under fire for its conduct of the war. Thus it was relatively easy for him to leave the army and return to the political arena in 1862.

As a soldier Vance had learned much, but, in the words of a leading North Carolina historian, "most important of all . . . [he] learned that effective war is made not by brave men and grand charges alone, but by food, medicine, clothes, arms, and supplies of all sorts. He learned how necessary cooperation is to achievement. He was . . . to be a better war governor for having been a soldier."[44]

One of the most critical problems facing Vance upon his assumption of the governorship was the presence of a sizable Federal occupation force in the eastern part of the state. Early he turned his attention to the task of driving the enemy from North Carolina soil. With much of the coastal region under Federal control and raids being conducted as far west as Goldsboro, he was swamped with requests for protection from those in the occupied areas. The governor, in turn, carried on a vigorous correspondence with Richmond in which he demanded that Confederate troops be ordered to North Carolina immediately. Much to his chagrin he met with no more success than Governor Clark, who had faced the same problem.[45] Neither Davis nor Lee was inclined to weaken the Virginia front to any great extent. In February 1863, however, D. H. Hill, who was very popular in North Carolina, arrived to take command. But his moves against New Bern and Washington accomplished very little, and in late May Lee began withdrawing troops from the state in preparation for an offensive across the Potomac.

Following its defeat at Gettysburg the Army of Northern Virginia saw little action for ten months. This enabled General Lee early in 1864 to write Davis: "The time is at hand when, if an attempt can be made to capture the enemy's forces at New Berne, it should be done. I can now spare the troops for the purpose, which will not be the case as spring approaches."[46] General George Pickett was given the assignment of capturing the important North Carolina town. Pickett, not the most competent of officers, failed in February and was soon back in Virginia. His able subordinate Robert F. Hoke of Lincolnton then took over command of the army and conducted successful operations in the spring against Plymouth and Washington, and was preparing for an attack on New Bern when ordered to Petersburg.

Hoke's departure for the Virginia front in May marked the end of the Confederate offensive in North Carolina, and fortunately for Vance the Federals launched no major operations until the last month of the year, when Fort Fisher came under attack. Thus during the summer and fall of 1864 the governor did not have to hound Richmond for troops. It is well that he did not because Lee, following the Wilderness, Spotsylvania, Cold Harbor, and Petersburg, had absolutely no men to spare.

In his efforts to defend the state Governor Vance not only appealed to Richmond for troops but also recommended to the General Assembly, as early as November 1862, that it raise at least ten regiments of reserves for use in North Carolina alone. Those recruited were to be over the conscription age. The lower house responded by passing a much broader bill than the governor had proposed, and one that would have resulted in conflict with Confederate authorities over conscription measures which Vance was trying to enforce. Fortunately for him, the Senate killed the bill.[47]

In another move designed to strengthen the state's defenses the governor prevailed upon the General Assembly to abolish the unsatisfactory militia system and replace it with the Guard for Home Defense, to consist of all whites between the ages of eighteen and fifty who were not liable to Confederate service nor exempt by state law. Although in 1864 Vance had twenty-five thousand enrolled in the guard, it was never as formidable a force as it appeared on paper.[48]

The governor's deep concern for his native state also extended to what he believed was President Davis's discrimination against North Carolina in both civil and military appointments. Only one cabinet position, that of attorney general, had been held by a North Carolinian, and of the full generals of the Confederacy none was from the state and only two of nineteen lieutenant generals called North Carolina home. In addition, Vance complained that "outsiders," in particular Virginians, were being appointed to command North Carolina troops. "It is mortifying" he wrote, "to find entire brigades of North Carolina soldiers in the field commanded by strangers and in many cases our own brave war-worn colonels are made to give place to colonels from distant states."[49] The appointment of T. P. August of Virginia to succeed Peter Mallett of Fayetteville as commandant of conscripts in North Carolina disturbed the governor greatly. He felt that the selection smacked "of discourtesy toward our people."[50]

Neither did the "outrageous" conduct of certain Confederate troops operating in the state go unnoticed. When Vance learned that some "armed soldiers from Georgia" had carried off several citizens from Cherokee County, he called out the militia and instructed the men to shoot the first person "who attempts to perpetrate a similar outrage."[51]

Word of the Shelton-Laurel "Massacre," an infamous affair in February 1863, both shocked and infuriated Vance. It occurred after a band of "Tories" from the Shelton-Laurel section of Madison County in western North Carolina raided Marshall, the county seat, to get salt and clothing. Colonel J. A. Keith of the Sixty-fourth North Carolina rounded up thirteen suspects, mostly old men and boys, and had them shot under the most cold-blooded circumstances. The governor ordered an investigation and swore that he would follow Keith to the gates of hell to see him punished.[52]

The depredations of cavalry units on detached service also aroused Vance's ire. Near the end of the war he wrote Secretary of War Seddon: "If God Almighty had yet in store another plague—worse than all others which he intended to have let loose on the Egyptians in case Pharaoh still hardened in his heart, I am sure it must have been a regiment or so of half armed, half disciplined Confederate cavalry. . . . Unless something can be done, I shall be compelled in some sections to call out the militia and levy actual war against them."[53]

One of the bitterest disputes between the state of North Carolina and the Confederacy centered around conscription. Soldiers, lawyers, newspapers, and the public in general condemned this practice. Although

Vance thought the acts "harsh and ordicius," he acquiesced in conscription, as Governor Clark had done, "as a matter of necessity." He used the militia to enroll conscripts, boldly proclaiming that resistance to the law was treason. So energetically did he work that North Carolina provided the Confederate army with seven thousand more conscripts than any other state. Still the governor had his troubles with Richmond. A bitter dispute developed when Confederate authorities reneged on their promise to allow a conscript to choose his regiment if he enrolled willingly. Since Vance had such a promise from the president both verbally and in writing, he virtually accused the chief executive of acting in bad faith.[54]

On the other hand, there were very few controversies with Richmond authorities when the governor turned his attention to the difficult task of returning deserters to the ranks. Desertion had become such a problem by the spring of 1863 that General Lee complained that unless it could be stopped immediately the number of North Carolina soldiers in the Army of Northern Virginia would be greatly reduced.[55] Vance sympathized with the deserters to a degree but realized at the same time that the practice could not be condoned. He knew it would soon ruin the armies in the field.

Vance ordered the militia to arrest Confederate deserters, only to have Judge R. M. Pearson, chief justice of the North Carolina supreme court and a strong critic of Confederate policies, rule that the state's chief executive had no authority to enforce Confederate laws. This meant that Vance could not use militiamen to arrest deserters from North Carolina regiments. There followed a "tortuous duel" between Vance and Pearson in which the governor sought legal means of helping the Confederacy keep the troops. In the process he found himself accused of "trampling the judiciary underfoot." This hurt Vance because in North Carolina a highly individualistic population very often resorted to the courts on constitutional grounds. Finally, a reluctant legislature authorized state forces to arrest deserters and recalcitrant conscripts.[56]

Throughout the war the Confederate government attempted to brush aside civil authority when it seemed to hamper the war effort, but every such move in North Carolina met the determined opposition of Governor Vance. Among the first civil rights clashes involved the arbitrary arrest by Confederate authorities of North Carolinians suspected of being disloyal. Those imprisoned were seldom charged and they were later released without being tried. This infuriated Vance. The fact that the Congress of the Confederacy had on February 27, 1862, authorized the suspension of the writ of habeas corpus under certain circumstances altered his thinking little. The governor considered the conduct of the Confederate officers "to be in defiance of North Carolina's civil law and in violation of the rights of her citizens." He declared it was his duty to protect the rights of the people, especially their right to a fair trial. Long after the war was over, one of Vance's proudest boasts was that in North Carolina "the laws were heard amidst the roar of cannon."[57]

Another serious problem developed in the spring of 1863 when Richmond began to ignore adverse decisions of state courts. Judge Pearson ruled that the Conscription Act of September 1862 did not apply to substitutes, though the War Department had ruled to the contrary.[58] Confederate authorities, already annoyed with Pearson for his rulings on the use of state troops to arrest deserters, decided to ignore the decision and so instructed the enrolling officers. This brought Vance into the controversy. He could not allow the substitution of martial law for civil law, and he made it clear to Secretary Seddon that the rulings of the state's judges must be respected by Confederate authorities until overturned by a higher judicial authority.[59]

The controversy with Seddon abated none in early 1864 when the Confederate Congress abolished substitution and made the principals of substitutes liable to military service. Judge Pearson, in the E. S. Walton case, ruled that Congress had no right to violate contracts made with principals of substitutes and discharged Walton, who had applied for a writ of habeas corpus on the grounds that having furnished a substitute he was exempt from military service. At the same time Judges W. H. Battle and M. E. Manly of the state supreme court in similar cases refused to issue the writ on the grounds that Congress had suspended it. Vance deplored the withdrawal of "this time-honored and blood-bought guard of personal freedom." The result of all this was total confusion. Ignoring the position of his colleagues, Pearson continued to release principals. Enrolling officers, in turn, ignored Pearson, which put Vance in a quandary. While he did not wish to deprive the Confederate army of badly needed replacements by protecting those released by Pearson, neither could he allow Richmond to defy the state judiciary. The controversy, certainly in Vance's best interest, was settled before he was forced to take any direct action against Confederate authorities. In June 1864 the North Carolina supreme court in a two to one decision overruled the chief justice and upheld the constitutionality of the act conscripting the principals of substitutes. With this decision the immediate crisis passed.[60]

Vance was seldom allowed to deal with one crisis at a time. While the dispute over substitution was in progress, he became involved in another wordy conflict with the Confederacy. This time it was the question of exemption from military service of state personnel. From the beginning Vance insisted that he had the authority to exempt from military service all men whom he considered necessary to administer state affairs. On March 20, 1863, he expressed this view in a letter to Colonel August, the Virginian commanding North Carolina conscripts: "All state officers and employees necessary to the operation of this government—of which necessity I must judge—shall not be interfered with by enrolling officers, and any attempt to arrest such men will be resisted."[61] August referred the letter to General G. B. Rains of the conscription bureau, who informed the governor that the law "exempts judicial and executive officers of State Government, except those liable to military duty. This, you will readily perceive, must be the rule of guidance for the agents of this bureau."[62]

Realizing that he stood little chance of getting the executive branch of the Confederate government to change its position, Vance turned with good results to the North Carolina delegation in the Confederate Congress. The legislative body passed a law in May 1863 that was completely satisfactory to the governor. It provided for the exemption of all officers whom Vance claimed were necessary for the "due administration" of the laws of the state, provided the General Assembly confirmed the list. By 1864 the number of those exempt had been extended to such a point that it even included textile workers in those factories where the state had contracts for the manufacture of clothing.[63]

The special arrangement with the Confederacy by which North Carolina had agreed to clothe its own troops was no less an issue for Vance than it had been for his predecessor Governor Clark.[64] In October 1862 Richmond abolished commutation for clothing and at the same time tried to persuade the state to share its textile products. Quartermaster General Myers requested that the governor turn over clothing contracts to the Confederacy. Vance not only refused but proceeded to negotiate new agreements. North Carolina, alone among Southern states, monopolized the entire output of its factories throughout the war.[65]

The clothing situation was extremely critical in the fall of 1862. Uniform material for over sixty thousand North Carolina troops had to be found. To get through the autumn and winter, Vance resorted to a number of temporary expedients, but he realized that a more permanent solution had to be found. It was under these circumstances that the governor turned to blockade-running. The idea was not his own. He entered this hazardous yet profitable business on behalf of the state at the suggestion of Adjutant General James G. Martin, who in August 1862 had asked Governor Clark for permission to buy supplies abroad and a ship to transport them. Since the governor's term was about to expire, he requested that the matter lie over until his successor took office. Vance hesitated momentarily because of strong opposition to the project in some quarters, but the opportunities were too inviting for him to ignore them for long.[66]

After perfecting his plans, he went before the legislature in closed session and prevailed upon that body to appropriate $2 million for the inauguration of the venture. With the appropriation the governor bought cotton and stored it. Warrants or certificates were issued on the basis of the cotton. The purchaser of the warrant was entitled to have cotton delivered to any port east of the Mississippi upon sixty days notice, but it was his responsibility to get the cotton out of the Confederacy. With the money from the sale of the warrants a steamer and supplies were to be purchased. After unloading its cargo in Wilmington, the vessel would take on cotton to finance the purchase of additional supplies by the state.[67] Only the Federal blockade threatened the success of the enterprise.[68]

Vance selected John White, a highly successful Scottish-born merchant of Warrenton, to be his European agent. White was to be assisted by Captain Thomas M. Crossan, a fellow townsman who had seen service in both the United States and Confederate navies. The performance of White was truly remarkable. Arriving in England in late 1862 with neither business connections nor influence, he managed to make favorable financial arrangements with the London banking house of Alexander Collie and Co. Shortly afterwards the fast steamer *Clyde* was purchased for $190,000. Rechristened the *Advance,* she unloaded her first cargo in Wilmington on June 26, 1863. By October Vance could boast that he could ensure clothing for North Carolina's troops until 1865.[69]

Blockade-running was so successful that part interest was acquired in three other vessels, the *Don, Hansa,* and *Annie.* Subsequently the state sold one-half interest in the *Advance* to Power, Lowe and Co. of Wilmington for the profitable sum of $350,000. In February 1864 Vance wrote E. J. Hale of Fayetteville that he had built up a credit for the state in the Bank of England of $400,000, had sent money to North Carolina soldiers in northern prisons, and had distributed thousands of uniforms, shoes, and blankets. He was elated also that "North Carolina warrants in England were commanding a premium."[70] However, he did not tell his friend that another acrimonious dispute with Richmond was beginning to cloud the picture considerably. The controversy had started in 1863 when the Confederacy began commandeering a third of the cargo space on all blockade-runners with the exception of state-owned vessels. Vance assumed that ships partially owned by the state of North Carolina would be exempt, but he was in for a surprise.

Confederate authorities, far from agreeing with him, upped their claim in the spring of 1864 to one-half the cargo space. The governor exclaimed that the "port of Wilmington is now more effectively blockaded from within than from without." It seemed most strange to him that his efforts at blockade-running, instead of being encouraged, were being met with "little else than downright opposition." This was most difficult for Vance to understand since his endeavors had been so beneficial to the Confederacy.[71]

North Carolina's blockade-runners, however, brought in goods for the civilian as well as the soldier in the field. A large portion of the cargoes consisted of nonmilitary items. This was not surprising because Vance brought to the governor's office in 1862 a deep concern for the welfare of the civilian who was already beginning to feel the hardships of war.

The governor believed that speculation in essential goods and hoarding were the primary causes of the distress. He persuaded the General Assembly in 1862 to give him permission to place an embargo on food and clothing, and for nearly a year it was illegal to ship certain "necessities" from the state. The embargo lowered some prices temporarily, but the permanent evils of speculation remained.[72]

In an effort to protect the supply of food further, Vance put through the legislature in late 1862 a drastic law prohibiting the distillation of liquor from "any kind of grain including rice, also potatoes, sugar cane, seed, syrup, molasses, peas, peanuts, and dried fruit of every description." The Raleigh *Progress* observed that the governor "thinks as all other honest people do that bread is better than whiskey." Curtailments were also placed on the planting of cotton and tobacco. In an eloquent appeal to the planters of North Carolina Vance proclaimed that "there is . . . but one danger to our speedy and triumph success, and that is the failure of our provisions."[73]

The governor's proclamation was issued in April 1863, shortly after the Confederate Congress had adopted impressment policies allowing quartermaster and commissary officers to impress food supplies and other produce at prices below the market price. This program hurt the small farmer most. It fell upon him with crushing severity and added greatly to the overall economic distress in the state.

Although Vance met with little success in his attempts to relieve suffering by striking at the causes, he was still able, with the help of the legislature, to provide the people with some of the necessities of life.[74] He turned to direct relief which he believed was a proper function of government. His first concern was salt, in which speculation was particularly grievous. More state saltworks were established on the coast, and thousands of bushels of this scarce item were distributed to the people at one-third the cost. Also, using state money Vance bought and stored provisions for resale at low prices to soldiers' families and the poor. The transactions were conducted through county agencies. During the war the state appropriated $6 million for relief, with counties furnishing additional funds. The governor wanted the General Assembly to assume the entire relief burden but the legislators refused.[75]

Vance without question did much to ease the burdens of war for the people. This accomplishment, more than any other one thing, gained for him their lasting affection. Their votes, in turn, made it easier for him to defeat the peace movement of 1864, which came at a time when many North Carolinians were sick of the war and longed for an end to hostilities.

There had been some manifestation of discontent early in the conflict,[76] but this disaffection did not take on serious proportions until the summer of 1863. In August of that year alone more than twenty counties held public meetings and adopted peace resolutions of remarkable similarity. These were published regularly in the Raleigh Standard whose editor, W. W. Holden, was emerging as the leader of the discontented. The governor at first moved cautiously, seeking to kill the movement by personally persuading Holden to abandon it, only to learn in December that if he refused to call a peace convention, the editor would oppose his reelection in 1864. "I cannot of course favour such a thing for any existing cause," wrote Vance. "I will see the Conservative party blown into a thousand atoms and Holden and his understrappers in hell . . . before I will consent to a course which I think would bring dishonor and ruin upon both State and Confederacy!"[77]

Having made the decision to fight Holden, his erstwhile political ally, Vance still waited two months before openly plunging into his campaign at Wilkesboro, a mountain town in the very heart of the disaffected area. On February 22 a crowd of two thousand turned out to hear the governor strike the first blow. A few days earlier a peace meeting had nominated Holden for the governorship, and in a special March edition of the Standard the editor officially announced his candidacy, promising the voters an honorable peace.

In the bitter gubernatorial contest of 1864 Vance urged the Confederate government to negotiate with the Union for peace, but he strongly denounced separate state action designed to end hostilities, which he insisted was his opponent's primary objective. He also called for a united front until independence was achieved.

On July 28 the soldiers went to the polls and gave Vance 13,209 out of 15,033 votes cast. The victory was made complete on August 4 when the civilians cast their ballots. Holden carried only three counties. Now there was no danger, if there ever had been, of North Carolina leaving the Confederacy.[78]

From the moment of his reelection to the end of the war Vance worked tirelessly in behalf of the Confederate cause, but his task was not easy. By the fall of 1864 Atlanta was in Federal hands and Lee was bottled up behind his fortifications at Petersburg. In January 1865 Fort Fisher fell. The next month Wilmington capitulated and in March General William T. Sherman entered the state, after having applied total war in its fullest to South Carolina. Fayetteville was occupied on the eleventh.

Governor Vance attempted to rally his people, but he had little to offer them other than encouragement and proclamations, which alone could not stop an army of over sixty thousand. After defeating Joseph E. Johnston at Bentonville on March 19–21, Sherman entered Goldsboro, where he remained until April 10. On that date he put his army in motion for Raleigh in pursuit of Johnston, who was retiring in the same direction.

During the evening of the eleventh Sherman learned of Lee's surrender at Appomattox, and the next day he was visited by peace commissioners David L. Swain and William A. Graham out of Raleigh. These two elderly ex-governors had been sent by Vance to confer with the general about the peaceful surrender of the capital.

When the commissioners failed to return by late afternoon of the twelfth, Vance decided to leave Raleigh, which was being evacuated by the Confederates. He lingered until midnight, then mounting his horse rode eight miles west to General Hoke's camp.[79] The next day he proceeded to Hillsboro, where he learned that President Davis wished to see him. The two leaders met at Charlotte.[80] From there Vance hastened to Greensboro, intending to go on to Raleigh and resume his duties as governor. However, he was not permitted to pass through military lines while the surrender negotiations between Sherman and Johnston were in progress at the James Bennett farmhouse near Durham. The original agreement signed by the generals on the eighteenth was turned down by Washington; so they met again at the Bennett homestead, where on the twenty-sixth Sherman granted and Johnston accepted terms similar to those Lee had received at Appomattox.

Shortly afterwards Vance issued his final proclamation to the people of North Carolina, urging them to remain at home and "to abstain from any and all acts of lawlessness."[81] He then surrendered himself to General J. M. Schofield, who, having no orders for the governor's arrest, told him to go to Statesville and remain with his family, which had earlier sought refuge there. Early on the morning of May 13,

Vance's thirty-fifth birthday, Federal cavalry surrounded his house and Major J. M. Porter presented an order for his arrest. Grant directed that the "late Rebel Governor of North Carolina" be sent to Washington under close guard. On the twentieth he was placed in the Old Capitol Prison where he remained until paroled on July 6, 1865. Vance returned to North Carolina and set up a law partnership in Charlotte. No explanation was ever given for his short imprisonment, and no charges were ever brought against him.[82]

While still in prison Vance filed an application for pardon which was granted on March 11, 1867. Three years later he was elected to the United States Senate, but he was never seated because of disabilities placed upon him by the Fourteenth Amendment. These were later removed, and in 1876 he ran successfully for the governorship on the Democratic ticket against Republican Thomas Settle of Rockingham County. The two candidates stumped North Carolina in one of the most dramatic campaigns in the state's history. Huge crowds turned out at every stop to hear the two able men debate.

Vance's third term as governor was marked by gains in education and railroad building as well by the end of political Reconstruction. He served only two of his four years, however, because the legislature by acclamation elected him to the United States Senate upon the expiration of A. S. Merrimon's term. Vance resigned the governorship in January 1879. Reelected to the Senate in 1885 and again in 1891, he remained in that body until his death. His career in the upper house of Congress was rather undistinguished. He opposed much of the important legislation of the day, including civil service reform, and became known as an opposition senator.

Vance's health began to fail in 1889. He died five years later at his home in Washington. His body was returned to Asheville for burial. As his funeral train wound its way slowly through North Carolina, thousands of people lined the tracks to pay their last respects to a beloved leader. Stations were thronged with mourners. On the day of the funeral it rained in Asheville, yet ten thousand marched in a procession through a city draped in mourning. That day and the next memorial services were held throughout the state. A friend commented: "No North Carolinian ever had such a funeral and it is doubtful if any citizen of the state . . . ever had a like funeral—such a universal going forth of the people."[83]

Vance was married twice. His first wife, Harriette Espy of Quaker Meadows, North Carolina, died in Raleigh on November 3, 1878, at the age of forty-six. In 1880 he married Florence Steele Martin, a widow from Louisville, Kentucky. She survived him.

"Zeb" Vance won the hearts and confidence of the great mass of people to a degree equaled by no other leader in the state's history. His role as war governor was largely responsible for this endearment. During the hard years of conflict he exhibited qualities of leadership that gained for him the people's lasting affection. "The crowning glory of his administration," observed one authority, "remains the untiring care and unstinted labor he devoted to the provision of every possible comfort for the soldiers and for their families. . . . He . . . [also] defended their liberties and preserved their priceless honor. These things were the solid foundations of his place in their minds and hearts, and of his place in history."[84]

SOUTH CAROLINA

John B. Edmunds, Jr.

outh Carolina was seething with emotion by the middle of November 1860. Abraham Lincoln had been elected president and the state was on the verge of secession. At this critical period Francis Wilkinson Pickens returned home from Russia where he had been serving as United States minister to the Court of Alexander II. Pickens enjoyed the reputation as a South Carolina moderate and conformed to that image on his journey home. He was distressed that many Europeans were laughing at the pretentious Palmetto State, and confessed to some of his fellow passengers that he believed the Carolinians were being foolishly precipitous and that he hoped to use his influence to urge them to pursue a course of moderation.[1]

Pickens's family had enjoyed prominence in South Carolina since the period of the Revolutionary War. His grandfather was the hero of the Battle of Cowpens, and his father had served the state as governor. Although Francis was born in Colleton District on April 7, 1807, he lived for most of his life in Edgefield. He attended South Carolina College and read law under his father-in-law, Eldred Simkins. He began practicing law in 1828 and managed several plantations which he had acquired by inheritance or marriage.

Well educated, wealthy, and a kinsman of John C. Calhoun, Pickens found politics irresistible. In 1832 he was elected to the General Assembly, where he took a prominent role in the Nullification controversy; and in 1834 he was elected to Congress, where for ten years he served as Calhoun's chief spokesman in the House. After his retirement from Congress he was elected to the state Senate, and in 1850 he took an active lead in urging South Carolina to reject the Compromise of 1850 and to secede from the Union. Two years later he joined with the moderates led by Benjamin F. Perry and James L. Orr and urged

South Carolina to abandon radicalism and cooperate with its sister southern states to promote southern unity. After losing a heated race for the United States Senate to James H. Hammond, the twice-widowed Pickens married Lucy Holcombe, a beauty from Texas who was many years younger than he, and departed for Russia after being named minister by President Buchanan. Upon hearing of the tension that was gripping the Union, he resigned his post in the spring of 1860.[2]

When Pickens arrived home he was not against secession but was opposed to separate state action, espousing the essentially moderate view of southern cooperation.[3] However, the infectious radicalism that took control in South Carolina following the election of Lincoln overwhelmed him. The Palmetto State was in the process of becoming the "Palmetto Republic," and the passion of the times was sweeping ordinarily moderate men into its vortex. In a speech delivered before the state legislature in Columbia on November 30, 1860, Pickens explained away his past moderation and excited the hot-blooded Carolinians with burning rhetoric, stating that he would be willing "to appeal to the god of battles—if need be, cover the state with ruin, conflagration and blood rather than submit." He was not only telling the attentive masses what they wanted to hear but was helping pave his way to the governor's office, where he would assist in leading his state down the road to ruin, conflagration, and bloodshed.[4]

The keenly observant Mary Boykin Chesnut, whose husband had recently resigned his seat in the United States Senate, commented on Pickens's reversal. "Wigfall [Louis T.]," she wrote, "says that before he left Washington, . . . Pickens and [William H.] Trescot were openly against secession. Trescot does not pretend to like it now but Pickens is a fire-eater down to the ground."[5]

State politicians widely predicted that Robert Barnwell Rhett, the so-called father of secession, would be elected governor, but many people opposed his election, fearing that he was too radical even for radical South Carolina. On December 16 the state legislature in joint session began the process of selecting a governor who would serve the state for the next two years. When the Rhett forces were unable to gather enough votes, Rhett dropped out of the contest on the fifth ballot, and Pickens won the race by a bare majority on the seventh ballot.[6]

Pickens's election aroused little enthusiasm. He won because he had not been a controversial figure during the years immediately preceding the secession controversy and because in the past he had advocated southern cooperation. His election broke a sixteen-year-old unwritten arrangement that had provided alternation of the governorship between up-country and low country. Many South Carolinians were hopeful that his election would bring harmony to the turbulent state. M. L. Bonham expressed the view of many when he wrote: "We see that Pickens is elected, but do not know what it indicates."[7] "All are for action now" was the way another contemporary expressed the feeling of the day,[8] but no one, including Pickens himself, knew what would be forthcoming from the new governor. One thing is certain: he was to have problems such as no other chief executive of South Carolina had experienced or would experience.

Some of his many difficulties were caused by misunderstandings; others were caused by outside influences. Unfortunately the new governor lacked the magnetism so essential for those in public life. He was a man of ideas, an acute observer but not a man of positive action.[9] His chief fault was his inability to draw men close to him. "I believe it my destiny," he wrote, "to be disliked by all who know me well."[10]

"South Carolinians had exasperated and heated themselves into a fever that only bloodletting could cure," wrote Mrs. Chesnut.[11] Now, as never before, the Palmetto State was in need of able leadership. On December 20, 1860, four days after Pickens took office, the secession convention proclaimed that South Carolina was no longer part of the Union.

Three days prior to secession, Pickens began trying to solve a problem that was irritating the Carolinians. The Federal forts in Charleston harbor were regarded as both a threat and an insult to the Palmetto State. Unfortunately, Pickens's first efforts at diplomacy were unsuccessful; instead of solving the problem, he further exacerbated it. He wrote President Buchanan claiming that the forts were being prepared to turn their guns on the city and the United States arsenal had been turned over to South Carolina. In this same letter Pickens requested the president to permit him to send a small force to take possession of Fort Sumter.[12] The president became alarmed and called in William H. Trescot, who was acting unofficially as South Carolina's representative in Washington. Trescot, who had hoped for moderation, became quite distressed after reading the governor's letter.

Pickens in this instance had made the first of many blunders. Actually the arsenal had not been turned over to South Carolina, and though General Winfield Scott was advocating that the forts be reinforced, this had not been ordered. Yet Pickens had now raised the critical issue of Fort Sumter. Trescot had hoped that the crucial situation would rest in a state of limbo until commissioners could be sent to bargain for the forts. A telegram was dispatched to the governor urging him to withdraw his letter. This Pickens did, but in this instance he proved that "his zeal was stronger than his discretion."[13]

South Carolina and its new governor seemed to Buchanan desirous of unleashing the war dogs. The frantic president sent his friend Caleb Cushing to South Carolina to find a means to maintain the status quo. However, it should have been apparent to Buchanan that nothing would calm the enraged South Carolinians. Already he had sacrificed his personal prestige by pandering to them.[14]

At this time the secession convention was in full progress in Charleston and excitement was even higher than usual. Pickens realized that there was to be no turning back and informed Cushing that there was no hope for Union.[15] The convention, which had assumed extraordinary powers, ordered Pickens to "prevent any garrisoning of the fortresses or mounting of guns thereon," and resolved that any attempt by the United States to build up the fortifications would be regarded "as an overt act of hostility."

The overt act of hostility that many thought would occur took place during the evening of December 26, 1860. The convention had requested the governor to exercise the utmost vigilance. This Pickens ordered done.[16] Charleston harbor was constantly patrolled to prevent any movement from Fort Moultrie to Fort Sumter by the small Union force under its new commander, Major Robert Anderson. Pickens had come under verbal fire prior to the movement of Anderson to Fort Sumter as a result of his refusal to order the forts seized. During this period Trescot had been assuring Pickens that Sumter would not be occupied by the military.[17] But Trescot's reassuring letter and Pickens's constant vigil did not prevent Major Anderson from moving his entire force from untenable Fort Moultrie to the strong bastion of Sumter. It was not until the next morning that the Carolinians discovered that Anderson had moved. The maneuver that Pickens had so carefully guarded against had been precipitated right under his nose. He had been criticized in the past, but he now knew what it was to be the target of a continuous barrage of abusive scorn. Wade Hampton referred to him as a "fool," and Mrs. Chesnut as a "sleeping dead head."[18] Pickens reacted to the clamor of public opinion and occupied the Federal properties in and around Charleston. Moultrie was occupied, and shortly afterwards Castle Pinckney was seized. The governor also ordered Morris Island in Charleston harbor fortified, and at the same time gave the order for the occupation of the United States arsenal and other Federal properties.

On the same day, December 30, 1860, Pickens ordered all communications between Anderson and the city cut off, except for food and the mails. He also forbade the sending of supplies to Fort Sumter. Activity of every description was taking place in Charleston harbor as South Carolina's commander in chief ordered the harbor fortified as quickly as possible. Up until this time no significant steps had been taken to place the Charleston area on a military footing. The governor's critics berated him, probably unfairly, because of the poor condition of the defenses.

Despite the criticism that he was receiving, Pickens still seemed to enjoy the confidence of the convention, which gave him extraordinary powers. It created an Executive Council which was to act as a cabinet. This council, consisting of the lieutenant governor and four other members, was designed to represent the convention within the administration and to serve both as an aid and a restraint upon Pickens. Council members were to be nominated by the governor and confirmed by the convention. Actually this council was simply an advisory board, with the governor retaining the right of final decision over any suggestions that it might present.[19] The governor was authorized by the convention to wage war, negotiate treaties, and send and receive ambassadors, and his appointive powers were greatly increased. Pickens was given the responsibility of negotiating with Buchanan and sending commissioners to other southern states to urge secession. In reality he was no longer a state governor in the usual sense of the word. Rather, he assumed the duties as the executive head of the sovereign Palmetto Republic.

Among the problems that confronted Pickens in this role was the need to erect coastal defenses and provide troops to man them. It appears that virtually everyone in the new republic wanted a commission or a position in the new government. The state militia was inadequate and had to be armed, trained, and provided with leadership. Before South Carolina joined the Confederacy all actions dealing with the military and logistics were the direct responsibility of South Carolina's chief executive. If the independent state was to be recognized by foreign powers, it was necessary that South Carolina inaugurate a program of diplomacy. Pickens tried his hand at diplomacy by attempting to form a relationship with the foreign power he knew best, Russia. All intelligence and engineering reports had to be reviewed and it was his decision as to how they would be handled. South Carolina had embarked on a new and dangerous experiment, and at the time of secession no plans had been formulated to provide the state with a government adequate to its needs. The problems that Pickens had to face would have been immense if secession had occurred under the most favorable circumstances, but with war clouds on the horizon and a frenzied populace, the pressures were immeasurable.[20]

"The Charlestonians are surrounding us with batteries on every point of land in the vicinity," reported Captain Abner Doubleday of the Fort Sumter garrison, ". . . this is done with the hope of preventing any vessel from coming to our assistance with a view to force us ultimately to surrender the fort."[21]

Buchanan decided that Fort Sumter should be reinforced, but took a long time in implementing his decision. At first he planned to send a warship to the fort, but he was dissuaded from taking such action. Instead he arranged to have a merchant vessel, the *Star of the West,* transport reinforcements to Charleston harbor. The ship set sail on January 5, 1861, bound officially for New Orleans. Louis T. Wigfall, a former Edgefield neighbor who had become United States senator from Texas, telegraphed Pickens that the *Star of the West* had set sail and should be expected in South Carolina waters.[22]

On January 9 an action took place that ordinarily would have precipitated war. On that morning the *Star of the West* entered Charleston harbor. The guns on Morris Island and Fort Moultrie fired on the ship, scoring several hits, but Major Anderson did not permit Fort Sumter's guns to retaliate. The Union commander asked the governor whether the attack on the ship was committed in obedience to his orders, and he warned Pickens that if the act were not disclaimed he would regard it as an act of war, and would not permit any vessel to pass within the range of the guns of Fort Sumter. Pickens explained that he had an understanding with Anderson's government to the effect that if Union troops were sent to reinforce Fort Sumter it would be regarded as an act of hostility. He continued: "In regard to your threat in regard to vessels, it is only necessary for me to say that you must judge of your responsibility." Anderson replied that he intended to turn the whole matter over to his government.[23]

The defenses around Charleston harbor were still in deplorable condition. The governor was reprieved by Anderson's decision not to use his cannon until he received instructions from Washington. The time that it would take Anderson's courier to reach Washington and return was put to good use. On the same day that the *Star of the West* was fired upon, Pickens called together three engineering officers and one ordnance officer to "consider and report the most favorable plan for operating upon Fort Sumter, so as to reduce the fortress, by batteries and other means in our possession."[24]

Isaac W. Hayne, the attorney general of South Carolina, was dispatched to Washington with a message to Buchanan in which Pickens stated that he regarded Fort Sumter as a threat and demanded that it be delivered to the state. Pickens instructed Hayne to tell the president that continued possession of Sumter by Anderson's troops would "inevitably lead to a bloody issue."[25] Hayne arrived in Washington on January 12, 1861, and had an unofficial interview with Buchanan two days later. The senators of other southern states that had seceded or were on the verge of secession requested Hayne to defer from delivering the governor's letter until they made suggestions to both Buchanan and Pickens.

By this time war had also become the concern of the other southern states. They were hopeful that hostilities could be avoided until after the meeting of the convention that was scheduled to assemble on February 4 in Montgomery, Alabama, to consider the formation of the Confederate States of America.[26]

Buchanan was content to leave matters in an unresolved state, but this Pickens could not do. Complicated maneuvering, which included an offer to purchase Sumter, was tried by the governor, but the president made it clear that he had no more right to cede Fort Sumter to South Carolina than he had the right to sell the capital of the United States to Maryland. The people of South Carolina were becoming more and more irritated with the situation. Buchanan had no desire to precipitate war; thus, he allowed the undeclared truce to remain in effect so long as South Carolina respected it. But it was becoming more difficult for Pickens to refrain from taking action. The highly critical *Mercury* asked: "Will South Carolina sit quietly with folded arms, and see a fort garrisoned by our enemies, armed with the power to forbid the egress and engress of vessels into and out the harbor? Never."[27]

Cooler heads were advising Pickens to make no move to increase tension until after the Confederacy was formed. Jefferson Davis believed that the *Star of the West* episode put the governor in the best position to stall until the Confederate government could "speak with a voice which all must hear and heed."[28]

In a letter to Davis, Pickens explained that he had no plans to take Fort Sumter. Yet the governor was faced with conflicting pressures as the month of January came to a close. Leaders of other southern states were urging forbearance, but in South Carolina the overwhelming sentiment was for an immediate storming of the fortress. The Columbia *Southern Guardian* asked: "Why is not Fort Sumter attacked?"[29] Criticism mounted. Pickens was accused of being negligent and of using poor judgment. James L. Petigru, the famous South Carolina Unionist, expressed the view that Pickens was a "windy," ineffective governor.[30] William Henry Ravenel, a prominent planter and botanist wrote, "There is great dissatisfaction prevailing at the course of Governor Pickens."[31]

The wrath of the firebrands increased, but still Pickens did not order an attack on Sumter. He seemed prepared to be personally vilified rather than permit the hotheads to have their way. Matters continued to drag on while tempers remained feverish. The South Carolina delegates at the Montgomery convention presented that assembly with a clear ultimatum to either unite and accept the Sumter problem as a common obligation or let South Carolina attack the fort. Robert Toombs, secretary of state of the new Confederacy, urged that Sumter not be attacked without the sanction of the Confederate government. In the situation Pickens saw an opportunity to lift the Sumter burden from his shoulders. He wrote Toombs that if the Confederate Congress would indicate jurisdiction, "then I could not hesitate to abide most cheerfully by your control."[32]

After the new Congress decided to shoulder the burden of Sumter, the governor abandoned his cautious attitude and joined the chorus of Carolinians in urging that the fort be taken immediately. He informed Toombs that he was prepared to take the necessary steps. In the last days of February he wrote his wife, who had gone to visit her family in Texas, that he fully intended to take the fort and had five hundred picked men ready to storm it.[33] In a speech to the Citadel cadets which he made while "about half drunk," he reiterated the often repeated promise of taking the fort.[34] On March 6, Brigadier General P. T. G. Beauregard arrived and ordered even more fortifications built in the harbor.

Meanwhile, Lincoln had been inaugurated on March 4. In his inaugural address he vowed that the power confided to him would be used to hold, occupy, and possess the property and places belonging to the government. There were attempts by the Confederate government at negotiating with the new president, but they were to no avail. When Lincoln ultimately determined to provision the fort, the inevitable occurred. Firing commenced on April 12, 1861, and Pickens was jubilant over what had been precipitated. After the cannonade those who in the past had cursed him applauded. Pickens, who had never been known for his humility, was puffed with pride when he spoke to the masses in the street from the balcony of the Charleston Hotel. In a speech full of "I's" he stated that the "triumphant and victorius results" were not attributable to his skill: nevertheless, he did not fail to remind the crowd that "I was determined to maintain our separate independence and freedom at any and every hazard. . . . when I knew we were prepared, I was ready to strike. . . . we have rallied: we have met them. . . . let it lead to what it might, even if it leads to blood and ruin. . . . we have defeated their twenty millions, we have met them and conquered them."[35] War was now the prospect, but in the closing days of April excitement and joy ruled the Palmetto State.

The brief moments of popularity that the governor enjoyed faded quickly. Critical decisions had to be made. Actions that affected the lives of numerous South Carolinians had to be taken. Pickens had to authorize the departure of military units from South Carolina. The units from the Palmetto State were better organized than similar units from other southern states. The ordering of volunteer regiments out of the state subjected the governor to bitter criticism. His action in support of the Confederate army was not the only thing that aroused critics. He had failed to consult the Executive Council that the secession convention had appointed to advise him. D. F. Jamison, president of the convention, became one of the governor's chief critics, and Secretary of State A. G. Magrath dissociated himself from the chief executive. For all practical purposes the Executive Council ceased to function after April 1861. Later, as the situation deteriorated in 1862, a new council was created.[36] William Gilmore Simms complained to James Hammond that "Pickens is such an ass that he will drive away from him every decent counselor. . . . his vanity throws him open to the most contemptible advisers, all who flatter him can rule him. He has caused the most infinite degree of blundering and has offended many."[37]

Pickens was unpopular, but it would appear that anyone who held his awesome responsibility would have met the same fate. The fact that it was necessary for him to declare martial law in the coastal regions of South Carolina in order to secure the areas against infiltration and attack diminished his popularity. South Carolina's troops had to be provisioned, not only with war materials but also with foodstuffs, medicines, and many other essentials. Certainly, no one appreciated having his goods or slaves requisitioned by the state's procurement officers. Another source of difficulty was the matter of appointments. The governor's office was besieged with requests for commissions and it was impossible to satisfy all those who clamored for office. These same problems were to vex not only Pickens but also the two future Civil War governors, M. L. Bonham and A. G. Magrath.

Some of the criticism leveled at Pickens was no doubt valid. He lacked tact and often equivocated in his decisions. Frequently he was overcautious, and there were times when his temperament led him to dramatic and impetuous actions. Throughout the summer and fall of 1861 public hostility continued unabated. In his annual message to the legislature on November 5, 1861, Pickens made no attempt to rally the people. Instead, he recalled the glories of secession and the onslaught against Fort Sumter.[38] Two days later a force of twelve thousand Union soldiers invaded the Port Royal region of South Carolina. This action revealed that the state's defenses had not been adequately prepared. There was real fear that Union soldiers might be able to take Charleston. Discontent increased. The *Courier* later claimed that "the governor was doing nothing for the benefit of the state, but much to produce confusion."[39]

Criticism aimed at Pickens and the legislature became extremely acute and developed into a crisis of faith. On December 27, 1861, during the height of the crisis, D. F. Jamison, the president of the secession convention, decided to take action to curb the governor. The convention was called back into session and Attorney General Isaac Hayne quickly assumed leadership. The convention decided to take steps to improve the state's defenses. Charleston was ordered strengthened against naval and land attacks, and a new Executive Council was created.

The convention, through the new council, assumed control over the governor and provided for an executive body unique in American political history. A plural executive was created that was to consist of the governor, the lieutenant governor, and three members to be elected by the convention. All decisions were to be made by a majority of the Executive Council. The council was to have control over the military and power to declare martial law, to arrest and detain disloyal and disaffected persons, and to impress private property for the public good, as well as control over the public treasury.[40]

Pickens was furious. He had expected some regulation, but complete emasculation of his office was something that he had never contemplated. He expressed his dismay to the convention when he wrote, "I seriously think the ordinance you have just passed, will, in its practical applications weaken the executive as created by the constitution."[41]

Jamison tried to placate the now virtually powerless Pickens by urging him in the name of patriotism to submit gracefully.[42] Eventually the tide of public opinion which had been running against Pickens began to turn in his favor. The loyal Edgefield Advertiser praised the governor and lamented the "denudation of his office by the sovereigns."[43]

The newly formed council was not to be South Carolina's panacea. Five men with varying personalities and desires could not possibly agree at all times with each other. The council from its very beginning was involved in both internal and external controversy. It became more dictatorial than the governor and possessed almost unlimited powers, which were used to adopt strong measures in order to meet the enemy. The council had more power than any government South Carolinians had ever known. It encompassed both executive and legislative prerogatives. The council's most important task was raising troops by means of conscription, a measure that proved to be increasingly more unpopular. More anger was generated as the council impressed slaves into service as laborers and made plans to confiscate gold, silver plate, and vital war materials.[44]

The Edgefield Advertiser called the council a "five headed dictatorship." A writer signing himself "South Carolina" wrote to the Mercury claiming that the supremacy of the council should give way to the Confederate government.[45] As the council carried out its plans to recruit more slaves for labor duty and cooperated with the Confederate government in drafting more and more men into military service its popularity waned and the popularity of the governor, who had been openly opposed to the council, increased. Mrs. Chesnut, whose husband was the member of the council in charge of the state's military operations, claimed that the council was losing popularity because of "Pickens' miserable jealousy."[46] As the council undertook more austerity measures, newspapers across the state published denunciations. The Charleston *Courier,* a Unionist paper, charged that the council was guilty of inefficiency and of squandering the public money "at will and pleasure." It was, in short, said the *Courier,* "a snake which ought to be scotched and killed."[47] Voices of the defenders of the experiment were lost in the clamor of criticism. As South Carolinians tired of the council, many demanded that the convention be reconvened. President Jamison issued a call for that body to meet on September 9, 1862. At this meeting a committee of twenty-one was given the task of reviewing the record of the council. The committee was impressed with the council's labors, but the people, swayed by emotion, were not. The convention decided that the future of the council should be left to the legislature. The convention adjourned on September 17, a few weeks before legislative elections were held in October.[48]

In his opening message to the General Assembly, Pickens lambasted the council. The legislature, feeling that the council had usurped its powers, was almost unanimous in its condemnation. Thus, on December 18, 1862, the legislature brought an end to South Carolina's unique experiment by abolishing the Executive Council and declaring all of its acts, resolutions, and proceedings to be invalid. Pickens emerged from the controversy with a popularity greater than he had ever enjoyed. One measure that caused the council to lose popularity was a plan to confiscate all gold and silver in private hands and issue paper on it. It is interesting to note that Pickens was the advocate and proposer of the plan. Yet, instead of causing the governor to lose popularity, it worked to his advantage in that the council received the blame for the proposed measure.[49]

There was some talk of extending his term, but this idea was denounced as being unconstitutional. The *Mercury* reminded the people that the controversial council had been created because of the governor's ineptness. There was also an attempt to secure a seat for Pickens in a Confederate Senate, but Senator James L. Orr refused to resign his seat and take the governorship which was offered him.[50] Pickens was at the height of his popularity when he returned to Edgefield on

December 18, 1862. Although he tried to involve himself in politics after the war, his failure to gain a pardon from President Andrew Johnson made political activity impossible. For the remainder of his life he devoted himself to planting. He died on January 25, 1869.

The retirement of Pickens and Orr's decision to remain in the Senate brought on a wild scramble for the governorship. John S. Preston, who had the promise of support from former Governor John L. Manning, was a strong candidate, but he made a decision which Charles E. Cauthen maintained cost him the governorship. Manning had earlier urged Preston to join the fight against the council, which certainly would have been good politics. But when Preston instead defended the council, Manning sensed the prejudice against Preston and decided to stand for the office himself. However, his expected victory did not materialize due to the appearance of a dark horse in the person of M. L. Bonham, then a member of the Confederate House of Representatives. Bonham was elected governor December 17, 1862, after the legislature, meeting in joint session, had taken three ballots. His nearest rival was former Governor Manning, who received 63 votes to 79 for Bonham.[51]

Milledge Luke Bonham was born in Edgefield District on December 25, 1813. After attending several local "old field" schools and academies, he entered South Carolina College and was graduated in 1834. He then read law and began practicing in the small upstate town of Edgefield where Pickens had already located. While Pickens was in Russia it was Bonham who had looked after his practice.

Bonham served in the General Assembly from 1840 to 1844 and in the United States House of Representatives from 1857 until 1860, having been elected a States' Rights Democrat to fill the unexpired term of his cousin Preston Brooks. But Bonham was best known for his military exploits. In the Seminole War he had commanded the South Carolina Brigade and during the Mexican War he had served as a lieutenant colonel in the Palmetto Regiment. His service in Mexico was partially motivated by a desire to avenge the death of his brother James, who had been killed by Santa Anna's troops at the Alamo. At the outbreak of the Civil War Bonham held the rank of major general and commander of the South Carolina Militia. In 1862 he resigned his commission as a brigadier general in the Confederate army upon being elected to the Confederate House of Representatives. He served in Congress until his election as governor.

On Thursday, December 18, the reins of power were transferred from Pickens to Bonham. Pickens, true to form, gave one of his long speeches, while the new governor was brief, yet "impressive and eloquent," in his remarks. The election of Bonham brought to the governor's office a man well equipped to provide the state with leadership in the difficult days ahead.[52]

The problems that had faced Pickens grew even more acute during the gubernatorial term of Milledge Bonham. Bonham did not have the albatross of the Executive Council as did Pickens. However, the years 1863 and 1864 were critical and as the war became more heated South Carolina's problems loomed greater. The state had cooperated fully with the Confederate government in supplying troops, materials, and revenue to the southern cause. Yet many South Carolinians began to feel that the Confederacy was more interested in the war in other areas than in protecting the Palmetto State from invasion by the Union army.

The feared invasion had taken place on November 7, 1861, by a fleet under flag officer Samuel L. Dupont. The taking of the Port Royal area caused alarm throughout the coastal region of the state. Prior to the invasion there was a patriotic fervor that resulted in a large number of voluntary enlistments. In an attempt to meet the emergency, Governor Pickens, acting under a resolution passed by the legislature, had asked for more volunteers to aid in the defense of Charleston. These troops were to be incorporated into the Confederate service. The results of Pickens's request were disappointing. Lieutenant Colonel John S. Preston, the state's conscription officer, wrote on November 23 that no troops were coming in "although twenty days have elapsed since Carolina's soil is desecrated—the deep mouthed curse—the fierce shout—the wild rush to arms and vengeance—aren't here."[53] Preston's statement sums up the chief problem that was to perplex both Pickens and Bonham. After initial successes the recruiting of soldiers for the defense of South Carolina quickly proved to be an unsolvable problem. While Pickens was governor, James Chesnut, as a member of the Executive Council, had the responsibility for procuring recruits. But after the demise of the council this responsibility was placed back in the governor's hands. Time after time the legislature changed the state's militia and conscription laws in order to make them conform more closely with Confederate acts, provide the state with more manpower for its own defense, and revitalize an utterly disorganized and inefficient militia. The state found itself in a precarious position. After First Manassas the Confederacy was requiring more and more troops to serve longer terms. These troops were to be used mainly in northern Virginia or in the West. Thus, South Carolina with its long unprotected coastline found itself left with a nominal number of Confederate troops and an unreliable, untrained, and often unwilling militia providing for its defense.

The Executive Council had been created chiefly for the purpose of raising troops to fill South Carolina's quota for the Confederacy and providing enough men for home defense. The council was given the power by the convention to suspend those militia laws that might interfere with the recruitment of troops. On March 20, 1862, it ended volunteering and relied exclusively on a plan of conscription which utilized sheriffs and tax collectors to aid in the drafting of white males between the ages of eighteen and forty-five. Shortly after the state passed its conscription act, the Confederacy followed suit. The Executive Council decided to support fully the Confederate law by giving the Confederate conscription officers all the rolls that were to be used by the state for conscription purposes. Since the Confederate law required at the outset service of men between the ages of eighteen and thirty-five, the state organized two militia corps composed of men over thirty-five for home defense. On September 28, 1862, a new Confederate act required the service of all men between the ages of eighteen and forty-five. This seriously upset South Carolina's defense posture and forced the state to call upon males between sixteen and sixty-five for militia duty.[54] Francis Pickens defended the acts on grounds of necessity, but was philosophically opposed to them as being "contrary to the spirit of the Constitution."[55]

When M. L. Bonham became governor, he inherited the defense and conscription problems. In his inaugural address the new governor made it clear that he intended to continue to carry out a policy "that in every legitimate way should sustain the Confederate authorities."[56] Beauregard, who commanded the Department of South Carolina and Georgia, reported that thirty thousand troops were the minimum needed for the defense of South Carolina. In January 1863 there were only ten thousand Confederate troops available for defense and these forces were constantly being drained away as the war in other theaters took priority. Thus, shortly after Bonham took office Beauregard was requesting from him arms that had been put aside for the use of the South Carolina Militia. Bonham became fearful that the Confederate government would lose sight of the necessity of providing adequate men and arms for the defense of coastal South Carolina.[57] Throughout the spring and summer of 1863 Union forces attempted raid after raid upon the sea islands in the Charleston area. On April 7, 1863, Commodore Dupont tried to destroy Fort Sumter, but was repulsed. At that time Beauregard's forces numbered about twenty-two thousand men. In spite of protests by Bonham and others, the Confederate army in South Carolina was being stripped as the need for troops grew more critical. By mid-summer Morris Island, Folly Island, James Island, and inland areas were all under attack by Union forces. On August 24 the Federals, who had been constantly shelling Fort Sumter, turned their guns on the city of Charleston. Throughout the fall and winter of 1863–64 the city suffered intermittent bombardment. Even though the enemy was very active in the coastal regions of South Carolina, because of needs elsewhere the Confederate forces in the area continued to dwindle.

In addition to having to cope with the military situation, Bonham had other responsibilities related to the state's impossible situation, such as the issuing of passports, planning the building of blockade-runners, the declaration of martial law in war zones, cooperating with the Confederate conscription authorities, providing arms and supplies for a weakened militia, receiving requests for commissions in the state and Confederate service, enforcing limitations on the planting of cotton so that more foodstuffs could be provided, and providing slave labor for work on fortifications. Several major concerns proved vexing to Bonham. The Confederate conscription law required service from all ablebodied men with only individuals in government or critical services being exempted. Overseers were not exempt by the terms of the Confederate act; yet there was the critical question of who was going to oversee the slaves and plant and harvest the crops. If the militia were called out to help defend the coastal region, the state ran the risk of having agricultural pursuits halted; furthermore, there was the fear that if the militia were mobilized, it would use up badly needed supplies while waiting for uncertain attacks. Because of the critical nature of the problems besetting him, Bonham moved cautiously. He refused to be stampeded into hastily planned actions. He felt that the Confederacy should assign Carolina regiments to the defense of their home state. Though being urged to call out the militia by many people, the governor continued to hold back, believing it would be foolish to rush an unorganized and inexperienced body of troops into the field with the probable result that the Confederacy would seize the opportunity to remove more soldiers from South Carolina.

By late February 1863, Beauregard demanded that all noncombatants leave the Charleston area. Despite misgivings, Governor Bonham finally ordered all white males sixteen to eighteen, and forty-five to fifty years of age mustered for the defense of the city. Three regiments were ordered to proceed to Charleston, but arming, equipping, and organizing the troops proved very difficult. The state had turned over all its supplies to the Confederate government, which by this time found itself woefully short of resources and in no position to help South Carolina. Confusion reigned. The legislature had declared all acts of the Executive Council null and void, thus necessitating a complete reorganization of the militia. President Davis was willing to accept the state troops for only three months' service (half the time authorized by Confederate law) provided the state could arm and equip its men. Bonham informed Davis that he could arm the troops, but had no equipment for them. Despite the lack of supplies the state continued to place its very limited military resources at the disposal of the Confederacy.[58]

This was quite different from the course that Zebulon Vance of North Carolina and Joseph E. Brown of Georgia were taking. Confederate laws exempted from military service those state officers whom the governor certified as necessary for state administration. The governors of Georgia and North Carolina had greatly abused this privilege, but in South Carolina Governor Bonham would not certify petty state officials as critical for state administration. Not until the end of 1864 did the state reverse its policy on exemptions. The reason for this change was the rising tide of opposition to the Davis administration, particularly its refusal to send reinforcements for the defense of South Carolina. There was the growing conviction that the state must reserve its remaining resources for defense against Sherman's approaching army.

But raising troops was not the only problem of manpower besetting Bonham. Slave labor was needed to build and maintain coastal fortifications. During the early days of Pickens's governorship there was little grumbling by planters in the coastal regions over the impressment of their slaves, but by the end of 1861 the increasing demands by both state and Confederate governments had caused them to complain. One of the reasons the Executive Council became so hated was that it and the military made arbitrary demands on the planters. At first only the counties directly affected by invasion were required to supply labor, but as the need for manpower became more desperate, labor was recruited from the entire state.[59] When Bonham became governor he was immediately faced with this problem. At the very time he was trying to build up the militia for defending the coast he was also calling upon the planters for more slave labor. The planters felt they were being treated unfairly; yet the Confederate military authorities were urging the impressment of more and more slaves. Unfortunately for Bonham, he was caught in the middle of a problem that was to last throughout his administration. Never were enough slaves raised for labor purposes. After it became apparent that planters would not cooperate with the state in supplying slave labor, General Beauregard announced in August 1863 that he would send agents under the authority of the Confederate government to impress slaves. This did have a positive but short-lived effect. In the month of September 1863, in addition to the seven hundred plus slaves that were impressed, the planters provided over 2,800 additional slaves. After that, despite stiffer penalties, planters became increasingly reluctant to give up their badly needed labor. In November 1863 Bonham requested the legislature to give him the authority to impress slave labor for a period of sixty days. The governor's request was honored and he was given the authority to order sheriffs and road commissioners to execute impressment orders. However, this labor law, like its predecessors, continued to prove ineffective. Planters claimed that the Negroes were ill treated, were not returned promptly, and were essential to agriculture. For all practical purposes the law was not well enforced as public opinion was against it.[60]

Disloyalty and desertion were other problems with which Bonham had to deal. By mid-1863 war weariness was becoming acute. This resulted in a disaffection for the Confederate cause that was most noticeable in the northwestern part of South Carolina. Bands of deserters who had fled to the mountains were terrorizing the citizenry. Though Bonham made serious efforts to curb desertion, neither he nor his successor, A. G. Magrath, succeeded in eliminating it.

As Confederate success waned in the West, a new fear gripped South Carolina. General James Longstreet's retreat in East Tennessee put more pressure on the governor to provide defense for the state. Bonham wanted the Confederate government to provide six or eight companies of mounted infantry and a battery of light artillery to serve in the mountainous region along the North Carolina border. In addition to the threat posed by the proximity of the Union armies, bushwhackers and deserters were also presenting a danger to Carolinians living in the northwestern area of the state. Bonham was urged to send in militia units to assert control over the region. However, the governor wanted the Confederate War Department to undertake this task. A real blow came to Carolina when in March 1864 General Beauregard was ordered to give up most of his cavalry for duty in Virginia. Though Bonham vehemently protested to Confederate Secretary of War James A. Seddon, his protests were to no avail. Simultaneous to the problems affecting South Carolina in its coastal and northwestern regions was the problem of General William T. Sherman's move into Georgia. By this time Governor Bonham had called out all of the state's reserve forces. The need for troops was at this time so desperate that proposals were made advocating the arming of slaves for the purpose of defending the South. General Robert E. Lee, who was assuming the role of supreme commander of the southern armies, endorsed the idea. Though most people in South Carolina were opposed to the arming of slaves in late 1864, public opinion changed as invasion became more imminent. In order to defend the state, Bonham urged the legislature to grant him authority to send state troops into Georgia to aid in the attempt to stop Sherman.[61] The Charleston *Courier* and other papers in the state published a proclamation issued by Bonham on December 5, 1864, urging all citizens to tear up roads and bridges on the route from Savannah to Port Royal in order to hamper the movement of Union forces. The governor ordered South Carolina's troops to concentrate at Hamburg, across the river from Augusta, Georgia.[62]

When the General Assembly met for its regular session on November 28, Bonham explained to it in detail what was transpiring and described the frustrations that he was encountering on every front. He recommended that a regiment of mounted infantry, a group of cavalry, and a battery of artillery be formed, and that Carolinians of all ages be liable for service anywhere in the state.[63] The labor problem which had proved so vexing throughout the war continued and Bonham recommended to the legislature that the state begin a policy of impressment to be carried out by state officials rather than by Confederate conscription officials. This act was passed by the legislature four days after Bonham left office.[64]

In Bonham's last days as governor he became acutely aware of the need for the state to maintain men for its own defense. Yet there were two ideals to which he clung. First, he believed that every ablebodied man should serve and that no one—not even state or Confederate officials—should be exempted from service. He felt that those soldiers who had been badly disabled could carry out their functions. Second, he felt that soldiers should be in the Confederate service rather than in state service. This is not to imply that he had modified his strong states' right views. Bonham was a practical man who had himself been a commander of soldiers and had seen the devastation of war. He felt that it was the responsibility of the Confederacy to provide the military strength necessary for the prosecution of the war. He tried to ensure that South Carolina's conscription and exemption acts were in conformity with Confederate laws, and he made it his policy not to directly interfere with Confederate officers operating in South Carolina. At the end of his term, when desperation ruled, he changed not because of a change in conviction but because the state faced a grave, hopeless situation.

At the end of Bonham's term the state legislature ended its cooperation with the Confederacy. Friction over slave labor, the impressment of supplies, the conscription issue, and numerous other irritations caused the Palmetto State once again to shoulder the mantle of states' rights and virtually nullify all important Confederate laws. Bonham's biographer is doubtful that the governor would have gone as far as the legislature in its anti-Confederate attitude. However, it is significant that Bonham did recommend to the legislature meeting in November and December of 1864 that the state should shoulder more responsibility for its own defense in the face of the mounting crisis.[65]

In February 1865 Bonham was reappointed brigadier general and he served as cavalry officer under Joseph E. Johnston until the end of the war. After the war he continued his interest in public affairs. He served in the legislature during presidential Reconstruction, but the Republican takeover in 1868 kept him on the sidelines for several years. In 1876 he took an active part in the Red Shirt campaign and in the restoration of white supremacy, and was rewarded in 1878 by an appointment as state railroad commissioner. He served in that position until his death on August 27, 1890.

The man who succeeded Bonham as governor late in 1864 was in complete harmony with the anti-Confederate attitude that was becoming more popular in South Carolina. Andrew Gordon Magrath was born on February 8, 1813, and reared in the cosmopolitan atmosphere of Charleston. His father had come to South Carolina from Ireland in 1789, fifteen years before Magrath was born. Andrew attended Bishop England's School in Charleston and graduated from South Carolina College in 1831. After graduation he read law in the office of the widely respected Unionist James L. Petigru. He studied law at Harvard and returned to Charleston in 1835. Like Pickens, during the period of the 1850s Magrath was known as a moderate in state politics. He was elected to the State House of Representatives in 1840 and 1842, and was picked as a delegate to the national Democratic convention in 1852. Prior to the meeting of the Democratic party, Magrath resigned to be appointed United States district judge for South Carolina. Shortly thereafter, Congressman William Aiken announced his retirement. Magrath desired the seat, but was hotly opposed by the Charleston *Mercury* and the Rhett faction, who accused him of rank political opportunism. This led to a duel between Magrath's brother Edward and the editor of the *Mercury,* William R. Taber. Taber was killed, and as a result of the controversy and the duel Magrath withdrew his candidacy.[66]

Magrath continued to serve as a Federal district judge until November 1860 when, realizing the popularity of the secession movement, he resigned from the judiciary by dramatically ripping off his robe in his courtroom and denouncing the United States. The resignation made him very popular with the masses. Thus, he was immediately elected to the state secession convention. In December 1860 he was elected secretary of state, and rapidly gained a reputation as a militant secessionist. After the death of the Executive Council in 1862, Magrath was appointed Confederate district judge for South Carolina. Initially he declared the Confederate conscription and sequestering acts constitutional, but as war wore South Carolinians down and the state became less inclined to support the Richmond government, the judge's opinions reflected a more states' rights bias. His decisions against the Confederate government made him popular with those in the state who believed that South Carolina should not depend too heavily upon the Confederacy.[67] On November 16, 1864, Magrath dined with James Chesnut, former United States senator, Confederate senator, and close friend of Jefferson Davis. Mrs. Chesnut, in her famous diary, wrote: "Judge Magrath dined here, he is besetting Mr. Chesnut to be a candidate for governor. I take it for granted he wants to be governor himself, and to use Mr. Chesnut in the canvass as a sort of lightning rod, to draw off the troublesome opposition of our friends."[68] Chesnut and his friends represented the faction in the state known as the Confederate party. Chesnut did not allow his name to be put forward; thus, the alternative was John S. Preston, who had served as chief of the Confederate Bureau of Conscription, a most unpopular post. He had had his name introduced in the governor's race in 1862, but lost because he had been closely connected with the hated Executive Council.[69]

Four names were put forward as candidates: Preston, Magrath, A. C. Garlington, and Samuel McGowan. The legislature met in joint session on December 13, and Magrath was able to defeat his opponents on the sixth ballot, which took place the following day. Both Magrath and the runner-up, Garlington, represented the anti-Confederate point of view. The results of the balloting clearly indicated the extent of the states' rights reaction in South Carolina. Magrath and Garlington received 79 and 52 votes respectively, whereas Preston, known for his pro-Confederate views, received only 11 votes on the final ballot.[70]

On Monday, December 19, the former judge was inaugurated. In his inaugural address the new governor declared that if the Confederacy was unable to defend South Carolina, then the state must defend itself and continue the war until freedom was secured. At this juncture Mrs. Chesnut wrote: "Red-hot resolutions are urged. . . . The temper of the House is roused, State's Rights are rampant. We are about to secede again from the Confederacy! No doubt the devil raved of Devil's rights in paradise."[71]

At the time of Magrath's inauguration, Sherman was completing his march across Georgia to Savannah. The legislature was in the process of passing the exemption acts, which gave the governor the authority to claim exemption from Confederate military service for those who served in virtually any capacity in state, county, or municipal government and those he deemed necessary for policing the country. Thus, in effect, the General Assembly had given Magrath the power to exempt whomever he pleased from Confederate service. At the same time the legislature passed another act which severely restricted the power of the Confederate government to impress slaves in South Carolina. However, the state continued to maintain its right of impressment.[72] Meanwhile, the people of the state were rapidly losing hope. Magrath's chief problem was to restore confidence and somehow save South Carolina and his beloved Charleston. On December 25 the governor wrote President Davis telling him that if Charleston were to be saved, help was immediately needed. If Charleston fell, he said, Richmond would fall also.[73] Magrath took stock of the supplies, public property, and forces he had with which to combat the Union forces. He began a continuous barrage of correspondence with those in Richmond whom he felt could help.

In early January 1865 word reached the governor that Beauregard had issued orders to General William J. Hardee, in command of the Charleston garrison, that he should evacuate the city rather than lose the garrison. Magrath became very bitter when he learned of Hardee's instructions. Once again the governor appealed to Davis, Lee, and other Confederate officials, urging them to save Charleston. "I tell you now that retreat from Charleston will be the dead march of the Confederation," he wrote. "The loss of Charleston is the loss of the Confederacy. . . . If Charleston cannot be defended, what can be defended . . . remember this state has held back not a single man; it has given all without question. Shall not any of these it has given for others, be now given back to it for its own defense?"[74]

At this time Sherman crossed into South Carolina. All of Magrath's pleas seemed to have fallen on deaf ears. Lee's army had its hands full trying to defend Petersburg and Richmond and could not be sent to Carolina. However, President Davis informed the governor that he was sending a brigade composed of Charlestonians to help in the situation. Magrath asked General Hardee to use the brigade to defend the vital railroad link between Charleston, Columbia, and Augusta.[75]

By the middle of January everything seemed to be coming unraveled, and deep despondency afflicted South Carolina. Magrath rationalized that the only possible salvation was for the state to cease depending on the Confederacy and appeal to its sister states to join in a pact of mutual assistance. The governor dispatched Colonel W. S. Mullins to meet with Governor Vance of North Carolina and William H. Trescot to meet with Brown of Georgia. The letters Magrath sent to Brown and Vance urged that the states initiate a policy of military cooperation utilizing the militias under the control of the governors to fight outside of their respective states. He believed that such a policy could lead to "deliverance," and if successful could be extended to include the states of Alabama, Florida, and Mississippi. Thus, the Confederacy could be saved.[76]

In the midst of these happenings the governor received news from Davis that Major General Butler's division of South Carolina Cavalry had been ordered home and that Wade Hampton's division would follow. General Beauregard was ordered to send General John B. Hood's shattered army to oppose Sherman. The governor had hoped that Georgia, North Carolina, and South Carolina acting jointly with Hood's army could defeat Sherman. Magrath discovered that rhetoric had replaced the needed cooperation. Governor Brown, though professing interest in Magrath's schemes, proved lukewarm towards his ideas, especially those dealing with sending state militia units outside of Georgia. By this time, however, Magrath's schemes for cooperation were of little consequence. By mid-February the governor was losing hope. Sherman's army was in the process of invading South Carolina and the state's only defense was composed of old men and children and remnants of worn-down armies. Magrath claimed that the "fatal heresy" was the policy of the states in yielding to every demand of the Confederate government.[77] In the last days the governor was still pleading with Hardee, Beauregard, and Davis not to abandon Charleston. He wrote Davis begging him to send troops to defend "the city which first proclaimed secession and the state which first adopted it." On February 7 the governor called upon citizens to defend their homes and destroy or carry off those things that were valuable to the enemy.[78]

For South Carolina the war was rapidly coming to an end. Refugees clogged the roads leading to Columbia. Sherman had left Savannah on February 1 and was marching on South Carolina. The Confederates thought his objective would be Charleston, but within two weeks he was on the outskirts of Columbia. On February 16 his armies were preparing to shell South Carolina's capital from the west bank of the Congaree River. That night Magrath fled Columbia and proceeded to Winnsboro. From there he moved the seat of government to Union. He still tried during this period to control the militia units. The fear in the northwestern portion of the state was that Union General George Stoneman would strike in a raid across the mountains from Tennessee. For this possibility the governor tried to get help from Beauregard and organize a force to resist Sherman's raiders. In the midst of this, Magrath moved his headquarters to Spartanburg. In addition to military difficulties, the situation was complicated by a virtual state of anarchy. The governor took steps to bring matters under control and ordered two companies of mounted infantry to proceed to Columbia to ascertain the extent of damage and restore order. By the end of March the situation had improved. The governor called for the General Assembly to convene in Greenville on April 25. However, Magrath was unable to get a sufficient number of the members to attend. The next day he called a secret session of those who had come to meet in the Greenville County courthouse. In the meeting he gave a candid assessment of the condition of South Carolina. The long-awaited raid by Stoneman took place on May 1, and Greenville fell into Union hands. Magrath fled back to Columbia and issued orders for all state officials to return to the shattered capital.[79]

The governor tried to maintain the "honor and independence" of South Carolina to the last. After the surrender of Joseph E. Johnston in North Carolina, Magrath used what power and influence he still possessed to maintain order and relieve suffering. He demanded that Confederate supplies be turned over to state agents in order to supply the needs of returning soldiers. By the middle of May, Union forces were firmly in control in South Carolina. On May 15 Union General Q. A. Gillmore issued an order charging the governor with treason and ordering the people to ignore Magrath's claims to function as a governor of South Carolina. On May 22, Andrew Gordon Magrath, the last Civil War governor of South Carolina, issued his last proclamation, which formally suspended the functions of his office, and on May 25 he was arrested. Later he was imprisoned in Fort Pulaski near Savannah. After his release from prison he resumed practicing law in Charleston until his death on April 9, 1893.[80]

The three wartime governors of South Carolina faced problems of incalculable magnitude. The state was invaded early and tenaciously fought against the Union. It gave a higher percentage of its resources in both men and supplies than any other Confederate state. Its zeal and its sense of duty and honor were tried; yet the will to continue the fight to the last was maintained in the face of certain defeat. Francis Pickens applauded the Confederacy and the coming of war. Milledge Bonham questioned the policies of the Confederacy, yet cooperated and continued the war. Andrew Magrath despised the Confederacy, thought of seceding from it, and helplessly encountered defeat.

TENNESSEE

Kermit L. Hall

istorians of the Civil War in Tennessee agree that Governor Isham Green Harris was the most energetic and influential spokesman for the Confederacy in the state. They disagree, however, over his role in bringing about separation of Tennessee from the Union and his success as governor.[1] An early generation of pro-Union historians labeled Harris a proslavery demagogue who trampled on the state constitution and the rights of the Union minority. In their view, Harris compounded treachery with administrative ineptitude and military blundering that burdened the state with an enormous debt and a military government. More recently, historians have adopted a revisionist view. They insist that Harris's actions reflected the wishes of most Tennesseans and that he administered the state government and organized the military with ability and energy. Taken alone, neither view is persuasive.

Harris was born on February 10, 1818, on a farm near Tullahoma, Tennessee, the son of Isham Harris, a Methodist minister and farmer, and his wife Lucy Davidson. He was educated by his parents and by teachers in the common schools of Franklin County and at the Winchester Academy. Harris's formal schooling ended at age fourteen, when he moved to Paris, Tennessee, to clerk in a local store. Seven years later he entered the law office of Judge Andrew McCampbell. After two years of study he began practice as one of fifteen lawyers serving the eight hundred residents of Paris. Through a dramatic courtroom style Harris emerged as an effective and prosperous trial lawyer. In 1860 he had an estimated $45,000 in real and personal property that included twenty slaves and a small plantation in Shelby County. In 1843 he married Martha Travis, daughter of Major Edward Travis.[2]

Political success accompanied professional advancement. In 1847, at the age of twenty-nine, Harris was elected a state senator from West Tennessee. Subsequently, he served two terms, from 1849 to 1853, in the United States House of Representatives, declining to seek a third term in favor of law practice in the bustling commercial city of Memphis. He remained there until elected governor in 1857.

The regional exigencies of Tennessee Democratic politics thrust Harris into the governor's mansion. The incumbent, Andrew Johnson, had the support of his yeoman farmer constituency in East Tennessee for the United States Senate, but he needed the cooperation of the southern rights wing of the Democratic party concentrated among the slaveholders of Middle and West Tennessee. They agreed to Johnson's nomination in return for East Tennessee Democrats accepting Harris as the gubernatorial nominee. Harris easily won election in 1857 and again in 1859. During both campaigns he extolled the virtues of Jacksonian Democracy and southern exceptionalism, insisted on the right of slaveholders to take their property into the territories, applauded the Dred Scott decision, denounced the Republican party, and rejected popular sovereignty. By 1860 Harris, who supported John C. Breckinridge for president, was the most powerful and popular leader of the southern rights wing of the Tennessee Democracy.[3]

Pro-Union historians have treated Harris as a prosouthern demagogue with an extraordinary ability to control events. "Tennessee never seceded," observed one historian, "Isham Harris seceded and carried Tennessee along with him."[4] The course that Harris and Tennessee followed in the secession crisis was circuitous and prolonged, not short and direct. Harris wanted to protect southern rights and to guarantee the autonomy of Tennessee, but he appreciated that many Tennesseans, especially in the eastern section of the state, doubted the wisdom of snapping the cords of Union. The governor, who in fifty years of public life never lost an election, was too politically astute to act precipitously. He recognized from the outset of the secession crisis that the fate of any state government—Confederate or Unionist— required perpetuation of interregional cooperation that had been the foundation of the defunct two-party system of Tennessee.[5]

The secession crisis in the state divided into two phases, both of which had an impact on Harris's tenure as Confederate governor. The first extended from the election of Lincoln to the firing on Fort Sumter. The second ran from Lincoln's call for troops following Sumter to the vote in favor of independence by Tennesseans on June 8, 1861. Throughout the first phase, the governor, whom Unionists correctly charged was "pretty well bent South," attempted to prepare for future conflict while compromising with Unionists.[6] Harris avoided any reference to secession; instead, he insisted that Tennesseans possessed a "right of revolution" that protected them from Federal coercion. To defend this right, Harris in January 1861 urged two measures on the General Assembly. First, he recommended a reorganization of the militia and appropriation of funds to purchase arms and ammunition. Second, he proposed a plebiscite on whether a state convention should be held "to take into consideration our federal relations, and determine what action shall be taken by the State of Tennessee for the security of the rights and powers of the citizens."[7] The Unionists in the General Assembly defeated the first measure; they accepted the second only because they sensed that it would draw less support than at a future date when "Tennesseans might be more agitated."[8] The rejection of Harris's first request resulted in a delay in obtaining arms and ammunition that subsequently haunted the governor. The electorate on February 9 rejected the call for a convention, leaving Harris at the mercy of events in Washington and Montgomery.

Lincoln's call for troops abruptly shifted political sentiment in Tennessee. The governor seized the initiative, although he scrupulously avoided offending recently converted Unionists. "Tennessee will not," Harris defiantly proclaimed in response to the president's call for troops, "furnish a single man for the purpose of coercion, but 50,000 if necessary for the defense of our rights and those of our Southern brothers."[9] The governor declined to justify publicly his actions on the basis of a theory of secession; Tennessee Unionists had long since rejected the idea as a constitutional impossibility. Instead, Harris, when he called the General Assembly into a second extraordinary session on April 25, argued for the right of revolution. Tennessee could declare its independence because of "the bloody and tyrannical policy of the Presidential usurper" and "his hordes of armed soldiary marching to the work of southern subjugation."[10] In conformance with the governor's wishes, the heavily disunionist General Assembly submitted to Tennessee residents a Declaration of Independence rather than an ordinance of secession.

Some recent historians, in reacting to the Unionist bias in much writing about the Civil War era in Tennessee, argue that Harris in the second phase of the secession crisis only followed the dictates of the majority of the population.[11] This assertion is disingenuous. The governor was the driving force behind disunion and the Confederate government in Tennessee. If he had not committed the prestige of his office and his energy, imagination, and aggressiveness to disunion, it is doubtful the state would have joined the Confederacy. This was underscored by his disregard for the Tennessee constitution. Harris approved the decision of the General Assembly to hold its proceedings in secret, including the debates and votes over the declaration and a measure authorizing the governor to raise an army.[12] The direct popular vote on the declaration and a companion ordinance authorizing Tennessee to join the Confederacy had the advantage of speed (something Harris needed in order to compensate for the effects of earlier delays in arming the state), but the procedure was unconstitutional. The state constitution provided that it could be amended only by an ad hoc convention or by an amendment passed by two-thirds of the legislature and approved by a majority vote in the next regular election.[13] The wanton disregard for constitutional procedure and evidence of fraud in the vote in favor of ratification of the declaration prompted East Tennessee Unionists, whom Harris had hoped to mollify, to denounce the governor as a traitor.[14] From the outset of his administration, Harris had to contend with substantial internal opposition.

Harris assumed the mantle of Confederate governor well before passage of the June 8 referendum. On April 20 he dispatched W. C. Whitthorne as a special envoy to facilitate cooperation between Tennessee and the Confederacy.[15] Two days later the governor informed Confederate Secretary of War Leroy P. Walker that he intended to "confer freely and co-operate most cordially" with the Montgomery government.[16] Although the state constitution prohibited the governor from commanding troops outside the state, Harris purposefully ignored this provision in dispatching three regiments to defend Virginia.[17] The governor also acted on his own authority to permit the Confederacy to erect fortifications at Memphis.[18] His most significant action, however, was to agree on May 7, with the acquiescence of the General Assembly, to place the state in a Military League with the Confederacy. As most historians have emphasized, the league pledged Tennessee troops to Confederate service, but it also ostensibly promised an umbrella of Confederate military protection for the state. The league did have the effect of rendering the June 8 referendum meaningless, but it must also be understood as a critical part of Harris's plan to prepare the state militarily.[19]

The exigencies of military necessity prompted the governor to abandon his prewar hostility to governmental interference in fiscal and commercial affairs. The state treasury in mid-1861 had a surplus of only $185,000—too little to raise a military force or to meet the $2 million Confederate war tax. At Harris's urging, the General Assembly on May 6, 1861, passed the Provisional Army of Tennessee Act, which authorized the governor to issue $5 million worth of bonds, to collect taxes on real and personal property to pay the interest and principal, and to serve as ex officio president of the Military and Financial Board whose duty it was to supervise the military fund.[20] When the directors of the three major banks in the state balked at purchasing the bonds, Harris coerced them into cooperating by threatening to place their assets in the hands of receivers friendly to the Confederacy. Harris also retreated from his prewar opposition to paper money. When the bond issue proved insufficient, he persuaded the General Assembly to issue $3 million in legal tender notes and countenanced the expanded issue of paper money by state banks.[21] These measures raised funds sufficient to put the Provisional Army into the field, but the massive indebtedness encumbered by the state fueled inflation.

The governor intervened or attempted to intervene in the state economy in other ways. He hoped to alleviate ruinous inflationary pressures by outlawing speculation. "In ordinary times," he argued, "an outraged public sentiment and the laws of trade" would prevent profiteering, but "in times . . . of war . . . the authorities cannot be too vigilant in their efforts to restrain the excess of avarice."[22] Harris urged the General Assembly to forbid profiteering in war commodities, but the legislators, in one of the few legislative reverses suffered by the governor, refused to act. The governor cited military necessity in refusing, despite his history of opposition to state support of internal improvements, to place into receivership eight railroads operating in Tennessee that had defaulted on interest payments on state bank construction loans.[23]

Harris gave his highest priority to military preparations. On April 25, 1861, he proposed the creation of a more perfect militia organization, "so that in case of necessity the whole force of the state can be speedily brought into action."[24] The General Assembly subsequently passed the Provisional Army of Tennessee Act, which established an army of fifty-five thousand volunteers—twenty-five thousand on active service and thirty thousand held in ready reserve. The act not only placed the governor at the head of the powerful Military and Financial Board but it made him commander in chief. Harris assumed responsibility for directing the military defense of the state, organizing the army, controlling the military fund, and making contracts for military supplies.[25]

Historians critical of Harris's administration have suggested the governor performed poorly as a military leader. Such judgments are insensitive to his successes and the difficulties he experienced in dealing with Confederate authorities. Harris harnessed the surge of popular support for the Confederacy following Fort Sumter to rapidly organize the Army of Tennessee. By August 7, 1861, Tennessee had turned over to Confederate control twenty-two regiments of infantry, two regiments of cavalry, ten companies of artillery, an engineering corps, and an ordnance bureau. Indeed, the troops could have been more quickly mustered into Confederate service had it not been for the inefficiency of authorities in Richmond.[26]

In planning the defense of the state, Harris was beset by a dilemma: the exposed position of Tennessee dictated that the Confederate military would have to defend it, but the strength of the Confederate army depended on the presence of Tennessee troops outside the state. Since the Richmond government gave priority to the defense of Virginia rather than the West, many of the Tennessee troops were assigned to Virginia. Harris threatened to withhold these troops if the Richmond government did not pledge to pay for part of the cost of raising them and to return them in case of Federal attack. Confederate authorities agreed to the first, but they were no more able than the Tennesseans to pay the enormous costs of raising an army. They rejected the second altogether.[27] Harris acted with magnanimity in cooperating with the Confederacy, but his hope for mutual cooperation was misplaced. When Federal armies menaced the state, Confederate authorities kept the Tennessee troops in Virginia.

The Richmond government was an impediment to the governor's plan to forge a political consensus between Democrats and Whigs throughout the state. During the three months that he commanded the Provisional Army of Tennessee, Harris selected Whigs as well as Democrats to serve as command and staff officers. When the Confederacy assumed control of the Army of Tennessee, Jefferson Davis replaced Harris's appointees with only "prominent Democrats and original secessionists" from Middle and West Tennessee. The governor was dismayed. "It is a matter of positive political necessity," he informed Davis, that "our former political opponents . . . be fully recognized in the appointments which are made in the state, especially when it can be done without injuring the public service."[28] Davis replied that the political composition of the appointments was "accidental," but he neither reversed his decision nor subsequently used the patronage to heal old political divisions in Tennessee.[29]

Harris and Davis disagreed over policy toward Kentucky. War preparations in Tennessee alarmed Governor Beriah Magofin of Kentucky, who asked Harris to recognize the neutrality of his state. The Tennessee governor promised to observe it; a neutral Kentucky, he concluded, would provide a buffer against the Federal armies. Davis, citing military necessity, overrode this agreement; in September 1861 Confederate troops occupied strategic positions in southern Kentucky.[30]

Officials in Richmond offered Harris little assistance in obtaining arms. The governor explained to Secretary of War Walker that it was "difficult, if not impossible, to procure arms"; the marketplace was already saturated by other southern states that had seceded earlier.[31]

Harris begged for assistance from Walker and arms merchants in New Orleans. The former had little to spare; the latter delivered only erratically and then at exorbitant prices. The Army of Tennessee did enter the field with sufficient arms, but by September 1861 the dearth of arms reached crisis proportions. On September 10 General Albert Sidney Johnston assumed command of Department Number Two with responsibility for the defense of Tennessee and the western flank of the Confederacy. Johnston expected Harris, who had just finished arming twenty-five thousand troops, to procure arms for an additional thirty thousand troops from Tennessee. Harris was anxious to cooperate with the new Confederate commander, but he warned that the lack of arms made recruitment difficult; potential volunteers refused to leave their families and property to pass idle days in camp waiting for arms. By early 1862 significant portions of Johnston's troops lacked arms; Tennessee enlistments, despite the governor's best efforts, plunged.[32]

Harris expected Tennesseans to provide the arms that could not be obtained from the Confederacy or weapons dealers. As the threat of Federal invasion heightened, the governor resorted to increasingly coercive measures. In mid-August he ordered constables throughout the state to make "diligent inquiry" at every home for muskets, rifles, and pistols.[33] When this scheme failed he issued a proclamation on November 12 that directed all male residents of the state not in military service to surrender their weapons. "If you refuse," the governor threatened, "prepare to take the field, for I am resolved to exhaust all resources before the foot of the invader shall pollute the soil of Tennessee."[34] Harris was victimized by a circular logic many Tennesseans accepted: they refused to disarm themselves because their best defense, the Confederate army, was inadequately armed. The weapons that were surrendered were unsatisfactory for field use; they were either in poor condition or sporting pieces ill-suited to combat. Harris attempted to deal with this problem by establishing four armories to repair and refurbish these weapons, but a scarcity of gunsmiths frustrated his plans. Despite equal doses of imagination and coercion, the governor was unable to provide arms for all of the troops that might have participated in the defense of the state.[35]

Harris wanted the state to become a major producer of ammunition and powder, but his hopes were largely abortive. He successfully encouraged the production of percussion caps in Nashville, but the central government siphoned much of this production to the Virginia front. Black powder was scarce. Harris promised that the powder mills of Nashville would produce ten thousand pounds of powder a day, but the governor failed to locate sufficient trained personnel, materials, or transport to fulfill this pledge. The mills of Nashville only produced about four hundred pounds a day.[36]

Some supporters of separation greeted the governor's intervention in the state economy with dissent or noncompliance. Some planters and merchants, for example, had to be restrained by the military from breaking the embargo on the sale of contraband goods to the North. More damaging to military preparations was the silent refusal of masters to provide slaves for military construction projects. Immediately after Tennessee declared its independence, Harris ordered the construction of Forts Henry and Donelson to defend respectively the Cumberland and Tennessee rivers and the erection of military works at Nashville. Slaveholders responded feebly to the governor's appeals; of the needed five thousand slaves, only five hundred were ever brought to service. Work on Forts Henry and Donelson proceeded fitfully; the military defenses of Nashville were never completed.[37]

East Tennessee Unionists presented the most serious internal threat to Harris's administration. Their hostility to the governor surfaced in the 1861 gubernatorial election. Anti-Harris forces coalesced around William H. Polk, brother of the former president. Harris was too involved in war preparations to campaign, but his followers in the Southern Rights party, through the major newspapers in the state, ran the campaign. Polk accepted separation, but he blasted Harris for acting as a "dictator," a "one-man power," and a "king." He insisted that the governor had endangered the state by wantonly disregarding the interests of East Tennessee Unionists, who were likely to rebel if Harris were returned to office.[38] Throughout July the struggle raged—Polk fighting Harris and Harris preparing to fight the North. The governor ultimately prevailed in a landslide of more than 31,000 votes, but this awesome majority was deceiving. Polk actually carried East Tennessee by more than twelve thousand votes; he polled over fifteen thousand votes in Middle and West Tennessee. The 43,342 votes cast for the challenger boded ill for the Confederate cause in Tennessee; every vote for Polk was either a protest against Harris or the Confederacy, or both.[39]

Initially, Harris hoped to prevent the development of a siege mentality among East Tennessee Unionists by lightly resting the hand of Confederate authority on them. In this he received the cooperation of President Davis. The Unionists posed a significant threat to the internal security of the Confederacy; an uprising in East Tennessee would threaten the major rail lines running from the Deep South to Virginia and require precious troops to quell. The governor persuaded Davis to assign Tennessee soldiers to duty in the major towns while stationing other Confederate troops in training camps removed from population centers. Davis also cooperated by appointing Felix Zollicoffer, a former

Whig and resident of East Tennessee, to command the Confederate troops there.[40]

Military necessity forced abandonment of this policy of accommodation. On the night of November 6, 1861, a small group of Unionists burned vital railroad bridges in East Tennessee. Harris was stunned and angered. He wrote Davis that "this rebellion must be crushed out instantly, the leaders arrested and summarily punished."[41] With the approval of Harris, Confederate authorities clamped martial law on East Tennessee and executed two of the bridge burners. These tactics produced the reaction the governor had earlier sought to prevent; Unionists retaliated with ambushes and bushwhacking parties.[42] Through Confederate military forces, Harris's government retained nominal control over East Tennessee until September 1863, when Union General Ambrose E. Burnside occupied Knoxville.

Two months after the bridge burning incident, a Federal army sliced into Middle Tennessee. Harris appreciated General Johnston's need for more men, arms, and equipment, but the governor had exhausted his resources. He asked Secretary of War Judah P. Benjamin to return some of the Tennessee troops in Virginia, to allow twelve-month volunteers to continue to enlist, and to provide badly needed arms. The secretary vetoed the first, but approved the latter two, although too late to affect the battle in the West. After the fall of Forts Henry and Donelson, Harris on February 23, 1862, with Nashville in panic, fled with members of the General Assembly to Memphis.[43]

Harris was the nominal governor of Tennessee until the end of the war. When he addressed the General Assembly for the last time in March 1862, he was bitter about the failure of many Tennesseans to cooperate with him in defending the state. "The country," he explained, "has not been sufficiently aroused to a full sense of danger. . . . There is scarcely a locality within our limits which could not have done more."[44] Immediately thereafter he joined the Confederate military, serving with distinction on the staffs of Johnston, Braxton Bragg, and Joseph E. Johnston. The Richmond government continued to seek his counsel, but as a governor without a state, Harris had slight impact on Confederate policies. This undoubtedly explains his wish to relinquish the post.[45] In May 1863 he issued a proclamation calling for the regular gubernatorial election as a way of exhibiting to the enemy "our unalterable firmness and determination to preserve and perpetuate our free institutions."[46] Harris refused to stand for election; the position went to Robert Caruthers, an elderly former judge of the Tennessee supreme court. The victor, whose vote was exceedingly small and confined to Confederate army camps, made no attempt to take office—nor could he had he desired. The legislature could not inaugurate him, since the Union military government of Andrew Johnson controlled civil affairs. The Tennessee constitution provided that the previous governor continue in office until the qualification of his successor; thus, Harris served until the inauguration of staunch Unionist William G. Brownlow on April 5, 1865.[47] With Brownlow's election, civil government was restored.

Harris only gradually reclaimed his political influence in the state after the war. As a result of a $5,000 reward issued by the Radical-dominated legislature, the former governor went into exile, first in Mexico and later in England. When the reward was withdrawn in 1867, he resumed law practice in Memphis. When "Bourbon" Democracy was restored a decade later in Tennessee, Harris was once again thrust into public life. The General Assembly in 1877 elected him to the United States Senate, where he served until his death in Washington on July 8, 1897.[48]

The governorship of Isham Green Harris defies the neat dichotomies of traditional and revisionist historians. The former correctly emphasize Harris's part in creating the Confederate government in Tennessee, but they obscure the pressures operating on him by insisting that he alone took Tennessee out of the Union and by claiming that his alleged one-man rule resulted in military catastrophe. Revisionists, on the other hand, fail to recognize that, after Lincoln's call for troops, Harris jettisoned many of his prewar beliefs in order to gain Unionist support and that he ignored the Tennessee constitution. Harris's major wartime achievement was the raising in sixty days of the Provisional Army of Tennessee, but this must be balanced against the realization that in doing so he disrupted the economy of the state. He was unable to procure sufficient arms and ammunition for the troops assigned to defend Tennessee, and construction of military fortifications lagged. These critical failures were not the result of Harris's ineptitude; instead, they are better understood as by-products of the delay of Tennessee in joining the Confederacy, the inability and unwillingness of the Richmond government to cooperate with the governor, the apathy of some Tennesseans who had voted for separation, and the opposition of a small but significant Unionist element in East Tennessee. Unlike some Confederate governors, Harris acted with magnanimity in fulfilling requests by authorities in Richmond for troops and supplies badly needed to defend Tennessee. This fateful decision to cooperate resulted from his commitment to southern nationhood and his recognition, shared by the Tennessee General Assembly, that the state, in its exposed military position, required Confederate troops in order to survive. When Richmond decided to give priority to the Virginia front, all of Harris's energy, imagination, and political sagacity could not repel a Union army.

TEXAS

Ralph A. Wooster

dward Clark, governor of Texas during the first year of the Civil War, became chief executive of the Lone Star State under unusual circumstances. Following voters' approval of an ordinance separating the state from the Union in the spring of 1861, the Texas secession convention voted to unite Texas with the newly formed Confederate States. However, Sam Houston, governor of the state and a longtime foe of secession, would not recognize this action of the convention. When called upon to take the oath of allegiance to the Confederacy, Houston refused to do so. The convention thereupon declared the office of governor vacant and elevated Clark, who was lieutenant governor, to the position.[1]

The new governor was not the obscure politician depicted by some writers.[2] The nephew of a former governor of Georgia and descendant of George Rogers Clark of the American Revolution, Clark was a member of one of the South's most distinguished families. Born in Louisiana on April 1, 1815, he moved to Montgomery, Alabama, when he was seventeen. There he studied law and was admitted to the bar. In 1842 he moved to Texas and opened a law practice in Marshall. Clark had previously been married in Alabama, but his wife died within a few months. In July 1849 he married Martha Malissa Evans of Marshall.

Clark was a delegate to the state constitutional convention of 1845, a member of the first state House of Representatives of Texas, and a senator in the second legislature. He served on the staff of General J. Pinckney Henderson in the Mexican War and received a citation for bravery in the Battle of Monterrey. From 1853 to 1857 he served as secretary of state under Governor Elisha M. Pease. He was appointed state commissioner of claims in 1858 and was elected lieutenant governor of the state as an independent Democrat in 1859.[3]

A tall, erect man who walked with a military bearing, Clark had bright blue eyes, black hair, and a full beard which he wore cut short. Contemporary accounts indicate he was a dignified, courtly man who spoke with eloquence and conviction.[4]

Clark faced momentous problems when he took the oath of governor on March 18, 1861. The state had a deficit of nearly one million dollars with little revenue coming in. The vast frontiers of the state were virtually unprotected from both Indian depredations and Federal invasion, decisions had to be made concerning the 2,800 Federal troops who were awaiting evacuation near Indianola under the terms of an agreement between General David Twiggs and the Committee on Public Safety created by the Texas secession convention, and state and Confederate government appointments had to be made.[5] In addition, there was concern that the Federal government would work with the former governor, Sam Houston, and other Unionists to prevent Texas from supporting the Confederacy.

Clark moved quickly to address the state's most pressing needs. The creation of a state regiment commanded by the veteran ranger-soldier John "Rip" Ford and consisting of volunteers from ten Texas counties gave a measure of stability and security to the Rio Grande border. Another regiment, recruited by Henry E. McCulloch under Confederate authority, was organized to protect the northwestern frontier of the state.[6] Meanwhile, upon Clark's recommendation, the legislature provided for issuance of one million dollars' worth of 8 percent interest bonds and the increase of the ad valorem tax from 12½ cents to 16½ cents and the poll tax from fifty cents to one dollar in an effort to stabilize the state's finances.[7]

The new governor was particularly anxious that the Confederate government bear the cost of frontier defense. On April 4, 1861, Clark wrote to Confederate President Jefferson Davis that "it is more than probable that an effort will soon be made by the submission party of this State, with General Houston at its head, to convert Texas into an independent republic." One of the most effective of the submissionists' arguments, contended Clark, "will be that the Confederate States have supplied the place of the 2,800 United States troops formerly upon our frontier with only a single regiment, and that Texas has at her own cost been forced to bring another regiment into the field, and to bear the burden of its maintenance."[8]

Four days after the governor had written to Davis, Secretary of War Leroy Walker wrote to Clark asking that three thousand volunteers be drilled, equipped, and held in readiness. The following day, April 9, Walked dispatched a second letter informing Clark that the volunteers should be recruited for infantry service, no small feat in Texas where citizen-soldiers overwhelmingly preferred cavalry service.[9]

Clark moved to meet Walker's request as rapidly as possible. On April 17 the governor announced that the state was being divided into districts and subdistricts for the purpose of recruiting and organizing the desired units. Six prominent Texans—Hugh McLeod of Galveston, Joseph L. Hogg of Rusk, Matthew F. Locke of Gilmer, James H. Murray of Huntsville, August Buchel of Indianola, and Thomas Green of Austin—were appointed to head these military districts.[10]

The firing upon Fort Sumter and the outbreak of fighting in the East placed additional military burdens upon Texas. On April 24, Governor Clark issued a call for five thousand additional troops to meet a new requisition received from Confederate authorities.[11] Meanwhile, the governor and other state officials searched desperately for weapons with which to arm the volunteers recruited. In May, Clark appointed Ebenezer B. Nichols, a prominent commission merchant from Galveston, as agent to purchase arms and ammunition and to negotiate the sale of the million-dollar bond issue authorized by the legislature before it adjourned in early April. Later in the summer others, including Samuel Maverick, Hamilton P. Bee, and Lemuel R. Evans, were also appointed as purchasing agents by Governor Clark.[12]

Throughout the late spring and early summer Clark continued to take steps he believed necessary for the state's defense. In a conference with Colonel Earl Van Dorn, newly appointed Confederate military commander for Texas, the governor expressed concern about the vulnerable condition of the Texas coast as well as the dangers from Indian attacks to the northwest. In an effort to prevent depredations by Mexican guerrillas and bandits, Clark wrote to Santiago Vidaurri, governor of the Mexican states of Nuevo and Coahuila, stating the desire of the southern and Texas people for continued friendly relations and goodwill. Clark also wrote to the governor of Tamaulipas expressing friendship and thanks for peaceful relations with that Mexican state.[13]

As the war grew in intensity, the recruitment and enrollment of troops required more and more attention. In June, Clark issued a proclamation reorganizing the archaic militia system of the state. Camps of instruction were set up in each of eleven militia districts. Militia men were to be mustered into volunteer companies and report to the camps for training while they awaited further orders from Confederate authorities. The troops were required to furnish their own weapons as the state and Confederate governments had exhausted their meager supplies.[14]

The new camp system worked reasonably well. Additional requisitions in the summer and fall were met by state officials, although there continued to be confusion caused by the Confederate War Department authorizing individuals to raise military units either without informing state officials or in competition with state efforts. In addition, some individuals were authorized to recruit cavalry in Texas, a privilege denied to state officials.[15]

In spite of the frustrations associated with the recruitment problem, Clark worked closely with Confederate authorities. When Secretary of War Walker wrote to Clark requesting help in obtaining supplies for the army, the governor asked the people of Texas to form committees and societies in each county for the purpose of collecting blankets, comforts, and warm clothing for the troops fighting in northern Arkansas, Kentucky, and Virginia. He further urged Texans to manufacture their own woolen clothing and blankets as a part of the war effort.[16] Shortly thereafter, Clark informed Secretary Walker that wool could be purchased in Texas and converted into cloth at the state penitentiary at the rate of a thousand yards a day. Soon various Confederate quartermasters throughout the South were contracting with penitentiary officials for the purchase of woolen cloth, a practice that continued throughout the war.[17]

Although the financial situation continued to look bleak as Commissioner Nichols reported he could find no buyers for Texas bonds, Clark was reasonably satisfied with his efforts as the state's chief executive. He was hopeful that the voters would reward his efforts by reelection in August. The state Democratic party had been unable to choose among Clark, former lieutenant governor Francis R. Lubbock, and Thomas Jefferson Chambers in its convention; consequently, all three offered themselves as candidates.

Although the war limited the campaigning of the principals, the 1861 election was nevertheless a spirited one. All three men pledged to prosecute the war with vigor and to cooperate with Confederate authorities in that objective. Although the influential *Texas State Gazette* of Austin was complimentary of Clark's conduct in recruiting and enrolling troops, most of the state's newspapers, including the *Gazette*, supported Lubbock, who was the favorite of Democratic party leaders. Charles DeMorse, editor of the Clarksville *Standard*, was especially critical of Clark. DeMorse accused Clark of being a Know-Nothing in the mid-fifties and of riding Houston's coattails to victory in 1859, only later to turn against Houston when he saw the opportunity to become governor.[18]

The outcome of the election was surprisingly close. Lubbock received 21,854 votes, Clark 21,730, and Chambers 13,733.[19] Thus Lubbock was chosen governor of Texas by a 124-vote margin. Although there were widespread rumors of fraud, Clark accepted the outcome of the election without protest.

Clark's eight-month tenure as chief executive came to an end with the inauguration of his successor on November 7, 1861. In his valedictory address to the legislature, Texas's first Civil War governor recounted some of the difficulties he faced as he moved to prepare the people for a war much larger than anyone had anticipated. He noted the successes of state authorities in supplying twenty thousand men for the Confederate army and described some of the problems in equipping such numbers for military service. He pointed with pride to the reorganization of the state's militia system, but admitted the failure to resolve the financial problems of the state. He concluded by thanking the people for their support and wishing his successor well.[20]

In her study of the Texas governorship, Fredericka Meiners notes that Clark "was not one to assume powers arbitrarily."[21] Certainly he had proceeded cautiously and within his constitutional limitations as governor. Even so, Texas's first Civil War governor had exercised more power than any previous chief executive in the recruiting, enrolling, and training of troops, in the purchasing of weapons and supplies, and in communicating not only with Confederate governmental and military officials but governors of Mexican states as well.[22] Subsequent events illustrate that his successors would be required to exercise even more authority.

Following his defeat in the governor's race, Clark received a commission in the Confederate army as colonel of the Fourteenth Texas Infantry Regiment. The regiment served as a part of Walker's Division in Louisiana during 1863 and 1864, and participated in the battles of Mansfield and Pleasant Hill in the Red River campaign. Clark himself was wounded in the leg while leading an attack at Pleasant Hill and subsequently discharged from the army. He was promoted to the rank of brigadier general before his discharge, but the promotion was never confirmed by Richmond authorities.[23]

When the war ended, Clark fled to Mexico with other prominent civil and military leaders of the Southwest. He remained there only briefly, however, and returned to his home in Marshall. After engaging in several business ventures with little success, he reopened his law practice. He died on May 4, 1880, and was buried in Marshall.[24]

Francis Richard Lubbock, who succeeded Edward Clark as governor in November 1861, was born in Beaufort, South Carolina, on October 15, 1815. He attended private schools until he was fourteen, when his father's death led him to take employment as a hardware clerk. After managing a cotton warehouse in Hamburg, South Carolina, Lubbock moved to New Orleans, where he opened a drugstore. In February 1835 he married Adele Baron, the daughter of a prominent New Orleans cotton merchant.[25]

In October 1836 Lubbock journeyed to Texas to look for his brother, who was a member of a military company fighting for Texas independence, and after locating the brother returned to New Orleans determined to make Texas his home. In January 1837 he moved to the new community of Houston, where he entered the mercantile business.[26] Lubbock quickly immersed himself in the political life of the new Republic. He was chosen assistant clerk of the Texas House of Representatives in 1837, and elevated to the post of chief clerk in 1838. Shortly thereafter, President Sam Houston appointed him comptroller of the Republic. Lubbock returned to private life when Houston's tenure as president ended, but resumed his duties as comptroller when Houston was reelected president in 1841. He resigned the post soon thereafter in order to serve as district clerk of Harris County.

During the 1840s Lubbock continued to serve as district clerk while operating a ranch south of Houston. He helped organize the Democratic party in Texas and in the 1850s broke with his old mentor Sam Houston over the Know-Nothing movement which Houston supported and Lubbock opposed.[27] In 1857 Lubbock was elected lieutenant governor of Texas on a ticket with Hardin Runnels, who was chosen governor. Two years later Runnels and Lubbock were defeated in their bid for reelection by the two men they had defeated in 1857, Sam Houston and Edward Clark.

In 1860 Lubbock served as one of eight Texas delegates to the national Democratic convention in Charleston. He was temporary chairman of the convention that later chose John C. Breckinridge as the southern candidate for president. When Lincoln was elected president in November 1860, Lubbock was among those Texans urging separation from the Union. His brother, Tom, was elected to the secession convention in January, and Francis made speeches and wrote letters supporting secession.[28]

Once Texas seceded, the Lubbock brothers moved in different ways to serve their state. Tom, the younger brother, traveled to Virginia almost at once and participated in the Battle of First Manassas and later helped to organize the Eighth Texas Cavalry Regiment. Francis, whose previous military experience had been confined to a brief campaign against the Indians in 1838, announced that he would be a candidate for governor in the summer elections. Following his narrow victory over Edward Clark in the August 1861 elections, Lubbock went to Richmond to confer with Confederate authorities prior to his inauguration. There he met with President Davis and discussed ways in which Texas could offer support for the Confederacy. After visiting Texas troops stationed in the Richmond area, the governor-elect returned to Texas.[29]

Lubbock was inaugurated on November 7. In his inaugural message the new governor praised the efforts that Texans had made to defend their liberties, but called for even greater sacrifices. While he commended the Davis administration for its ability and integrity, he encouraged his fellow Texans to strengthen their own defenses "against the polluted trends of abolition hordes." He also pointed to the need for frontier protection against Indian attacks and urged Texans to pay both Confederate and state taxes in order that the government could operate efficiently.[30]

Lubbock elaborated upon these points in his message to the legislature delivered on November 15. Because of the failure to sell the million dollars in bonds authorized by the last legislature, the public treasury was empty. Lubbock recommended an increase in the ad valorem tax from 16½ cents to 25 cents per $100. In order to provide public funds until new revenue could be collected, the governor recommended the issuance of noninterest-bearing treasury warrants, payable at the treasurer's office out of monies not otherwise appropriated. He also requested that the legislature formulate a system for frontier protection, revise the militia law to validate and improve practices begun by the previous administration, establish a state cannon foundry, and expand the facilities of the state penitentiary.[31]

The legislature worked throughout December and early January to meet the governor's recommendations. On Christmas Day a new militia act was approved. The act divided the state into thirty-three brigade districts, each commanded by a brigadier general, and made all white males liable for military service. It also provided that companies assemble every two weeks for training. Regimental or battalion drill was to be held every two months. The law gave the governor the power to resort to a draft by lottery if the response to a call for volunteers was not sufficient.[32]

In December the legislature also passed legislation creating a frontier regiment. The companies of this regiment were to be stationed along the frontier at posts approximately twenty-five miles apart. The legislature instructed Lubbock to attempt to get the Davis administration to accept the unit into Confederate service, but stipulated that the regiment was always to be subject to state control and could not be moved outside of Texas.[33]

On January 11, 1862, the legislature passed a revenue act containing most of the features recommended by Governor Lubbock. The ad valorem tax was raised to 25 cents per $100 valuation, the poll tax was increased from 50 cents to one dollar, and an earlier practice of imposing a license fee upon doctors, lawyers, and dentists was reinstituted. State treasury warrants and Confederate treasury notes were made receivable for state taxes and state lands.[34]

The same day the legislature enacted the tax bill it also passed an act creating the Texas State Military Board. Creation of the board, "the only governmental agency the state set up to deal with the immediate needs of the war,"[35] was the result of a request from acting Secretary of War Judah P. Benjamin to Governor Lubbock to exchange U.S. 5 percent indemnity bonds held by Texas for Confederate 8 percent bonds so that the U.S. bonds could be used by Confederate authorities for the purchase of arms and ammunition. In January, Lubbock recommended acceptance of the proposal to the legislature. Two days later the legislature responded with two measures, one creating the Texas State Military Board consisting of the governor, treasurer, and comptroller, and the other authorizing the board to replace any bonds held by the state with an equal amount of Confederate bonds. The board was also empowered to use $500,000 of the state bonds authorized in April 1861 for the purchase of military supplies and was instructed to establish an ordnance foundry and small-arms factories.[36]

The new board, consisting of Governor Lubbock, Comptroller C. R. Johns, and Treasurer C. H. Randolph, went to work almost at once. Early efforts to exchange the U.S. indemnity bonds for badly needed war materials were largely unsuccessful, in part due to foreign investors' fears relating to the policy of the Federal government toward the bonds and in part due to the ineptness of the agents employed by the board.

The board was only slightly more successful in its efforts to exchange Texas cotton for war materials. In February 1862 it asked the people of Texas to sell their cotton to the board in exchange for 8 percent state bonds. The cotton would then be used to pay for goods coming from Mexico and Europe. Although some supplies were obtained in this manner, transportation problems, high prices, border unrest, and untrustworthy agents limited the successes of the board.[37]

The Military Board worked diligently throughout Lubbock's administration. A foundry was established in Austin in 1862, but turned out only a few brass cannon. The cap and cartridge factory also established by the board at Austin was apparently more successful. Governor Lubbock notes in his memoirs that the board was "almost in continuous session" throughout 1862 and 1863, although he confessed that his own attendance was frequently interrupted by other duties.[38]

Like his predecessor, Lubbock spent much time attempting to fill Confederate requisitions for troops. In early February 1862 he received a call from Secretary Benjamin requesting that the state furnish an additional fifteen regiments for Confederate service. To fulfill this levy, Lubbock issued a proclamation to the people of Texas on February 26, urging them to respond to the call for troops. While he believed that patriotic Texans would respond, he cautioned that if necessary he would draft troops to fill the quota.[39]

During the spring and summer months Lubbock received additional requests for troops. He continued to cooperate with Confederate authorities, but frequently criticized what he considered to be mistakes. Like Edward Clark, Lubbock was particularly unhappy with independent recruiters who operated without the restrictions played upon state authorities.

The passage of a general conscription law by the Confederate Congress in April 1862 relieved state officials from the necessity of instituting a local draft. The measure did increase the hostility of Unionist elements to the Confederacy. This opposition was particularly strong in the German counties of central Texas. Lubbock received many reports from loyal southerners during the summer months reporting rumors of Unionist meetings and activities, but he himself remained calm and left the matter for the Confederate government to resolve. When Confederate military authorities did institute martial law, they received Lubbock's full support.[40]

Lubbock considered the possibility of a Union invasion a greater threat than the activities of Texas Unionists. He was especially concerned about the defense of the state's largest seaport, Galveston. On December 7, 1861, he wrote to General Paul O. Hebert, the new Confederate commander of Texas, emphasizing the importance of the isle city. "Every effort should be made to prevent the enemy from effecting a landing," wrote Lubbock. The loss of Galveston would be a serious blow to Texas; "it would dispirit the people from one end of the state to the other." Lubbock urged that every effort be made to defend the city, and, that failing, the city itself should be destroyed rather than allow the enemy its control.[41]

Lubbock's letter to General Hebert aroused concern from Galvestonians that the governor intended to burn the city. This Lubbock denied, both in a letter to Galveston Mayor Thomas M. Joseph and in a speech he delivered in Galveston.[42]

The threat to Galveston became a reality in May when Captain Henry Eagle, commanding U.S. naval forces off Galveston, demanded its surrender. General Hebert refused to surrender the city, but did order all civilians, livestock, and excess provisions off the island. Lubbock, in Houston at the time, issued a proclamation organizing the removal and calling upon Texans to provide food, clothing, and other assistance to the refugees.[43]

Union military forces were active in other parts of the Confederate Southwest in the spring and summer of 1862. The fall of New Orleans and Memphis caused fear in the Trans-Mississippi states that they would be abandoned. In June, Governor Henry M. Rector of Arkansas issued a statement indicating that his state, Texas, and Missouri might withdraw from the Confederacy and form their own government.

Lubbock wrote to President Davis assuring him of Texas's loyalty to the Confederacy. Davis in turn sent Major Guy M. Bryan, a Texan serving on Hebert's staff, to confer with Lubbock. At Bryan's suggestion, Lubbock issued a general invitation to Governors Rector of Arkansas, Thomas O. Moore of Louisiana, and Claiborne Jackson of Missouri to meet with him at Marshall for the purpose of preparing plans for the defense of the Trans-Mississippi states.[44]

Neither Governor Rector nor Moore attended the Marshall conference held in late July. Nevertheless, Lubbock and Jackson prepared a letter to President Davis and a proclamation to the people which both Rector and Moore endorsed. In the letter to Davis, the governors urged that a commanding general over all the states west of the Mississippi be appointed, that a branch of the Confederate treasury with power to issue money be established, and that twenty thousand to thirty thousand small arms be provided for equipping soldiers from the Southwest states.[45] In their address to the people, the governors reiterated their support for Confederate leadership and urged their citizens to make even greater sacrifices for the common good. "Gird on your swords, shoulder your rifles, and be ready for the word of command when given by the government of our choice and affection," the address concluded.[46]

Lubbock believed the Marshall meeting was beneficial in quieting some dissatisfaction within the state, but felt the central government could give little assistance to the states of the Southwest. President Davis's reply to the governor's letter offered some reassurance that the Trans-Mississippi was not being forgotten. The president pointed out that General Theophilus Holmes had been appointed commander of the newly created Department of the Trans-Mississippi and that efforts were being made to provide more supplies and money for the department.[47]

While Davis's letter afforded hope, events of early autumn were discouraging. In September authorities in North Texas uncovered evidence of a Unionist plot that resulted in a series of hangings. Governor Lubbock was not directly involved but was no doubt concerned about the existence of similar plots elsewhere in the state.

In early October, Lubbock received the startling news that Galveston had fallen to the enemy without a fight. He set off for the coast at once. In Houston he conferred with Confederate military authorities and local officials about steps to defend Houston and the mainland from further advances.[48]

Lubbock was pleased when the Confederate War Department removed General Paul Hebert from command of Texas. Hebert had never been popular with Texans; his emphasis upon military protocol had offended frontier Texans from the start, and with the loss of Galveston without a fight, they were convinced Hebert was a coward as well.[49]

The new commander for Texas, John B. Magruder, was popular with Texans. Although he had a courtly bearing that gained him the nickname "Prince John," Magruder was an experienced campaigner who had a reputation as a fighter. Almost immediately he began planning for the recapture of Galveston.

Lubbock met with Magruder in Houston in mid-December. The governor approved Magruder's plans for retaking Galveston and planned to accompany him in the effort. The press of official duties and an attack of rheumatism brought on by a cold contracted in Houston while helping to quell a jail riot, however, prevented Lubbock from participating in the recapture of the isle city on January 1, 1863.[50] The governor was jubilant over Magruder's success, which Lubbock characterized as "the most daring affair of the war." He assured Magruder that "you have fixed yourself permanently in the hearts of Texans."[51]

Although the recapture of Galveston buoyed Lubbock's spirits, other matters continued to cause concern. Opposition to conscription led to mass meetings in several central Texas communities and rumors of Unionist activities spread throughout the state. In early January, Lubbock issued a proclamation demanding that all efforts to resist constitutional authorities cease. Martial law was declared in three counties and General Magruder sent troops to arrest ringleaders of the resistance. Lubbock himself went to La Grange to talk with opposition leaders. By late January, conditions in central Texas had improved.[52]

The growing problems associated with providing troops for the Confederacy and Lincoln's Emancipation Proclamation led Lubbock to call the legislature into special session in February. In his message to the lawmakers, the governor called upon them to support the Davis administration in its determination to resist Lincoln's plan "to Africanize the Southern Confederacy." He described the efforts of his office to provide troops and supplies for the military and urged the legislature to take bold measures to support the war effort. These included approving a new plan for defending the frontier, providing greater support for the families of soldiers, enforcing limitations upon the planting of cotton while encouraging the production of grain crops, and the raising of new tax dollars. In closing, Lubbock thanked the legislators for their support and announced that he would not seek reelection as he planned to enter the Confederate army at the end of his term.[53]

The legislature remained in session for a month, February 5 to

March 6, 1863. During this period the lawmakers carefully considered Lubbock's proposals. The ad valorem tax was raised to 50 cents per $100 as the governor had recommended, and additional taxes were imposed upon loans, monetary transactions, spiritous liquors, and certain occupations. A joint resolution to limit the planting of cotton was approved in both houses, but a bill which would have provided the method of enforcing such a limitation was defeated in the Senate.[54] A bill providing $600,000 for the relief of soliders' families was adopted on the last day of the session. Although the governor believed that a larger sum should have been voted, he considered this the most important measure adopted by the special session.[55]

The lawmakers only partially met the governor's request relating to frontier protection. While the legislature approved Lubbock's creation of the Mounted Regiment of Texas State Troops, only $800,000 was appropriated for its expense, half of that the governor believed necessary. Again the legislature authorized the transference to Confederate service, but with the stipulation that "the regiment shall be retained upon the Indian frontier of Texas," a condition which President Davis found unacceptable.[56]

Lubbock continued to wrestle with problems of war throughout the spring and summer of 1863. A special legislative committee appointed to investigate the textile operations at the state penitentiary made its report in late April. While the committee was critical of some management practices at the penitentiary, the officers of the institution were exonerated from any criminal wrongdoing, much to the governor's satisfaction. The possibility of a Union invasion led to a new call for troops in June. The fall of Vicksburg and Port Hudson the following month meant that Texas and the Southwest were now cut off from the rest of the Confederacy. The seriousness of the situation caused Edmund Kirby Smith, who now commanded the Trans-Mississippi Department, to call a meeting of the Southwest governors in Marshall in early August.

The second Marshall conference was better attended than the first. In addition to Lubbock, who was chosen chairman of the conference, Governors Thomas O. Moore of Louisiana and Thomas C. Reynolds of Confederate Missouri were in attendance, as was also Marshall attorney Pendleton Murrah, who had just been elected to succeed Lubbock as governor of Texas. Governor Harris Flanagin of Arkansas was not present, but was represented by Robert M. Johnson, Confederate senator from that state. Several other judges and senators from the four states were also in attendance.[57]

The Marshall conference lasted several days with Kirby Smith first presenting items for consideration, the items being referred to committees appointed by the chairman, and then discussion of committee recommendations. Resolutions recommending the appointment of an agent to deal with French and Mexican authorities in Mexico, calling upon Smith to assume greater powers in matters relating to the defense of the department, and expressing confidence in Smith's handling of the department were approved. The Texas delegation to the conference favored a plan to pay for impressed cotton in certificates redeemable in Confederate bonds, but this proposal was defeated.[58] In closing the conference, the governors issued a proclamation to their people expressing their determination to remain a part of the Confederacy in spite of the obstacles they faced.[59]

Lubbock was well satisfied with the results of the second Marshall conference. He returned to Austin where he spent the last months of his administration responding to various pleas for money, men, and supplies. In September and October he received two most unusual requests. One, from B. Théron, the French consul at Galveston, implied that if Texas would resume its independent status as a nation it would receive French assistance. This suggestion Lubbock, a determined and loyal Confederate, treated with scorn. After advising Théron that Texas had no intention of leaving the Confederacy, the governor forwarded the correspondence to President Davis, who expelled the Frenchman.[60]

A similar request came from John Tyler, son of former President Tyler. In a letter addressed to Lubbock, Murrah, and other state officers, Tyler pointed out that Texas, once a part of the Louisiana Territory, had the right to appeal to the French government for protection. Lubbock considered this a scheme to divide the South and dismissed the matter as "many pages of beautiful English" wasted to no purpose.[61]

In his message to the legislature which assembled on November 4, Lubbock reemphasized the need for unity of all citizens in support of the Confederacy. In his farewell address delivered the next day, Lubbock urged lawmakers to punish deserters, control extortioners and speculators, force shirkers into military service, and eliminate exemptions from military service. That evening Lubbock appeared at Governor Murrah's inaugural ball in the uniform of a lieutenant colonel in the Confederate army. His career as a politician was ended for now; his service as a military officer was beginning.[62]

Lubbock could look back upon his administration with satisfaction. The frontier was safe from Indian attack, the financial condition of the state was reasonably sound, the enemy had been driven from Galveston and repulsed at Sabine Pass, troop quotas had been met, and soldiers' families were receiving relief. The Trans-Mississippi was cut off from the rest of the Confederacy, but Lubbock did not consider this fatal. Although there was a growing weariness on the part of the people, Lubbock refused to countenance defeatist talk. The recent Confederate victory at Chickamauga convinced him that the war could be won if the southern people were willing to sacrifice.

In December, Lubbock joined the staff of General Magruder. After brief service as inspector of field transportation, the former governor was reassigned to the staff of Major General John A. Wharton in Louisiana. In August 1864 he became an aide-de-camp to President Davis. Lubbock accompanied Davis when Richmond was evacuated in April 1865 and was with the Confederate president when he was captured near Irwinsville, Georgia, on May 10, 1865.

Lubbock was held in Union prison at Fort Delaware for several months. Upon his release, he returned to Texas where he resumed his business activities. After sustaining financial reverses in the beef-packing industry, he reentered politics. In 1878 he was elected state treasurer, a post he held for twelve years. He served on the State Board of Pardons under James Stephen Hogg, finally retiring from public service in 1895 at the age of eighty. He spent the last years of his life in Austin, where he died on June 22, 1905. He was buried in the state cemetery in a coffin draped with both Confederate and United States flags.[63]

Pendleton Murrah was not as well known as the two men who preceded him as chief executive of Civil War Texas. He was apparently born in South Carolina in the late 1820s and raised in an orphanage. Murrah entered Brown University in 1845 and was graduated in 1848. He then migrated to Alabama, where he studied law, but he suffered from tuberculosis and in 1850 went to Texas seeking the relief of a dry climate. He opened his law office in Marshall, the center of northeast Texas cotton production and county seat of Harrison County. There he met Sue Ellen Taylor, daughter of a wealthy planter, and after a brief courtship the two were married on October 16, 1850.[64]

By the mid-1850s Murrah was one of Marshall's most successful attorneys. In 1855 he was an unsuccessful Democratic candidate for the state legislature. He ran again in 1857 and was victorious. The following year he was chosen as a member of the Democratic State Executive Committee. He announced as a candidate for the Confederate Congress in 1861 but withdrew due to ill health. He served briefly as an officer in the Fourteenth Texas Infantry Regiment commanded by former Governor Edward Clark, but poor health forced him to resign his commission.[65]

Murrah's health improved sufficiently so that he entered the governor's race in the summer of 1863. At first it appeared there would be a wild scramble for the post being vacated by Lubbock as various individuals including Murrah, Thomas Jefferson Chambers, William P. Ballinger, Guy M. Bryan, Fletcher Stockdale, Henry E. McCulloch, and even Sam Houston were mentioned as potential contenders. Eventually, only Murrah and Chambers, a wealthy Gulf coast planter who had previously run for governor three times, were candidates in the election. Although Murrah was much less well known than Chambers, the Harrison lawyer benefited from Chambers's reputation as a political maverick and a foe of the Davis administration. Party leaders and newspaper editors regarded Murrah, whose political views were not well known, as a safer candidate.[66]

Murrah's victory over Chambers in the August elections was interpreted by most observers as an endorsement of the Davis administration and an indication that state officials would continue to work closely with Confederate authorities. Although the new governor spoke of the necessity for defining boundaries of power and authority between state and Confederate officials in his inaugural address, he also pledged continued support of the Confederacy and stressed the need for personal sacrifice by the people.[67] In his message to the legislature delivered three weeks later, Murrah reemphasized positions of his predecessors—the need for better frontier protection, more arms and ammunition, a stable currency, militia reorganization, and penitentiary reform.

Indication that Murrah intended to chart a more independent course first came in a controversy with General Magruder over impressment of slaves. In December 1863 Magruder issued an appeal to Texas planters and farmers for the use of their slaves in building military fortifications. His superior, Kirby Smith, convinced Magruder to amend the call to include only 25 percent of the male slave population, but this modification did not satisfy Governor Murrah. In a ten-page letter to the general, Murrah indicated that, unlike his predecessor, he did not intend to allow military authorities a free hand in the matter of impressment. He advised Magruder to limit the number of slaves called to those actually needed and suggested that the army try to contract for slave labor rather than impressing it.[68]

Murrah's disagreement with Confederate military authorities extended to the enrollment of troops for the army. Since November 1862 the state had been enrolling individuals subject to Confederate conscription in the state militia. Although the Conscript Bureau of the Confederate Trans-Mississippi Department objected to the practice, General Magruder had not intervened. Eight thousand state troops had been placed under Confederate command for a six-month period in

1863 to defend the Texas coast, and Magruder hoped that the legislature would eventually pass laws turning these troops over to the Confederate army for the remainder of the war.[69]

The militia act passed by the tenth Texas legislature in December 1863 made no provision for transferring Texas troops to Confederate service as Magruder wished. Upon recommendation of Governor Murrah, the legislature continued the policy of enrolling individuals between eighteen and fifty years of age in the state militia. Those living in border counties would be formed into frontier defense companies and those living elsewhere would be subject to the governor's call.[70]

The new Texas law and Governor Murrah's proclamation implementing it caused much confusion. Many Texas soldiers who were residents of frontier counties but who were serving elsewhere believed the new law applied to them and left their units to return home. Others interpreted Murrah's proclamation as meaning that they could serve only in state units and not in Confederate organizations. Still others, convinced that their period of service under Confederate command was over, headed home.[71]

For the next two months there was bickering between Magruder and Murrah over the enrollment of troops, especially conscripts. Magruder, whose patience had worn thin, contended that the Confederate conscription laws had superiority over state legislation and ordered all conscripts enrolled in Confederate service. Murrah, determined to uphold state sovereignty, criticized Magruder's high-handed tactics and insisted that in cases where the state and Confederacy had concurrent jurisdiction, such as he believed this to be, the Confederacy should give ground.[72]

In early February 1864, Murrah and Magruder met with district commander Kirby Smith in Houston in an effort to resolve their disagreements over conscription. Murrah continued to argue that the Confederacy had no right to draft men from the organized militia, a position which Magruder refused to accept. Kirby Smith, who wanted to avoid an open break with the Texas governor, proposed a compromise whereby the state could retain those militiamen already under arms provided that all or part of the militia might be subordinated to Confederate authority in case of an emergency. Murrah accepted the substance of Kirby Smith's proposal but did not promise to exclude potential Confederate conscripts from the militia in the future. Magruder was not totally satisfied with this arrangement, but temporarily the friction between state and Confederate authorities was reduced.[73]

The controversy between Murrah and Magruder was reopened in mid-March when it became evident that the Union advance up the Red River posed a major threat to the security of the Trans-Mississippi

Department. Magruder, under orders from Kirby Smith to strip manpower from Texas to reinforce Confederate troops in Louisiana, called upon Murrah to transfer control of state troops to Confederate authorities. Murrah objected unless the militiamen were permitted their state officers and brigade organizations and were guaranteed that they would not be employed outside the state. Magruder, who intended to use state troops to relieve Confederate forces in Texas for service in Louisiana, readily acceded to Murrah's request to keep militiamen within the state, but informed the Texas governor that under Confederate law he could not accept organized state brigades into Confederate service. Murrah at first refused to yield, but after receiving a second plea from Magruder on April 6 reluctantly agreed to Confederate demands. "I shall be forced, in view of the dangers surrounding the state and country," he wrote Magruder, "to co-operate with you in organizing them under the recent law of Congress."[74]

Murrah's concession came too late to have any effect upon the Red River campaign, but it did end the controversy between state and Confederate officials over the state militia and the general question of conscription. Murrah and the Texas legislature never conceded a special claim over potential conscripts who resided in the frontier counties. Murrah continued to maintain that frontier residents should serve in state forces defending the frontier and were not liable to Confederate conscription. In the summer and fall of 1864 the Conscription Bureau of the Trans-Mississippi Department attempted to obtain control of conscripts in the frontier counties, but state authorities refused to budge. Kirby Smith finally agreed to submit this matter to the Davis administration to settle, but the war ended before the issue could be resolved.[75]

An even more bitter controversy between Murrah and Confederate military authorities occurred concerning cotton purchases. In an effort to obtain badly needed money and supplies for his department, Kirby Smith had established a Cotton Bureau for the purpose of purchasing and selling cotton. Headquarters for the bureau were located in Shreveport, Louisiana, but a branch, known as the Texas Cotton Office, was established in Houston. The Cotton Office, which opened its doors in early December 1863, was authorized to purchase half of a planter's cotton with specie certificates which the Confederate government would later honor. The planter would also receive an exemption from impressment for the other half of his cotton and for the teams needed to transport it. Planters refusing to sell their cotton to the Cotton Office ran the risk of losing all of it under the Confederate Impressment Act of 1863.[76]

Texas planters and farmers were quick to criticize the activities of the newly established Cotton Office. Under the procedures established by Colonel William J. Hutchins, chief of the office, owners of the cotton were required to pay the cost of transporting cotton purchased by Hutchins's agents to Cotton Office depots, a charge which many Texans believed unfair. Too, there was no guarantee that the Richmond government would pay for the cotton purchased. Confidence in the Confederacy's ability to honor its financial commitments was declining rapidly and many planters had no desire to exchange half of their crop for depreciating Confederate certificates. Also, there was resentment towards the impressment of cotton from uncooperative owners. Texans believed they had contributed much to the Confederacy and opposed this additional intrusion into their lives.[77]

In response to the public criticism of the Cotton Office, Governor Murrah and the Texas legislature developed a "State Plan" for the purchase of cotton which, while satisfying the angry cotton planters, threatened to undermine the efforts of Kirby Smith's Texas Cotton Office. Under the plan, a new state organization called the Texas Loan Agency offered to purchase cotton at a fair market price, payable in 7 percent Texas bonds (payable in Texas land warrants rather than depreciated currency).[78] The State Plan also offered owners a way to protect their own cotton from Confederate impressment as the Loan Agency would transport all consigned cotton to the Rio Grande. Since the cotton in transit belonged to the state it was safe from Confederate impressment. Once the cotton reached the border, half would be returned to the owner and the other half would be purchased by the state with the 7 percent bonds.

The new State Plan was the immediate subject of controversy. Planters and farmers, pleased to obtain the 7 percent Texas bonds and at the same time protect their remaining cotton from the Cotton Office, responded eagerly to the efforts of the state agents. By March 1864 nearly half of the baled cotton in Texas had been sold to the state and officers of the Loan Agency were attempting to purchase the remainder. Colonel W. A. Broadwell, chief of the Cotton Bureau in Shreveport, complained to President Davis that state authorities would soon control all the cotton in the state. Pleas to Murrah from Broadwell, Hutchins, Magruder, and Kirby Smith failed to convince the governor that Texas should abandon its plan. Murrah did agree to suspend temporarily the purchase of additional cotton when Colonel Guy Bryan, Smith's aide, convinced him that speculators and profiteers were taking advantage of the State Plan. The controversy continued throughout the late spring, however, with charges and countercharges made by both sides. Officials of the Cotton Office claimed that state agents were still buying cotton in spite of Murrah's assurances to

Colonel Bryan. State authorities charged that Confederate officials were interfering with the free movement of state-owned cotton.[79]

New laws passed by the Confederate Congress to regulate export trade strengthened Kirby Smith's determination to control the cotton business. In early June 1864, Smith issued new regulations for the overland trade between his department and Mexico. Under these regulations only merchants licensed by the Cotton Bureau could engage in foreign commerce and only those merchants who shipped nothing but government cotton or agreed to import nothing but machinery, agricultural tools, ordnance, and quartermaster stores would be licensed. The effect of the regulations would be to give Confederate military authorities total control over the cotton trade.[80]

Smith's regulations touched off another round of correspondence between Texas and Confederate officials. In a series of letters to Smith, Murrah protested the new action as a violation of state sovereignty and interference with the rights of Texas citizens. Furthermore, the governor questioned the legality of Smith's actions. In forceful language, Smith replied that the State Plan threatened the interests of the Confederacy and weakened the department's capacity to defend itself against the enemy. While he admitted that his regulations were severe, Smith argued that they were in conformity with Confederate laws.[81]

At the Texas governor's invitation, Smith met with Murrah at Hempstead, Texas, in the second week of July 1864. No transcript of the meeting has survived, but Smith's appeals apparently had their effect upon Murrah. On July 19 the governor issued an address to the people of Texas in which he acceded to Smith's requests. In this message Murrah told the people that the survival of Texas depended upon the army's ability to import military supplies. To obtain these supplies, Murrah admitted, the army must have cotton for exchange. He appealed to patriotic Texans to deliver their cotton to the army's agents for compensation, and announced that the state would no longer extend protection to shipments of privately owned cotton.[82]

Murrah's capitulation at Hempstead ended the controversy between state officials and Kirby Smith over cotton. Ironically, the complaints made by Texas planters and Murrah against the impressment practices of the army led the Davis administration to take control of the cotton trade away from Smith's Cotton Bureau. On August 3, 1864, one year after the creation of the Cotton Bureau and two weeks after Murrah's address urging Texans to cooperate with army officials, the Confederate secretary of war directed Smith to transfer control of cotton transactions to the newly created Trans-Mississippi Treasury Department.[83]

While much of Murrah's time was devoted to defending state interests in the debates over conscription and impressment, there were
other issues that could not be ignored. The currency situation was a
matter of great concern to Texans in 1864. As the Confederate currency depreciated rapidly, the state government, which accepted Confederate notes at par value in payment for taxes, faced increased difficulty in maintaining financial solvency. The special session of the
legislature called by Governor Murrah in May 1864 did little to resolve
the financial difficulties of the state. The legislators did provide for the
exchange of the old issue of Confederate notes for a new issue authorized by the Confederate Congress.

The continued inflationary spiral and depreciation of Confederacy
currency forced Murrah to call another special session of the legislature in October. Upon Murrah's recommendation the legislature made
certain taxes payable in specie, state warrants, or state bond specie
coupons. The legislature also repealed a previous measure authorizing
one million dollars in warrants for relief and enacted a plan to distribute penitentiary cloth to the state's needy citizens. Unfortunately,
these efforts did little to turn the tide and the state's financial situation, as that of the Confederacy as a whole, continued to worsen.[84]

There was a growing weariness and despair by many Texans during
the winter months of 1864–65 as the South sustained additional military defeats. In an effort to boost morale, Governor Murrah addressed
the people of Texas on January 14, 1865. In a ringing message more
characteristic of Lubbock than Murrah the governor insisted that independence could still be won if the people would put aside their personal
ambitions and make sacrifices in defense of their liberty.[85]

Murrah's address apparently had little impact, however. New military reversals in Virginia and the Carolinas convinced most citizens
that the cause was hopeless. Even after the news of Lee's surrender
reached Texas, Murrah and Kirby Smith continued to urge resistance,
but widespread desertion and increased lawlessness demonstrated that
this was impossible. At a conference held in Marshall in early May
(which Murrah was unable to attend because of illness), Smith and the
Trans-Mississippi governors attempted unsuccessfully to find new
ways to end the fighting without a formal surrender. Murrah made an
effort to prevent Union military occupation by sending Ashbel Smith
and William P. Ballinger as special commissioners to negotiate with
Union officials in New Orleans, but the Texas delegation was informed
that terms for surrender had been negotiated already and were awaiting Kirby Smith's approval. Smith affixed his signature to the surrender document on June 2, 1865.[86]

Murrah had naively hoped that Union authorities would not interfere with the civil government of the state. In late May he announced an election on June 19 for delegates to a state convention which would meet in July to restore Texas to the Union. He also called a special session of the legislature to meet later in July. At the same time he called upon local sheriffs to preserve law and protect property in the transition period.

In early June, Murrah heard rumors that the Union government meant to punish Confederate political and military leaders. Since he continued to suffer from the debilitating effects of tuberculosis, he decided to avoid a long imprisonment by escaping to Mexico. On June 12 he vacated his office, leaving Lieutenant Governor Fletcher Stockdale in charge, and joined other Confederate and state officials who were traveling southward with General Joseph D. Shelby and his cavalry.

The long trip to Mexico was too much for Murrah. He was confined to bed upon reaching Monterrey and on August 4, 1865, Texas's last Civil War governor died.[87]

As governor, Pendleton Murrah had faced more difficult tasks than either Edward Clark or Francis Lubbock, who had served as chief executive before the war had taken such a toll upon the resources of the state and the South. From the beginning Murrah had tried to uphold and defend what he considered to be the fundamental rights of the state. In doing so he received much criticism from Confederate officials and some civilians who considered him an obstructionist. Indeed, most historians have been similarly critical of Murrah, charging him with being obstinate, with quibbling over details, and with being provincial.[88] The most recent study of Murrah, by Fredericka Meiners, however, notes that he did "place Confederate interests ahead of state ones when necessary for the department."[89] In the controversies over both conscription and the cotton trade it was Murrah who gave in to Confederate authorities when convinced that the good of the Confederacy depended upon it.

Like Clark and Lubbock before him, Murrah had to make many adjustments to meet the changing conditions which confronted him. He found cooperation with Confederate military authorities more difficult than either of his predecessors. In part this was due to his strong views on states' rights; in part it was the result of new circumstances which forced state and Confederate officials to compete for the same limited resources of men, money, and materials. All three of Texas's wartime governors, Clark, Lubbock, and Murrah, had been required to expand the powers of their office far beyond those exercised by the state's antebellum governors. In raising and equipping troops, purchasing and selling raw materials, establishing manufactories, and dealing with military authorities, the Civil War governors moved into areas in which prewar Texas chief executives had little experience.

VIRGINIA

F. N. Boney

ohn Letcher, the first of Virginia's two Civil War governors, was born on March 28, 1813, and grew up in a stable, middle-class environment at Lexington, a small commercial center in the heart of the Shenandoah Valley. He and his brother and sister were part of a loving and affluent family, but some tensions developed as the children matured. John rejected the stern Methodist puritanism of his parents and never really accepted traditional Christianity. He became a gregarious young man who smoked, drank, and partied enthusiastically. His father, a self-made businessman, was not pleased, and when his twenty-two-year old son casually dropped out of Washington College he was put to work as a manual laborer and told to sink or swim on his own.

Almost overnight John Letcher matured. He began reading law as a clerk for a local lawyer, and he joined his father in the ranks of the Democrats who were led by President Andrew Jackson and opposed by the emerging Whig party. Letcher soon became the lieutenant of James McDowell, a leading Democrat in the Valley who would become governor the state in 1843. An ambitious, energetic lawyer-politician, Letcher remained friendly and unpretentious, but, motivated by marriage and a fast-growing family, for the rest of his life he labored relentlessly at his calling—more influenced by his parents than he might have realized. A typical American on the make, Letcher had charted the course of his life, but he could not dream of the terrible challenges that lay ahead.[1]

Always an optimist, young Letcher was not discouraged by the Whig predominance in his native Rockbridge County. In 1839 McDowell made him editor of the Lexington *Valley Star,* a new Democratic newspaper, but even at the peak of his youthful enthusiasm Letcher demonstrated a characteristic moderation. Emphasizing issues rather than personalities, on the national level he advocated traditional states' rights and strict constitutional construction and rejected protective tariffs, monopolies, abolition, and internal improvements by the Federal government. On the state level he favored state aid for internal improvements in his isolated western part of the state and championed democratic reform of Virginia's antiquated government. Unfazed by Whig counterattacks, Letcher considered himself a Jacksonian crusader riding the wave of the future. Certainly within conservative Virginia he was a liberal young politician.

Like most Virginians living west of the Blue Ridge Mountains, Letcher resented a governmental system which allowed the east to continue to dominate the state even though it no longer contained a majority of the white population. He frequently denounced this undemocratic system and in 1847, during a heated debate in Lexington, Letcher, the owner of a few slaves, even briefly supported a call for a division of the state and gradual emancipation in the west if the east did not yield to reform. Finally, in 1850, the legislature authorized a constitutional convention. Letcher was elected a delegate and played a significant role in the writing of a new state constitution which greatly increased the number of elected officials, including the governor, proclaimed universal white manhood suffrage, and provided for the gradual equalization of representation in the legislature.[2]

Letcher had helped Jacksonian Democracy triumph in conservative old Virginia, and he quickly took advantage of his new popularity in the west by running for Congress in 1851. He recanted his one superficial flirtation with emancipation and won easily in a Democratic district where even the Whig minority was pleased with his performance at the state constitutional convention. His support in the Valley was secure and he remained in Congress for four consecutive terms through the 1850s.

The moderate liberal from Virginia soon became the moderate conservative in Washington. He had accomplished all the reform he wanted back home, and in Congress he found himself in a national setting where the South was increasingly a minority under fire. Times were changing rapidly. The dying Whig party was soon replaced by a Republican party determined to contain slavery. The abolitionists in the North and the secessionists in the South were gaining strength, and the old middle ground of moderates like Letcher was eroding. Letcher rejected secession but at the same time defended the traditional rights and privileges of the South. Avoiding sectional controversy most of the time, he championed compromise and reconciliation, but he put most of his energy into a crusade for honesty and economy in the Federal government, and he became known as "Honest John Letcher, Watchdog of the Treasury."[3]

Letcher's congressional activities were reduced in 1858 when he made his bid for the governorship of Virginia. A quarrelsome Democratic convention gave him the nomination, and then he waged an intense campaign against the Whigs, who bitterly attacked "Emancipation John" for his 1847 flirtation with the abolition heresy. In the May 1859 election Letcher won a narrow victory, thanks to strong support in northwestern Virginia, an area the new governor would soon find hostile. But many Virginians, especially secessionists, were uneasy about their new governor who had once seemed receptive to emancipation and who still favored compromise with the hated North.[4]

On January 1, 1860, the forty-six-year-old Lexingtonian began his four-year term as governor of Virginia as the nation drifted toward civil war. Although often distracted by routine problems, Letcher worked hard to frustrate the secession movement in Virginia which had been stimulated by John Brown's raid at Harpers Ferry late in 1859. His inaugural address on January 7 gave him an opportunity to try to calm rising passions. He urged the legislators to call a convention of all the states to try to reach another sectional compromise, but he also called for increased spending on Virginia's military forces. Letcher opposed secession and war but he knew war was probably coming, and he felt obliged to recommend the very sort of military preparations which would help undermine his own moderate position. The legislators eagerly voted for increased military appropriations but delayed a call for a national convention for a whole year, and when the Peace Convention did finally convene in February 1861, it was too late for any meaningful compromise.

Governor Letcher also championed moderation within the Democratic party in Virginia, but the disruption of the national party at Charleston drove most Virginia Democrats into the camp of John C. Breckinridge, the candidate of the southern Democrats. Not the governor. On August 22 Letcher publicly called for "prudence and moderation . . . conciliation and compromise" and threw his support to Stephen A. Douglas, the candidate of the northern Democrats. In November Virginia went for John Bell instead of Breckinridge by the very narrow margin of only 358 votes out of a total of 167,000 cast. Over 16,000 Virginians, mostly Democrats, followed Letcher and voted for Douglas, depriving Breckinridge of a key state and leaving Virginia secessionists frustrated and furious.[5]

The election of Lincoln ended the old Union. South Carolina seceded immediately, and by February 1861 the rest of the Deep South had followed and the new Confederate States of America was being established. Virginia and the other border slave states wavered. The most populous and industrialized of all the southern states, Virginia was absolutely essential for the survival of the new Confederacy.

The secessionists made steady gains in Virginia, but Governor Letcher refused to yield. He opposed calling a state convention, the vehicle which had carried the deep southern states out of the Union, but finally in January 1861 he yielded to intense legislative pressure and issued a call for a convention to be held the following month. Still, he was encouraged when a clear majority of the delegates voted against secession in February and March. Desperately Letcher sought support from the enigmatic new president-elect, but Lincoln refused to speak out before his inauguration and the ranks of southern Unionists thinned rapidly.

Still trying to calm the rising passion of the people, Letcher moved very cautiously as he directed the gradual strengthening of Virginia's disorganized military forces. Then on April 12 Confederate artillery opened fire on Fort Sumter, and President Lincoln called for troops to suppress the rebellion. Governor Letcher curtly refused the Federal government's request for Virginia troops, and on April 17 the convention in secret session voted to secede.[6]

Suddenly a new era began, and Letcher found himself the wartime leader of the most powerful southern state. The time for moderation had passed; now it was his responsibility not only to prepare his state for bloody war but also to supervise its orderly integration into the Confederacy. During this early period of frantic activity, Letcher worked at a grueling pace. He occasionally delayed major policy decisions while he wrestled with routine red tape, but overall he operated efficiently to solve a mass of urgent new problems. Even some of the more fanatic prewar secessionists grudgingly admitted that the governor was a vigorous leader. Actually Letcher was what he had always been, a loyal Virginian with a practical bourgeois ability to adjust to the demands of the hour.

Like the other American states, Virginia mobilized enthusiastically but erratically, unaware of the horrors to come. Following convention orders, Letcher appointed a three-man Advisory Council which included his old friend Colonel Francis H. Smith, superintendent of the Virginia Military Institute, and Captain Matthew Fontaine Maury, who had resigned from the U.S. Navy to follow his native state. The governor was fully aware of his lack of military experience and he often followed his council's advice, but the responsibility was always solely his own. One of his most important early military duties was to appoint high-ranking officers, and he usually, but not always, selected capable men. He offered command of all state forces to U.S. Army

Colonel Robert E. Lee, who accepted and was enthusiastically approved by the convention. Despite complaints, he also commissioned Professor Thomas Jonathan Jackson of VMI a colonel and later supported the eccentric Jackson in a bitter dispute with Confederate authorities. Thus Governor Letcher was instrumental in the recruitment of two of the Confederacy's greatest generals.

Virginia's hectic, confused mobilization quickly produced hordes of volunteers but far too few weapons and other pieces of military equipment. Many unequipped volunteers had to be sent home, but, nevertheless, Letcher loaned some scarce weapons to other Confederate states. A practical man, he realized that the southern states would have to cooperate with one another in order to survive the coming holocaust.[7]

Letcher also realized that unity could only be achieved if the proud individual states yielded many traditional rights and powers to President Jefferson Davis's new central government which was moving to Richmond. This commonsense approach speeded up the effective organizing of the troops which were massing to defend the state from an expected Federal offensive. Not every southern governor was willing to cooperate so fully with the new Confederate government, and the complex, sensitive process of integrating Virginia into the Confederacy caused even Letcher to waver occasionally, but only one early dispute with Confederate authorities led to significant trouble.

At the time of secession Virginia forces had seized the famous Federal arsenal at Harpers Ferry. Modern rifle-making machinery there was vital in the agrarian South, so it was all quickly shipped to a state arsenal in Richmond and put into operation. Soon Confederate officials requested control of this machinery as part of the general transfer of all Virginia forces to Confederate command, but Letcher balked. For months he held on to the machinery despite pleas from Josiah Gorgas, head of Confederate ordnance, Secretary of War Leroy Pope Walker, and President Davis himself. Letcher only yielded under direct orders from the convention, and even then legalistic and bureaucratic hassles further delayed the actual transfer of the machinery until September, more than a month after the first major battle in Virginia at Manassas.[8]

This kind of obstructionism was uncharacteristic of Governor Letcher. He was not entirely immune to the old concepts of states' rights and strict legalism, powerful traditions which greatly weakened the southern war effort, but generally he was able to subordinate them to the more immediate and vital demands of victory in battle. His pragmatic determination to cooperate with Confederate authorities, even the more inept and obnoxious ones, was the main theme of his wartime administration.

Letcher's admiration for Jefferson Davis made cooperation easier. He believed that the aristocratic Mississippian was the best leader for the Confederacy in what Letcher expected would be a long, desperate struggle for independence. But the governor had little confidence in some of the president's key aides, especially Secretary of War Walker, Secretary of the Navy Stephen R. Mallory, Judah P. Benjamin, who held several cabinet posts during the course of the war, and to some extent Secretary of the Treasury Christopher G. Memminger. Unlike many southern politicians, Letcher, for the sake of unity, seldom publicly attacked Confederate authorities, but in private correspondence to friends he freely denounced those he considered inept.[9]

As he feared, the war dragged on and on despite some spectacular southern victories. Americans found themselves waging a modern war of attrition, and the outnumbered Confederates moved dramatically to maintain their battered armies in the field. In order to keep one-year volunteers from going home and to tap large reservoirs of ablebodied men who had never served, the Confederate government in April 1862 enacted the first national draft in American history. This radical violation of old individual and states' rights generated a storm of protests. In a hurried exchange of confidential correspondence between the southern governors Letcher joined the general denunciation of conscription, calling it unnecessary, unconstitutional, and "the most alarming stride towards consolidation that has ever occurred." He wanted only the states to draft, naively assuming that every southern state would be equally conscientious about mobilizing its unwilling manpower. But Letcher went much further and recommended supporting the unconstitutional Confederate draft until the war was won and then challenging it in the courts. Again he was the practical southern nationalist, supporting a controversial Confederate policy, realizing that the temporary abandonment of some precious rights was the only way to avoid military defeat and the permanent loss of much more. Governor Letcher publicly ordered Virginia officials to help enforce the unpopular new draft act.

Going even further, he cooperated with Confederate requests for call-ups of the state's rapidly dwindling militia units during emergencies. Despite waves of protests from the affected areas, the governor always activated militia units requested by Confederate field commanders. Sometimes only a few disgruntled men actually appeared for temporary service, but Letcher did what he could to reinforce Confederate defenses.[10]

From the very beginning Virginia had been the main battleground of the war, and the constant menace of Union military power had encouraged Letcher's cooperation with the Confederacy. Still, he worried that the Confederates might overlook some of Virginia's vital defense needs. He was an early exponent of guerrilla warfare, especially in the northwest, which had given him massive support in the gubernatorial election but was shifting toward the Union despite his every appeal and manipulation. Letcher actually organized a few "ranger" detachments but they performed poorly and were soon disbanded. Finally, in May 1862, the governor with the authorization of the legislature organized the Virginia State Line. This small state army was not designed as a refuge for draft-dodgers; only men ineligible for Confederate conscription were accepted. Still, it performed very little useful service. Never coming near its authorized strength of ten thousand troops, inadequately equipped, and poorly led by discredited General John B. Floyd, it was almost as much of a nuisance to the Confederates as it was to the Yankees. The Line demonstrated the inadvisability of fielding an independent state force in a larger Confederate theater of operations, but Governor Letcher, who had become a bit of an "armchair general" as the war raged on in his state, continued to champion the Line. By February 1863 the Line had accomplished little more than spending over a million dollars in state funds, so the legislature stepped in and, despite the governor's protests, disbanded this inept force.[11]

One of the reasons for the establishment of the Line was the vulnerability of vital salt works in western Virginia. Cut off from normal peacetime imports, the Confederacy was desperately short of this essential preservative, and prices soared. In the fall of 1862 the legislature passed this ticklish new problem on to the governor along with sweeping new powers. Letcher could do virtually anything to see that salt was produced and distributed at reasonable prices. He had no experience at being a salt czar, and he balked at extreme actions like price fixing and outright seizure. While trying to set up and operate a distribution system for Virginia, he became entangled in red tape. An organization was finally established, and a host of administrators fanned out over the state, but the new system did not function efficiently. It was not a complete failure, but the governor's unwillingness to use his full powers crippled it. Early in 1863 the legislature transferred the salt program to the Board of Public Works, which had no better luck with the problem.[12]

Letcher's failure to solve the salt problem was only part of the general failure of the wartime South to organize the home front efficiently, to mobilize its limited resources adequately. Like President Davis, Governor Letcher sometimes bogged down in details while delaying major decisions. Occasionally each acted more like a chief clerk than a chief executive, but this tendency was widespread among a whole generation of southern political leaders who were woefully unprepared for the administrative demands of modern war.

The most serious internal problem for the South was inflation. Often Governor Letcher publicly condemned "speculators" and "extortioners," even equating them with drunkards, adulterers, and fornicators in a speech in January 1863, but neither he nor the legislature, nor for that matter the Confederate government, could check the soaring prices which were relentlessly undermining the war effort on the home front.

Letcher also failed to stop northwest Virginia from pulling free of the South and establishing itself as the new Union state of West Virginia, but this would have required a major commitment of Confederate troops which were simply not available. And he never really fired his people with his oratory. His speeches were usually the long, dry, statistical summaries of a dutiful executive officer and never the clarion calls of a charismatic leader, but only Lincoln and perhaps a few others were ever able to truly stir the masses in this era.[13]

Governor Letcher had flaws aplenty, the flaws of a whole generation of southern politicians, but more than most he was able to rise above tradition and environment. In comparison to most Confederate state governors he was a model of selfless patriotism, a staunch Confederate nationalist. Even as the tide turned gradually against the South and war weariness increased, Letcher continued to cooperate with the Confederates and refused to consider anything less than victory and independence. He continued to support Jefferson Davis wholeheartedly, even as it became increasingly fashionable to blame every reversal on the embattled president. Letcher even tolerated Confederate impressment, the seizure of civilian property by government authorities. He detested this practice and had refused to do it himself while salt czar, but, as usual, for the sake of harmony and unity he seldom tried to hinder impressment despite rising protests from all over the state. He even supported Confederate impressment of slave laborers for temporary work on fortifications, a procedure which infuriated some influential planters.[14]

Letcher's support of the war effort was sometimes so enthusiastic that the Confederates were placed in an awkward position. In the summer of 1862 he advocated selecting a few of the captured Union soldiers from northwestern Virginia and trying them in state courts for treason. Any such action would have brought swift Union retaliation, so Confederate authorities declined to turn any Virginia prisoners of war over to Virginia "justice." As usual, Letcher agreed to abide by the decision of the central government. He also wanted to try some captured Union officers in state courts for the capital crime of inciting slave insurrections. President Davis and the Confederate Congress made similar threats in reaction to the Union's evolving emancipation policy and increased recruitment of black soldiers who were mostly former slaves, but once again the certainty of Union retaliation caused Confederate authorities to avoid an ugly confrontation. And again Letcher quietly accepted a Confederate decision.[15]

Letcher's policy of cooperating with the Confederates knew almost no limits, but the governor, an experienced politician, was fully aware of the risks involved. Early he spotted rising popular discontent with his strong executive leadership and consistent support of Confederate policies. This growing dissatisfaction was mirrored and even intensified in the legislature as the war dragged on and on. Some prewar secessionists in the legislature were itching to get even with Letcher, and many more moderate members were concerned that the governor had usurped too much of their power during the emergency.

Traditionally the legislature had dominated Virginia state government. The new constitution of 1851 had made the governor elective and enhanced his prestige, but the legislature still considered itself predominant. Virginia's Confederate legislature was an unimpressive body which seldom responded adequately to the governor's pleas for quick action. Letcher often operated independently without much liaison with the legislature, which grew increasingly resentful of his new aggressiveness and assertiveness. Trouble was inevitable.

At first Letcher received only scattered, uncoordinated criticism from individual legislators, pinprick assaults easily ignored. But soon the legislature initiated investigations of the governor's policies—his handling of the salt shortage, his cooperation with Confederate impressment, and especially his frequent mobilizations of state militia units in rapid response to the requests of Confederate generals. Letcher presented defenses which were always full of details and statistics and usually rather persuasive. Generally he performed well in wrestling with the complex problems of modern war—sometimes hopeless messes that the legislature had quickly passed on to him. Letcher clearly made some mistakes, but even some of the legislators grudgingly conceded that the governor had acted with complete honesty and considerable competency in attempting to lead his people to victory. Letcher was never officially censured, but these investigations were still a clear warning to him: be more cautious and restrained; do not be so eager to put Confederate interests ahead of the traditional rights and privileges of Virginia and its people.[16]

Letcher was too seasoned a politician to miss this message, and he did begin to act a little more cautiously and hesitantly. Gradually his leadership lost a little of its vitality as he depended more on legal opinions by Attorney General John Randolph Tucker. But Letcher was too much a Confederate patriot to fundamentally alter his policies. He tacked a little with the wind without changing his basic course. He continued to serve as an intermediary between a grumbling legislature which represented an increasingly disaffected population and the Confederate government which was struggling to mobilize its full strength against a powerful and relentless foe. Letcher performed this political juggling act admirably. He was an impressive leader, one of the most effective of the Confederate governors.

During 1863, Letcher's final year as governor, the rapidly expanding Confederate bureaucracy and the increasingly hostile state legislature assumed some of his responsibilities, but as the chief executive of the state where so much of the Civil War was actually fought, he remained very busy, much busier than prewar governors had ever dreamed of being. Still ambitious and optimistic, Letcher planned to continue his political career in the Confederate House of Representatives after he left the Governor's Mansion. In April he formally announced his candidacy to his old congressional constituents in the Valley.

The voters of the Confederacy were too distracted by the war to show their usual interest and enthusiasm, and the governor had no time for traditional politicking anyway. His local supporters conducted a brief, restrained campaign and then a very light turnout of voters decided the gubernatorial, legislative, and congressional contests on May 28. For the first time in his career Letcher lost a major election.

He was rejected by many of the same voters who had sent him to Congress for four consecutive terms before the war. The incumbent, John B. Baldwin, was a competent opponent, but the main reason for Letcher's defeat was clear enough. The people of the Valley—and the rest of the state, for that matter—did not approve of his wartime leadership. He had been too vigorous a leader, had asked too much of a proud, brave people who simply did not understand just how much times had changed. He had infringed too much on his people's ancient rights and subordinated old Virginia too much to the new upstart Confederacy. In a sense he had known too well what was needed to win and had been too successful in his policies.

Already depressed by the recent death of his friend "Stonewall" Jackson and financially strapped by Richmond's raging inflation, Letcher was shocked by this defeat in his home area. But, a firm believer in democracy, he accepted the will of the people with outward stoicism and got on with the business of the last months of his administration. He remained loyal to President Davis and the Confederacy, but increasingly his stubborn optimism was based on his faith in General Robert E. Lee—somehow, even after the debacle at Gettysburg, Lee's Army of Northern Virginia would gain the final victory.[17]

At the end of the year Governor Letcher's four-year administration was completed, and early in January 1864 he returned to Lexington to spend the rest of the war supporting the Confederacy as a private citizen. He was at peace with himself. He had done his best, risking popular disapproval to pursue policies he knew were essential. He had paid the price, losing the congressional election of 1863; now the struggle would have to be carried on by others, especially the new governor, William Smith.[18]

Born into a prominent family on September 6, 1797, Governor Smith was raised on a plantation in King George County near Fredericksburg. He received a sound basic education at a series of private academies but did not attend college. Instead he prepared for a legal career by clerking at several law offices, and in 1818 he began to practice in Culpeper, a small town in the upper piedmont. He married well and soon his own rapidly growing family spurred him to greater activity.

In 1827 he began a mail-coach service which soon became quite extensive. As a mail contractor he often received additional compensation from the United States Post Office for extra services rendered, and he soon became known as "Extra Billy." Spread too thin as a lawyer, a mail contractor, and increasingly as a politician, Smith was frequently in economic difficulties.[19]

He entered politics as a Jeffersonian Republican championing states' rights, strict constitutional construction, democracy, and frugal, honest government, and he retained these commitments when he became a Jacksonian Democrat in the late 1820s. An outstanding speaker and debater, he served from 1836 to 1841 in the state Senate, where he opposed monopolies and advocated strict regulation of banking and extensive internal improvements. Generally a liberal, he became a leading Virginia Democrat with more popular support in the west than in the east.

In 1841 he won a bitter campaign against the Whigs and went to the House of Representatives in Washington. There he concentrated on economic affairs, opposing protective tariffs and championing reduced expenditures by the Federal government. Pragmatic rather than doctrinaire, he relied heavily on facts and statistics in his numerous speeches. He was defeated for reelection in 1843 when his congressional district was redrawn by the state legislature to favor the Whigs.[20] Smith then moved from Culpeper to nearby Warrenton in Fauquier County. He concentrated on his law practice but also engaged in farming with a few slaves. He campaigned effectively as James K. Polk and the Democrats carried Virginia in 1844, and in return was elected governor by the Democratic legislature in 1845. Still financially insecure, Smith preferred a more lucrative seat in the

United States Senate, but, twice frustrated by the political power of the east, he concentrated on his crucial governorship.

On January 1, 1846, the forty-eight-year-old laywer-politician began his three-year term as governor, and four months later the United States was at war with Mexico. The new governor enthusiastically supported the war effort. He cooperated with the national government's efforts to mobilize troops, and, despite the state's initial unpreparedness and rising opposition to the war, he fielded the large regiment of volunteers requested. This experience in wartime administration would serve him well later.

Sectional controversy increased even as the United States was winning the war and Governor Smith denounced northern efforts to restrict slavery from territory taken from Mexico. He also found time to present a considerable domestic program during the war. He strongly advocated the removal of all free blacks from the state, but the legislature refused to act. His proposal for two major state-owned, east-west railroads and his suggestions for judicial reform were largely ignored too. Smith completed his administration on December 31, 1848, but he would once again face an independent-minded wartime legislature sixteen years later.[21]

Financially strapped as usual, Smith went alone to California in April 1849. He prospered practicing law and speculating in land and, inevitably, dabbling in Democratic politics. Three years later he returned to his family in Virginia, financially secure at last. Almost immediately he was reelected to Congress, where he served from 1853 to 1861. There he joined John Letcher in the Virginia delegation. Like Letcher, Smith became more conservative as the sectional controversy grew in the 1850s, but he was much more strident in his defense of the South and slavery, on one occasion even engaging in a brief fight on the floor of the House. He supported Letcher in the gubernatorial contest of 1859 and Breckinridge in the presidential election. After Lincoln's victory he favored the secession of the Deep South but wanted Virginia and the other border states to remain in the Union to mediate the controversy.[22]

When the fighting began at Fort Sumter, Smith followed his native state out of the Union. Although sixty-three years old and without military experience, Smith sought combat and Governor Letcher appointed him colonel of the Forty-ninth Virginia Infantry Regiment. Soon in Confederate service, Smith participated in many battles, showing more bravery than tactical skill. Wounded in the Peninsula campaign and again at Antietam, he returned to action as a brigadier general at Chancellorsville and Gettysburg. During the first half of the war Smith had also served briefly in the Confederate Congress by taking leaves from the army during inactive periods early in 1861 and 1863. He concentrated mainly on financial and military affairs and generally supported the Davis administration. Then early in 1863 he announced his candidacy for the governorship. The people were distracted by the war and paid little attention to the election, but Smith, with a sizable majority of the army vote, won over his main opponent, George Wythe Munford, one of Governor Letcher's assistants in the state government bureaucracy.[23]

Governor Smith began his second war-time administration on January 1, 1864. Like Letcher he was sometimes too preoccupied with routine duties, but, again like Letcher, overall he performed quite ably. He cooperated with the Confederate central government and urged Virginians to yield old rights and privileges to the demands of the hour and make an even greater effort for victory. Inevitably he often clashed with the recalcitrant state legislature.

In spite of legislative opposition, he organized some new home defense forces, but expanding Confederate conscription soon weakened this operation. Smith not only yielded to the draft but also called out his dwindling forces whenever the Confederates requested temporary, emergency reinforcements, again angering the legislators. He also cooperated with Confederate efforts to reduce the number of state and local officials exempt from the draft, and this led to another bitter feud with the legislature. Smith the combat veteran wanted to exempt only absolutely essential officials, and he was especially opposed to allowing continued exemptions for thousands of local officials who had refugeed from Union-held areas of the state. Occasionally the governor yielded to local pressures, but generally he was very sympathetic to increasing Confederate efforts to mobilize all ablebodied men in the besieged South.[24]

Governor Smith also cooperated with Confederate impressments of slave laborers, despite increasing protests from the planters and the legislators. This was a continuation of his predecessor's policy, but in August 1864 Smith even ordered state seizure of an uncooperative salt works in the southwest, something Letcher had never done. He also accepted almost complete Confederate control of the state's transportation and manufacturing facilities, but despite every exertion the South was gradually weakening before the ever-increasing power of the North.[25]

Desperate, last-ditch measures were needed as the Confederacy's armies were relentlessly decimated in battle. In January 1864 Confederate General Patrick R. Cleburne proposed freeing all the slaves and recruiting the ablebodied men into the Confederate army, but President Davis quickly refused. In September of that year Louisiana Gov-

ernor Henry W. Allen's confidential call for the use of black troops
leaked to the public. Then the following month Smith and the governors of the Carolinas, Georgia, Alabama, and Mississippi met in Augusta, Georgia, and, under prodding from Smith, issued a resolution
cautiously calling for "a change in policy" and the use of slaves "under
proper regulations . . . to the public service as may be required."[26]
President Davis and the Confederate government slowly, grudgingly
shifted toward the use of black troops.

With Grant's huge army poised to attack Lee's depleted forces in
Virginia in the spring, Smith wanted immediate action. In December
he appealed to the legislature to begin arming the slaves for combat.
He still considered blacks inferior and slavery desirable, but, a pragmatic Confederate nationalist, he felt arming blacks was essential,
especially since the North had started doing it as early as 1862. The
people of Virginia and the legislature were divided on this controversial issue; but when Lee called for black troops early in January of
1865 Smith renewed his appeals and finally, in the first week of
March—only a month before Appomattox—the Virginia legislature
agreed to furnish black troops to the Confederate army.[27] Then on
March 16 the Confederate Congress—by a margin of one vote in the
Senate—provided for the use of black troops but said nothing about
emancipation. Governor Smith pushed hard for a guarantee of freedom
for honorable service, the only practical and just policy in his view, and
the Confederate War Department's new regulations for black soldiers
did indeed promise freedom. A few black Confederate soldiers were
actually drilling in Richmond before the war ended, but the South,
which had gone to war to defend slavery, had waited far too long to
make this radical change of policy advocated by foresighted leaders
like Cleburne and Allen and Smith.

Governor Smith pushed for other new, drastic programs to meet
other challenges. From the beginning of his administration he pleaded
with the legislature to establish controls on soaring prices, but the
conservative legislators would not act, and the Confederate government also failed to control inflation, which continued to undermine the
home front.[28]

Soaring prices and other factors like inadequate civilian transportation facilities and Confederate impressment created severe local short-
ages of food and other goods. The governor tried to cope with this
problem, not by attacking Confederate policies but by requesting funds
from the legislature so the state could employ its own agent to run the
blockade and its own agent to purchase supplies in other areas of the
Confederacy. When the state Senate rejected his appropriation request, Smith in desperation gathered $80,000 of his own contingency

funds, borrowed $30,000 more from a Richmond bank, and started running his own supply program independently. He talked the Confederates into allowing him exclusive use of one supply train and sent his purchasing agent into the Deep South. Soon corn and rice were being shipped by train into Virginia and sold far below inflated market prices. Governor Smith also expanded his efforts to run supplies in through the blockade by purchasing a part interest in several steamers which were placed under state control. These emergency efforts did bring in some scarce supplies and generated enough profit to allow the governor to pay off his original debt and continue operations, but they were far too limited and too late to have any significant effect on the deteriorating economy.[29]

The governor instituted a similar program to combat the shortage of cotton and cotton cloth, and he was even able to obtain an appropriation of $500,000 from the legislature. An official commercial agent was placed at the head of a new bureaucracy charged with the responsibility of buying cotton and cotton cards and selling them at reasonable prices to the people. Smith also talked the Confederates into relinquishing control of one Virginia cotton mill where cloth could be manufactured for the people, again at reasonable prices. Purchasing agents had difficulty obtaining cotton in the Deep South, and transportation was even more of a problem. Once again the governor's efforts to alleviate a severe shortage met with only very limited success as the Confederacy began to crumble.[30]

Military operations in 1864 doomed the Confederacy. During the spring and summer Lee's fading army, fighting desperately, was driven relentlessly back and finally besieged at Petersburg. Union forces devastated the Shenandoah Valley, burning former Governor Letcher's home at Lexington in the process, and Governor Smith bitterly denounced his old commander, Jubal Early, for not protecting that vital agricultural region. Sherman took Atlanta and marched through Georgia to Savannah, and as the year ended he was preparing to coordinate an invasion of the Carolinas with Grant's final grand offensive in Virginia in the spring of 1865.

The death throes of the Confederacy began on April 1, 1865, when Lee's lines were breached at Petersburg. The next day the Confederate government evacuated Richmond, and the following day Governor Smith fled just ahead of onrushing Federal troops. He and a nucleus of state government went first to Lynchburg and then on farther westward to Danville. Even after learning of Lee's surrender on April 9, Governor Smith contemplated countinuing the struggle. He unsuccessfully suggested that President Davis turn over all remaining Confederate forces in Virginia to his command, and he toyed with the idea of waging guerrilla warfare against the conquering Yankees. But as he moved about western Virginia he saw that his people had had enough, and on June 8 he turned himself in to Federal officials in Richmond. In the meantime his predecessor, John Letcher, had been arrested in Lexington and briefly imprisoned in Washington, D.C. By July both former governors were free on parole.[31]

Both men accepted the verdict of the battlefield and were soon moderately successful in earning a peacetime living, Letcher as a lawyer and Smith as a farmer. Both returned to politics in a minor way, and they even served together in the state legislature in the mid-1870s as they had served together in Congress in the 1850s. Both had reached the high points of their political careers during the Civil War as they shared the responsibility of the wartime governorship of Virginia. Influenced by the presence of the Confederate government in Richmond and by massive Union armies on Virginia soil, they had been vigorous, effective war leaders. Both had cooperated with the Confederacy and both had urged their fellow Virginians to make ever greater adjustments and ever greater sacrifices. And both had been repeatedly frustrated by the ingrained conservatism of their people.[32] Both had been loyal Americans and then loyal Confederates and then loyal Americans again. Letcher died on January 26, 1884, and Smith three years later, on May 18, 1887. Both had always been true to their first loyalty, Virginia.

NOTES

INTRODUCTION

1. *State Rights in the Confederacy* (Chicago: University of Chicago Press, 1925), 1.
2. Black, *The Railroads of the Confederacy* (Chapel Hill: University of North Carolina Press, 1952).
3. Josiah Gorgas, "Notes on the Ordnance Department of the Confederate Government," *Southern Historical Society Papers,* 12:69.
4. Vandiver, *Ploughshares into Swords: Josiah Gorgas and Confederate Ordnance* (Austin: University of Texas Press, 1952).
5. Wells, *The Confederate Navy: A Study in Organization* (University, Ala.: University of Alabama Press, 1971).
6. *Confederate Finance* (Athens: University of Georgia Press, 1954).
7. Wesley, *The Collapse of the Confederacy* (Washington: Associated Publishers, 1937).
8. *Salt as a Factor in the Confederacy* (University, Ala.: University of Alabama Press, 1965).
9. *King Cotton Diplomacy* (Chicago: University of Chicago Press, 1931).
10. Lebergott, "Why the South Lost: Commercial Purpose in the Confederacy, 1861–1865," *Journal of American History* 70 (June 1983): 58–74.
11. Escott, *After Secession: Jefferson Davis and the Failure of Confederate Nationalism* (Baton Rouge: Louisiana State University Press, 1978).
12. Nelson, *Bullets, Ballots, and Rhetoric* (University, Ala.: University of Alabama Press, 1980).
13. Brief but excellent accounts of the development of the constitutional position of the southern governors from Revolutionary times to the Civil War may be found in Fletcher M. Green, *Constitutional Development in the South Atlantic States, 1776–1860* (Chapel Hill: University of North Carolina Press, 1930), and in Ralph A. Wooster's two monographs, *Politicians, Planters and Plain Folk* (Knoxville: University of Tennessee Press, 1975) and *The People in Power* (Knoxville: University of Tennessee

Press, 1969). Interesting, but less satisfying, is Leslie Lipson, *The American Governor from Figurehead to Leader* (Chicago: University of Chicago Press, 1939). All of the state constitutions and their amendments are in Francis N. Thorpe, comp., *The Federal and State Constitutions, Colonial Charters,* 7 vols. (Washington: Government Printing Office, 1909).

14. Sydnor, *Gentlemen Freeholders* (Chapel Hill: University of North Carolina Press, 1952), 96.

15. Jefferson, *Notes on the State of Virginia* (New York: Harper & Row, 1964), 113.

16. Henry Reeve, trans., *Democracy in America by Alexis de Tocqueville* (New York: Edward Walker, 1847), 1:83.

17. Merriam, *American Political Ideas* (New York: Macmillan and Co., 1920), 135.

18. *Politicians, Planters and Plain Folk,* 78. Professor Wooster has also pointed out the fact that the governor of Louisiana, because of certain reductions in his appointive power, was actually losing power in the 1850s. See Ralph A. Wooster, "The Structure of Government in Late Antebellum Louisiana," *Louisiana Studies* 14 (Winter 1975): 371–72.

19. For an interesting account of how this system operated, see Lee A. Wallace, Jr., "Raising a Volunteer Regiment for Mexico, 1846–47," *North Carolina Historical Review* 25 (January 1958): 20–33.

20. For instance, two recent studies of Davis take quite different interpretations of his presidency. See Escott, *After Secession,* and Clement Eaton, *Jefferson Davis* (New York: Free Press, 1977).

21. Soon to be published is a comprehensive analysis by Richard Beringer, Archer Jones, Herman Hattaway, and William Still of why the South lost the Civil War.

22. Escott, *After Secession,* 22.

23. See p. 215.

ALABAMA

1. Thomas M. Owen, *History of Alabama and Dictionary of Alabama Biography,* 4 vols. (Chicago: S. J. Clarke Publishing Company, 1921), 4:1222; Willis Brewer, *Alabama: Her History, War Record, and Public Men* (Montgomery: Barrett & Bowen, 1872), 490–91; William Garrett, *Reminiscences of Public Men in Alabama for Thirty Years* (Atlanta: Plantation Publishing Company, 1872), 720–22; Obituary in Mobile *Daily Register,* April 10, 1873.

2. Brewer, *Alabama,* 491.

3. Quoted in Virginia Knapp, "William Phineas Browne: Business Man and Pioneer Iron Operator," *Alabama Review* 3 (April 1950): 116.

4. Lewy Dorman, *Party Politics in Alabama from 1850 through 1860* (Wetumpka: Wetumpka Printing Company, 1935), 137–38: J. Mills Thornton, *Politics and Power in a Slave Society: Alabama, 1800–1860* (Baton Rouge: Louisiana State University Press, 1978), 265–66, 360, 363–64;

Albert B. Moore, *History of Alabama* (Tuscaloosa: Alabama Book Store, 1951), 412–13; Moore's second inaugural in Montgomery *Weekly Confederation,* December 10, 1859.

5. Clarence Denman, *The Secession Movement in Alabama* (Montgomery: State Department of Archives and History, 1933), 76–77.

6. Governor's Message to the General Assembly, January 17, 1860, in *Journal of the Senate of the State of Alabama, 1860,* 176–77.

7. Draft of a letter of Andrew Barry Moore to W. H. Gist, April 2, 1860, in Andrew Barry Moore Collection, Alabama State Department of Archives and History, Montgomery. Unless otherwise stated, the letters of all three Civil War governors cited are in ADAH.

8. A. B. Moore to E. C. Bullock, October 16, 1860.

9. See letter of Citizens to Moore and Moore's letter to Citizens, in William R. Smith, *The History and Debates of the Convention of the People of Alabama, Begun and Held in the City of Montgomery, on the Seventh Day of January, 1861* (Montgomery: White, Pfister and Co., 1861), 12–15.

10. *War of the Rebellion: A Compilation of the Official Records of the Union and Confederate Armies,* 128 vols. and index (Washington: Government Printing Office, 1880–1901), ser. 4, vol. 1, 1–89, hereinafter cited as *Official Records;* Roy F. Nichols, *The Disruption of American Democracy* (New York: Macmillan Company, 1948), 377, 553.

11. Joseph E. Brown to A. B. Moore, January 2, 1861; Thomas J. Butler to A. B. Moore, December 24, 25, 1860; Danville Ledbetter to A. B. Moore, December 28, 1860.

12. A. B. Moore to Col. J. B. Todd, First Regiment of Volunteers, General Order No. 1, January 3, 1861; Explanation of General Order No. 1, January 3, 1861; Smith, *History and Debates,* 42, 49.

13. A. B. Moore to President James Buchanan, January 4, 1861, in *Official Records,* ser. 1, vol. 1, 327; Smith, *History and Debates,* 41, 452–55; Ruth K. Nuermberger, *The Clays of Alabama* (Lexington: University of Kentucky Press, 1958), 181.

14. Smith, *History and Debates,* 36–40; Message to the legislature, January 8, 1861, in *Official Records,* ser. 4, vol. 1, 30–33; Walter L. Fleming, *Civil War and Reconstruction in Alabama* (New York: Columbia University Press, 1905), 162–63.

15. J. R. Powell to A. B. Moore, November 18, 20, 21, 25, 28, 29, December 3, 4, 6, 7, 11, 14, 18; A. B. Moore to J. R. Powell (telegram), December 14, 1860.

16. Smith, *History and Debates,* 52, 124, 161–63, 211–13.

17. *Journal of the House of Representatives of the State of Alabama at the Called Session, January 14, 1861,* 9, 57–59, 120, 123; *Acts of the Called Session, January, 1861,* 9, 16.

18. T. R. R. Cobb to his wife, February 3, 1861, in A. L. Hull, ed., "Correspondence of T. R. R. Cobb, 1860–62" *Publications of the Southern Historical Association* 11, (May 1907), 160.

19. F. M. Gilmer, Memoir, May, 1880, in Dunbar Rowland, ed., *Jefferson*

Davis, Constitutionalist: His Letters, Papers and Speeches, 10 vols. (Jackson: Mississippi Department of Archives and History, 1923), 8:461–63.

20. *Acts of the Called Session, January, 1861,* 46–48; *Journal of the Senate of Alabama at the Called Session, January 14, 1861,* 11, 17, 77. For Green's appointment, see Special Order No. 4, Moore Order Book.

21. A. B. Moore to Col. Percy Walker, July 15, 1861.

22. Governor's Proclamation against Extortioners, Oct. 2, 1861, in Frank Moore, ed., *The Rebellion Record: A Diary of American Events,* 11 vols. (New York: D. Van Nostrand Company, 1861–68), 3:159; Pratville *Autauga Citizen,* November 14, 1861; Bessie Martin, *Desertion of Alabama Troops* (New York: Columbia University Press, 1932), 17.

23. A. B. Moore to Messrs. H. G. Humphries and Colin J. McRae, July 16, 1861; A. B. Moore to Col. Percy Walker, July 3, 1861; A. B. Moore to W. T. Ayers, July 30, 1861; J. W. Withers to A. B. Moore, November 5, 1861.

24. A. B. Moore to William M. Brooks, January 12, 1861, in *Official Records,* ser. 1, vol. 52, pt. 2, 5; J. J. Seibels to Tennent Lomax, January 13, 1861, ibid., 11; J. J. Seibels to John H. Forney, February 7, 1861, ibid., 17; Tennent Lomax to A. B. Moore, July 27, 1861.

25. W. Hunsgrove to A. B. Moore, July 16, 1861; J. H. Vail to A. B. Moore, July 9, 1861; Houston to A. B. Moore, August 1, 27, 1861; A. B. Moore to Josephus W. Hampton, July 12, 1861. For letters from all the counties named, see folder marked "sedition" in Moore Papers.

26. Frank L. Owsley, *State Rights in the Confederacy* (Chicago: University of Chicago Press, 1925), 10–16; *Journal of the Senate of Alabama, 1861,* 698, 705; Albert B. Moore to Braxton Bragg, November 8, 1861, in *Official Records,* ser. 4, vol. 1, 69; S. B. Buckner to Andrew B. Moore, September 15, 1861, *Official Records,* ser. 4, vol. 1, 69. Albert S. Johnston to Albert B. Moore, September 16, 1861.

27. *Journal of the Second Called Session of the Senate, 1862,* 9, 20, 29–30.

28. John G. Shorter to A. B. Moore, December 12 and 28, 1861, March 9 and 24, 1862, and February 10, 1863; A. B. Moore to John G. Shorter, October 24, 1862, in *Official Records,* ser. 4, vol. 2, 148–49; Troy *Southern Advertiser,* January 22, 1862.

29. Edwin M. Stanton to E. R. S. Canby, May 16, 1865, in *Official Records,* ser. 1, vol. 49, pt. 2, 810.

30. Owen, *History of Alabama,* 4:1222.

31. Montgomery *Advertiser and Mail,* April 6, 1873.

32. Garrett, *Reminiscences,* 722–23; Brewer, *Alabama,* 126; Ralph N. Brannen, "John Gill Shorter: War Governor of Alabama, 1861–63" (Master's thesis, Auburn University, 1956).

33. Dorman, *Party Politics in Alabama,* 36; John Gill Shorter to Joseph E. Brown, January 3, 1861, in *Official Records,* ser. 4, vol. 1, 16–17; John Gill Shorter to George W. Crawford, January 16, 1861, *Official Records,* ser. 4, vol. 1, 54–55.

34. *Journal of the House of Representatives of Alabama, 1862,* 117–18; Bran-

nen, "Shorter," 12–18; M. C. McMillan, ed., *The Alabama Confederate Reader* (University: University of Alabama Press, 1963), 233.

35. Brewer, *Alabama,* 126; John Gill Shorter to the Gentlemen of the Senate and House of Representatives, December 2, 1861, in *Official Records,* ser. 4, vol. 1, 771–74.

36. Albert S. Johnston to John G. Shorter, December 13, 1861, in *Official Records,* ser. 1, vol. 7, 762–63; Brannen, "Shorter," 22–23; Montgomery *Weekly Advertiser,* July 15, 1863.

37. Brannen, "Shorter," 23–24; Shorter's address to the people in Montgomery *Weekly Advertiser,* July 15, 1863; John G. Shorter to John Tyler Morgan, September 2, 1862; John G. Shorter to Major General Barclay, February 12, 1862; John G. Shorter to C. C. Clay, March 22, 1862.

38. John G. Shorter to George W. Randolph, April 5, 1862; John G. Shorter to Judah P. Benjamin, March 18, 1862.

39. Montgomery *Weekly Advertiser,* July 15, 1863.

40. John G. Shorter to Brigadier General Thomas S. Butler, December 20, 1861; John G. Shorter to Judah P. Benjamin, March 5 and 23, 1862; General Braxton Bragg to John G. Shorter, December 31, 1861.

41. Montgomery *Weekly Advertiser,* July 15, 1863.

42. John G. Shorter to Judah P. Benjamin, March 4, 1862, in *Official Records,* ser. 1, vol. 52, pt. 2, 281–82.

43. John G. Shorter to Judah P. Benjamin, March 23, 1862, ibid.

44. John G. Shorter to T. H. Claiborne, December 15, 1861; John G. Shorter to William Alley, January 25, 1862; John G. Shorter to Brigadier General Thomas J. Butler, February 25, 1862; Governor's Proclamation Book, March 1, 1862.

45. *Acts of Alabama, 1861,* 49; *Journal of the House of Representatives of Alabama, Special Session, 1863,* 48–49; Brannen, "Shorter," 49.

46. Report of the Board of Trustees, in *Journal of the House of Representatives of Alabama, 1862,* 148–49; John G. Shorter to Nicholas Davis, December 4, 1861; John G. Shorter to George W. Randolph, April 28, 1862; John G. Shorter to Jefferson Davis, May 1, 1862.

47. John G. Shorter to John F. Morgan, February 14, 1862; John G. Shorter to George W. Randolph, May 30, 1862.

48. John G. Shorter to George W. Randolph, September 19, 1862, in *Official Records,* ser. 4, vol. 2, 87; John G. Shorter to James A. Seddon, December 23, 1862, ibid., 258.

49. Gideon J. Pillow to Benjamin S. Ewell, July 28, 1862, ibid., 680; John G. Shorter to Jefferson Davis, January 10, 1863, ibid., ser. 1, vol. 15, 939–40; James G. Shorter to James A. Seddon, January 14, 1863, ibid., 946–48; Montgomery *Weekly Advertiser,* February 4 and May 13, 1863.

50. Moore, ed., *Rebellion Record,* 6:291.

51. *Journal of the Senate of Alabama, Called Session, 1862,* 19.

52. John G. Shorter to Joseph E. Johnston, August 4, 1863, in *Official Records,* ser. 1, vol. 26, pt. 2, 139–40.

53. *Journal of the Senate of Alabama, Third Regular Session, 1863,* 8–17;

Montgomery *Weekly Advertiser,* October 19 and 29, 1863; *Acts of Alabama, 1863,* 3–8.

54. P. 258.

55. *Journal of the Senate of Alabama, Called Session, 1862,* 5–10.

56. Martin, *Desertion of Alabama Troops,* 171–72.

57. *Acts of Alabama, 1862,* 11; Brannen, "Shorter," 56.

58. Brannen, "Shorter," 59–60; Paul W. Gates, *Agriculture and the Civil War* (New York: Alfred A. Knopf, 1965), 97.

59. John G. Shorter to Messrs. Dennis, English and Thomas, April 22, 1862; *Journal of the Senate of Alabama, Regular Session, 1862,* 90; Brannen, "Shorter," 71.

60. George W. Randolph to John G. Shorter, October 2, 1862, in *Official Records,* ser. 4, vol. 2, 106; A. B. Moore to John G. Shorter, ibid., 148–49; Shorter's proclamation to planters, March 16, 1863.

61. *Acts of Alabama, 1862,* 37–40; *Journal of the Senate of Alabama, Regular Session, 1862,* 8–9. Shorter's letters to the ADAH about fortifications at the bluffs are too numerous to cite.

62. John G. Shorter to Major General S. B. Buckner, March 3, 1863; John G. Shorter to Dabney H. Maury, August 14, 1863.

63. John G. Shorter to Dabney H. Maury, August 14, 1863.

64. Milo B. Howard, "Alabama State Currency," *Alabama Historical Quarterly* 25 (Spring-Summer 1963), 70–82; Governor's message, *Journal of the Senate, 1862,* 83.

65. Troy *Southern Advertiser,* April 3, 1862; Frank L. Owsley, *King Cotton Diplomacy* (Chicago: University of Chicago Press, 1931), 476–77.

66. Montgomery *Weekly Advertiser,* July 15, 1863; John G. Shorter to Braxton Bragg, July 24, 1863.

67. Frank E. Vandiver, *Ploughshares into Swords: Josiah Gorgas and Confederate Ordnance* (Austin: University of Texas Press, 1952), 73; Garrett, *Reminiscences,* 722–23; John G. Shorter to William T. Hardee, September 8, 1863.

68. Eufaula *Daily Times,* May 31, 1872; Brannen, "Shorter," 86.

69. Allen Johnson et al., eds., *Dictionary of American Biography,* 20 vols. (New York: Charles Scribner's Sons, 1928–44), 10:557, hereinafter cited as *DAB.* Garrett, *Reminiscences,* 723–25; Brewer, *Alabama,* 460–61; Lewis E. Atherton, "The Problem of Credit Rating in the Ante-bellum South" *Journal of Southern History* 12 (November 1946), 549, 360.

70. Thomas H. Watts to S. J. Bolling and L. D. Steele, November 10, 1860, is an excellent exposition of why Watts thought the time for secession had come. See also Montgomery *Weekly Post,* November 14, 1860; Jeanne Hall Lynch, "Thomas Hill Watts: Civil War Governor of Alabama, 1863–65" (Master's thesis, Auburn University, 1957), 7–9; and Smith, *History and Debates,* 68–70.

71. Lynch, Thomas Hill Watts, 12–14; Election returns in *Journal of the House of Representatives of Alabama, 1861,* 117–18.

72. Thomas H. Watts to Daniel S. Troy, May 24, 1862.

73. Rembert W. Patrick, *Jefferson Davis and His Cabinet* (Baton Rouge: Louisiana State University Press, 1944), 304–309, 366 and fns.

74. McMillan, ed., *Alabama Confederate Reader* 233–35; Election returns in *Journal of the House of Representatives of Alabama, 1863,* 110.

75. McMillan, ed., *Alabama Confederate Reader,* 233–38.

76. Lynch, "Thomas Hill Watts," 20–21.

77. Garrett, *Reminiscences,* 724.

78. Troy *Southern Advertiser,* September 20, 1864.

79. Jefferson Davis to Major General D. H. Maury, September 2, 1863, in *Official Records,* ser. 1, vol. 39, pt. 2, 812.

80. *Governor's Message, November 17, 1864* (pamphlet, Manuscript Room, ADAH). Fleming, *Civil War and Reconstruction in Alabama,* 90, 92.

81. Fleming, *Civil War and Reconstruction in Alabama,* 98; *Acts of Alabama,* December 12 and 14, 1864.

82. Quoted in Albert B. Moore, *Conscription and Conflict in the Confederacy* (New York: Macmillan Co., 1924), 242–43.

83. Thomas H. Watts to Lt. Col. P. C. Powell, April 1, 1865.

84. Moore, *Conscription and Conflict in the Confederacy,* 251–52; *Alabama Reports, 1868,* 609–10.

85. F. L. Owsley, "Local Defense and the Overthrow of the Confederacy" *Mississippi Valley Historical Review* 11 (March 1925), 490; Bessie Martin, *Desertion of Alabama Troops,* 233.

86. McMillan, ed., *Alabama Confederate Reader,* 380.

87. Martin, *Desertion of Alabama Troops,* 145, 216–17.

88. Thomas H. Watts to Dabney H. Maury, August 15, 1864, in *Official Records,* ser. 1, vol. 39, pt. 2, 780; Thomas H. Watts to John Dent, April 14, 1864; Thomas H. Watts to Major T. I. Walker, January 19, 1864.

89. Resolutions of the Conference of Governors, in *Official Records,* ser. 4, vol. 3, 735–36; Thomas H. Watts to Jefferson Davis, December 14, 1864, ibid., ser. 2, vol. 7, 1222–25; *Governor's Message, November 17, 1864;* Montgomery *Daily Mail,* January 19, 1874.

90. Taken from the numerous letters on this controversy in the Watts Collection, ADAH.

91. Montgomery *Daily Mail,* September 30, 1864.

92. Lynch, "Thomas Hill Watts," 50–52.

93. Ibid., 77–78.

94. Ibid., 75–76.

95. Thomas H. Watts to Andrew Magrath, February 13, 1865.

96. Ibid.; Thomas H. Watts to ex-Governor John L. Manning, February 14, 1865.

97. James L. Rushing to Thomas H. Watts, October 20, 1864.

98. Montgomery *Daily Advertiser,* March 3, 1865.

99. In a letter to the editor of the *Daily Advertiser,* October 15, 1933, J. F. Eley said that as a boy of fifteen he witnessed Watts's arrest at his father's house in Union Springs. See also Brig. Gen. T. J. Lucas to Major S. L. Woodward, June 23, 1865, in *Official Records,* ser. 1, vol. 69, pt. 1, 305–307.

100. Watts's postbellum career is treated at length in *Representative Men of the South* (Philadelphia: C. Robson & Co., 1880), 52–70.

ARKANSAS

1. Powhatan *Advertiser*, December 17, 1857, quoted in Little Rock *Arkansas State Gazette*, January 2, 1858. See also Michael B. Dougan, *Confederate Arkansas: The People and Policies of a Frontier State in Wartime* (University, Ala.: University of Alabama Press, 1976), 1–11; Harry S. Ashmore, *Arkansas: A History* (New York: W. W. Norton and Company, 1978), 1–78.
2. Clio Harper, comp. "Prominent Members of the Early Arkansas Bar," manuscript in Arkansas History Commission, Little Rock, 296; Josiah Shinn, *Pioneers and Makers of Arkansas* (Little Rock: Genealogical and Historical Publishing Company, 1908), 370–410; *DAB*, 8:436.
3. Harper, comp., "Arkansas Bar," 296; Shinn, *Pioneers*, 401; *DAB*, 8:436; Little Rock *Arkansas State Gazette*, November 21, 1838. Rector's first wife died in 1857 and in 1860 he married Ernestine Flora Linde of Memphis.
4. Little Rock *Arkansas Gazette Centennial Edition*, June 15, 1936, 100, 102; Little Rock *True Democrat*, July 7, 1860; Pulaski County Tax Books, 1860, microfilm, Arkansas History Commission.
5. Rector's period on the court is contained in 20 and 21 *Arkansas Reports;* Pocahontas *Advertiser and Herald*, n.d., quoted in Fayetteville *Arkansian*, August 4, 1860.
6. Van Buren *Press*, December 30, 1859; Letter of William Quesenbury, Little Rock *Arkansas State Gazette*, June 2, 1860. The Washington *Telegraph*, November 2, 1853, identified Rector as "among the most reliable and devoted friends" of his cousin Governor Conway. Apparently family relations soured, partially over money, as revealed in *Rector* v. *Conway*, 20 *Ark.* 79 (1859).
7. Dougan, *Confederate Arkansas*, 12–22; Michael B. Dougan, "A Look at the 'Family' in Arkansas Politics, 1858–1865," *Arkansas Historical Quarterly* 29 (Summer 1970), 99–111.
8. Brian G. Walton, "The Second Party System in Arkansas," *Arkansas Historical Quarterly* 28 (Summer 1969), 120–55; Gene W. Boyett, "Quantitative Differences Between the Arkansas Whig and Democratic Parties, 1836–1850," *Arkansas Historical Quarterly* 34 (Autumn 1975), 214–26; Michael B. Dougan, "Thomas C. Hindman: Arkansas Politician and General," in James I. Robertson, Jr., and Richard M. McMurry, eds., *Rank and File: Civil War Essays in Honor of Bell Irvin Wiley* (San Rafael, Calif.: Presidio Press, 1976), 21–38; Bobby Leon Roberts, "Thomas C. Hindman, Jr.: Secessionist and Confederate General" (Master's thesis, University of Arkansas, 1972), passim.
9. Little Rock *Old Line Democrat*, May 24, 1860; Letter of William Quesenbury, Little Rock *Arkansas State Gazette*, June 16, 1860.

10. Dougan, *Confederate Arkansas,* 18–21.
11. Little Rock *Arkansas State Gazette,* July 28, 1860; Letter of William Quesenbury, Little Rock *Arkansas State Gazette,* June 2, 1860.
12. Dougan, *Confederate Arkansas,* 21–22; Little Rock *Old Line Democrat,* December 20, 1860; Little Rock *True Democrat,* August 25, 1860.
13. Inaugural Address of Henry M. Rector, Little Rock *Arkansas State Gazette,* November 24, 1860.
14. Dougan, *Confederate Arkansas,* 37; *Special Message of the Governor on Federal Relations* (Little Rock: Johnson and Yerkes, n.d.).
15. Dougan, *Confederate Arkansas,* 38–40.
16. Ibid., 41–42; Anonymous Diary, February 7, 1861, Arkansas History Commission.
17. Dougan, *Confederate Arkansas,* 42–43; Anonymous Diary, February 8, 1861.
18. Dougan, *Confederate Arkansas,* 43–44; Anonymous Diary, February 8, 1861.
19. Dougan, *Confederate Arkansas,* 42; Anonymous Diary, February 11, 1861. At least one observer, Little Rock doctor and sometime editor C. Van Meador, felt that Rector was being duped by his aides, especially Ben T. DuVal and Edmund Burgevin. See Little Rock *National Democrat,* June 11, 1864.
20. Dougan, *Confederate Arkansas,* 47–56.
21. Ibid., 61. However, the appointment of Napoleon Bonaparte Burrow, a Rector man, to command the captured arsenal led to criticism in the press: "Things have been carried on in a manner at once so extravagant and so pompously unmilitary as to render the pronunciamentos and home wars of Mexico almost respectable." Little Rock *Arkansas State Gazette,* May 18, 1861.
22. Dougan, *Confederate Arkansas,* 62–67; C. C. Danley to W. W. Mansfield, April 23, 1861, in Mansfield Papers, Arkansas History Commission; Note of Henry M. Rector, April 7, 1861, in Kie Oldham Collection, Arkansas History Commission; J. William Demby, *The War in Arkansas, or a Treatise on the Great Rebellion of 1861* . . . (Little Rock: Egis Print, 1864), 52.
23. Dougan, *Confederate Arkansas,* 75–76.
24. David Hubbard to L. P. Walker, June 2, 1861, in *Official Records,* ser. 1, vol. 3, 589–90; Ben McCulloch to L. P. Walker, May 20, 1861, ibid., 578–80; Governor Rector to L. P. Walker, June 12, 1861, ibid., 590–91; L. P. Walker to Governor Rector, June 22, 1861, ibid., 597; Little Rock *True Democrat,* July 4, 1861; Little Rock *Arkansas State Gazette,* July 20, 1861. All citations in this chapter from the *Official Records* are from Series 1.
25. Dougan, "Hindman," 28–29; Dougan, *Confederate Arkansas,* 78–80.
26. Dougan, *Confederate Arkansas,* 81; Governor's Message, Little Rock *True Democrat,* November 7, 1861.
27. Dougan, *Confederate Arkansas,* 83; Little Rock *Arkansas State Gazette,* December 14, 1861; Little Rock *Daily State Journal,* November 29, 1861.

28. Dougan, *Confederate Arkansas,* 81–83.
29. Ted R. Worley, "The Arkansas Peace Society of 1861: A Study in Mountain Unionism," *Journal of Southern History* 24 (November 1958), 445–56; Ted R. Worley, "Documents Relating to the Arkansas Peace Society of 1861," *Arkansas Historical Quarterly* 17 (Spring 1958), 82–111.
30. Dougan, *Confederate Arkansas,* 84–85; Little Rock *True Democrat,* December 26, 1861; Helena *Southern Shield,* n.d., quoted in the Little Rock *True Democrat,* February 20, 1862.
31. Robert G. Hartje, *Van Dorn: The Life and Times of a Confederate General* (Nashville: Vanderbilt University Press, 1967), 12; Walter L. Brown, "Pea Ridge: Gettysburg of the West," *Arkansas Historical Quarterly* 15 (Spring 1956), 3–16.
32. Dougan, *Confederate Arkansas,* 86–87; Governor Rector to Francis W. Pickens, April 11, 1862, photocopy, University of Arkansas.
33. Proclamation of Governor Rector, Little Rock *True Democrat,* May 8, 1862; Earl Van Dorn to Jefferson Davis, June 9, 1862, in *Official Records,* vol. 13, 831.
34. Dougan, "Hindman," 29–30; Dougan, *Confederate Arkansas,* 89–91.
35. Dougan, *Confederate Arkansas,* 88–89.
36. Ibid., 94–95; *Danley and Johnson, ex parte,* 24 *Ark.* 1–6 (1862).
37. Dougan, *Confederate Arkansas,* 95.
38. Ibid., 95. Thomas Fletcher was born in Nashville on May 15, 1815. He attended the University of Tennessee, graduating in 1836, and was admitted to the bar two years later. He practiced law and served as a probate judge at Natchez, Mississippi. He was the U.S. marshal of the Southern District of Mississippi before coming to Arkansas in 1850, settling at Red Fork in Desha County. Elected to the state Senate in 1858, he was chosen president of the Senate (making him next in line to the governor in succession). He held that office in three assemblies. He died in Little Rock on February 25, 1880. A notable descendant was Pulitzer Prize–winning poet John Gould Fletcher. See Harper, comp., "Arkansas Bar," 296.
39. Anonymous Diary, May 15, 1862; Dougan, *Confederate Arkansas,* 123.
40. Rector to Pickens, April 11, 1862, University of Arkansas; *Message to Senate, November 11, 1861* (Little Rock: Johnson and Yerkes, 1861); Shinn, *Pioneers,* 404.
41. *DAB,* 3:454; Farrar Newberry, "Harris Flanagin," *Arkansas Historical Quarterly* 17 (Spring 1958), 3–20.
42. Newberry, "Flanagin," 5; Little Rock *True Democrat,* November 5, 1862; Jonathan W. Callaway to J. H. Thomas, October 27, 1862, Arkansas History Commission. Flanagin's own papers, in the Arkansas History Commission, contain only a telegram informing him of the election and his diary entry indicating the same.
43. Dougan, *Confederate Arkansas,* 96.
44. Dougan, "Hindman," 29–31; Dougan, *Confederate Arkansas,* 96–99; Harris Flanagin to Kirby Smith, July 11, 1864, in Oldham Collection.

45. Thomas H. Compere to Harris Flanagin, November 21, 1864, in Oldham Collection; Dougan, *Confederate Arkansas,* 99–118.
46. Dougan, *Confederate Arkansas,* 102–103.
47. Ibid., 103; Governor Flanagin to Kirby Smith, June 15, 1863, in Oldham Collection; Jonathan K. Smith, *The Romance of Tulip* (Baltimore: Deford and Company, 1966), 64–66.
48. Washington *Telegraph,* August 18, 1863; Dougan, *Confederate Arkansas,* 102–104. Flanagin reported that his efforts with the old men did not turn out well, "for want of skill or experience." Governor Flanagin to General Holmes, October 18, 1863, in *Official Records,* 53, 901.
49. Dougan, *Confederate Arkansas,* 124; Governor Flanagin to R. W. Johnson, February 14, 1865 (draft), in Oldham Collection; Washington *Telegraph,* May 18, 1864; John Hugh Reynolds, ed., "Official Orders of Governor Flanagin," *Publications of the Arkansas Historical Association* 2:369–423.
50. Dougan, *Confederate Arkansas,* 124.
51. H. H. Coleman to Governor Flanagin, May 10, 1865, J. N. Smith to Governor Flanagin, October 18, 1864, in Oldham Collection.
52. J. J. Reynolds to Adjutant General, May 27, 1865, in *Official Records* 48, pt. 2, 626–31.
53. Robert L. Kerby, *Kirby Smith's Confederacy: The Trans-Mississippi South, 1863–1865* (New York: Columbia University Press, 1972), 150, suggests that Flanagin displayed a stronger states' rights sentiment prior to the loss of Little Rock than after.
54. Arkadelphia *Southern Standard,* October 24, 1874.
55. *DAB,* 8:436; *The Hot Springs Cases,* 92 *U.S.* (2 Otto) 698 (1875); Walter L. Brown, "The Henry M. Rector Claim to the Hot Springs of Arkansas," *Arkansas Historical Quarterly* 15 (Autumn 1956), 281–92; Margaret Ross, "Chronicles of Arkansas," Little Rock *State Gazette,* February 8, 1959; Arkadelphia *Southern Standard,* August 3, 1878. The bulk of items in the Henry M. Rector Papers, Arkansas History Commission, deals with the Hot Springs property. Unfortunately the family is attempting to repossess them, and they were closed to this researcher.

FLORIDA

1. John E. Johns, *Florida During the Civil War* (Gainesville: University of Florida Press, 1963), 1–9.
2. Biographical information on Perry is scarce. The following is from Robert Sobel and John Raimo, eds., *Biographical Directory of the Governors of the United States, 1789–1978,* 2 vols. (Westport, Conn.,: Meckler Books), 1:253; and Junius E. Dovell, *Florida: Historic, Dramatic, Contemporary,* 4 vols. (New York: Lewis Historical Publishing Company, 1952), 1:336.
3. Quoted in Johns, *Florida During the Civil War,* 5.
4. Ibid., 6.
5. *A Journal of the Proceedings of the Senate of the General Assembly of the State of Florida . . . 1860,* 10–14.

6. William Watson Davis, *The Civil War and Reconstruction in Florida* (Gainesville: University of Florida Press, 1964), 48–64.
7. Ibid., 71–82; Johns, *Florida During the Civil War*, 23–30.
8. Johns, *Florida During the Civil War*, 31–33. Perry had received a telegram from several important secession leaders stating: "We think no assault should be made. The possession of the Fort is not worth one drop of blood to us. Measures pending unite us in the opinion bloodshed now may be fatal to our cause." John Slidell et al. to Governor Perry, January 18, 1861, in *Official Records,* ser. 1, vol. 1, 445.
9. *Journal of the Senate of Florida, 1861,* 249–53.
10. Johns, *Florida During the Civil War,* 34–35.
11. Ibid., 36–39; Davis, *Civil War and Reconstruction in Florida,* 91–96.
12. M. S. Perry to L. P. Walker, June 1, 1861, in *Official records,* ser. 1, vol. 1, 469.
13. Johns, *Florida During the Civil War,* 34, 82.
14. *DAB,* 13:21; William L. Gammon, "Governor John Milton of Florida, Confederate States of America" (Master's thesis, University of Florida, 1948), chaps. 6 and 7.
15. Milton wrote President Davis that "Governor Perry is, I reckon, as you would have perceived, a man of strong prejudices, without very extraordinary intellectual abilities." John Milton to Jefferson Davis, October 29, 1861, in *Official Records,* ser. 1, vol. 6, 300–303.
16. Johns, *Florida During the Civil War,* 84–86. For Milton's lengthy analysis of Florida's coastal defenses and the incapacity of Perry's appointees to direct then, see *Official Records,* ser. 1, vol. 6, 290–427 passim.
17. Johns, *Florida During the Civil War,* 86–88.
18. *Journal of the Senate of Florida, 1862,* 52.
19. *Journal of the Proceedings of the Convention of the People of Florida. . .,* 71–72; *Journal of the Senate of Florida, 1862,* 38–39.
20. Johns, *Florida During the Civil War,* 89–93.
21. *Acts of Florida, 1861,* 43–46, 86.
22. John Milton to the Senators and Representatives of Florida, August 18, 1862, in *Official Records,* ser. 4, vol. 2, 57.
23. Johns, *Florida During the Civil War,* 99, 108.
24. John Milton to Jefferson Davis, December 9, 1861, in *Official Records,* ser. 1, vol. 6, 341–42; John Milton Papers, Florida Historical Society, Tampa. The legislature had agreed with Milton on this principle, for on December 14, 1861, it had resolved that the act of Congress authorizing the president to receive militia from a state "without requisition upon the Governor . . . and without the consent of the state authority, is . . . without warrant in the Constitution, and a dangerous infraction of the rights of the sovereign States." *Acts of Florida, 1861,* 74.
25. *Journal of the Senate of Florida, 1861,* 28–34, 71.
26. Johns, *Florida During the Civil War,* 114–15.
27. R. E. Lee to Governor John Milton, February 19, 1862, in *Official Records,* ser. 1, vol. 6, 393.

28. John Milton to Judah P. Benjamin, March 5, 1862, in Milton Papers.
29. John Milton to P. G. T. Beauregard, November 6, 1863, ibid.; John Milton to the Senators and Representatives from Florida, August 18 and September 11, 1862, in *Official Records,* ser. 4, vol. 2, 56, 93.
30. John Milton to the Senators and Representatives from Florida, September 11, 1862, in *Official Records,* ser. 4, vol. 2, 56, 93.
31. John S. Preston to James A. Seddon, November 23, 1863, ibid., 851.
32. Florida law required that at least one white adult male reside on each plantation where slaves lived. Congress never repealed this law drafting some overseers, and the shortage of white males in plantations remained a serious problem. For an elaboration of Milton's arguments, see John Milton to Jefferson Davis, February 17, 1863, in *Official Records,* ser. 4, vol. 2, 401–402.
33. James A. Seddon to John Milton, October 31 [29], 1863, ibid., 879–80.
34. John F. Reiger, "Deprivation, Disaffection, and Desertion in Confederate Florida," *Florida Historical Quarterly* 48 (January 1970): 284; Johns, *Florida During the Civil War,* 119.
35. John Milton to the Senators and Representatives of Florida, November 23, 1863, in *Official Records,* ser. 4, vol. 2, 972–76.
36. Johns, *Florida During the Civil War,* 120.
37. For a full account of this controversy, see Robert C. Black, *Railroads of the Confederacy* (Chapel Hill: University of North Carolina Press, 1952), 208–13.
38. John Milton to James C. Dawkins, June 14, 1864, in *Official Records,* ser. 1, vol. 53, 357.
39. For a full analysis of Milton's hostility to private blockade-running, see Davis, *Civil War and Reconstruction in Florida,* 199–200. For the resolution mentioned, see *Acts of Florida, 1863,* 59.
40. John Milton to George W. Randolph, June 25, 1862, and endorsement, in *Official Records,* ser. 4, vol. 1, 1173–74.
41. John Milton to Joseph E. Brown, April 14, 1864, in John Milton Letterbook, Florida State Library, Tallahassee.
42. Johns, *Florida During the Civil War,* 141; *Florida Sentinel,* March 3, 17, 31, 1863; *Florida Senate Journal, 1864,* 21; *Acts of Florida, 1863,* 42–43.
43. Johns, *Florida During the Civil War,* 124–26; John Milton to James A. Seddon, June 17, 1864, in *Official Records,* ser. 4, vol. 3, 499.
44. *Acts of Florida, 1862,* 65; *Journal of the Senate of Florida, 1863,* 52–53; Johns, *Florida During the Civil War,* 126–27.
45. Ella Lonn, "The Extent and Importance of Federal Naval Raids on Salt Making in Florida, 1862–1865," *Florida Historical Quarterly* 10 (April 1932): 167–68.
46. *Journal of the Senate of Florida, 1863,* 21; *Acts of Florida, 1862,* 77; Lieutenant W. Fisher to the Governor of Florida, January 9, 1863, in *Official Records,* ser. 1, vol. 14, 753.
47. Johns, *Florida During the Civil War,* 109–11.

48. *Florida Sentinel,* January 13, 1863; Proclamation of Governor Milton to "Citizens of Florida," October 21, 1863, in Milton Papers.
49. C. C. Yonge to John Milton, April 2, 1864, quoted in Samuel Proctor, ed., *Florida a Hundred Years Ago* (Coral Gables: Florida Library and Historical Commission, 1960–1965).
50. For a comprehensive analysis of Unionism and desertion, see Davis, *Civil War and Reconstruction in Florida,* 243–61.
51. For a detailed account of this episode, see Johns, *Florida During the Civil War,* 165–67.
52. John Milton to Maj. Gen. Patton Anderson, May 5, 1864, in *Official Records,* ser. 1, vol. 53, 352.
53. John Milton to the People of Florida, July 30, 1864, in *Official Records,* ser. 1, vol. 53, 371–73; Johns, *Florida During the Civil War,* 202–205. For other descriptions of how Milton possibly met his end, see Johns, 241.

GEORGIA

1. Joseph H. Parks, *Joseph E. Brown of Georgia* (Baton Rouge: Louisiana State University Press, 1977), 23–25; Peter Reeve Wallenstein, "From Slave South to New South: Taxes and Spending in Georgia from 1850 through Reconstruction" (Ph.D. dissertation, Johns Hopkins University, 1973), chaps. 1–3. A major revision of taxes in 1852 had greatly reduced the burdens of urban property owners by doubling the taxes of many nonslaveholding farmers.
2. Full treatment of the internal history of the Confederacy is impossible here. For more detailed coverage, see Paul D. Escott, *After Secession: Jefferson Davis and the Failure of Confederate Nationalism* (Baton Rouge: Louisiana State University Press, 1978). See also James L. Roark, *Masters Without Slaves* (New York: Norton, 1977) and Thomas B. Alexander and Richard E. Beringer, *The Anatomy of the Confederate Congress* (Nashville: Vanderbilt University Press, 1972), chaps. 9 and 10 and pp. 339–41.
3. The author disclaims any intention of explaining Brown's own perception of his political activities. As he responded to political pressures, Brown may have felt no inconsistencies in his appeals to planters and yeomen. From an analytical perspective, however, he was serving two masters, each made more aware of its class interests by the stresses of war.
4. Parks, *Brown,* 2–6.
5. Ibid., 6–18.
6. Ibid., 45–49, 66, 112–17. See also Joseph E. Brown to David Walker, April 19, 1861, in Georgia, Executive Department, Governors' Letter Books, Georgia Department of Archives and History, Atlanta.
7. Allen D. Candler, ed., *The Confederate Records of the State of Georgia,* 6 vols. (Atlanta: Chas. P. Byrd, 1910), 2:19–20.
8. L. P. Walker to Joseph E. Brown, May 22, 1861, in *Official Records,* ser. 4, vol. 1, 348–50; Joseph E. Brown to J. A. Seddon, July 10, 1863,

ibid., vol. 2, 620–23; Joseph E. Brown to J. A. Seddon, August 21, 1863, ibid., 737–39; Joseph E. Brown to Howell Cobb, October 15, 1863, ibid., 878; Candler, ed., *Confederate Records of Georgia,* 3:188–89, 206–209.

9. Louise Biles Hill, *Joseph E. Brown and the Confederacy* (Chapel Hill: University of North Carolina Press, 1939), 113–19.

10. Candler, ed., *Confederate Records of Georgia,* 3:192–98, 213–14, 362.

11. Ibid., 200; Rowland, ed., *Jefferson Davis,* 5:256; Joseph E. Brown to Jefferson Davis, June 21, 1862, in *Official Records,* ser. 4, vol. 1, 1160–61; Candler, ed., *Confederate Records of Georgia,* 3:252, 253, 258–59, 268, 280–81, and 2:192.

12. Candler, ed., *Confederate Records of Georgia,* 3:299, 301–12.

13. Hill, *Brown and the Confederacy,* 206–12; Resolutions on the suspension of the habeas corpus, March 19, 1864, in *Official Records,* ser. 4, vol. 3, 234; James Z. Rabun, "Alexander H. Stephens and Jefferson Davis," *American Historical Review* 58 (1953): 307–310. For another view, see John R. Brumgardt, "Alexander H. Stephens and the State Convention Movement in Georgia: A Reappraisal," *Georgia Historical Quarterly* 59 (1975): 38–49.

14. Ulrich B. Phillips, ed., *The Correspondence of Robert Toombs, Alexander H. Stephens, and Howell Cobb* (New York: Da Capo Press, 1970 [1913]), 431–32ff.

15. Rome *Weekly Courier,* November 21, 1862; Hill, *Brown and the Confederacy,* 120; Wallenstein, "From Slave South to New South," 204, 223. Toombs refused to reduce his cotton crop. For reaction, see Charleston *Mercury,* February 1, 1862 (which also quotes the Augusta *Constitutionalist*), and the Rome *Weekly Courier,* June 20 and July 4, 1862.

16. Charles W. Ramsdell, *Behind the Lines in the Southern Confederacy,* ed. Wendell H. Stephenson (Baton Rouge: Louisiana State University Press, 1944), 34–37; Rome *Weekly Courier,* May 16 and June 27, 1862, and January 23, March 6, October 2, November 12, 20, and 27, 1863.

17. Hill, *Brown and the Confederacy,* 118–19.

18. Joseph E. Brown to Howell Cobb, May 20, 1864, in *Official Records,* ser. 4, vol. 3, 431–39; Annual message to legislature, November 3, 1864, in Candler, ed., *Confederate Records of Georgia,* 2:761; Brown to Brigadier General Anderson, May 2, 1861, in *Official Records,* ser. 4, vol. 3, 372–75.

19. Wallenstein, "From Slave South to New South," 190, 206.

20. Ibid., 190, 196–99, 206; *Acts of the General Assembly of the State of Georgia Passed in Milledgeville at the Annual Session in November and December, 1863; also Extra Session of 1864,* 8, 67.

21. Wallenstein, "From Slave South to New South," 206, 223–25.

22. Angus McSwain to Brown, August 3, 1864, William H. Hillis to Brown, April 1, 1864, Ladyes [*sic*] of Green County to Brown, —— 18, 1864, and P. McDaniel to Brown, May 14, 1864, all in Georgia, Executive Department, Letters to the Governor, Georgia Department of Archives and History.

23. Candler, ed., *Confederate Records of Georgia,* 3:418–19, 431, 438–39; Joseph E. Brown to J. A. Seddon, November 9, 1863, in *Official Records,* ser. 4, vol. 2, 943–44.

24. Captain John McGrady to Captain Geo. A. Mercer, March 11, 1863, Joseph McWhorter to Brown, March 21, 1865, Benjamin H. Hill to Brown, January 15, 1862, Thos. A. McLarty to Brown, March 10, 1862, and Reuben Herndon to Brown, May 29, 1862, all in Georgia, Executive Department, letters to the Governor; *Official Records,* ser. 4, vol. 3, 851, 866–70, 776–79, 1112.

25. John Milton to Brown, April 14, 1864, in *Official Records,* ser. 4, vol. 3, 303–304; Brown to Howell Cobb, May 5, 1864, ibid., 380–86; Brown to C. G. Memminger, May 21, 1864, ibid., 439; Howell Cobb to Brown, May 23, 1864, ibid., 442; Atlanta *Daily Intelligencer,* July 1, 1864; Rowland, ed., *Jefferson Davis,* 6:297–98, 336, 400–401; and James D. Richardson, comp., *A Compilation of the Messages and Papers of the Confederacy, Including the Diplomatic Correspondence, 1861–1865,* 2 vols. (Nashville: United States Publishing Company, 1906), 466–70, 505–13.

26. Wilfred B. Yearns, *The Confederate Congress* (Athens: University of Georgia Press, 1960), 54–59. See also Escott, *After Secession,* chaps. 6 and 7.

27. Substitution finally was eliminated in 1864, but the exemption of overseers continued through the end of the war.

28. See Escott, *After Secession,* chaps. 3–5, 8–9.

29. Parks, *Brown,* 296–99, 315–23.

30. Ibid., 355, 359, 408–409, 451–55, 506–507.

31. Ibid., 364–67, 418, 422–24, 412–13, 432–33, 451–55, 476, 487, 513–18, 529, 534, 555.

KENTUCKY

1. "Conference at Russellville, Ky.," in Frank Moore, ed., *The Rebellion Record,* 11 vols. (New York: G. P. Putnam, 1861–63; D. Van Nostrand, 1964–68), 3:259–61.

2. "Proceedings of the convention held at Russellville, November 18, 19, and 20, 1861," in *Official Records,* ser. 4, vol. 1, 741–43.

3. Jefferson Davis to Howell Cobb, November 25, 1861, in *Official Records,* ser. 4, vol. 1, 755–56.

4. "Memoirs of Hon. Henry V. Johnson of Scott County, Kentucky, 1852–1931," typescript in Kentucky Historical Society, Frankfort, 1–10.

5. G. Glenn Clift, *Governors of Kentucky* (Cynthiana, Ky.: Hobson Press, 1942), 136–38; Hagan Trammel, Assistant Archivist, Transylvania College, to author, July 11, 1978; J. Stoddard Johnston, "Gov. George W. Johnson," in Ed Porter Thompson, *History of the Orphan Brigade* (Louisville: Lewis W. Thompson Co., 1898), 516–22; Basil W. Duke, *Reminiscences of General Basil W. Duke, C.S.A.* (Garden City, N.Y.: Doubleday, Page & Co., 1911), 146–50.

6. Johnson to Davis, November 21, 1861, in *Official Records,* ser. 4, vol. 1, 743–47.

7. E. Merton Coulter, *The Civil War and Readjustment in Kentucky* (Chapel Hill: University of North Carolina Press, 1926), 138–39; Frankfort *Daily Yeoman,* December 16, 1861; Arndt M. Stickles, *Simon Bolivar Buckner* (Chapel Hill: University of North Carolina Press, 1940), 112–14.

8. *Official Records,* ser. 4, vol. 1, 905–906; Covington *Journal,* December 28, 1861.

9. Louisville *Daily Democrat,* January 1, 24, 1862; Stickles, *Buckner,* 113.

10. Louisville *Daily Democrat,* January 10, 1862; Frankfort *Tri-Weekly Yeoman,* January 14, 1862.

11. Louisville *Daily Democrat,* April 3, 1862.

12. Johnson to Johnston, December 26, 1861, in Special Collections, Margaret I. King Library, University of Kentucky; Johnson to his wife, February 15, 1862, in "Letters of George W. Johnson," *Register of the Kentucky State Historical Society* 40 (October 1942): 346.

13. Johnson to his wife, February 15, 1862, in "Letters of Johnson," 346–47; Covington *Journal,* March 29, 1862.

14. Glasgow *Times,* undated clipping, in Johnson Family Papers, Box 1, The Filson Club, Louisville; Report of General P. G. T. Beauregard, April 11, 1862, in *Official Records,* ser. 1, vol. 10, pt. 1, 389; Report of Col. Robert P. Trabue, April 15, 1862, in *Official Records,* ser. 1, vol. 10, pt. 1, 614, 618.

15. "Memoirs of Henry V. Johnson," 20–22; Chaplain James F. Jaquess to Mrs. Johnson, April 15, May 29, 1862, in Johnson Family Papers, Box 1.

16. Clift, *Kentucky Governors,* 138–39; Richard Hawes to Charles Lanmon, October 27, 1859, in Charles Lanmon Collection, The Filson Club.

17. Marshall to General S. Cooper, January 27, 1862, in *Official Records,* ser. 1, vol. 52, pt. 2, 260; Marshall to General S. Cooper, February 13, 1862, ibid., vol. 7, 879.

18. Resolution of the council, August 27, 1862, in *Official Records,* ser. 1, vol. 7, pt. 2, 342; Hawes to Davis, September 2, 1862, in Special Collections, Margaret I. King Library; Davis to Hawes, September 12, 1862, in *Official Records,* ser. 1, vol. 16, pt. 2, 814.

19. Bragg to Leonidas Polk, October 3, 1862, in *Official Records,* ser. 1, vol. 16, pt. 2, 903.

20. Hawes to Editors, the Louisville *Courier,* July 9, 1866, in Clift, *Kentucky Governors,* 140–41; Owensboro *Monitor,* October 22, 1862; Lewis and Richard H. Collins, History of Kentucky, 2 vols. (Covington: Collins and Co., 1874), 1:133.

21. Thomas Lawrence Connelly, *Autumn of Glory* (Baton Rouge: Louisiana State University Press, 1971), 20.

22. Hawes to Davis, March 4, 1863, in *Official Records,* ser. 4, vol. 2, 417–18. Several Hawes letters are in the *Official Records.*

23. Collins, *History of Kentucky,* I:175; Ibid., 2:82; Clift, *Kentucky Governors,* 141–42; Paris *True Kentuckian,* May 30, 1877.

LOUISIANA

1. In the following sequence footnotes are kept at a minimum. Material concerning Governor Moore is to be found in the Department of Archives and Manuscripts, Louisiana State University, Baton Rouge. The best printed source is "The Political Career of Thomas Overton Moore, Secession Governor of Louisiana," by Van D. Odom in the *Louisiana Historical Quarterly* 26 (October 1943) 975–1054. Materials of a more personal and genealogical nature can be found in Claude Hunter Moore, *Thomas Overton Moore: A Confederate Governor* (Clinton, N.C.: Commercial Printing Company, 1960). Archival records of Governor Allen are sparser although twenty years of research have not dispelled the persistent reports that such records exist, unidentified and unclassified. Much pertinent data on Allen's career appears in Sarah Dorsey's *Recollections of Henry Watkins Allen* (New York: M. Doolady, 1866) and in Luther Edward Chandler, "The Career of Henry Watkins Allen" (Ph.D. dissertation, Louisiana State University, 1940). Vincent H. Cassidy and Amos E. Simpson, *Henry Watkins Allen of Louisiana* (Baton Rouge: Louisiana State University Press, 1964) includes the bulk of pertinent materials known. For an overall view, see John D. Winters, *The Civil War in Louisiana* (Baton Rouge: Louisiana State University Press, 1963).
2. Plantation document, March 15, 1858, in the Thomas Overton Moore Papers, Department of Archives and Manuscripts, Louisiana State University.
3. Moore to Halsey, August 11, 1859, ibid.
4. R. I. Brent to T. O. Moore, May 29, 1859, ibid.
5. The estimates vary. Moore himself claimed thirty thousand men "fully armed and equipped" by May 1862. Moore to President Davis, May 21, 1862, in *Official Records,* ser. 1, vol. 15, 740.
6. Braxton Bragg to Moore, May 2, 1861, in G. P. Whittington, "Papers of Thomas O. Moore," *Louisiana Historical Quarterly* 13 (January 1930), 10–31.
7. Bragg to Moore, May 7, 1861; July 25, 1861; August 2, 1861; August 13, 1861; September 5, 1861; October 31, 1861, in Whittington, "Papers," 23–30.
8. Bragg to Moore (with enclosure), November 18, 1861, Moore Papers.
9. Bragg to Moore, November 14, 1861, in Whittington, "Papers," 30–31.
10. Moore to Davis, April 1, 1862, in *Official Records,* ser. 1, vol. 6, 869.
11. Randolph, Secretary of War, to Moore, June 27, 1862, ibid., 768–69.
12. Moore to Davis, June 11, 1862, ibid., vol. 53, 812.
13. Moore to Randolph, July 8, 1862, Moore Papers.
14. Moore to Davis, July 23, 1862, in Whittington, "Papers," 12–13.
15. Moore to Randolph, July 8, 1862, Moore Papers.
16. Moore "Address," June 18, 1862, Moore Papers.
17. Petition from Private of 17th Louisiana to Moore, September 30, 1862, Moore Papers.
18. Petition to Moore, December 1, 1862, Moore Papers.

19. J. H. Ransdell to Moore, May 24, 1863; J. C. Younger to Moore, May 27, 1863, Moore Papers. The Ransdell letters to Moore are extensively treated in "Concerning the Loyalty of Slaves in North Louisiana in 1863," *Louisiana Historical Quarterly* 14 (October 1931), 487–502.
20. Ransdell to Moore, "Loyalty of Slaves," 498.
21. Ransdell to Moore, June 6, 1863, "Loyalty of Slaves," 499–500.
22. Moore, "Annual Message," January 18, 1864, Moore Papers.
23. Cassidy and Simpson, *Henry Watkins Allen of Louisiana*, 98–100.
24. Dorsey, *Recollections*, 251–52.
25. Allen, "Annual Message," January 1865. Cassidy and Simpson, *Henry Watkins Allen of Louisiana*, 113.
26. Dorsey, *Recollections*, 284.
27. Cassidy and Simpson, *Henry Watkins Allen of Louisiana*, 117.
28. Ibid., 127–28.

MISSISSIPPI

1. Reuben Davis, *Recollections of Mississippi and Mississippians* (Boston: Houghton Mifflin Company, 1890), 378; *Mississippi Senate Journal, 1859,* 55–56.
2. Donald M. Rawson, "Democratic Resurgence of Mississippi, 1852–1853," *Journal of Mississippi History* 26 (August 1964), 1–27.
3. For a comprehensive study of this period, see Donald M. Rawson, "Party Politics in Mississippi, 1850–1860" (Ph.D. dissertation, Vanderbilt University, 1964).
4. Robert W. Dubay, *John Jones Pettus, Mississippi Fire-Eater: His Life and Times, 1813–1867* (Jackson: University Press of Mississippi, 1975), 4–6.
5. Ibid., 10–11, 16–17; John E. Gonzales, "Henry Stuart Foote: A Forgotten Unionist of the Fifties," *Southern Quarterly* 1 (January 1963), 135.
6. Dubay, *John Jones Pettus,* 8; Walter L. Fleming, "Jefferson Davis' First Marriage," *Publications of the Mississippi Historical Society* 12 (1912), 21–36.
7. See index of *Mississippi House Journal, 1846* for votes on related bills. Also see *Mississippi Senate Journal, 1848,* 537; Z. T. Leavell, "The Ante-Bellum Historical Society of Mississippi," *Publications of the Mississippi Historical Society* 8 (1904), 321; Jackson *Semi-Weekly Mississippian,* August 2, 1859.
8. *Mississippi Senate Journal, 1850,* 712–13; Dunbar Rowland, *History of Mississippi: The Heart of the South,* 2 vols. (Jackson: S. J. Clarke Company, 1925), 1:764.
9. Natchez *Weekly Courier,* July 9, 1859; Jackson *Semi-Weekly Mississippian,* July 12, August 2, 1859; Jackson *Weekly Mississippian,* August 31, 1859; DeKalb *Democrat,* August 10, 1859; Vicksburg *Weekly Whig,* September 7, 1859.
10. Jackson *Semi-Weekly Mississippian,* July 12, 1859; Vicksburg *Weekly Whig,* November 2, 1859; J. W. R. Taylor to J. F. H. Claiborne, August 30,

1860, in J. F. H. Claiborne Papers, Southern Historical Collection, University of North Carolina, Chapel Hill.

11. *Mississippi Senate Journal, 1859,* 105–109.

12. Robert W. Dubay, "Mississippi and the Proposed Atlanta Convention of 1860," *Southern Quarterly* 1 (April 1967), 347–62.

13. Pettus to Gist, April 7, May 12, 1860, in Governor's Executive Journal, 1856–66, Mississippi Department of Archives and History, Jackson; Moore to Gist, April 2, 1860, in Andrew B. Moore Papers, Alabama Department of Archives and History, Montgomery.

14. R. W. James to Pettus, December 24, 1859, in John J. Pettus Papers, Mississippi Department of Archives and History.

15. *Mississippi Senate Journal, 1859,* 164–65; Eli Whitney Arms Company to Pettus, January 1860, in Governor's Records, vol. 33, Mississippi Department of Archives and History; Pettus to R. W. James, March 9, 1860, in Governor's Executive Journal, 1856–66.

16. Natchez *Mississippi Free Trader,* June 13, 1860; Fernandina *East Floridian,* October 31, 1860; Jackson *Semi-Weekly Mississippian,* October 31, 1860.

17. Gist to Pettus, November 8, 1860, in Governor's Records.

18. Jackson *Semi-Weekly Mississippian,* November 16, 1860; Jefferson Davis Bragg, *Louisiana in the Confederacy* (Baton Rouge: Louisiana State University Press, 1941), 51.

19. Davis, *Recollections of Mississippi,* 392; Jackson *Clarion,* June 5, 12, 1878; Jackson *Times,* July 6, 1878.

20. *Mississippi Senate Journal, Called Session, November, 1860,* 11–12, 23, 25; *Laws of the State of Mississippi, Called Session, November, 1860,* 32.

21. Adams to Pettus, December 11, 1860, in *Mississippi Senate Journal, Called Session, January, 1861,* Appendix, 88–91; Natchez *Mississippi Free Trader,* December 20, 1860; Edmund W. Pettus to A. B. Moore, January 21, 1861, in *Official Records,* ser. 4, vol. 1, 76–77.

22. Pettus to Davis, December 27, 1860, Davis to Pettus, January 4, 1861, in Robert M. McElroy, *Jefferson Davis: The Unreal and the Real,* 2 vols. (New York: Harper and Brothers, 1937), 1:242–43; Pettus to Davis, December 16, 31, 1860, in Jefferson Davis Papers, Duke University Library, Durham.

23. Ralph A. Wooster, *The Secession Conventions of the South* (Princeton: Princeton University Press, 1962), 30–35. The convention president did not vote and the ordinance of secession was not formally signed until January 15. See *Journal of the State Convention and Ordinances and Resolutions Adopted in January, 1861,* 16, 27–28, 119–22.

24. Hudson Strode, *Jefferson Davis: American Patriot, 1808–1861* (New York: Harcourt, Brace and Company, 1955), 1:397; John J. Pettus to John B. Floyd, December 31, 1860, in *Official Records,* ser. 3, vol. 1, 22.

25. Davis, *Recollections of Mississippi,* 403–404; A. Rozie to Pettus, January 25, 1861, in Governor's Records, vol. 33.

26. Horace S. Fulkerson, *A Civilian's Recollections of the War Between the*

States (Baton Rouge: Otto Claitor, 1939), 47; Pettus to A. B. Moore, January 12, 1861, in Andrew B. Moore Papers; Baxter McFarland, "A Forgotten Expedition to Pensacola in January, 1861," *Publications of the Mississippi Historical Society* 9 (1906), 18–21.

27. Dunbar Rowland, *The Official and Statistical Register of the State of Mississippi* (Nashville: Brandon Printing Company, 1908), 421–22; Pettus to H. H. Miller, January 11, 1861, in Governor's Executive Journal, 1856–66; Charles E. Hooker, "Mississippi," in Clement A. Evans, ed., *Confederate Military History,* 12 vols. (Atlanta: Confederate Publishing Company, 1899), 7:17–18.

28. Hooker, "Mississippi," 17–18; W. L. Sykes to John J. Pettus, January 18, 1861, in *Official Records,* ser. 4, vol. 1, 61–67.

29. Pettus to Thomas O. Moore, January 20, 1861, in Governor's Executive Journal, 1856–66; McFarland, "A Forgotten Expedition to Pensacola," 18–21; Thomas D. Duncan, *Recollections of Thomas D. Duncan, A Confederate Soldier* (Nashville: McQuiddy Printing Company, 1922), 10–11; A. B. Moore to Wm. M. Brooks, January 28, 1861, in *Official Records,* ser. 1, vol. 1, 446.

30. *Journal of the Mississippi State Convention, 1861,* 122–32, 136.

31. Resolutions of the Brandon Artillery Company to Pettus, December 27, 1860, O. B. Young to Pettus, December 26, 1860, in Governor's Records, vol. 33.

32. A M. Williamson et al. to Pettus, February 16, 1861, ibid.

33. *Laws of Mississippi, Called Session, January, 1861,* 43–44.

34. Benjamin to Pettus, February 1, 1861, in Governor's Records, vol. 33.

35. Davis to Pettus, February 12, 1861, in Rowland, ed., *Jefferson Davis,* 5:46.

36. Natchez *Daily Courier,* March 6, 1861.

37. John J. Pettus to L. P. Walker, March 28, 1861, in *Official Records,* ser. 1, vol. 52, pt. 2, 31; Minutes of the Military Board of the State of Mississippi, ser. 50, vol. 86, March 26, 1861, Mississippi Department of Archives and History.

38. Pettus to W. L. Barry, March 28, 1861, in Governor's Records, 33.

39. *Laws of Mississippi, Called Session, November, 1860,* 21–23; *Laws of Mississippi, Called Session, January, 1861,* 17; *Journal of the State Convention, 1861,* 85–86, 92, 94–95, 126–32; Natchez *Daily Courier,* March 14, 1861.

40. Richardson, comp., *Messages and Papers of the Confederacy,* 1:78; Frank A. Montgomery, *Reminiscences of a Mississippian in Peace and War* (Cincinnati: Robert Clarke Company, 1901), 39; Pettus to Leroy P. Walker, March 17, 18, 1861, in Telegrams Received by the CSA Secretary of War, 1861–65, National Archives.

41. Samuel G. French, *Two Wars: An Autobiography of General Samuel G. French* (Nashville: Confederate Veteran Publishers, 1901), 137–39.

42. Davis to Pettus, April 8, 1861, John Fowler to Pettus, in Governor's Records, vol. 33; Natchez *Mississippi Free Trader,* April 19, 1861.

43. Pettus to Walker, March 31, 1861, in Telegrams Received by the CSA Secretary of War; Pettus to Walker, April 13, 1861, in *Official Records,* ser. 1, vol. 52, pt. 2, 46; Pettus to Walker, April 17, 1861, in *Official Records,* vol. 53, 672.

44. Percy L. Rainwater, ed., "W. A. Montgomery's Record of the Raymond Fencibles," *Journal of Mississippi History* 6 (April 1944), 113; Natchez *Daily Courier,* May 1, 1861; John J. Pettus to L. P. Walker, April 8, 1861, in Telegrams Received by the CSA Secretary of War.

45. Natchez *Daily Courier,* May 2, 1861; Vicksburg *Weekly Whig,* May 4, 1861.

46. Pettus to Jefferson Davis, May 18, 1861, in *Official Records,* ser. 4, vol. 1, 334; Pettus to Pillow, May 18, 1861, in John J. Pettus Papers; L. P. Walker to Pettus, May 18, 1861, in Telegrams Sent by the CSA Secretary of War, National Archives.

47. Clark to Pettus, June 10, 1861, Davis to Pettus, June 10, 1861, in Governor's Records, vol. 34; Davis, *Recollections of Mississippi,* 405–406.

48. Pettus Proclamation, June 23, 1861, in Moore, ed., *Rebellion Record,* 2:195–96.

49. Minutes of the Military Board, July 20, 1861.

50. *Mississippi House Journal, Called Session, July 1861,* 6–7, 9.

51. Davis, *Recollections of Mississippi,* 411.

52. I. M. Patridge to Pettus, May 10, 1861, in Governor's Records, vol. 24; William Howard Russell, *My Diary North and South* (New York: Harper and Brothers, 1863), 113, 299–300; William Howard Russell, *Pictures of Southern Life, Social, Political and Military* (New York: James G. Gregory Company, 1861), 116.

53. Davis, *Recollections of Mississippi,* 414; Jackson *Weekly Mississippian,* July 14, 1861.

54. E. B. Gardner to Pettus, August 3, 1861, John Marshall to Pettus, August 30, 1861, in Governor's Records, vol. 35.

55. Davis, *Recollections of Mississippi,* 413–14.

56. Pettus to McAfee, August 8, 1861, in Governor's Records, vol. 35; Jackson *Weekly Mississippian,* September 18, 1861.

57. Paulding *Eastern Clarion,* August 23, 1861.

58. Report of Commander Melancton Smith, September 30, 1861, in Moore, ed., *Rebellion Record,* 3:125; Pettus to Jefferson Davis, September 20, 1861, in Telegrams Received by the CSA Secretary of War; Richard P. Weinert, "The Neglected Key to the Gulf Coast," *Journal of Mississippi History* 31 (August 1969), 289–300.

59. Twiggs to Pettus, September 19, 21, 1861, in Governor's Records, vol. 35.

60. Davis, *Recollections of Mississippi,* 415; Jefferson Davis to Leonidas Polk, September 15, 1861, in *Official Records,* ser. 1, vol. 4, 188; Pettus Proclamation, September 28, 1861, in Governor's Executive Journal, 1857–1870; Natchez *Daily Courier,* October 4, 1861.

61. *Mississippi House Journal, November, 1861,* 38–39.

62. Entry for November 6, 1861, in Thomas B. Webber Diary, Duke University Library.

63. Pettus to A. Sidney Johnston, September 28, 1861, in *Official Records,* ser. 1, vol. 4, 432; Pettus to Judah P. Benjamin, December 3, 7, 1861, January 6, 1862, in Telegrams Received by the CSA Secretary of War.

64. A. B. Moore to Pettus, November 14, 1861, in Andrew B. Moore Papers.

65. *Mississippi House Journal, November, 1861,* 10–16.

66. Pettus to Legislature, December 4, 1861, in Governor's Executive Journal, 1857–70.

67. Pettus to A. Sidney Johnston, December 2, 1861, in *Official Records,* ser. 1, vol. 7, 732–33; A. S. Johnston to Pettus, January 7, 1862, ibid., 823–24; Pettus to A. Sidney Johnston, January 31, 1862, ibid., 851; Thomas Brach to Pettus, January 22, 1862, in Governor's Records, vol. 37.

68. D. L. Smythe to Pettus, March 4, 1862, Governor's Records, vol. 37; Edward Fontaine to Pettus, January 11, 1862, ibid.

69. S. Durham to Pettus, April 15, 1862, ibid.; Montgomery, *Reminiscences of a Mississippian,* 77–78.

70. Pettus to Judah P. Benjamin, March 18, 1862, in Telegrams Received by the CSA Secretary of War; C. G. Dahlgren to Pettus, March 8, 1862, E. C. Eggleston to Pettus, April 7, 1862, in Governor's Records, vol. 37.

71. Macon *Beacon,* April 16, 1862.

72. Vicksburg *Daily Whig,* May 15, 1862; Pettus to Earl Van Dorn, July 25, 1862, in Earl Van Dorn Letters and Telegrams, Library of Congress.

73. William P. Johnston to Pettus, July 29, 1862, in Governor's Records, vol. 38; Pettus to Jefferson Davis, July 27, 1862, in *Official Records,* ser. 1, vol. 52, pt. 2, 332.

74. *Official Records,* ser. 4, vol. 1, 1110.

75. Davis to Pettus, June 19, 1862, in Rowland, ed., *Jefferson Davis,* 4:282.

76. Pettus to Randolph, October 28, 1862, in Governor's Records, vol. 38; Pettus to James H. Rives, November 17, 1862, ibid., vol. 39.

77. D. S. Pattison to Pettus, November 18, 1862, Pettus to A. M. West, December 2, 1862, H. O. Dixon to Pettus, November 4, 1862, in Governor's Records, vol. 39.

78. Pettus to R. S. C. Foster, November 1, 1862, D. A. Holman to Pettus, November 1, 1862, ibid.

79. Pemberton to Pettus, December 19, 1862, ibid.

80. James Phelan to Pettus, December 8, 1862, Pettus to Jefferson Davis, December 9, 1862, ibid.; Davis to Mississippi Legislature, December 26, 1862, in Moore, ed., *Rebellion Record,* 6:295–300.

81. *Mississippi Senate Journal, Called Session, December, 1862–January, 1863,* 4, 7–11.

82. *Laws of Mississippi, Called Session, December, 1862–January, 1863,* 67, 79, 81–89, 95–96.

83. Seddon to Pettus, January 10, 1863, in Governor's Records, vol. 39.

84. Pettus to W. L. Lowry, March 14, 1863, ibid., vol. 40.

85. A. P. Anderson to Pettus, March 22, 1863, L. Curtis to Pettus, March 19, 1863, L. Andrews to Pettus, March 28, 1863, ibid.

86. P. T. Moore to Pettus, March 27, 1863, L. Curtis to Pettus and James Thompson to Pettus, March 31, 1863, ibid.

87. Jefferson Davis to Pettus, September 20, 1863, in Rowland, ed., *Jefferson Davis,* 5:347.

88. Vicksburg *Daily Whig,* February 3, 1863; "A New Orleans Refugee" to Pettus, March 3, 1863, in Governor's Records, vol. 40; Hamilton Basso, *Beauregard: The Great Creole* (New York: Charles Scribner's Sons, 1933), 217.

89. Jackson *Daily Mississippian,* April 16, 1863; William P. Chambers, "My Journal," in *Publications of the Mississippi Historical Society* 5 (1925), 240.

90. Edmund Pettus to Mary Pettus, April 21, 1863, in Edmund Winston Pettus Papers, Alabama Department of Archives and History; Jackson *Daily Mississippian,* April 24, 1863.

91. John C. Pemberton to Pettus, May 2, 9, 1863, C. C. Bennett to Pettus, May 5, 1863, John Adams to Pettus, May 6, 1863, in Governor's Records, vol. 40.

92. James Rives to Pettus, May 2, 1863, ibid.

93. Pettus to Jefferson Davis, May 8, 1863, in *Official Records,* ser. 1, vol. 52, pt. 2, 468; Mobile *Daily Advertiser and Register,* May 2, 1863.

94. Natchez *Daily Courier,* May 9, 1863.

95. Junius Henri Browne, *Four Years in Secessia: Adventures Within and Beyond the Union Lines* (Hartford: O. D. Case and Company, 1865), 248–49.

96. Walter Lord, ed., *The Fremantle Diary: Being the Journal of Lieutenant Colonel James Lyon Fremantle, Coldstream Guards, on His Three Months in the Southern States* (Boston: Little, Brown and Company, 1954), 88.

97. Albert T. Goodloe, *Confederate Echoes: A Voice From the South in the Days of Secession and of the Southern Confederacy* (Nashville: Smith and Lemar Company, 1907), 275–76; James Rives to Pettus, May 15, 1863, in Governor's Records, vol. 40.

98. J. Gholson to Pettus, May 21, 1863, in Governor's Records, vol. 40; Pettus to Jefferson Davis, May 21, 1863, in *Official Records,* ser. 1, vol. 52, pt. 2, 475–76.

99. Natchez *Daily Courier,* June 3, 1863.

100. French, *Two Wars,* 183; D. W. Yandell to John M. Pettus, June 17, 1863, in Rowland, ed., *Jefferson Davis,* 6:3.

101. Pettus to Davis, July 9, 1863, Davis to Pettus, July 11, 1863, in Governor's Records, vol. 40.

102. Entry for July, 1863, in Wimer Bedford Diary, Library of Congress; James W. Garner, *Reconstruction in Mississippi* (New York: Macmillan Company, 1901), 51–53.

103. Dubay, *John Jones Pettus,* 189–92.

104. *Mississippi Senate Journal, November, 1863,* 89–100.

105. Dubay, *John Jones Pettus,* 194–95.

106. *Mississippi House Journal, November, 1863,* 85, 112–14, 141–51, 167–71; Russell, *My Diary North and South,* 308.

107. Florence W. Sillers, *History of Bolivar County, Mississippi* (Jackson: Hederman Brothers, 1948), 428; Annie E. Jacobs, "The Master of Doro Plantation: An Epic of the Old South," typescript in Mississippi Department of Archives and History, 1–9; Robert Lowry and William H. McCardle, *A History of Mississippi* (Jackson: R. H. Henry and Company, 1891), 350.

108. James Clark to Charles Clark, March 18, July 25, 1831, November 12, 1833, in Charles Clark Papers and Correspondence, 1830–90, Mississippi Department of Archives and History.

109. Sillers, *History of Bolivar County,* 433; Florence S. Ogden, "A Famous Indian Lawsuit," *Journal of Mississippi History* 8 (1946), 127.

110. 1860 Population Schedule, Bolivar County, Mississippi, microfilm copy in Mississippi Department of Archives and History, roll 578; Charles Clark's Cotton Plantation Record and Account Book, Mississippi Department of Archives and History.

111. Hooker, "Mississippi," 246.

112. *Mississippi House Journal, November 1863,* 159.

113. Ibid., 159, 202–204.

114. Clark Proclamation, December 11, 1863, in Governor's Executive Journal, 1857–70; Clark to G. J. Pillow, December 24, 1863, in Governor's Executive Journal, 1856–66; Clark to Jefferson Davis, November 18, 1863, in *Official Records,* ser. 1, vol. 31, pt. 3, 712.

115. *Laws of Mississippi, November, 1863,* 106–107.

116. Clark to James A. Seddon, February 6, 1864, Clark to J. C. Dennis, January 31, 1864, Clark to T. S. Blount, April 1, 1864, all in Governor's Executive Journal, 1856–66.

117. *Mississippi Senate Journal, Called Session, March–April, 1864,* 6–11.

118. Alex Vintreps to Clark, February 6, 1864, Samuel J. Gholson to Clark, April 16, 1864, Z. P. Stubbs to Clark, April 24, 1864, Clark Proclamation, November 16, 1864, all in Governor's Records, vol. 57.

119. G. W. Bradley to Clark, February 8, 1864, M. H. Quarles to Clark, March 28, 1864, Robert S. Hudson to Clark, October 26, 1864, Clark Proclamation, November 16, 1864, ibid.

120. *Mississippi Senate Journal, Called Session, March–April, 1864,* 13; Forrest to Clark, June 24, 1864, in Military Telegrams, Governor's Records, vol. 56; Clark to Forrest, June 30, 1864, in Governor's Executive Journal, 1856–66.

121. Clark to Henry Maury, November 28, 1864, Clark to Richard Taylor, February 11, 1865, Clark to T. J. Wharton, March 13, 1865, all in Governor's Executive Journal, 1856–66.

122. Clark to Osband, May 22, 1865, in Governor's Records, vol. 60.

123. Edwin M. Stanton to Major General Canby, June 3, 1865, in *Official Records,* ser. 1, vol. 49, pt. 2, 952.

124. Dubay, *John Jones Pettus,* 196–98.

MISSOURI

1. *Journal of the Senate, Extra Session of the Rebel Legislature, Called by a Proclamation of C. F. Jackson, Begun and Held at Neosho, Newton County, Missouri, on the Twenty-first of October, 1861* (Jefferson City: Emory S. Foster, Public Printer, 1865); Howard L. Conard, ed., *Encyclopedia of the History of Missouri: A Compendium of History and Biography for Ready Reference*, 6 vols. (New York, Louisville, St. Louis: Southern History Company, 1901), 5:551; *Official Records*, ser. 1, vol. 53, 752–58. The claim of a lack of a quorum arose as early as 1862. The *Senate Journal*, discovered in Kentucky, in 1863 contains no roll calls.

2. *DAB*, 9:538.

3. Thomas L. Snead, *The Fight for Missouri from the Election of Lincoln to the Death of Lyon* (New York: Charles Scribner's Sons, 1888), 18.

4. William E. Parrish, *Turbulent Partnership: Missouri and the Union, 1861–1865* (Columbia: University of Missouri Press, 1963), 1–6.

5. Buel Leopard and Floyd C. Shoemaker, eds., *The Messages and Proclamations of the Governors of the State of Missouri*, 16 vols. (Columbia: State Historical Society of Missouri, 1922–51), 3:328–42.

6. Snead, *The Fight for Missouri*, 30–33; William E. Parrish, *A History of Missouri, 1860 to 1875*, vol. 3 of Parrish, ed., *The Missouri Sesquicentennial Edition* (Columbia: University of Missouri Press, 1973), 4–5.

7. Walter Harrington Ryle, *Missouri: Union or Secession* (Nashville: George Peabody College for Teachers, 1931), 181–86; Snead, *The Fight for Missouri*, 105–10; Parrish, *Turbulent Partnership*, 10–14.

8. Frank P. Blair, Jr. to Simon Cameron, April 19, 1861, in *Official Records*, ser. 1, vol. 1, 668–69; C. F. Jackson to Simon Cameron, April 17, 1861, ibid. ser. 3, vol. 1, 82–83.

9. Leopard and Shoemaker, *Messages and Proclamations*, 3:343–48, 384; Snead, *The Fight for Missouri*, 148–51; Duke, *Reminiscences*, 43–45; Jefferson Davis to C. F. Jackson, April 23, 1861, in *Official Records*, ser. 1, vol. 1, 688; C. F. Jackson to L. P. Walker, May 5, 1861, in *Official Records*, ser. 1, vol. 1, 690.

10. Snead, *The Fight for Missouri*, 167–72; James Peckham, *Gen. Nathaniel Lyon and Missouri in 1861: A Monograph of the Great Rebellion* (New York: American News Company, 1866), 136–56; N. Lyon to L. Thomas, April 30, 1861, in *Official Records*, ser. 1, vol. 1, 675–76; Capture of Camp Jackson, near St. Louis, Mo., in *Official Records*, ser. 1, vol. 3, 4–9.

11. Snead, *The Fight for Missouri*, 172–74, 180–81.

12. Thomas C. Reynolds, "General Sterling Price and the Confederacy," manuscript in Thomas C. Reynolds Papers, Missouri Historical Society, St. Louis, 21–35; Sterling Price and William S. Harney *To the People of the State of Missouri*, May 21, 1861, in *Official Records*, ser. 1, vol. 3, 375.

13. Peckham, *Gen. Nathaniel Lyon*, 202–27, 244–48; Thomas W. Knox, *Camp-Fire and Cotton-Field: Southern Adventure in Time of War* (Cin-

cinnati: Jones Bros. & Co., 1865), 33–36; Snead, *The Fight for Missouri,* 186–92, 197–200.

14. Leopard and Shoemaker, *Messages and Proclamations,* 3:385–89; Snead, *The Fight for Missouri,* 206–208.

15. Snead, *The Fight for Missouri,* 210–28; Engagement at Booneville, Mo., June 17, 1861, in *Official Records,* ser. 1, vol. 3, 11–19, 384–400.

16. Report of Maj. Gen. Sterling Price . . . of operations from July 25 to August 11, 1861, *Official Records,* ser. 1, vol. 3, 98–100; L. Polk to L. P. Walker, July 23, 1861, *Official Records,* ser. 1, vol. 3, 612–14; General Orders Nos. 2 and 3, *Official Records,* ser. 1, vol. 53, 710–11.

17. William E. Parrish, *David Rice Atchison of Missouri: Border Politican* (Columbia: University of Missouri Press, 1961), 216–17; Reynolds, "General Sterling Price," 44–49; Thomas C. Reynolds to Jefferson Davis, January 20 and November 13, 1880, in Reynolds Papers.

18. Gideon J. Pillow to L. Polk, August 6, 1861, in *Official Records,* ser. 1, vol. 3, 631; C. F. Jackson to E. C. Cabell, August 8, 1861, ibid., 639; L. Polk to L. P. Walker, August 13, 1861, ibid., vol. 53, 721–25; Leopard and Shoemaker, *Messages and Proclamations,* 3:389–93; Parrish, *Turbulent Partnership,* 33–47.

19. Sterling Price to Ben McCulloch, November 10, 1861, and McCulloch to Price, November 11, 1861, in *Official Records,* ser. 1, vol. 3, 736–38; Siege of Lexington, Mo., September 13–20, 1861, ibid., vol. 53, 437–52; Leopard and Shoemaker, *Messages and Proclamations,* 3:394.

20. Price's declining fortunes are described in *Official Records,* ser. 1, vol. 8, 711–57 passim. See also E. A. Pollard, *Southern History of the War,* 2 vols. in 1 (New York: Charles B. Richardson, 1866), 1:159–60.

21. Robert E. Shalhope, *Sterling Price: Portrait of a Southerner* (Columbia: University of Missouri Press, 1971), 192–97.

22. The Battle of Pea Ridge and its aftermath is detailed in *Official Records,* ser. 1, vol. 8, 189–330 passim.

23. Sterling Price to Judah P. Benjamin, March 19, 1862, ibid., 792; Special Orders, No. 41, April 7, 1862, ibid., 812–13.

24. Arthur Roy Kirkpatrick, "Missouri, the Twelfth Confederate State" (Ph.D. dissertation, University of Missouri, 1954), 139–43.

25. Ibid., 144.

26. Ibid., 146, 157–59, 168–70, 354–58.

27. George W. Randolph to Sterling Price, June 24, 1862, in *Official Records,* ser. 1, vol. 13, 841; Thomas C. Reynolds to James A. Seddon, January 31 and February 5, 1863, J. A. Seddon to E. Kirby Smith, February 5, 1863, ibid., vol. 22, pt. 2, 780–83; Reynolds, "General Sterling Price," 41–77.

28. Reynolds, "General Sterling Price," 92–105.

29. Kirkpatrick, "Missouri, the Twelfth Confederate State," 266–70.

30. Ibid., 173–74, 233.

31. F. R. Lubbock to Jefferson Davis, September 11, 1863, in *Official Records,* ser. 1, vol. 22, pt. 2, 1004–10; Thomas O. Moore et al. To the People of Louisiana, Texas, Arkansas, and Missouri, August 18, 1863, ibid., vol.

53, 892–94; Thomas C. Reynolds to Sterling Price, December 4, 1863, ibid., 918; Reynolds, "General Sterling Price," 125–32; Circular dated August 20, 1863, Reynolds Papers.

32. Parrish, *History of Missouri,* 3:50–51.

33. Ibid., 51.

34. Howard N. Monnett, *Action Before Westport: 1864* (Kansas City, Mo.: Westport Historical Society, 1964).

35. Kirkpatrick, "Missouri, the Twelfth Confederate State," 359–72; Record of the Price Court of Inquiry, April 21–May 3, 1863, in *Official Records,* ser. 1, vol. 41, pt. 1, 701–28.

NORTH CAROLINA

1. This section of Rowan became part of Davidson County in 1822.

2. The parents of Mary White, his first wife, were former residents of Salisbury. Mary died two months after their marriage. In 1858 Ellis married Mary Daves of New Bern, who bore him two daughters.

3. Ellis knew that Lincoln's election would not take North Carolina out of the Union. In October he had written Governor Gist of South Carolina: "Upon the whole, I am decidedly of opinion that a majority of our people would not consider the event referred to, as sufficient ground for dissolving the Union of States." John W. Ellis to William H. Gist, October 19, 1860, in Noble J. Tolbert, ed., *The Papers of John Willis Ellis,* 2 vols. (Raleigh: State Department of Archives and History, 1964), 2:469–70.

4. John W. Ellis to General Assembly of North Carolina (message), November 20, 1860, in Tolbert, ed., *Papers of Ellis,* 2:514–15.

5. W. Buck Yearns and John G. Barrett, *North Carolina Civil War Documentary* (Chapel Hill: University of North Carolina Press, 1980), 5.

6. John W. Ellis to Charles C. Lee, January 19, 1861, in Tolbert, ed., *Papers of Ellis,* 2:562–63.

7. John W. Ellis to Simon Cameron, April 15, 1861, ibid., 612.

8. John W. Ellis to Jefferson Davis, April 17, 1861, ibid., 623.

9. John W. Ellis to General Assembly of North Carolina (message), May 1, 1861, ibid., 697–704.

10. L. P. Walker to Messrs. Graham and Ruffin, June 23, 1861, in *Official Records,* ser. 4, vol. 1, 396–98.

11. The governor was very proud of the regiment's performance at Big Bethel Church, Virginia, June 10, 1861, the first major engagement of the war.

12. Raleigh *State Journal,* May 22, 1861.

13. Ellis was buried in the family cemetery in Davidson County.

14. "John Willis Ellis," in Tolbert, ed., *Papers of Ellis,* 1:104.

15. The office of lieutenant governor was created by the North Carolina constitution of 1868.

16. Clark's father, James West Clark, had represented Edgecomb County in the state Senate from 1812 to 1815.

17. No major changes were made in the personnel and policies of the previous administration.

18. *Ordinances and Resolutions Passed by the State Convention of North Carolina, 1861–1862,* 141–42. The convention met four times between May 1861 and November 1862. It served as a legislative body during this period.

19. D. H. Hill, Jr., *North Carolina* (Atlanta: Confederate Publishing Company, 1899), vol. 4 of Clement A. Evans, ed., *Confederate Military History,* 12 vols. (Atlanta: Confederate Publishing Company, 1899), 5–31.

20. D. H. Hill, Jr., *A History of North Carolina in the War between the States. Bethel to Sharpsburg,* 2 vols. (Raleigh: Edwards and Broughton Company, 1926), 1:159; John G. Barrett, *The Civil War in North Carolina* (Chapel Hill: University of North Carolina Press, 1963), 182.

21. Barrett, *Civil War in North Carolina,* 26–27.

22. Josiah Gorgas to J. A. Seddon, December 31, 1864, in *Official Records,* ser. 4, vol. 3, 987; Josiah Gorgas, "Notes on the Ordnance Department of the Confederate Government," *Southern Historical Society Papers* 12 (January–February 1884), 77.

23. A. C. Myers to H. T. Clark, June 12, 1862, F. & H. Fries to H. T. Clark, April 18, 1862, both in Governors' Papers, State Department of Archives and History, Raleigh.

24. Frontis W. Johnston, ed., *The Papers of Zebulon Baird Vance* (Raleigh: State Department of Archives and History, 1963), 429n.

25. H. T. Lefler and A. R. Newsome, *The History of Southern State. North Carolina* (Chapel Hill: University of North Carolina Press, 1954), 430.

26. Lefler and Newsome, *North Carolina,* 442. Davis most often chose to accept those troops which had volunteered for the duration of the war.

27. The first conscription act was passed April 16, 1862.

28. H. T. Clark to W. B. Gulick, August 23, 1862, W. B. Gulick to G. W. Randolph, August 27, 1862, W. B. Gulick to H. T. Clark, September 4, 1862, all in Governors' Papers (Clark).

29. General Orders No. 30, War Department, Richmond, April 28, 1862, required, among other things, that "application will be made immediately to the Governors of the several states for permission to employ State Officers for said enrollment." *Official Records,* ser. 4, vol. 1, 1097.

30. Johnston, ed., *Papers of Vance,* 175n.

31. Ibid., 254n.

32. Barrett, *Civil War in North Carolina,* 38; *Official Records of the Union and Confederate Navies in the War of the Rebellion,* 30 vols. (Washington, D.C.: Government Printing Office, 1894–1927), ser. 1, vol. 6, 137; H. T. Clark to S. L. Fremont, September 2, 1861, in Governors' Papers (Clark); Forts Oregon and Ocracoke on the Outer Banks were abandoned without a fight.

33. J. W. Graham to his father, September 22, 1861, in Max R. Williams and J. G. de Roulhac Hamilton, eds., *The Papers of William Alexander Graham,* 6 vols. (Raleigh: North Carolina Office of Archives and History,

1973), 5:296; Journal of David Schenck, September 11, 1861, Southern Historical Collection, University of North Carolina.

34. H. T. Clark to L. P. Walker, September 8, 1861, H. T. Clark to J. P. Benjamin, October 25, 1861, both in Governors' Papers (Clark); Hill, *Bethel to Sharpsburg,* 1–185.

35. Lefler and Newsome, *North Carolina,* 441.

36. On February 17 Governor Clark announced that the invasion of the state had "infused quite a spirit of volunteering for the war." H. T. Clark to J. P. Benjamin, February 17, 1862, in Governors' Papers (Clark). The convention meeting in Raleigh, however, discussed the Roanoke Island disaster and the "total incapacity" of the governor. Journal of David Schenck, February [?], 1862.

37. H. T. Clark to R. E. Lee, August 3, 1862, R. E. Lee to H. T. Clark, August 8, 1862, both in Governors' Papers (Clark).

38. H. T. Clark to J. P. Benjamin, November 16, 1861, in *Official Records,* ser. 1, vol. 52, pt. 2, 209.

39. Native Unionists in eastern North Carolina were called "Buffaloes."

40. Richard E. Yates, *The Confederacy and Zeb Vance, Confederate Centennial Studies,* 8 (Tuscaloosa, Ala.: Confederate Publishing Company, 1958), 13–18; "Zebulon Baird Vance," in Johnston, ed., *Papers of Vance,* 1:43.

41. Clark suffered severe economic losses during the years of conflict. His home was plundered by Federal troops and much property was destroyed.

42. Glen Tucker, *Zeb Vance: Champion of Personal Freedom* (Indianapolis: Bobbs-Merrill, 1965), 164.

43. Clement Dowd, *Life of Zebulon B. Vance* (Charlotte: Observer Publishing and Printing House, 1897), 441.

44. "Zebulon Baird Vance," in Johnston, ed., *Papers of Vance,* 1:41.

45. Federal troops were never driven from eastern North Carolina.

46. R. E. Lee to Jefferson Davis, January 2, 1862, in R. E. Lee Papers, Duke University, Durham, N.C.

47. Richard E. Yates, "Zebulon B. Vance as War Governor of North Carolina, 1862–1865," *Journal of Southern History* 3 (February 1937), 52–53; "Zebulon Baird Vance," in Johnston, ed., *Papers of Vance,* 1:50.

48. "Zebulon Baird Vance," in Johnston, ed., *Papers of Vance,* 1:51. The Home Guard was created also to arrest deserters.

49. Lefler and Newsome, *North Carolina,* 441.

50. Z. B. Vance to J. A. Seddon, January 26, 1863, in *Official Records,* ser. 4, vol. 2, 375.

51. T. N. Grant to Z. B. Vance, February 26, 1863, Z. B. Vance to J. A. Seddon, March 31, 1863, both in Governors' Papers (Vance).

52. A. S. Merrimon to Z. B. Vance, February 24, 1863, in *Official Records,* ser. 1, vol. 18, 893; Yates, *The Confederacy and Vance,* 52. After the war Keith was arrested and jailed in Asheville to await trial in Federal court. He managed to escape trial and punishment, however.

53. Z. B. Vance to J. A. Seddon, December 21, 1863, in *Official Records,* ser. 4, vol. 2, 1061–62.

54. Z. B. Vance to G. W. Randolph, October 10, 1862, ibid., 114–15; Z. B.

Vance to Jefferson Davis, October 25, 1862, ibid., 146–47; Jefferson Davis to Z. B. Vance, November 1, 1862, ibid., 154; Lefler and Newsome, *North Carolina,* 442.

55. R. E. Lee to J. A. Seddon, April 18, 1863, in *Official Records,* ser. 1, vol. 18, 998.

56. Yates, "Vance as War Governor," 57–58; J. G. de Roulhac Hamilton, "The North Carolina Courts and the Confederacy," *North Carolina Historical Review* 4 (October 1927), 369; J. G. de Roulhac Hamilton, "The State Courts and the Confederate Constitution," *Journal of Southern History* 4 (November 1938), 438.

57. Dowd, *Vance,* 453; Lefler and Newsome, *North Carolina,* 445; Z. B. Vance to Jefferson Davis, November 11, 1862, in *Official Records,* ser. 1, vol. 51, pt. 2, 644–45; Z. B. Vance to J. A. Seddon, December 8, 1864, ibid., ser. 2, vol. 7, 1205.

58. J. A. Campbell to Peter Mallett (copy), May 11, 1863, in Governors' Papers (Vance).

59. J. A. Seddon to Z. B. Vance, May 22, 1863, Z. B. Vance to J. A. Seddon, June 8, 1863, both in Governors' Papers (Vance); Hamilton, "North Carolina Courts and the Confederacy," 370–75. Vance did not have to worry because there was no Confederate supreme court.

60. "Zebulon Baird Vance," in Johnston, ed., *Papers of Vance,* 1:58; Hamilton, "North Carolina Courts and the Confederacy," 399; Yates, "Vance as War Governor," 60–61; Jefferson Davis to the Senate and House of Representatives of the Confederate States, February 3, 1864, in *Official Records,* ser. 4, vol. 3, 69; Z. B. Vance to J. A. Seddon, February 29, 1864, in *Official Records,* ser. 4, vol. 3, 176–77; J. A. Seddon to Z. B. Vance, March 5, 1864, in *Official Records,* ser. 4, vol. 3, 197–98; General Orders, No. 31, March 10, 1864, in *Official Records,* ser. 4, vol. 3, 203–204.

61. Z. B. Vance to T. P. August, March 20, 1863, in Governors' Papers (Vance).

62. G. B. Rains to Z. B. Vance, March 25, 1863, in *Official Records,* ser. 4, vol. 2, 458.

63. C. D. Douglas, "Conscription and the Writ of Habeas Corpus in North Carolina During the Civil War," *Historical Papers of the Trinity College Historical Society* 14 (1922), 8.

64. Ibid., 7–8.

65. A. R. Lawton to J. A. Seddon, September 28, 1864, in *Official Records,* ser. 4, vol. 3, 691; Owsley, *State Rights in the Confederacy,* 76–149.

66. "Zebulon Baird Vance," in Johnston, ed., *Papers of Vance,* 1:52; Barrett, *Civil War in North Carolina,* 254; Tucker, *Zeb Vance,* 219–20.

67. "Zebulon Baird Vance," in Johnston, ed., *Papers of Vance,* 1:53.

68. It is estimated that as late as 1865 one out of every two blockade-runners still managed to make it safely through the blockade.

69. Z. B. Vance to E. J. Hale, October 26, 1863, in E. J. Hale Papers, Southern Historical Collection, University of North Carolina.

70. Z. B. Vance to E. J. Hale, February 11, 1864, ibid.

71. Yates, *The Confederacy and Vance,* 80; Z. B. Vance to J. A. Seddon, January 7, 1864, in *Official Records,* ser. 4, vol. 3, 10–11.
72. Yates, "Vance as War Governor," 66; Z. B. Vance to Jefferson Davis, November 12, 1862, in *Official Records,* ser. I, vol. 18, 771–73; Z. B. Vance to the Honorable General Assembly, November 17, 1862, ibid., ser. 4, vol. 2, 182.
73. Tucker, *Zeb Vance,* 174; Moore, ed., *Rebellion Record,* 6:524–25.
74. Public education was not one of the "necessities" of life, but all three of the state's war governors adopted a favorable attitude toward the public school system. It continued to operate throughout the war, and all efforts to divert school funds to the military were defeated.
75. "Zebulon Baird Vance," in Johnston, ed., *Papers of Vance,* 1:47–49; Lefler and Newsome, *North Carolina,* 435; Tucker, *Zeb Vance,* 189–90.
76. In November 1861 a "so-called" convention of Unionists was held on Hatteras Island and the Reverend Marble Nash Taylor was selected provisional governor of the state. But the whole movement was so deceptive that it soon died. Then, in May 1862, Lincoln appointed Edward Stanley military governor of North Carolina, only to have him resign in January 1863 following a bitter attack on the president's emancipation proclamation.
77. Z. B. Vance to W. A. Graham, January 1, 1863 [1864], in William A. Graham Papers, State Department of Archives and History, Raleigh.
78. Yates, *The Confederacy and Vance,* 85–107.
79. Earlier Vance had begun the transfer of state records and military stores to Graham, Greensboro, and Salisbury for safekeeping. However, on the day the governor departed from Raleigh General Stoneman's Federal cavalry arrived in Salisbury and commenced the destruction of public buildings and military supplies.
80. Davis appeared still full of hope and mentioned the possibility of retreating across the Mississippi. He intimated that he would like for Vance to join him with North Carolina troops. But the governor wished to remain in North Carolina and do what he could for his people.
81. Proclamation by the Governor of North Carolina, April 28, 1865, in Governors' Papers (Vance).
82. Dowd, *Vance,* 96–99.
83. Tucker, *Zeb Vance,* 479.
84. "Zebulon Baird Vance," in Johnston, ed., *Papers of Vance,* 1:63–64.

SOUTH CAROLINA

1. George Templeton Strong, *Diary of the Civil War,* ed. Allan Nevins (New York: Macmillan Co., 1952), 76.
2. John B. Edmunds, Jr., "Francis W. Pickens: A Political Biography" (Ph.D. dissertation, University of South Carolina, 1967), 1–195.
3. Samuel W. Crawford, *The History of the Fall of Fort Sumter* (New York: S. L. McLean & Co., 1889), 80. Laura A. White, *Robert Barnwell Rhett: Father of Secession* (New York: Century Co., 1931), 185.

4. Charleston *Courier,* December 3, 1860.
5. Mary Boykin Chesnut, *Mary Chesnut's Civil War,* ed. C. Vann Woodward (New Haven: Yale University Press, 1981), 40.
6. Pickens defeated Benjamin J. Johnson 64 to 63. For an excellent analysis of how Rhett's radicalism caused South Carolinians to reject his leadership at this stage, see White, *Robert Barnwell Rhett,* 185.
7. Bonham to W. H. Gist, December 16, 1860, Bonham Papers, South Caroliniana Library, University of South Carolina, Columbia.
8. B. T. Watts to James H. Hammond, December 1, 1860, Beaufort T. Watts Papers, South Caroliniana Library.
9. Lowry Ware, "The South Carolina Executive Councils of 1861 and 1862" (Master's thesis, University of South Carolina, 1952), 27.
10. Pickens to Lucy Pickens, February 23, 1860, in possession of A. T. Graydon, Columbia.
11. Chesnut, *Mary Chesnut's Civil War,* 4.
12. Pickens to Buchanan, December 17, 1860, in W. A. Harris, *The Record of Fort Sumter* (Columbia: South Carolina Steam Press, 1862), 7–8.
13. W. H. Trescot to Pickens, December 21, 1860, in Harris, *The Record of Fort Sumter,* 9–11; *Message No. 1 of His Excellency Francis W. Pickens to the Legislature Meeting in Extra Session, November 5, 1861;* W. A. Swanburg, *First Blood* (New York: Charles Scribner's Sons, 1957), 84–85.
14. W. H. Trescot to Pickens, December 21, 1860, in Harris, *The Record of Fort Sumter,* 9–11.
15. Charles M. Fuess, *The Life of Caleb Cushing,* 2 vols. (New York: Harcourt Brace, 1923), 2:273.
16. *South Carolina Secedes,* ed. by John A. May and Joan R. Faunt (Columbia: University of South Carolina Press, 1960), 19.
17. Trescot to Pickens, December 21, 1860, in Harris, *The Record of Fort Sumter,* 9.
18. Manley Wade Wellman, *Giant in Gray* (New York: Charles Scribner's Sons, 1949), 47; Chesnut, *Mary Chesnut's Civil War,* 4.
19. Ware, "The South Carolina Executive Councils," 8–10.
20. For an excellent analysis of the problems facing South Carolina when it attempted to revert to a sovereign nation, see Charles E. Cauthen, *South Carolina Goes to War, 1860–1865* (Chapel Hill: University of North Carolina Press, 1950), passim.
21. Abner Doubleday to General Legoine, January 6, 1861, in Charleston *Mercury,* January 19, 1861.
22. Louis T. Wigfall to Pickens (telegram), January 8, 1861, in Francis W. Pickens Papers, South Carolina Archives, Columbia.
23. The Anderson-Pickens exchange of letters is found in the Edgefield *Advertiser,* January 16, 1861.
24. Pickens to Cols. Gwyn et al., January 9, 1861, in Harris, *The Record of Fort Sumter,* 21.
25. Pickens to Anderson, January 11, 1861, in Crawford, *The History of the Fall of Fort Sumter,* 192.

26. Crawford, *The History of the Fall of Fort Sumter,* 218–20; I. W. Hayne to Francis W. Pickens, January 16, 1861, Pickens-Bonham Papers, Library of Congress.

27. Charleston *Mercury,* January 19, 1861; Crawford, *The History of the Fall of Fort Sumter,* 226–34.

28. Jefferson Davis to Pickens, January 13, 1861, in *Jefferson Davis,* ed. Rowland, 5:40–41.

29. Columbia *Southern Guardian,* quoted in Edgefield *Advertiser,* January 30, 1861.

30. J. L. Petigru to Jane Petigru North, January 29, 1861, in *Life, Letters, and Speeches of James Louis Petigru,* ed. James Petigru Carson (Washington, D.C.: W. A. Loudermilk and Co., 1920), 367.

31. A. R. Childs, ed., *The Private Journal of Henry William Ravenel, 1859–1887* (Columbia: University of South Carolina Press, 1947), 51.

32. Pickens to Robert Toombs, February 9, 1861, in Crawford, *The History of the Fall of Fort Sumter,* 267.

33. Pickens to Lucy Pickens, February 23, 1861, in possession of A. T. Graydon, Columbia.

34. Robert L. Cooper to Thomas B. Fraser, February 23, 1861, in T. B. Fraser Papers, South Caroliniana Library.

35. Charleston *Mercury,* April 16, 1861.

36. W. G. Simms to W. P. Miles, May 11, 1861, in William Porcher Miles Papers, Southern Historical Collection, University of North Carolina, Chapel Hill; Ware, "The South Carolina Executive Councils," 27.

37. W. G. Simms to Hammond, June 14, 1861, in Mary Simms Oliphant, *Letters of William Gilmore Simms,* 5 vols. (Columbia: University of South Carolina Press, 1955), 4:366–67.

38. *Message No. 1 of Governor Pickens to the Legislature, November 5, 1861.*

39. Charleston *Courier,* July 25, 1862.

40. Ware, "The South Carolina Executive Councils," 31–32.

41. Pickens to the President and members of the convention, January 8, 1862, in Pickens–Dugas Papers, Southern Historical Collection, University of North Carolina.

42. D. F. Jamison to Pickens, March 5, 1862, in Pickens Papers, Duke University Library, Durham, N. C.

43. Edgefield *Advertiser,* January 30, 1862.

44. Cauthen, *South Carolina Goes to War,* 144–51.

45. Charleston *Mercury,* September 8, 1862.

46. Chesnut, *Mary Chesnut's Civil War,* 426.

47. Quoted in Ware, "The South Carolina Executive Councils," 64–65.

48. Cauthen, *South Carolina Goes to War,* 156–63.

49. Ibid.

50. F.W.P. to M. L. Bonham, September 15, 1862, Bonham Papers, South Caroliniana Library; Charleston *Courier,* December 8, 1862; Charleston *Mercury,* December 1, 1862; F.W.P. to B. F. Perry, July 8, 1865, Benjamin

F. Perry Papers, Southern Historical Collection, University of North Carolina.

51. Cauthen, *South Carolina Goes to War,* 162–63.
52. Ibid., 164.
53. Ibid., 137.
54. Ibid., 134–38, 144–46.
55. *Message No. 1 of His Excellency F. W. Pickens to the Legislature in Regular Session, November 1862.*
56. Charleston *Mercury,* December 22, 1862.
57. Bonham to Beauregard, January 17, 1863, in Pickens Papers, Duke University Library.
58. Milledge Lipscomb Bonham, "Unpublished Biography of Milledge L. Bonham," 638, 653–59, unpublished manuscript in the South Caroliniana Library.
59. Cauthen, *South Carolina Goes to War,* 168–70, 180.
60. Edgefield *Advertiser,* March 4, 1863; Charleston *Mercury,* August 28, 1863; Cauthen, *South Carolina Goes to War,* 180–81.
61. Bonham, "Unpublished Biography," 681–93, 704–706; Cauthen, *South Carolina Goes to War,* 220–22; Charleston *Mercury,* December 12, 1864.
62. Charleston *Courier,* December 7, 1864; Bonham to Braxton Bragg, December 3, 1864, Pickens-Bonham Papers, Library of Congress.
63. Charleston *Courier,* November 30, 1864.
64. Bonham, "Unpublished Biography," 726–28.
65. Ibid., 744–49.
66. *DAB,* 12:203; Charleston *Mercury,* September 24, 1856.
67. Joel R. Williamson, "The Disruption of State Government in South Carolina During the Magrath Administration" (Master's thesis, University of South Carolina, 1951), 42–43.
68. Chesnut, *Mary Chesnut's Civil War,* 451.
69. Cauthen, *South Carolina Goes to War,* 162–63.
70. Charleston *Courier,* December 16–18, 1864.
71. Chesnut, *Mary Chesnut's Civil War,* 456.
72. Williamson, "Disruption of State Government in South Carolina," 42–43.
73. A. G. Magrath to Jefferson Davis, December 25, 1864, in *Official Records,* ser. 1, vol. 44, 986–88.
74. A. G. Magrath to W. J. Hardee, January 11, 1865, in A. G. Magrath Papers, South Carolina Historical Society, Charleston.
75. A. G. Magrath to W. J. Hardee, January 6, 1865, in A. G. Magrath Papers, South Caroliniana Library.
76. A. G. Magrath to Z. B. Vance and J. E. Brown, January 11, 1865, in Magrath Papers, South Carolina Historical Society.
77. Cauthen, *South Carolina Goes to War,* 226–27.
78. A. G. Magrath to Jefferson Davis, January 22, 1865, in *Official Records,* ser. 1, vol. 47, pt. 2, 1035–36; Charleston *Mercury,* February 7, 1865.
79. Williamson, "Disruption of State Government in South Carolina," 79–85.
80. Cauthen, *South Carolina Goes to War,* 228–29; *DAB,* 12:203.

TENNESSEE

1. Historians are divided over Harris's guilt in precipitating the secession crisis, his effectiveness as governor, and his success as a military leader. For the revisionist, pro-Harris view, see Stanley F. Horn, *The Army of Tennessee* (Indianapolis: Bobbs-Merrill, 1941); Gerald M. Capers, *The Biography of a River Town* (Chapel Hill: University of North Carolina Press, 1939); Horn, "Isham G. Harris in the Pre-War Years," *Tennessee Historical Quarterly* 19 (September 1960), 195–207; Peter F. Walker, "Building a Tennessee Army, Autumn, 1861," *Tennessee Historical Quarterly* 16 (June 1957), 101; John H. Deberry, "Confederate Tennessee" (Ph.D. dissertation, University of Kentucky, 1967); and George W. Wayne, "Isham Green Harris, Civil War Governor and Senator from Tennessee, 1818–1897" (Ph.D. dissertation, Florida State University, 1977). The traditional, pro-Union, anti-Harris view is argued in James W. Fertig, *The Secession and Reconstruction of Tennessee* (Chicago: University of Chicago Press, 1898); James Welch Patton, *Unionism and Reconstruction in Tennessee* (Chapel Hill: University of North Carolina Press, 1934); Stanley J. Folmsbee, Robert E. Corlew, and Enoch Mitchell, *History of Tennessee,* 4 vols. (New York: Lewis Historical Publishing Company, 1960), 2:37–42; Joseph H. Parks, *John Bell of Tennessee* (Baton Rouge: Louisiana State University Press, 1950); Clifton R. Hall, *Andrew Johnson: Military Governor of Tennessee* (Princeton: Princeton University Press, 1916); J. M. Keating, *History of the City of Memphis and Shelby County, Tennessee,* 2 vols. (Syracuse, N.Y.: D. Mason and Company, 1888), 2:209; and Wooster, *Secession Conventions of the South.* The most balanced yet critical assessment of Harris's military role is Thomas L. Connelly, *Army of the Heartland: The Army of Tennessee, 1861–1862* (Baton Rouge: Louisiana State University Press, 1967), 25–45. On the impact of Harris's administration on civil affairs, see Peter Maslowski, *Treason Must Be Made Odious: Military Occupation and Wartime Reconstruction in Nashville, Tennessee, 1862–65* (Millwood, N.Y.: KTO Press, 1978).
2. *DAB,* 11:310–11; "Paper on Isham Green Harris, Governor and Senator of Tennessee," typescript in Tennessee State Library and Archives, Nashville; Census of 1860, Free Schedule, Shelby County, Tennessee, Record Group 29, "Records of the Bureau of the Census," National Archives, Microcopy 653, p. 143; Slave Schedule, Shelby County, Tennessee, RG 29, NA, Microcopy 653, p. 50.
3. Robert Love Partin, "The Administration of Isham G. Harris" (Master's thesis, George Peabody College for Teachers, 1928), 27–28, 45–50; John E. Tricamo, "Tennessee Politics, 1845–1861" (Ph.D. dissertation, Columbia University, 1965), 173–75.
4. Folmsbee, Corlew, and Mitchell, *History of Tennessee,* 2:37.
5. Nashville *Union and American,* November 24, 25, December 9, 1860; Robert H. White, ed., *Messages of the Governors of Tennessee, 1857–1869,*

7 vols. (Nashville: Tennessee Historical Commission, 1959), 5:270–72; Horn, "Isham G. Harris in the Pre-War Years," 200.

6. Pister Miller to Andrew Johnson, February 27, 1861, in Leroy P. Graf and Ralph W. Haskins, eds., *The Papers of Andrew Johnson,* 6 vols. to date (Knoxville: University of Tennessee Press, 1967–), 4:341.

7. White, ed., *Messages of the Governors of Tennessee,* 5:272; Isham G. Harris to John B. Floyd, November 20, 1860, Floyd to Harris, November 26, 1860, in *Official Records,* ser. 3, vol. 1, 6, 9.

8. C. D. Faxon to Andrew Johnson, February 11, 1861, in Graf and Haskins, eds., *Papers of Andrew Johnson,* 4:274; *Acts of Tennessee, First Extraordinary Session, 1861,* chapter 1.

9. Isham G. Harris to Simon Cameron, April 17, 1861, in Isham G. Harris Papers, Tennessee State Library and Archives, Nashville.

10. White, ed., *Messages of the Governors of Tennessee,* 5:288.

11. See, for example, Horn, *The Army of Tennessee,* 47, and Walker, "Building a Tennessee Army," 101. For a useful corrective, see Connelly, *Army of the Heartland,* 26–27.

12. *Acts of Tennessee, Second Extraordinary Session, 1861,* 3–11; *House Journal, Second Extraordinary Session,* 2–5; Henry Hilliard to Robert Toombs, April 29, 1861, in *Official Records,* ser. 1, vol. 52, pt. 2, 76.

13. *Constitution of Tennessee,* 1835, art. 11, sec. 1, 3. Of course, the declaration also violated the United States Constitution by absolving state officers of their oaths, by entering into an alliance with other states, and by surrendering the military forces of the state to a foreign power.

14. Knoxville *Whig,* May 11, 1861; John Lellyett to Andrew Johnson, June 10, 1861, in Andrew Johnson Papers, Library of Congress.

15. Isham G. Harris to Leroy Walker, April 20, 1861, in *Official Records,* ser. 1, vol. 52, pt. 2, 57.

16. Harris to Walker, April 22, 1861, ibid., 63.

17. Ibid.

18. Ibid.

19. Harris to Walker, April 20, 1861, ibid., 57.

20. White, ed., *Messages of the Governors of Tennessee,* 5:347; *Acts of Tennessee, 33rd General Assembly, 1861,* 21–22.

21. *Acts of Tennessee, Second Extraordinary Session, 1861,* Chapter 14; Robert H. *White, Development of the Tennessee State Educational Organization, 1796–1929* (Kingsport: University of Tennessee Press, 1929), 278–79.

22. White, ed., *Messages of the Governors of Tennessee,* 5:344.

23. Ibid., 286.

24. Ibid.

25. *Acts of Tennessee, Second Extraordinary Session, 1861,* chapter 1.

26. White, ed., *Messages of the Governors of Tennessee,* 5:341–42; Walker, "Building a Tennessee Army," 101–3. The most critical assessment is in Connelly, *Army of the Heartland,* 45.

27. Leroy P. Walker to Gideon J. Pillow, July 1, 2, 1861, Pillow to Walker,

July 2, 1861, in *Official Records*, ser. 1, vol. 53, 375; Leonidas Polk to Walker, July 20, 1861, ibid., vol. 4, 371–72; Harris to Jefferson Davis, July 2, 1861, in Harris Papers.

28. Harris to Davis, July 13, 1861, in Harris Papers.

29. Davis to Harris, July 15, 1861, ibid; Keating, *History of Memphis*, 2: 211–13.

30. Harris to Davis, September 13, 1861, Davis to Leonidas Polk, September 15, 1861, in *Official Records*, ser. 1, vol. 4, 188–90.

31. Harris to Walker, April 20, 1861, ibid., vol. 52, pt. 2, 57.

32. Harris to Perkins and Company, May 25, 1861, Harris to Gideon J. Pillow, May 24, 1861, in Harris Papers; Nashville *Union and American*, September 26, 1861; Albert S. Johnston to Harris, November 3, 1861, Johnston to Judah P. Benjamin, January 12, 1862, in *Official Records*, ser. 1, vol. 7, 505, 827–28; William P. Johnston, *The Life of Albert Sidney Johnston* (New York: Appleton, 1879), 291.

33. Nashville *Union and American*, August 11, 1861; Moore, ed., *Rebellion Record*, 2:521.

34. Nashville *Union and American*, November 11, 1861.

35. Ibid., November 28, 1861; R. D. Stewart, "How Johnny Got His Gun," *Confederate Veteran* 33 (1924), 166.

36. Benjamin to Harris, October 4, 1861, in *Official Records*, ser. 1, vol. 4, 436; Deberry, "Confederate Tennessee," 145. Harris did succeed in making Nashville a major depot, but the Virginia front enjoyed a priority on these supplies until General Johnston, with Harris's approval, began summarily to confiscate them for use by troops assigned to defend Tennessee. See Walker, "Building a Tennessee Army," 111.

37. Horn, *Army of the Tennessee*, 78; Harris to Johnston, December 31, 1861, in *Official Records*, ser. 1, vol. 7, 811–12.

38. Nashville *Republican Banner*, July 3, 20, 1861. Harris had contemplated not seeking reelection in order to assume a military command or take a seat in the Confederate Senate. Landon G. Haynes to Harris, June 15, 1861, in Harris Papers; Partin, "The Administration of Isham G. Harris," 15.

39. Nashville *Union and American*, August 15, 1861.

40. Harris to Walker, August 3, 12, 1861, in *Official Records*, ser. 1, vol. 1, 389, 830; Thomas W. Humes, *The Loyal Mountaineers of Tennessee* (Knoxville: Ogden Brothers & Company, 1888), 123–24.

41. Harris to Davis, November 12, 1861; Johnston to Harris, November 9, 1861, in *Official Records*, ser. 2, vol. 1, 838.

42. J. G. M. Ramsey to Harris, March 18, 1862, in Harris Papers.

43. Johnston to Harris, November 19, December 25, 1861, in *Official Records*, ser. 1, vol. 4, 564; Johnston to Benjamin, December 16, 1861, Harris to Johnston, December 31, 1861, Johnston to Benjamin, January 12, 1862, Polk to Harris, January 31, 1862, Benjamin to Harris, February 11, 1862, all in ibid., vol. 7, 769, 811–12, 851, 872; *The Great Panic, by an Eye Witness* (Nashville: Johnson and Whiting, 1862).

44. White, ed., *Messages of the Governors of Tennessee*, 5:366.

45. Harris to Davis, September 29, 1862, Davis to Harris, September 30, October 25, 1862, Report of C. G. Memminger to Confederate States of America, January 10, 1863, all in *Official Records,* ser. 4, vol. 2, 99, 148, 323.

46. As quoted in John Trotwood Moore and Austin P. Foster, *Tennessee: The Volunteer State,* 4 vols. (Chicago: S. J. Clarke Publishing Co., 1923), 1:521.

47. *Constitution of Tennessee,* 1835, art. 11, sec. 1, 3. The Tennessee legislature had adjourned *sine die* on March 20, 1862. Thus, there was no way for Caruthers to qualify himself for office.

48. *DAB,* 11:311.

TEXAS

1. *Journal of the Secession Convention of Texas, 1861,* edited from the original in the Department of State by E. W. Winkler (Austin: Austin Printing Co., 1912), 100–102, 178–79, 184–85. Details of the removal of Governor Houston are given in William Mumford Baker, "A Pivot Point," *Lippincott's Magazine* 26 (November 1880), 566; Llerena Friend, *Sam Houston: The Great Designer* (Austin: University of Texas Press, 1954), 339–45; and Edward R. Maher, Jr., "Sam Houston and Secession," *Southwestern Historical Quarterly* 60 (April 1952), 448–58.

2. The late John F. Kennedy, in his *Profiles in Courage* (New York: Harper & Brothers, 1955), 116, relying on contemporary observer Amelia Barr, *All the Days of My Life: An Autobiography* (New York: D. Appleton and Co., 1913), 226–27, described Clark as "an insignificant creature, contemptible, spry, and pert." Allan C. Ashcraft, "Texas, 1860–1866: The Lone Star State in the Civil War" (Ph.D. dissertation, Columbia University, 1960), 66, refers to him as "the very obscure Edward Clark."

3. "Sketch of life of Edward Clark by his son John E. Clark," photostat in Edward Clark Papers, University of Texas Archives, Austin: J. T. Robinson to John Clark, May 4, 1908, in Clark Papers; Tinsie Larison, "Edward Clark," in W. C. Nunn, ed., *Ten Texans in Gray,* (Hillsboro, Tex.: Hill Junior College Press, 1968), 22–23. *Handbook of Texas,* ed. Walter P. Webb and H. Bailey Carroll, 2 vols. (Austin: Texas State Historical Association, 1952), 1:354, incorrectly states that Clark was born in Georgia, the son of Governor John Clark. This is corrected in volume 3 of the *Handbook,* edited by Eldon Stephen Branda (1976).

4. John E. Clark to James T. DeShields, July 17, 1907, in Clark Papers; Ross Phares, *The Governors of Texas* (Gretna, La.: Pelican Publishing Co., 1976), 98. For more on Clark's early career, see Justin W. Dart, Jr., "Edward Clark, Governor of Texas, March 16 to November 7, 1861" (Master's thesis, University of Houston, 1954), 1–28.

5. Reports and correspondence relating to the surrender of Federal property in Texas are found in *Official Records,* ser. 1, vol. 1, 503–16. Unless otherwise indicated, all citations are to series 1.

6. Edward Clark to John Ford, March 22, 1861, in Executive Record Book, Texas State Archives, Austin; L. P. Walker to Ben McCullock, March 4, 1861, in *Official Records*, vol. 1, 609–10; H. E. McCulloch to L. P. Walker, March 30, 1861, *Official Records*, vol. 1, 617–18.

7. Edward Clark to the Legislature, March 29, 1861, in Executive Record Book; Fredericka Ann Meiners, "The Texas Governorship, 1861–1865: Biography of an Office" (Ph.D. dissertation, Rice University, 1974), 13–17.

8. Edward Clark to Jefferson Davis, April 4, 1861, in *Official Records*, vol. 1, 621.

9. Leroy Walker to the Governor of Texas, April 8, 1861, ibid., vol. 1, 290–91; Walker to the Governor of Texas, April 9, 1861, ibid., ser. 4, vol. 1, 213; Stephen B. Oates, "Texas Under the Secessionists," *Southwestern Historical Quarterly* 67 (October 1963), 186.

10. Edward Clark to the People of Texas, April 17, 1861, in Executive Record Book.

11. L. P. Walker to Edward Clark, April 16, 1861, in Governors' Letters, Texas State Archives; Clark to the People of Texas, April 24, 1861, in Executive Record Book.

12. Appointment of Nicholas, May 13, 14, 1861, in Executive Record Book; *Handbook of Texas,* 2:278–79; Meiners, "Texas Governorship, 1861–1865," 48–50.

13. Fredericka Meiners, ("Texas Governorship, 1861–1865," 40) points out that Clark exceeded his authority by negotiating with a foreign power. See Ronnie C. Tyler, *Santiago Vidaurri and the Southern Confederacy* (Austin: Texas State Historical Association, 1973), 45–49; Clark to Governor of Tamaulipas, July 13, 1861, in Executive Record Book; Clark to Earl Van Dorn, May 6, 1861, in Clark Papers.

14. Proclamation of Governor Clark, June 8, 1861, in Executive Record Book; Oates, "Texas Under the Secessionists," 186–87.

15. Edward Clark to the Delegation of Texas in the Confederate Congress, August 22, 1861, in Executive Record Book; Albert B. Moore, *Conscription and Conflict in the Confederacy,* 8–12.

16. Edward Clark to the People of Texas, August 31, 1861, in *Official Records,* vol. 1, 102.

17. Edward Clark to L. P. Walker, September 7, 1861, ibid., vol. 1, 101; James L. Nichols, *The Confederate Quartermaster in the Trans-Mississippi* (Austin: University of Texas Press, 1964), 32, 34–35.

18. *Texas State Gazette,* June 22, 1861; Clarksville *Standard,* July 20, 1861; Nancy Head Bowen, "A Political Labyrinth: Texas in the Civil War, Questions in Continuity" (Ph.D. dissertation, Rice University, 1974), 27–38; Francis R. Lubbock, *Six Decades in Texas: The Memoirs of Francis Richard Lubbock, Confederate Governor of Texas,* ed. C. W. Raines (Austin: Pemberton Press, 1968), 323–24.

19. James M. Day, ed., *Senate Journal of the Ninth Legislature of the State of Texas, November 4, 1861–January 14, 1862* (Austin: Texas State Library, 1963), 6–9.

20. Edward Clark to the Legislature, November 7, 1861, in Day, ed., *Senate Journal, Ninth Legislature, 12–14.*
21. Meiners, "Texas Governorship, 1861–1865," 78.
22. For the governor's powers in Texas prior to the Civil War, see Fred Gantt, Jr., *The Chief Executive in Texas* (Austin: University of Texas Press, 1964), 15–27.
23. Joseph Blessington, *The Campaigns of Walker's Texas Division* (New York: Lange, Little and Company, 1875), 53; Larison, "Edward Clark," 30–32.
24. *Handbook of Texas,* 1:354.
25. Lubbock, *Six Decades in Texas,* 1–24; Leann Cox Adams, "Francis Richard Lubbock," *Ten Texans in Gray,* 76; *Handbook of Texas,* 2:89.
26. Lubbock, *Six Decades in Texas,* 48.
27. Ibid., 190–208.
28. Ibid., 267–313; Adams, "Francis Richard Lubbock," 79–80.
29. Ibid., 325–28.
30. Day, comp. and ed., *Senate Journal, Ninth Legislature,* 14–17.
31. Ibid., 49–59.
32. Lubbock, *Six Decades in Texas,* 359–60; James M. Day, comp. and ed., *House Journal of the Ninth Legislature, Regular Session of the State of Texas* (Austin: Texas State Library, 1964), 102–21; James B. Warner, "A Legislative History of Texas During the Civil War" (Master's thesis, Lamar University, 1971), 43–44.
33. Fredericka Meiners ("Texas Governorship, 1861–1865," 105) notes that this was another attempt by the state to "have its protection and its money too." After months of effort Lubbock did succeed in getting the Frontier Regiment accepted into Confederate service, but without the conditions as to service and command. Ibid., 105–109.
34. Edmund T. Miller, *A Financial History of Texas. Bulletin of the University of Texas, No. 37* (Austin: A. C. Baldwin & Sons, 1916), 140–47.
35. Meiners, "Texas Governorship, 1861–1865," 100.
36. J. P. Benjamin to Governor Lubbock, December 2, 1861, in *Official Records,* ser. 4, vol. 1, 774–75; Day, comp. and ed., *Senate Journal, Ninth Legislature,* 238–39; Charles W. Ramsdell, "The Texas State Military Board, 1862–1865," *Southwestern Historical Quarterly* 27 (April 1924), 257–58.
37. Lubbock, *Six Decades in Texas,* 365–71; Ramsdell, "Texas State Military Board," 259–67; Ronnie C. Tyler, "Cotton on the Border, 1861–1865," *Southwestern Historical Quarterly* 73 (April 1970), 456–77; Fredericka Meiners, "The Texas Border Cotton Trade, 1862–1863," *Civil War History* 23 (December 1977), 293–306.
38. Lubbock, *Six Decades in Texas,* 369; Ramsdell, "Texas State Military Board," 268–69.
39. Lubbock, "Proclamation to the People of Texas," in *Official Records,* ser. 4, vol. 1, 980.
40. Lubbock to Hamilton P. Bee, May 1, 1862; Bee to Lubbock, May 5, 1862, in Governors' Letters, Texas State Archives.

41. Lubbock to General Paul O. Hebert, December 7, 1861, in Executive Record Book.
42. Lubbock to Thomas M. Joseph, December 19, 1861, in Executive Record Book; Lubbock, *Six Decades in Texas,* 380.
43. Lubbock, *Six Decades in Texas,* 384–88.
44. Ibid., 388–90; Lubbock to Jefferson Davis, June 27, 1862, Lubbock to Governor Rector, June 27, 1862, Lubbock to Governor Jackson, June 27, 1862, Lubbock to Governor Thomas O. Moore, June 27, 1862, all in Executive Record Book.
45. Lubbock, *Six Decades in Texas,* 391–92; Lubbock, Jackson, Moore, and Rector to Jefferson Davis, July 28, 1862, in Executive Record Book.
46. Lubbock, *Six Decades in Texas,,* 392–94.
47. Davis to Governors Lubbock, Jackson, Moore, and Rector, September 12, 1862, in *Official Records,* vol. 53, 879–80.
48. Lubbock, *Six Decades in Texas,* 416–21; Adams, "Francis Richard Lubbock," 89.
49. Stephen B. Oates ("Texas Under the Secessionists," 194) says that Hebert "was a superb example of the type of officer Texans despised."
50. For the recapture of Galveston, see *Official Records,* vol. 15, 211–20; Alwyn Barr, "Texas Coastal Defense, 1861–1865," *Southwestern Historical Quarterly* 45 (July 1961), 14–18; and Charles C. Cumberland, "The Confederate Loss and Recapture of Galveston, 1862–1863," *Southwestern Historical Quarterly* 51 (October 1947), 109–30.
51. Lubbock to John B. Magruder, January 6, 1863, in Executive Record Book.
52. *Official Records,* vol. 15, 886–90, 928–35, 945–46, 955–56.
53. James M. Day, comp. and ed., *House Journal of the Ninth Legislature, First Called Session of the State of Texas* (Austin: Texas State Library, 1963), 4–38; Lubbock, *Six Decades in Texas,* 465–70.
54. Day, comp. and ed., *House Journal, Ninth Legislature, Called Session,* 49; James M. Day, comp. and ed., *Senate Journal of the Ninth Legislature, First Called Session of the State of Texas* (Austin: Texas State Library, 1963), 53–54, 96–97, 108.
55. Lubbock, *Six Decades in Texas,* 477.
56. Meiners, "Texas Governorship, 1861–1865," 206–9.
57. Lubbock, *Six Decades in Texas,* 493.
58. Ibid., 493–501.
59. Governors to the People of Louisiana, Texas, Arkansas, and Missouri, and the Allied Indian Nations, August 18, 1863, in *Official Records,* vol. 53, 892–94.
60. Lubbock, *Six Decades in Texas,* 511–12.
61. Ibid., 513; John Tyler to Lubbock, Governor Elect, and State Authorities, October 27, 1863, in Governors' Letters, Texas State Archives. See also Charles W. Ramsdell, "Lost Hope of the Confederacy—John Tyler to the Governor and Authorities of Texas," *Quarterly of the Texas State Historical Association* 14 (October 1910), 129–45.

62. Lubbock, *Six Decades in Texas,* 515–25.
63. *Handbook of Texas,* 2:89; Adams, "Francis Richard Lubbock," 95–98.
64. The exact place and date of his birth are unknown. Phares (*Governors of Texas,* 100) says he was probably born in 1807. The manuscript Federal census returns for Harrison County, 1850 and 1860, indicate that Murrah was born between 1826 and 1828. See also Benny E. Deuson, "Pendleton Murrah," in Nunn, *Ten Texans in Gray,* 122–23.
65. James T. DeShields, *They Sat in High Places* (San Antonio: Naylor Company, 1940), 247–48.
66. Nancy H. Bowen, "A Political Labyrinth: Texas in the Civil War," *East Texas Historical Journal* 11 (Fall 1973), 3–11.
67. Inaugural Address, November 5, 1863, in James Day, comp. and ed., *Senate Journal of the Tenth Legislature, Regular Session of the State of Texas, November 3, 1863–December 16, 1863* (Austin: Texas State Library, 1964), 48–55.
68. Pendleton Murrah to General John B. Magruder, January 17, 1864, in Governors' Letters, Texas State Archives.
69. Meiners, "Texas Governorship, 1861–1865," 293–94.
70. Austin *Tri-Weekly State Gazette,* December 16, 1863.
71. Robert P. Felgar, "Texas in the War for Southern Independence" (Ph.D. dissertation, University of Texas, 1936), 212.
72. Murrah to Magruder, January 12, 1864, in *Official Records,* vol. 53., 926–30; Magruder to Murrah, January 17, 1864, in Governor's Letters, Texas State Archives; General Orders, No. 14, January 20, 1864, in Governors' Letters; Moore, *Conscription and Conflict in the Confederacy,* 247–48.
73. Kerby, *Kirby Smith's Confederacy,* 277.
74. Magruder to Murrah, March 23, 1864, in *Official Records,* vol. 34, pt. 2, 1093–95; Magruder to Murrah, April 2, 1864, ibid., pt. 3, 739–41; Murrah to Magruder, ibid., 747–50.
75. Meiners, "Texas Governorship, 1861–1865," 314–16; Felgar, "Texas in the War for Southern Independence," 210–25.
76. Kerby, *Kirby Smith's Confederacy,* 176–77.
77. Ibid., 177–78; Ashcraft, "Texas: 1860–1866," 179–80, 218–21.
78. In her excellent study of the Texas governorship, Fredericka Meiners notes that practically all historians, including Charles W. Ramsdell, have assumed that the Texas Military Board purchased the cotton. Meiners points out that Judith Gentry in a paper, "Government Cotton Exports from Texas During the Civil War: A Study in Confederate-State Relations," presented to the Texas State Historical Association, March 9, 1973, showed that the Texas Loan Agency, not the Military Board, bought and sold the cotton with the state bonds under Murrah's state plan.
79. W. A. Broadwell to Jefferson Davis, April 6, 1864, in *Official Records,* vol. 53, 979–80; Kirby Smith to Pendleton Murrah, March 1, 1864, John B. Magruder to Pendleton Murrah, March 28, 1864, in Governors' Let-

ters, Texas State Archives; "Message of Governor Murrah to the Tenth Legislature," May 11, 1864, in Executive Record Book.

80. Kerby, *Kirby Smith's Confederacy,* 201–202.

81. Murrah to Kirby Smith, June 17, 21, 24, 25, 28, 1864, in Governors' Letters, Texas State Archives; Kirby Smith to Murrah, July 4, 1864, July 5, 1864, in *Official Records,* vol. 53, 1008–15.

82. Murrah to the People of Texas, July 19, 1864, in Governors' Proclamations, Texas State Archives.

83. Kerby, *Kirby Smith's Confederacy,* 203–207.

84. Warner, "Legislative History of Texas During the Civil War," 105–12.

85. Murrah to Fellow Citizens, January 14, 1865, in Governors' Proclamations, Texas State Archives.

86. See Charles W. Ramsdell, "Texas from the Fall of the Confederacy to the Beginning of Reconstruction," *Southwestern Historical Quarterly* 11 (January 1908), 199–219.

87. Deuson, "Pendleton Murrah," 133–34.

88. Felgar, "Texas in the War for Southern Independence," 223–24; Ila Mae Myers, "The Relations of Governor Pendleton Murrah, of Texas, with the Confederacy Military Authorities" (Master's thesis, University of Texas, 1929), 111–12; Joseph Howard Parks, *General Edmund Kirby Smith, C.S.A.* (Baton Rouge: Louisiana State University Press, 1954), 355–57; Florence Elizabeth Holladay, "The Powers of the Commander of the Confederate Trans-Mississippi Department," *Southwestern Historical Quarterly* 21 (April 1918), 349–51.

89. Meiners, "Texas Governorship, 1861–1865," 355.

VIRGINIA

1. For a complete biography of Letcher, see F. N. Boney, *John Letcher of Virginia: The Story of Virginia's Civil War Governor* (University Ala.: University of Alabama Press, 1966). For briefer summaries of his life, see Boney, "John Letcher: Pragmatic Confederate Governor," in Edward Younger and James Tice Moore, eds., *The Governors of Virginia, 1860–1978* (Charlottesville: University Press of Virginia, 1982), 8–19, and Boney, "Governor John Letcher, Virginian," *Civil War Times Illustrated,* 11 (December 1972), 10–19.

2. Boney, *John Letcher,* 27–50; Boney, "Governor John Letcher, Virginian," 11–12; Charles Henry Ambler, *Sectionalism in Virginia from 1776 to 1861* (New York: Russell & Russell, 1964), 244, 251–72. See also William Gleason Bean, "The Ruffner Pamphlet of 1847: An Antislavery Aspect of Virginia Sectionalism," *Virginia Magazine of History and Biography* 61 (July 1953), 260–82.

3. Boney, *John Letcher,* 50–73, 81–83; Boney, "Governor John Letcher, Virginian," 12. See also David M. Potter, "The Impending Crisis, 1848–1861 (New York: Harper & Row, 1976), passim.

4. Boney, *John Letcher,* 74–90; Boney, "Governor John Letcher, Virginian,"

12. See also William Gleason Bean, "John Letcher and the Slavery Issue in Virginia's Gubernatorial Contest of 1858–1859," *Journal of Southern History* 20 (February 1954), 22–49.

5. Boney, *John Letcher*, 91–100. For the complete speeches, see Richmond *Daily Whig*, August 22, 1860, and *Message of the Governor and Accompanying Documents* (Richmond, 1861), in Executive Papers, Virginia State Library, Richmond.

6. Boney, *John Letcher*, 100–14. See also George H. Reese, ed., *Proceedings of the Virginia State Convention of 1861, February 13–May 1,* 4 vols. (Richmond: Virginia State Library, 1965), passim, and Henry T. Shanks, *The Secession Movement in Virginia, 1847–1861* (Richmond: Garrett and Massie, 1934), passim.

7. Boney, *John Letcher*, 114–30; James I. Robertson, Jr., ed., *Proceedings of the Advisory Council of the State of Virginia, April 21–June 19, 1861* (Richmond: Virginia State Library), 1977, xi–xxiii, 116, 125, 132–34.

8. Boney, *John Letcher*, 115–16, 125, 132–34. See also Merritt Roe Smith, *Harpers Ferry Armory and the New Technology: The Challenge of Change* (Ithaca, N.Y.: Cornell University Press, 1977), passim.

9. F. N. Boney, "Governor Letcher's Candid Correspondence," *Civil War History* 10 (June 1964), 173–76. Letcher's private letters criticizing Confederate officials were mainly written to Francis H. Smith, James D. Davidson, and William Weaver, all old friends from the Valley.

10. Boney, *John Letcher*, 136–41, 150–63, 173, 181–82, 194, 197. The quotation is from a letter to Governor John Gill Shorter, August 11, 1862, in Executive Papers, Virginia State Library.

11. Boney, *John Letcher*, 128–29, 136–44, 152, 153, 157–65, 179–81, 188; Boney, "Governor John Letcher, Virginian," 17; Lee A. Wallace, Jr., comp., *A Guide to Virginia Military Organizations. 1861–1865* (Richmond: Virginia State Library, 1964), 235–42.

12. Boney, *John Letcher*, 150, 164, 168–72, 197, 285–86. See also Ella Lonn, *Salt as a Factor in the Confederacy* (University, Ala.: University of Alabama Press, 1965), passim.

13. Boney, *John Letcher*, 134–201. For Letcher's bitterest attack on war profiteers, see *Message of the Governor* (Richmond, January 7, 1863), Executive Papers, Virginia State Library. See also Virginius Dabney, *Virginia: The New Dominion* (Garden City, N.Y.: Doubleday, 1971), 328.

14. Boney, *John Letcher*, 146, 170–76, 184–85, 189, 191, 199. For recent analyses of Confederate nationalism, see Emory M. Thomas, *The Confederate Nation, 1861–1865* (New York: Harper & Row, 1979), and Raimondo Luraghi, *The Rise and Fall of the Plantation South* (New York: New Viewpoints, 1978). Letcher's support of slave impressments was especially lukewarm.

15. Boney, *John Letcher*, 165–66, 178, 183–84, 199; J. G. Randall and David Donald, *The Civil War and Reconstruction* (Lexington, Mass.: D. C. Heath and Company, 1969), 391–95.

16. Boney, *John Letcher*, 160, 173, 186, 197. See also May Spencer Ringold,

The Role of the State Legislatures in the Confederacy (Athens: University of Georgia Press, 1966), passim.

17. Boney, *John Letcher,* 182–200; Boney, "Governor John Letcher, Virginian," 17–18.

18. Boney, *John Letcher,* 201–15.

19. Alvin Arthur Fahrner, "The Public Career of William 'Extra Billy' Smith" (Ph.D. dissertation, University of North Carolina, 1953), 1–12; Alvin A. Fahrner, "William 'Extra Billy' Smith, Governor of Virginia, 1864–1865: A Pillar of the Confederacy," *Virginia Magazine of History and Biography* 74 (January 1966), 68; Alvin A. Fahrner, "William ('Extra Billy') Smith: Governor in Two Wars," in Edward Younger and James Tice Moore, eds., *The Governors of Virginia,* 21–22.

20. Fahrner, "The Public Career of William 'Extra Billy' Smith," 12–85; Fahrner, "William 'Extra Billy' Smith, Governor of Virginia," 68.

21. Alvin A. Fahrner, "William 'Extra Billy' Smith, Democratic Governor of Virginia, 1846–1849," *East Carolina College Publications in History* 2 (1965), 36–53; Fahrner, "The Public Career of William 'Extra Billy' Smith," 85–161.

22. Fahrner, "The Public Career of William 'Extra Billy' Smith," 162–217; Shanks, *Secession in Virginia,* 110, 122.

23. Fahrner, "The Public Career of William 'Extra Billy' Smith," 218–51. See also Yearns, *The Confederate Congress,* and Alexander and Beringer, *Anatomy of the Confederate Congress.* Munford remained secretary of the commonwealth under Governor Smith.

24. Fahrner, "The Public Career of William 'Extra Billy' Smith," 252–58, 270–78; Clifford Dowdey, *Experiment in Rebellion* (Garden City, N.Y.: Doubleday & Company, 1946). 376. Dowdey briefly criticizes Smith for granting too many exemptions, but Fahrner's detailed study of this situation is more persuasive.

25. Fahrner, "The Public Career of William 'Extra Billy' Smith," 267–69, 278–85; Lonn, *Salt in the Confederacy,* 155–56.

26. Quoted in Robert F. Durden, *The Gray and the Black: The Confederate Debate on Emancipation* (Baton Rouge: Louisiana State University Press, 1972), 99–100. This is an exhaustive study of the debate in the Confederacy of whether emancipation should be a part of the plan to recruit black soldiers. See also Fahrner, "The Public Career of William 'Extra Billy' Smith," 285–94.

27. *Official Records,* ser. 4, vol. 3, 905–26; *Calendar of Virginia State Papers and Other Manuscripts,* 11 vols. (Richmond: Virginia State Library, 1875–1893), 11:261–62.

28. Fahrner, "The Public Career of William 'Extra Billy' Smith," 253, 266–67. See also Richard Cecil Todd, *Confederate Finance* (Athens: University of Georgia Press, 1954), passim.

29. Fahrner, "The Public Career of William 'Extra Billy' Smith," 258–62; Emory M. Thomas, *The Confederacy as a Revolutionary Experience* (Englewood Cliffs, N.J.: Prentice-Hall, 1971), 71–72. See also John W. Bell,

Memoirs of Governor William Smith of Virginia: His Political, Military, and Personal History (New York: Moss Engraving Company, 1891), 57–59.

30. Fahrner, "The Public Career of William 'Extra Billy' Smith," 262–66.

31. Boney, *John Letcher,* 205–208, 214–21; Fahrner, "The Public Career of William 'Extra Billy' Smith," 296–306.

32. Boney, *John Letcher,* 230–47; Fahrner, "The Public Career of William 'Extra Billy' Smith," 307–43. See also Jack P. Maddex, Jr., *The Virginia Conservatives, 1867–1879: A Study in Reconstruction Politics* (Chapel Hill: University of North Carolina Press, 1970), passim.

CONTRIBUTORS

JOHN G. BARRETT is General Edwin Cox Distinguished Professor of History at the Virginia Military Institute. He is the author of *The Civil War in North Carolina.*

F. N. BONEY is professor of history at the University of Georgia. He is the author of *John Letcher of Virginia.*

VINCENT H. CASSIDY is professor of history at the University of Akron. He is the author (with Amos E. Simpson) of *Henry Watkins Allen of Louisiana.*

MICHAEL B. DOUGAN is professor of history at Arkansas State University. He is the author of *Confederate Arkansas: The People and Politics of a Frontier State in Wartime.*

ROBERT W. DUBAY is academic dean and professor of history at Bainbridge Junior College, Bainbridge, Georgia. He is the author of *John Jones Pettus, Mississippi Fire-Eater.*

JOHN B. EDMUNDS, JR., is professor of history at the University of South Carolina at Spartanburg. He is working on a biography of Francis W. Pickens.

PAUL D. ESCOTT is professor of history at the University of North Carolina at Charlotte. He is the author of *After Secession: Jefferson Davis and the Failure of Confederate Nationalism.*

KERMIT L. HALL is associate professor of history and law at the University of Florida. He is the author of *The Politics of Justice: Lower Federal Judicial Selection and the Second Party System, 1829–1861.*

LOWELL H. HARRISON is professor of history at Western Kentucky University. He is the author of *The Civil War in Kentucky.*

MALCOLM C. MCMILLAN is Emeritus Hollifield Professor of Southern History at Auburn University. He is the author of *The Alabama Confederate Reader*.

WILLIAM E. PARRISH is professor and head of the Department of History at Mississippi State University. He is the author of *A History of Missouri, 1860–1875*.

RALPH A. WOOSTER is Regents Professor of History and dean of faculties at Lamar University. He is the author of *The Secession Conventions of the South*.

W. BUCK YEARNS is professor of history at Wake Forest University. He is the author of *The Confederate Congress*.

INDEX

DATE DUE

DATE DUE			
DE 1 8 '90			
APR 2 3 1994			
			PRINTED